Marketing Strategy

Edited by Dale Littler and Dominic Wilson

Butterworth-Heinemann Ltd
Linacre House, Jordan Hill, Oxford OX2 8DP

A member of the Reed Elsevier plc group

OXFORD LONDON BOSTON
MUNICH NEW DELHI SINGAPORE SYDNEY
TOKYO TORONTO WELLINGTON

First published 1995

© Dale Littler and Dominic Wilson 1995

British Library Cataloguing in Publication Data
A catalogue record for this book is available from the British Library.

ISBN 0 7506 0662 2

Composition by Deltatype, Ellesmere Port
Printed and bound in Great Britain

Contents

Preface

Strategy is a dominant feature of the contemporary lexicon of management. When it became part of common management parlance – significantly after the Second World War – its military connotations seemed especially apt in a world of intense competition where businesses were seen as 'fighting' for market share and profits. The same post-war era also saw the rise of marketing as an ideology and an increasingly important management function and it was only natural that, as with many other business activities, strategy should become a kin of marketing.

Now marketing strategy is a burgeoning area of interest, often being presented as at least a contributor to organizational performance, despite the fact that empirical research has failed to demonstrate a definite relationship between the two. At its simplest, marketing strategy can be viewed as encompassing the definition of clusters of customers as market targets and the corresponding development of appropriate offerings, including the means of delivering, promoting, packaging, pricing, and branding them in product markets which the firm has defined for itself.

Various prescriptive models for strategic marketing planning have been developed, and, increasingly, note is being taken of the significant behavioural influences that can affect the implementation of the resultant marketing plans. However, the impact of uncertainty on the strategic planning process does not yet seem to have extensively pervaded marketers' consideration of the process by which marketing strategies develop and are implemented. Perhaps, as some organizational theorists argue, strategy cannot be clearly predetermined in the form of documented plans to be applied slavishly by those lower down in the organizational hierarchy. Apart from the fact that organizations have for various reasons been going through a process of streamlining, so that 'hierarchy' is increasingly regarded as having inappropriate if not pejorative overtones, this 'planning' perspective may be regarded as somewhat naive given the complex political maelstrom within which many managers have to operate, the differences in organizational cultures, the baggage of experience, and the prejudices which individual managers bring to the dialogue. Marketing strategy should be regarded as a process in which, as Mintzberg notes, *thinking* cannot be separated from *doing* in a context where uncertainty can have a powerful hand in shaping the outcome. Accident may have a greater influence than is often admitted, with strategy often becoming the 'jockey of happenstance'.

The readings collected here present different perspectives on various aspects of marketing strategy. They have been selected after an extensive culling of the many articles and papers which we have examined in the area. We believe collectively they are a challenging read, and although our own prejudices may shine through, we believe the reader is left to decide their own stance towards the subject of marketing strategy.

In preparing this text, we are particularly indebted to our secretary, Miss Patrizia Venosa who, apart from having to tolerate our idiosyncrasies, has managed to make sense of the numerous scribblings and has generally ensured that the manuscript was in the appropriate order. We are also very grateful to the assistance of Mrs Debbie Taylor and Mrs Carol Jamieson who persevered in typing some of the manuscript.

Dale Littler
Dominic Wilson

Part One
Marketing Strategy and Strategic Decisions

Over the past few decades the meaning of the terms *marketing* and *marketing strategy* has developed considerably. Earlier studies of marketing tended to treat the subject as a practically-oriented management function with several interrelated subdivisions such as product development, distribution, packaging, purchasing, promotion, and pricing – these being referred to collectively as the 'marketing mix'. Many of these areas had also been studied for some time by scholars with perspectives quite different to 'marketing', for example pricing by industrial economists, product development by scholars of innovation theory, purchasing by experts in production management, and buying behaviour by psychologists. It has taken time therefore for the distinctive perspective of marketing to emerge and to be accepted as a field of management theory.

In 1985, following considerable debate over many of these issues, the American Marketing Association (AMA) adopted the following revised definition of marketing:

> Marketing is the process of planning and executing the conception, pricing, promotion and distribution of ideas, goods and services to create exchanges that satisfy individual and organizational objectives.

Reflecting the domination of US scholars in the early development of marketing theory, this definition, or close variants of it, has been widely used in many marketing textbooks (e.g. Kotler, 1991; Dibb *et al.*, 1991; McCarthy and Perreault, 1990) though its adequacy is beginning to be questioned in some European textbooks (e.g. Foxall, 1984; Baker (*ed.*), 1987). It could be said that the AMA definition is more of a list than a definition and is therefore clumsy and inconvenient to use; that it cannot ever be comprehensive; and that it fails to provide a demarcation as to what necessarily is or is not *marketing*. Hooley *et al.* (1990) point out that the AMA definition presents marketing as a functional process conducted by the organization's marketing department, whereas the general thrust of the more recent literature on marketing theory is that marketing is increasingly being conceptualized as an organizational philosophy or 'an approach to doing business'. This strategic, as opposed to functional, approach to marketing is captured by McDonald (see Chapter 21, Part Four of this book):

> Marketing is a management process whereby the resources of the whole organization are utilized to satisfy the needs of selected customer groups in order to achieve the objectives of both parties. Marketing, then, is first and foremost an attitude of mind rather than a series of functional activities. (McDonald, 1989, p. 8)

Thus two discernible but interdependent emphases might be seen to be emerging in marketing theory, loosely labelled 'marketing management' and 'marketing strategy'.

McDonald's definition of marketing emphasizes the central role of marketing in business or corporate strategy and echoes the observation of Wind and Robertson (1983) that marketing strategy 'focuses explicitly on the quest for long run competitive and consumer advantage'. Wind and Robertson recognize that this entails a considerable overlap between marketing strategy, business strategy and, by implication, corporate strategy but they clarify this linkage:

> Marketing strategy's difference is that it serves a boundary role function between the firm and its customers, competitors and other stakeholders. Marketing is uniquely able to assess consumer needs and the firm's potential for gaining competitive advantage, which ultimately must guide the corporate mission. (Wind and Robertson, 1983, p. 12)

Wind and Robertson (1983) conclude that the role of marketing is to anticipate and manage the application of an organization's strategies to the competitive and consumer environments, and that this places a very high priority on the contribution of marketing to strategy both at the business and at the corporate levels. In his article later in this section, Gordon Greenley echoes the conclusion of Wind and Robertson in his emphasis on the *operational* role of marketing strategy. In other words, not only does marketing contribute to the development and formation of business and corporate strategy, but marketing then also contributes to the implementation of strategy in terms of the decisions and actions taken within the context of marketing operations. These marketing decisions and actions can be referred to collectively as marketing strategy.

At a more general level there is also considerable discussion over the meaning of the term *strategy*, reflecting differences among management scholars largely as to how the process of strategy formation is best understood. The classic view of strategy at the corporate level is that of Andrews[1] which assumes that corporate executives are free to conceive and direct strategies as they see fit. Mintzberg (1978) points out that organizational factors and environmental constraints restrict executive discretion so that strategy should be seen more as an outcome than as an intention. Thus Mintzberg favours historical explanations of strategy as 'patterns in a stream of activities' or similarities over time in the way in which an organization responds to its environment (Mintzberg, 1977, 1990). Others have stressed the influence of organizational culture and politics (Pettigrew, 1985), the limiting effect of managerial perception and prejudice (Gronhaug and Falkenberg, 1989), and even the importance of luck (Barney, 1986) in understanding how strategy is formed.

Nevertheless, a broad consensus is discernible in the strategic management literature concerning the distinctive features of *strategic decisions*, namely that they: involve the deployment of significant resources; are regarded by those involved at the time as being 'important'; are concerned with competitive activity; are recognized as having long-term implications; and are generally complex, unstructured, lack clear parallels and require a degree of creativity or innovation in devising appropriate responses (Weitz and Wensley, 1988, p. 3). Many of these criteria could be challenged. For example, decisions which seem tactical and 'internal' at the time may later be seen, with the benefit of hindsight, as having dramatic strategic consequences.[2]

The similarity in agenda between *marketing strategy* and *business strategy* is also evident in the process of planning typically associated in most textbooks with both forms of strategy. In each case the planning process is usually depicted as a sequence of stages starting with the corporate mission and its expression in terms of corporate 'objectives'. The sequence progresses through analysis of the organization's position internally and externally (strengths, weaknesses, opportunities, and threats – familiar as the SWOT analysis) with respect both to environmental trends and competitive prospects. Then the focus is supposed to turn to the identification of strategic options, often supported by scenario analysis, and the sequence concludes with the selection and implementation of the preferred strategy. There may also be mention of the importance of 'feedback loops' comparing the outcome of strategy implementation with the initial corporate mission and objectives.

Whereas this process has some merit as a convenient model for teaching and presentation purposes, it has many failings as a realistic model of strategic or marketing planning in practice. For example, these 'stages' may well occur simultaneously rather than sequentially; some may even be superfluous (such as SWOT or scenario analyses) when managers are under pressure to devise strategies quickly, as may often be the case, or when they have confidence in their collective experience and feel familiar with their competitive situation. The model also ignores the inherently ambiguous nature of 'strength', 'weakness', 'opportunity', and 'threat' in markets where such key variables as technology, demand and rival offerings can change rapidly and with little obvious warning. It is easy to dismiss such models as unrealistic or irrelevant but until superior alternatives become available it would be unwise to abandon what little support they do offer.

Against this background the definition of *marketing* continues to be debated[3] and the role of marketing in strategic decision-making remains open to discussion.

In the first of the articles in Part One, Biggadike (1981) discusses what he considers to be the five most important contributions of marketing theory to a better understanding of strategic management. These are the marketing concept *per se*, which shares with strategic planning a prime focus on the customer, and the marketing concepts of segmentation, positioning, mapping (including matrix techniques), and product life cycle analysis. These concepts and their associated analytical techniques provide a systematic rationale not only to marketing and environmental analysis but also to strategic planning and to strategic management more generally.

There are some writers, for example contingency theorists,[4] who would challenge Biggadike's apparent preoccupation with academic marketing research as necessarily seeking general theories of marketing regardless of contingent variation. Such critics might also dispute Biggadike's conclusions that these are the most important contributions to understanding strategic management. For example, one might also point to the recognition of collaborative inter-organizational relationships as the basis of marketing in organizational markets (Gummesson, 1987; Ford, 1990), an insight which has profound implications for competitive analysis and strategic management.

In the second article of Part One, Day (1992) re-examines the contribution of marketing to the field of strategy development a decade after Biggadike's forthright analysis. Day suggests that the importance of marketing's contribution to strategy development is so profound that the two activities may eventually merge resulting in the deceptive disappearance or 'internalization' of marketing as a separate function. Here Day is going beyond the similarity in planning between marketing and strategy that others have noted.[5] He argues that this absorption of marketing would be consistent with the academic marginalization of marketing over the last decade due to the apparent preoccupation of marketing researchers with marketing management issues, and due to the sequestration of some of marketing's more strategic level contributions by rival academic fields, notably industrial economics and organizational behaviour. Day describes some of the challenges facing those seeking to develop a better understanding of marketing strategy in the 1990s, as many of its assumptions are questioned, and concludes that understanding strategy issues will increasingly require an interdisciplinary approach. Kerin and Varadarajan take a more positive view of marketing's role in the development of strategy, arguing that marketing has powerful potential to contribute to two increasingly important aspects of organizational competitiveness, namely innovation (Kerin, 1992) and competitive analysis (Varadarajan, 1992).

In parallel with developments in marketing theory, it can be said at a general level that markets have become more competitive over the latter part of the century with many more products and services on offer, of better quality, from more efficient suppliers, and to increasingly affluent and sophisticated customers. One important consequence of increasing competition has been to encourage the development of a more strategic approach to marketing. Marketing strategy involves not only the coordination of the traditional elements of the marketing mix but also the coordination of marketing as a whole with other organizational functions in order synergistically to pursue over-arching objectives which are informed by a richer appreciation of long-term environmental and competitive dynamics.

Given these developments, it is not perhaps surprising that there remains some controversy about how *marketing* and *marketing strategy* should be understood. Seeking to resolve this controversy, in the third article, Greenley (1989) reviews the literature on marketing strategy and shows that, by and large, the subject tends to be approached from the perspective of the marketing mix. He argues that some confusion has arisen between the process and the objectives of marketing strategy and he attempts to resolve this by outlining a fundamental understanding of marketing strategy which is universally applicable. This view of marketing strategy, not unlike that of Biggadike, is founded on five components all of which carry long-term implications: the marketing mix; the two integrating elements of marketing positioning (i.e. segmentation and targeting) and product positioning (i.e. product portfolio development); and the two operational elements of market entry (i.e. how the strategy is to be prosecuted – through acquisition, collaboration, or internal development) and competitive timing (based largely on life cycle analysis).

The fundamental issue of competitive timing is the focus of Abell's article, the fourth reading in Part One, which argues convincingly that the pace of change in the competitive environment is accelerating and that there is a limited – and narrowing – 'window of strategic opportunity' within which organizations must take strategic action if they are not to miss competitive opportunities. Close environmental monitoring, speed of competitive response and readiness to accept considerable change are crucial prerequisites to taking advantage of strategic windows. Abell suggests that traditional models of marketing analysis such as product portfolios, sales forecasts and product life cycles are not adequate to capture the dynamics of contemporary competitive environments. His short article focuses on the radical nature of change often required of organizations facing 'strategic windows' but he is less specific about how to recognize (much less anticipate) them.

The increasing urgency of competitive reaction recognized by Abell has encouraged a number of writers to view marketing strategies through a military analogy, as in the fifth article of Part One, by Kotler and Singh (1980).[6] The military analogy provides an attractive and compelling perspective which resonates clearly with the popular language of marketing (advertising campaigns, price-wars, 'car wars', battling for shelf-space, . . .). The analogy is also encouraged by the combative style of popular media analysis (aimed more often at attracting readers than at generating insight) where rival companies are often compared head-to-head (in terms of products, strategies, markets) and progress is measured in zero-sum terms such as market share, winning key contracts and contested acquisitions. The analogy often appeals to students of strategy, not least because of its colourful imagery, clear-cut objectives and the role of strong leadership. However, it is important to ask 'what is the role of the customer in military marketing'. In Kotler and Singh the only reference to consumer satisfaction (arguably the ultimate objective of marketing) is in terms of the 'terrain' over which rival suppliers struggle. Often the customer seems to be regarded implicitly by advocates of the military analogy as the 'spoils of war' to be looted by the victor. Pennings (1985) points out also that the degree of control exercised by a general over an army in the exceptional conditions of warfare (including imprisonment and execution for desertion) is far greater than that granted even to the most charismatic leader of an organization where commitments of history, culture and established product offerings curtail strategic options. It is perhaps easy to forget that warfare is a means to an end rather than an end in itself; a more profitable analogy may be developed from comparison between marketing strategy and diplomatic strategy which lists warfare as one (and generally the last resort) of many strategies available in pursuit of the best interests of a populace.

The five articles in Part One are primarily conceptual in that they are not argued directly from a body of empirical research, though all were prompted either by extensive empirical research[7] or by considerable experience with commercial organizations. The articles also reveal something of the limitations in our emerging understanding of marketing strategy. For example, there is an implicit assumption in all five articles that strategy is appropriately conceived as proactive, long-term planning by decision-makers capable of foresight and objective analysis.[8] This may be a convenient starting point for understanding marketing strategy and decision-making, especially for teaching purposes, but it underestimates crucial organizational and circumstantial limitations on managerial discretion.[9] There also seems to be a persistent assumption that marketing strategy is typified by large corporations involved in highly competitive markets and offering manufactured products. Significantly less attention has been given (though this is changing) to the nature of marketing strategy (as opposed to marketing management) and decision-making in services markets, in not-for-profit markets and in small organizations. Some of these assumptions are reflected revealingly in the frequency with which strategy *formation* is referred to in the literature as strategy *formulation*. There are writers who are developing perspectives from research into strategy processes and organizational decision-making which can be applied to the context of marketing and which recognize some of the limits on managerial control,[10] but these concerns are not yet in the mainstream of scholarly marketing research. Some of these issues are discussed further in Part Four on Strategy Implementation.

References

Abell, D.F. (1978), 'Strategic Windows', *Journal of Marketing*, volume 42, number 3, July 1978, pp. 21-26.

Albaum, G. (1992), 'What is Marketing? A Comment on "Marketing is . . ." ', *Journal of the Academy of Management Science*, volume 20, number 4, 1992, pp. 313-316 [comment on Hunt, S.D. (1992), 'Marketing is . . .', *Journal of the Academy of Management Science*, volume 20, number 4, 1992, pp. 301-311].

Andrews, K.R. (1971), '*The Concept of Corporate Strategy*', Dow Jones-Irwin, Homewood, IL, 1971 [second edition, 1980; third edition, 1987].

Barney, J., (1986), 'Strategic Factor Markets: Expectations, Luck and Business Strategy', *Management Science*, volume 32, number 10, 1986, pp. 1231-1241.

Biggadike, E.R. (1981), 'The Contributions of Marketing to Strategic Management', *Academy of Management Review*, volume 6, number 4, pp. 621-632, 1981.

Crosier, K., (1975), 'What exactly is Marketing', *Quarterly Review of Marketing*, Winter, 1975.

Day, G.S. (1992), 'Marketing's Contribution to the Strategy Dialogue', *Journal of the Academy of Management Science*, volume 20, number 4, 1992, pp. 323-329.

Eisenhardt, K.M. and Zbaracki, M.J. (1992), 'Strategic Decision Making', *Strategic Management Journal*, volume 13, Winter 1992, pp. 17-37.

Ford, D. (ed.) (1990), *Understanding Business Markets: Interaction, Relationships and Networks*, Academic Press, London.

Greenley, G.E. (1987), 'An Exposition of Empirical Research into Marketing Planning', *Journal of Marketing Management*, volume 3, number 1, July, 1987, pp. 83-102.

Greenley, G.E. (1989), 'An Understanding of Marketing Strategy', *European Journal of Marketing*, volume 23, number 8, 1989, pp. 45-58.

Gronhaug, K. and Falkenberg, J.S. (1989), 'Exploring Strategy Perceptions in Changing Environments', *Journal of Management Studies*, volume 26, number 4, 1989, pp. 349-359.

Hunt, S.D. (1976), 'The Nature and Scope of Marketing', *Journal of Marketing*, vol. 40, July, pp. 17-28.

Hunt, S.D. (1992), 'Marketing is . . .', *Journal of the Academy of Management Science*, volume 20, number 4, 1992, pp. 301-311.

Johnson, G. (1988), 'Rethinking Incrementalism', *Strategic Management Journal*, volume 9, number 1, 1988, pp. 75-91.

Kerin, R.A. (1992), 'Marketing's Contribution to the Strategy Dialogue Revisited', *Journal of the Academy of Management Science*, volume 20, number 4, 1992, pp. 331-334.

Kotler, P. and Singh, R. (1980), 'Marketing Warfare in the 1980s', *Journal of Business Strategy*, volume 1, number 3, Winter 1980, pp. 30-41.

Mintzberg, H. (1977), 'Strategy Formulation as a Historical Process', *International Studies of Management and Organization*, volume 7, number 2, pages, 28-40.

Mintzberg, H. (1978), 'Patterns in Strategy Formation', *Management Science*, volume 24, number 9, May 1978, pp. 934-948.

Mintzberg, H. (1987), 'Crafting Strategy', *Harvard Business Review*, volume 65, July/August, 1987.

Mintzberg, H. (1990), 'Strategy Formation: Ten Schools of Thought', in Frederickson, J.W. (ed.), *Perspectives on Strategic Management*, Harper Business, New York, pp. 105-135.

Pennings, J.M. (1985), 'On the Nature and Theory of Strategic Decisions', in Pennings, J.M. (ed.), *Organizational Strategy and Change: New Views on Formulating and Implementing Strategic Decisions*, Jossey-Bass, San Francisco, pp. 1-34.

Pettigrew, A.M. (1985), 'Examining Change in the Long-Term Context of Culture and Politics', in Pennings, J.M. (ed.), *Organizational Strategy and Change: New Views on Formulating and Implementing Strategic Decisions*, Jossey-Bass, San Francisco, pp. 269-318.

Piercy, N.F. and Giles, W., (1989), 'The Logic of Being Illogical in Strategic Marketing Planning', *Journal of Marketing Management*, vol. 5, no. 1, Summer 1989, pp. 19-31.

Thomas, H. and McGee, J., (1986), 'Introduction: Mapping Strategic Management Research', in McGee, J. and Thomas, H. (eds.) *Strategic Management Research: a European Perspective*, John Wiley & Sons, Chichester, pp. 1-18.

Varadarajan, P.R. (1992), 'Marketing's Contribution to Strategy: the View from a Different Looking Glass', *Journal of the Academy of Management Science*, volume 20, number 4, 1992, pp. 335-343.

Weitz, B.A. and Wensley, R. (eds.) (1988), *Readings in Strategic Marketing: Analysis, Planning & Implementation*, Dryden Press, Harcourt Brace Jovanovich, New York.

Notes

1 In a recent review of research in strategic management, Thomas and McGee (1986) recommend Andrews' definition of corporate strategy as a well-accepted expression of the intentions (as opposed to the process) of corporate strategy:

   "Corporate strategy is the pattern of major objectives, purposes or goals and essential policies or plans for achieving those goals, stated in such a way as to define what business the company is in or is to be in and the kind of company it is or is not to be." (Andrews, 1971, p. 28)

2 It is also worth noting that it seems unlikely that strategic managerial decisions will always be unanimous, or even unanimously regarded as strategic, which implies that there may often be an important degree of doubt in the minds of managers themselves as to what is or is not a *strategic* decision.

3 For those wishing to examine the evolving understanding of the meaning and role of marketing, Hunt (1976) provides a scholarly review and Crosier (1975) discusses 48 definitions of the term *marketing*. A more recent reflection on the current state of the debate is given by a number of authors in the 1992 special edition of the *Journal of the Academy of Marketing Science* (volume 20, number 4, Fall, 1992 – see particularly Hunt's article and Albaum's subsequent comment).

4 For a review of contingency theory in the context of strategic management see Ginsberg, A. and Venkatraman, N., 'Contingency Perspectives on Organizational Strategy: a Critical Review of the Empirical Research', *Academy of Management Review*, volume 10, 1985, pp. 421-434; or Drazin, R. and Van de Ven, A., 'An Examination of Alternative Forms of Contingency Theory', *Administrative Science Quarterly*, volume 30, 1985, pp. 514-539. There is also an interesting article describing contingency research specifically in UK markets: Grinyer, P.H., Al-Bazzaz, S. and Yasai-Ardekani, M., 'Towards a Contingency Theory of Corporate Planning: Findings in 48 UK Companies', *Strategic Management Journal*, volume 7, pp. 3-28, 1986.

5 For example:

   "in the practical setting there is frequently difficulty in distinguishing marketing planning from corporate or strategic planning. Indeed, in practical terms at the company level, the difference is often largely semantic." (Piercy and Giles, 1989, p. 20)

6 For a more extensive development of the military analogy in marketing see: James, B.G., *Business Wargames: Business Strategy for Executives in the Trenches of Market Warfare*, Abacus Press, 1984 [also Penguin Books, Harmondsworth, 1985].

7 Greenley's article in particular was prompted by his extensive research into marketing planning which concluded that formal marketing planning as described in the literature was not widely practised (Greenley, 1987) and that managers claiming to operate marketing strategies (the vast majority) often found it difficult to specify what these strategies were or how they had emerged.

8 All five also clearly assume a model of 'top-down' strategic decision-making by executive management. Others have argued that strategy formation can also be seen as a 'bottom-up' process where tactics can steer the direction of strategy (Piercy and Giles, 1989), and where the restraining influences of corporate culture and

bureaucratic systems combine to restrict the strategic options to incremental adjustments of historic positions (Mintzberg, 1977, 1978, 1987). On the other hand, it is also recognized that the pace of environmental change is generally too great to enable organizations to remain competitive for long just by incremental strategic adjustments (Abell, 1978; Johnson, 1988; Grönhaug and Falkenberg, 1989).

9 A recent review of the literature on strategic decision-making and its alternative theoretical approaches, including that of rationality, is provided by Eisenhardt and Zbaracki (1992).

10 For example: Andrew Pettigrew's (1985) work on the political and cultural restraints on managerial discretion, that of Grönhaug on perceptual limitations (Grönhaug and Falkenberg, 1989), and that of Mintzberg (1977) on historical constraints hedging strategic options.

1 The contributions of marketing to strategic management[1]

E. Ralph Biggadike

Strategic management issues are usually defined to be those affecting the relationship of an organization to its environment. They include the choice of both strategy and structure. A simple paradigm of strategic choice is:

$$\text{environment} + \text{organization capabilities} +$$
$$\text{current competitive position} = \text{strategy.}$$

Environment is defined as 'technological, economic, social, and political' influences (Learned *et al.* 1965, p. 170). *Organization capabilities* refer to human and physical resources, and *current competitive position* is the firm's reputation, markets served, relative market share, and so on. *Strategy* is the choice of markets the firm will attempt to serve, or a choice about the scope of the firm's domain, including decisions about expansion, defense, and contraction of that domain.

Issues in strategic management occur at both the corporate and business unit levels. It is at the business unit level that we have seen a proliferation of models and matrices to help resolve strategic management issues (Allen, 1976; Boston Consulting Group, 1970; Little, n.d.; Schoeffler *et al.*, 1974). Although there are important differences among them, they do require essentially similar steps in tackling business unit strategic choice issues. I have combined the strategic choice paradigm shown above and these steps into one in order to assess the contributions of marketing at both the corporate and business unit levels. My combination paradigm is shown in Table 1.

[1] Thanks to Neil H. Borden, Jr., and Robert D. Buzzell for discussions on this topic.

Table 1 Combination Paradigm of Strategic Management at the Corporate and Business Unit Levels

Corporate and Business Unit Levels	{ Environmental Analysis (technological, economic, social, political) Organizational Analysis (strengths weaknesses, personal values)
Business Unit Level	{ Define the business and market Assess industry or market attractiveness Assess current competitive position Select appropriate strategy, given market attractiveness, competitive position, and risk assessment Identify needed functional strategies, employee behavior, and information, control, evaluation, and compensation systems to achieve implementation Measure performance appropriately (e.g., share for new businesses, ROI for established businesses)

Overall, I judge that marketing has made a number of conceptual contributions but few theoretical ones. The contributions occur most frequently at the environmental analysis stage and at the business unit level. Also, marketing has contributed more to the choice of strategy than to the choice of structure. Marketing concepts and techniques such as market segmentation, positioning, and perceptual mapping help define the environment and frame strategic choices in customer terms. The product life cycle concept helps dynamic analysis of the environment and different strategic options. Essentially, marketing sees strategic management as being market-driven, and provides aids for hypothesizing about customer needs and competitor behavior.

Marketing: a definition and paradigm

Marketing scholars (for a review, see Hunt, 1976) agree that marketing is concerned with the external environment. There is no unifying paradigm for the entire marketing field, but there is a paradigm for marketing management

(McCarthy, 1971, p. 38). Figure 1 shows this paradigm which suggests that marketing management tries to satisfy customers (C) within the context of the environment and the firm's resources and objectives (the uncontrollable factors) by designing an appropriate marketing mix (the four P's - controllable factors).

There is considerable overlap between the strategic management and marketing management paradigms. First, both share a concern with the environment, because the target of marketing decisions is the customer and the marketing decision variables - product, price, place, and promotion - are heavily influenced by external elements, such as customers and competitors (unlike all the 'controllables' in other functions). Another reason for the overlap is that both fields share one 'controllable' - the product.

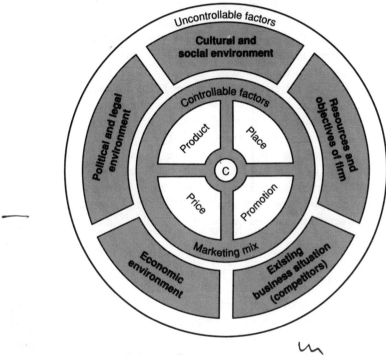

Figure 1 *A popular marketing paradigm*

The major difference between the two paradigms is that two of the marketing 'controllables' - place and promotion - are not often at the heart of strategic management issues. And, of course, some variables that are at the heart of strategy issues (e.g., choice of technology, level of vertical integration, type of manufacturing process, and capital intensity) are not marketing variables. Another difference is in emphasis. For example, although both fields study organization capabilities, it is rare that marketers explicitly study the influence of executives' personal values and leadership style.

Research in marketing

Research in marketing has not concentrated on specifying and validating the relationships suggested by the paradigm. For example, we do not have in marketing a set of propositions along the lines of:

> In an environment (segment) of high growth, fragmented customers, slow cultural change, and relatively larger competitors, an incremental innovation should be introduced at a skim price, with more emphasis on personal selling and service than on advertising and, initially, selective distribution.

One reason for this lack of marketing management theory is that it is easier to build theory in narrowly defined areas. Marketers have specialized in subfields, such as information processing theory, communications theory, and attitude change theory. Marketing scholars have chosen one element of the marketing management paradigm and have studied this element from the perspective of, and with the research methods of, a related academic discipline. An example is advertising (promotion) and the social psychology approach to attitude change. This level of specialization has prevented comprehensive development of marketing management theory.

A related reason is that business administration academics have been under pressure to be more 'problem oriented' and more 'scientific' (read 'quantitative'). These pressures have led to a preoccupation with applying technique to what I will call commercial marketing research problems - e.g., multidimensional scaling applied to segmentation. This kind of research has met some criteria of managerial and academic respectability, but it is not theory-building research.

The specific output of research in marketing over the 25-year period of 1952-1977 has recently been documented by the American Marketing Association's Commission on the Effectiveness of Research and Development for Marketing Management (Myers *et al.*, 1979). The Commission identified 64 examples of 'new theories, concepts, methods, and techniques,' and these are shown in Table 2. Their summary conclusions are that this research has had 'relatively little impact on improving marketing management practice' (p. 27); that theory building, or what the commissioners called 'general facts and laws,' is 'comparatively rare' (p. 27); and that 'marketing is still in a rather primitive state of development' (p. 27).

I have assessed each of the 64 new knowledge examples identified by the commissioners against the strategic management paradigm explained earlier. I judge that about 60 per cent have not made a contribution for one of three reasons: some knowledge is, as one would expect, at a functional level; other knowledge was derived from a narrow unit of analysis; and some is, simply, still undiffused.

Table 2 Examples of knowledge development in marketing, 1952-1977

Discipline-based theories	Managerial frameworks and approaches	Models and measurement	Research methods and statistical techniques
Demand and utility theory	Marketing concept	Stochastic models of brand	Motivation research and
Market segmentation	Marketing mix – 4Ps	choice	projective techniques
General and middle-range	Development of marketing	Market share models	Survey research
theories of consumer	cases	Marginal analysis and linear	Focus groups and depth
behavior	DAGMAR	programming	interviewing
Image and attitude theory	Product life cycle	Bayesian analysis	Experiential and panel
Theories of motivation,	Marketing plan	Advertising models; e.g.,	designs – ANOVA
personality, social class,	State approaches to strategy	Mediac, Pomsis,	Advances in probability
life style, and culture	development	Admesim, Brandaid,	sampling
Expectancy-value theory	Product portfolio analysis	Adbug	Hypothesis formulation,
Theories of advertising	Physical distribution manage-	Causal models	inference, significance test
processes and effects	ment	Sensitivity analysis and	Multivariate dependence
Information processing	Marketing information	validity tests	methods – mutiple regres-
theory	systems	Response functions	sion and multiple discrimi-
Attitude change theories	Product positioning and	Weighted belief models,	nant analysis, canonical
(consistency and	perceptual mapping	determinant attributes	correlation
complexity theories)	Segmentation strategies	Simulation and marketing	Multivariate interdependence
Attribution theory	New marketing organization	games	methods – cluster and factor
Perceptual processes	concepts; e.g., brand	Multidimensional scaling and	analysis, latent structure
Advertising repetition	management	attitude measurement	analysis
Distribution theory	Territory design and	Sales management models;	Advances in forecasting
Refutation and distraction	salesman compensation	e.g., Detailer, Callplan	econometrics, and time
hypotheses	Marketing audit	New product models; e.g.,	series analysis
Theories of diffusion, new	Demand state strategies	Demon, Sprinter, Steam,	Trade-off analysis and conjoint
product adoption, and	Creative approaches and	Hendry	analysis
personal influence	styles	Bid pricing models	Psychographics and AIO
Prospect theory	New search and screening	Computer-assisted marketing	studies
	approaches	cases	Physiological techniques – eye
	Refinements in test	Product planning models,	camera, GSR, CONPAAD
	marketing approaches	perceptor, accessor	Unobtrusive measures,
			response latency, nonverbal
			behavior.

From Myers, John G.; Greyser, Stephen A.; and Massy, William F. The effectiveness of marketing's 'R&D' for marketing management: An assessment. *Journal of Marketing*, 1979, 43, 7-29. Reprinted with permission.

In Table 3, I list the knowledge developments in marketing that I consider to be contributions. The most significant of these are the marketing concept, market segmentation, positioning, mapping, and the product life cycle. In the balance of this article, I will discuss these contributions.

Five major contributions of marketing

The marketing concept

Scholars and practitioners agree that this concept describes the function of marketing. One widely used definition is:

a management orientation that holds that the key task of the organization is to determine the needs, wants, and values of a target market and to adapt the organization to delivering the desired satisfactions more effectively and efficiently than its competitors. (Kotler, 1976, p. 14)

McKitterick describes how the concept was developed at General Electric as a response to a changed environment and corporations grown too large to use profit as an objective. Instead, corporations had to focus on 'customer betterment': that is, management is 'not so much to be skillful in making the customer do what suits the interests of the business, as to be skillful in conceiving and then making the business do what suits the interests of the customer' (1957, p. 78).

Table 3 Contributions to Strategic Management from Knowledge Development in Marketing, 1952-1977[a]

Strategic Management Combination Paradigm	Discipline-Based Theories	Managerial Frameworks And Approaches	Models and Measurement	Research Methods And Techniques
Environmental Analysis	market segmentation theories of diffusion consumer behavior theories theories of motivation, etc.	marketing concept marketing information systems product life cycle product positioning and perceptual mapping		survey research focus groups advances in forecasting psychographics
Organization Competence and Resources		marketing audit		
Business Unit Level				
Define the business and the market	market segmentation	product positioning and perceptual mapping	multidimensional scaling	
Assess environmental attractiveness	theories of diffusion	product life cycle		all the methods and techniques listed above
Assess competitive position		marketing audit product positioning and perceptual mapping product-portfolio analysis	market share models	
Select appropriate strategy		marketing mix – the 4 Ps product-portfolio analysis segmentation strategies demand state approaches development of marketing cases marketing plan	Bayesian analysis simulation and marketing games market share models	trade-off analysis and conjoint analysis
Implementation		new marketing organization concepts territory design and salesman compensation		
Performance				

[a]Some contributions are of relevance to more than one aspect of strategy formulation and process, and are therefore listed more than once.

One contribution of marketing, then, is a perspective that emphasizes at least one element - the customer - of an organization's environment. Indeed, marketers would argue that the now fashionable pre-occupation with the external environment and strategy started with the articulation of the marketing concept. Up to the mid 50s, business had concentrated primarily on internal considerations.

Marketers would also argue that the marketing concept is both a philosophy and a practical guide-line. For example, Bennett (1979) writes that the more a company has adopted the concept, the more 'the gap between a company's strategic plan and its marketing plan narrows.' Strategic management issues often entail trade-offs between the short and long run, between financial and market performance, between private and public goals. The marketing concept provides a clear, if somewhat utopian, direction for resolving these trade-offs: in favor of the customer and the long run.

Market segmentation and positioning

I think market segmentation and its counterpart, positioning, must rank as marketing's most important contributions to strategic management. Market segmentation is defined as 'the subdividing of the market into distinct subsets of customers' (Kotler, 1976, p. 144) according to their needs and the way they buy and use a product or service. Positioning is a decision to serve a particular segment with a program tailored to those specific customer needs. Thus, these two concepts deal directly with analyzing a firm's environment so as to make a strategic decision about the extent of the firm's domain in that environment.

To illustrate, a suggested segmentation of the typewriter industry is shown in Figure 2 with my imputed positioning of IBM's Office Products Division and SCM's Smith-Corona Group.

Typewriter characteristics	Market Segment			
	Business buyers		Personal buyers	
Automatic	IBM			
Office	OPD		?	
Portable		?	SCM	

Figure 2 *Hypothesized segmentation of the typewriter industry and competitor positioning*

SCM's strategic choices can be framed as:

1 *Expansion* Should they try to serve additional segments, such as personal buyers needing office machine capabilities and business buyers needing portability?
2 *Defense* Is their current dominance of the personal buyer segment defensible against competitors who are dominant in another segment (e.g., IBM)?

Marketers have developed an arsenal of research techniques to help them segment markets and position competitors. One of these is *perceptual mapping* - plots of customer's perceptions constructed by multivariate analytic techniques, such as multi-dimensional scaling and multiple discriminant analysis (Greene and Carmone, 1970). Figure 3 shows a map of customers' perceptions of retail stores on the segmentation dimensions of 'fashion' and 'value for money.' For example, the discounter/mass merchandiser type of store (indicated by a solid triangle) is positioned in Quadrant 3, representing lower fashionability and lower value.

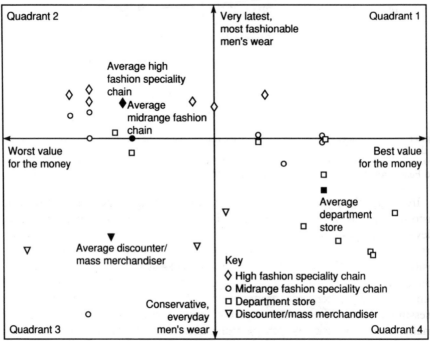

Figure 3   *Two-dimensional perceptual space: store positions on fashionability and value for the money. (From C.W. King and L. Ring (1980), 'Market positioning across retail fashion institutions: a comparative analysis of store types', Journal of Retailing, 56(1), 37-55. Reprinted with permission)*

This map suggests strategic questions. Note that Quadrant 1 is 'under-occupied.' This space might represent a market opportunity for a new type of store. Note also that individual department stores (indicated by light squares) are widely dispersed over Quadrants 3 and 4, while the department store *type* (solid square) is almost in the middle of Quadrant 4. The dispersion might suggest customer confusion and an opportunity for retailers 'to build clarity of offering and to differentiate their offerings from the average.'

Another map, in Figure 4, shows that customers tended to distinguish banks on 'their personalism' (horizontal axis) and 'their ability to change' (vertical axis). The authors report that executives of Bank A were disturbed to be positioned so close to Banks C and F - both suffering declining market shares. Bank A executives launched programs to reposition their bank.

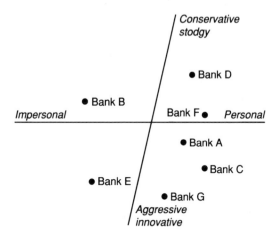

Figure 4 Multidimensional mapping/two-dimensional configuration. (Reprinted by permission of the Harvard Business Review. Exhibit from 'Quantitative rechniques for today's decision makers' by D.A. Heenan and R.B. Addleman (May-June 1976). Copyright © by the President and Fellows of Harvard College; all rights reserved)

In using these concepts, marketers first ask the question, 'How do customers define the environment?' (That is, what needs or problems are relevant to them?). Second, 'How do customers perceive different competitors' attempts to solve their problems?' Having segmented customers and positioned competitors, marketers next ask, 'How will environmental change alter the map (the market)?' For example, some segments might contract or even disappear; others will grow. Next, marketers analyze competitors by assessing their relative ability to serve existing and prospective segments. Finally, marketers ask, 'Which part of the market should we serve, against which kind of competitors?' In answering these questions, marketers have developed some strategic rules of thumb:

1 *Look for the hole.* The best strategic opportunity might be an unserved segment (e.g., Quadrant 1 in Figure 3).
2 *Don't squat between segments.* Any advantage from squatting (such as a larger target market) is offset by your failure to satisfy one segment. In decision theory terms, the intent here is to avoid sub-optimization by trying to serve more than one objective function.
3 *Don't serve two segments with the same strategy.* Usually, a successful strategy with one segment cannot be directly transferred to another segment.
4 *Don't position yourself in the middle of the map.* The middle usually means a strategy that is not clearly perceived to have any distinguishing characteristics. Obviously, this rule varies with the number of competitors (when

there are two, as in U.S. presidential elections, the middle becomes the preferred strategic positioning).

In summary, these rules stress the importance of achieving a focus in strategy: choose a segment of the market and serve it.

To guard against specious segmentation and to assess the attractiveness of a segment, marketers examine six aspects of a proposed segment. Experience has shown that after consideration of these aspects, there are probably only two or three ways of segmenting a market:

1 *Measurability* How many buyers are in the segment? Doubtless, there are automobile buyers who want high performance, styling, status, and luxury. But, are there enough of them to enable John de Lorean (ex-GM) to build a business?
2 *Accessibility* Can we reach the segment with product and promotion? Doubtless, there is a geriatric segment but distribution channels for geriatrics are not well developed.
3 *Substantiality* Can the segment profitably support a tailored strategic effort? The demise of The Saturday Evening Post was attributed to a declining segment for that kind of product.
4 *Defensibility* Are the costs of serving the segment unique to that segment? The alleged unprofitability of Hewlett-Packard's personal calculator business could be attributed to their strategy of concentrating on the engineer/scientist segment. This segment has few barriers to separate it from other segments, so that mass market competitors such as Texas Instruments have enormous 'shared experience' cost benefits in all segments.
5 *Durability* Are the differences between segments likely to endure or erode as buyers gain experience and technology diffuses? Data Terminal Systems has built a $150 million business in eight years serving small- and medium-sized retailers with stand-alone electronic cash registers. But medium-sized retailers are becoming more sophisticated about data processing, and competitive point-of-sale systems are becoming cheaper and simpler. As a result, Data Terminal's segment might erode.
6 *Competitiveness* Do we have a relative advantage in the types of skills required to serve the segment? One might suggest that Hewlett-Packard or The Saturday Evening Post should serve broader segments, but given the skills of the company's executives, such an expansion in domain would not be accomplished easily.

Marketers have not progressed beyond these kinds of rules and criteria to a theory of segmentation and positioning. The thousands of market segmentation studies have not led to a theory of segmentation that can specify segmentation dimensions and a taxonomy of positions for a specific strategic situation. Wind (1978) suggests four reasons why: (1) a lack of systematic effort to build a cumulative body of substantive findings about customer behavior, (2) a lack of specific models that link behavior to descriptor variables and thus predict which descriptor variables should be used, (3) the nonrepresentative nature of most of the academic studies with respect to sample design, and (4) a lack of comparable conceptual and operational definitions of variables across studies.

Segmentation/positioning and market/business definition

To marketers, segmentation and positioning concepts are the entry point for the strategic issues of market and business definition. Abell's (1977, 1980, Chapter 2) pioneering clinical work led him to conclude that businesses may be defined along three dimensions: (1) the type of customer groups that are targeted, (2) the customer functions that are performed for each customer group, and (3) the technologies that are employed to perform the functions. These three dimensions for the personal financial transactions market are illustrated in Figure 5. The strategic questions for a competitor in this market – Docutel, the largest producer of automatic teller machines (ATMs) but a small company absolutely – concern the *scope* of its business (how many customer functions and groups should it attempt to serve, with what technology?), and how it should *differentiate* itself (add software capability to interface with IBM/Burroughs systems to outperform other ATM component manufacturers?).

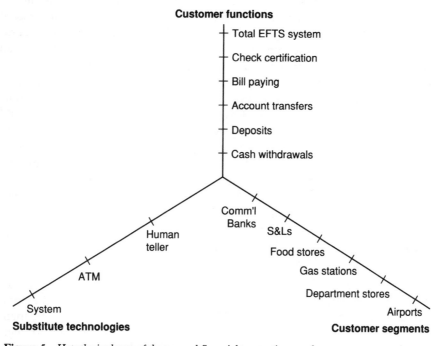

Figure 5 *Hypothesized map of the personal financial transactions market*

The way in which these questions are answered is to analyze:

1   Similarities and differences in the resource requirements of the different business functions (manufacturing, marketing, R&D, etc.)
2   Customer needs (do they need several functions to be performed together or not? – e.g., dispense cash only, or dispense and deposit functions)
3   The company's relative ability to actually span the resource requirements associated with serving a variety of customer functions in a variety of market segments.

Product life cycle

This familiar concept has had an enormous impact on the study of strategic management issues. Two leading consulting houses use the concept as a critical variable in their approach to strategic management (Boston Consulting Group, 1970; Little, n.d.). Hofer argues that 'the most fundamental variable in determining an appropriate business strategy is the stage of the product life cycle' (1975, p. 798).

The value of the concept derives from the fact that the stage of the product life cycle (PLC) is a useful indicator of what might be appropriate strategies (Levitt, 1965). For example, increasing vertical integration is often appropriate in the mature stage but inappropriate in the growth stage. The concept also helps strategists to think about strategy and financial flows over time. Indeed, the postulated flows of costs, investment, revenue, and break-even according to PLC stage pre-dated the Boston Consulting Group's matrix. But perhaps most important, the PLC enables marketers to think dynamically. The segmentation and positioning concepts discussed earlier are static until cast in a PLC. It helps prediction of the likely future bases of competition and how a strategy may have to be modified. It aids understanding of the evolution of a broader market or industry by recognizing product class cycles, product category cycles, and brand cycles.

The concept has not, however, been developed into a precise tool. The slope and duration of each stage of the cycle for particular products requires much judgment and varies from industry to industry; the PLC is not a completely independent variable - it is itself heavily influenced by the very strategies it predicts; and, unlike biological life cycles, a PLC stage can be renewed, through opening up a new segment (Buzzell *et al.*, 1969; Cox, 1967; Dhalla and Yuspeh, 1976; Enis *et al.*, 1977; Polli and Cook, 1969); others argue that it is a descriptive concept - we cannot predict when it will apply and when it will not (e.g., Porter, 1980).

Partly in response to these criticisms, marketers and others are now moving to extend the PLC to a theory of market evolution. This work is still in its early stages (Abell, 1980; Biggadike, 1980; Buzzell, 1979; Day, 1980), but I will sketch its direction and content. Our first objective is to get away from focus on a product to focus on the market for a particular generic need (for example, the personal financial transactions market as distinct from the automated teller machines product). This shift should help us to see discontinuous changes in the environment (in the spirit of Levitt's (1965) famous 'transportation industry' advice to the airlines).

This shift also facilitates the study of supply (as emphasized by industrial organization economists). Thus, in forecasting the evolution of a market, we are studying:

Demand   How are the market boundaries changing over time? What is the nature and extent of segmentation over time? What is the nature of customers' buying behavior? What is the growth rate?

Supply   How many competitors will there be over time? What will be their relative sizes and shares? How will the value-added structure change over time?

Analysis of the demand side suggests the extent of differentiation in a market. Analysis of the supply side suggests the level of concentration. These judgments lead to a simple taxonomy of markets: Concentrated-Differentiated, Fragmented-Differentiated, Concentrated-Undifferentiated, Fragmented-Undifferentiated. Thus, if a market is expected to evolve to a Concentrated-Undifferentiated type in maturity, share-building objectives in the embryonic and growth stages are important so that the business has the lowest cost position in maturity. Such an emphasis on share building, however, would be disastrous in a Fragmented-Differentiated market type (such as the furniture industry or many distribution industries). Here, strategies that position rivals against specific segments are indicated.

Of course, the analytical tasks of forecasting the extent of differentiation and concentration remain. To facilitate this work, we are trying to identify 'environmental drivers' – which influence the characteristics of a market (such as whether or not there is an experience curve effect, the magnitude of economies of scale, the heterogeneity in customer demand) – and examine to what extent different values on these drivers predetermine evolution, at what pace, to what kind of market. For example, an experience curve and homogeneous demand (e.g., an electronic component) are likely to lead to a Concentrated-Undifferentiated market type. But, if demand is sufficiently heterogeneous (as perhaps in the case of automobiles), experience curve and scale economy effects can be partially offset and a Concentrated-Differentiated type results. This market type permits the survival of segmented strategies, such as those followed by Mercedes-Benz, Rolls Royce, and Porsche.

Abell's (1980) research in industrial markets suggests that in the early stages of market evolution, customers are seeking solutions to single problems or functions (for example, cash dispensing). In our taxonomy, these customer needs beget competitors offering components and a Fragments-Differentiated market. Later, customers take more of a system view of their needs and competitors offering systems have a relative advantage. Because of the resources that a systems-based strategy requires, we might expect a more Concentrated market. Next, the systems competitors ignore some segments and we may see re-emergence of component competitors and a Fragmented-Differentiated market.

Work on market evolution also deals with the task of forecasting which stage a market is in and when it is about to move. For example, the guidelines shown in Table 4 help identify stages of market development.

Table 4   Indicators helpful in identifying stages of market evolution

Indicator	Early stages	Late stages
Growth rate	high	low
Mass merchandiser		
% of total sales	low	high
Competitor entry	high	low
Competitor exit	low	high
New feature		
introductions	low	high
Age of products/services	young	old
Rate of technological		
change	high	low
R&D/sales revenue ratio	high	low
Marketing/sales		
revenue ratio	high	low
Real price behavior	rapid decline	stable
Replacement sales		
% of total sales	low	high
Customer emphasis		
on education	high	low
Customer emphasis		
on price	low	high

As to when a market will change stages, Levitt (1965) offers this prescription: the mature stage will last as long as there are no substitutes, no shift in customer values, no changes in demand for complementary products, and no changes in the rate of obsolescence of the product or in the rate of product modifications.

The common premise behind this work is that we can understand and predict market evolution only after analysis of the drivers and market characteristics: customer needs, problems, or functions (of both end users and channels); competitor strategies; substitute and complementary products; technology and cost/price characteristics (see also Porter, 1980).

Concluding remarks

The distinctive feature of marketing for strategic management studies is that, although it is one of the business functions, it is a function that is directly concerned with the organization's environment. Consequently, marketing has a perspective that is critical to strategic management. This perspective is captured by the marketing concept, which provides strategic management students with both a philosophy and an operational method for resolving strategic management issues and for integrating the activities of the business: make 'the business do what suits the interests of the customer' (McKitterick, 1957, p. 78).

Marketers operationalize the marketing concept by segmenting customers and positioning competitors on perceptual maps. This work frames the strategic choice issue as decisions about which segment of the market to serve, and with whom to compete. Normatively, segmentation and positioning research have shown the importance of focus and concentration in strategy. Finally, marketers help strategy students to conduct dynamic analysis with the concept of the product life cycle and an emerging theory of market evolution.

The enormous and diverse array of research in marketing has not led to many 'general facts and laws' – either for marketing or for strategic management issues. Marketing does, however, have a rich basis for hypothesizing about strategic situations and a growing body of techniques to explore these hypotheses. Most reported research, however, is ad hoc problem-oriented research with little attempt to integrate and extend relationships to other situations. I judge that many marketers today are not scientists in the theory-building sense but technological virtuosi in solving problems at a brand or, occasionally, product level.

This survey therefore leaves me both optimistic and pessimistic. I am optimistic in believing that marketers have concepts and tools to attack strategic management issues. I am pessimistic in doubting that this attack will lead to theory, primarily because of the data acquisition problems that all researchers in strategy face, which will therefore perpetuate ad hoc, firm-specific, problem-oriented research. Also, I am not convinced that many marketers are interested in raising their level of aggregation to the business-unit or industry-unit level and their time horizon to the long run. It is reasonably straightforward to apply a quantitative technique to a brand over the next twelve months. It is far less straightforward to apply the same technique to a product class over the next five, ten, or twenty years.

What I see, then, over the next few years from marketers, is more conceptual development (e.g., market evolution), improved technical expertise (e.g., market definition and quantitative models), and, of course, more methods for surveying, segmenting, and positioning customers. In other words, we can expect more of the same – concept and methods. It will be up to strategic management students to make the transfer to their issues.

References

Abell, Derek F. Business definition as an element of the strategic decision. In Allan D. Shocker (Ed.), *Analytic approaches to product and marketing planning.* Cambridge: Marketing Science Institute, 1977.

Abell, Derek F. *Defining the business: The starting point of strategic planning.* Englewood Cliffs, N.J.: Prentice-Hall, 1980.

Allen, Michael G. *Strategic problems facing today's corporate planner.* Paper presented at the annual meeting of the Academy of Management, Kansas City, 1976.

Bennett, Peter D. Review of *Strategic Planning and Policy* by William R. King and David I. Cleland. *Journal of Marketing*, 1979, 43(2), 131-132.

Biggadike, E. Ralph. *Market evolution.* Unpublished manuscript, 1980.

Boston Consulting Group. *Product portfolio: Growth/share matrix perspective.* Cambridge: Boston Consulting Group, 1970.

Buzzell, Robert D. *Are there 'natural' market structures?* Working Paper 73-79, Harvard Business School, 1979.

Buzzell, Robert D., Cook, Victor, Peterson, James and Hase, Paul. *Product life cycles.* Cambridge: Marketing Science Institute, 1969.

Cox, William E. Product life cycles as marketing models. *Journal of Business*, 1967, 40(4), 375-384.

Day, George S. *Strategic market analysis: Top down and bottom up approaches.* Cambridge: Marketing Science Institute, 1980.

Dhalla, Nariman K. and Yuspeh, Sonia. Forget the product life cycle concept. *Harvard Business Review*, 1976, 54(1), 102-112.

Enis, Ben M., La Garce, Raymond and Prell, Arthur E. Extending the product life cycle. *Business Horizons*, 1977, 20(3), 46-56.

Green, Paul E. and Carmone, Frank J. *Multidimensional scaling and related techniques in marketing analysis.* Boston: Allyn & Bacon, 1970.

Hofer, Charles N. Toward a contingency theory of business strategy. *Academy of Management Journal*, 1975, 18(4), 784-810.

Hunt, Shelby D. *Marketing theory: Conceptual foundations of research in marketing.* Columbus, Ohio: Grid, 1976.

Kotler, Phillip. *Marketing management.* Englewood Cliffs, N.J.: Prentice-Hall, 1976.

Learned, Edmund P., Christensen, C. Roland, Andrews, Kenneth R. and Guth, William D. *Business policy: Text and cases.* Homewood, Ill.: Irwin, 1965.

Levitt, Theodore. Exploit the product life cycle. *Harvard Business Review*, 1965, 43(6), 81-94.

Little, Arthur D., Inc. *A system for managing diversity.* Cambridge: Arthur D. Little, Inc., n.d.

McCarthy, E. Jerome. *Basic marketing* (4th ed.). Homewood, Ill.: Irwin, 1971.

McKitterick, J.B. What is the marketing management concept? In Frank M. Bass (Ed.), *The frontiers of marketing thought and action.* Chicago: American Marketing Association, 1957.

Myers, John G., Greyser, Stephen A. and Massy, William F. The effectiveness of marketing's 'R&D' for marketing management: An assessment. *Journal of Marketing*, 1979, 43(1), 17-29.

Polli, Rolando and Cook, Victor. Validity of the product life cycle. *Journal of Business*, 1969, 42(4), 385-400.

Porter, Michael E. *Competitive strategy.* New York: Free Press, 1980.

Schoeffler, Sidney, Buzzel, Robert D. and Heany, Donald F. Impact of strategic planning on profit performance. *Harvard Business Review*, 1974, 52(2), 137-146.

Wind, Yoram. Issues and advances in segmentation research. *Journal of Marketing Research*, 1978, 15(3), 317-337.

2 Marketing's contribution to the strategy dialogue

George S. Day

Marketers appear comfortable with the assertion that marketing should play the lead role in charting the strategic direction of a business. The logic behind this assertion is straightforward. Strategic planning is about keeping the business in step with the anticipated environment, and marketing has traditionally served as the boundary function between the firm and its customer, channel, and competitor environment. It follows that marketing should have the most to say about the match of the competencies of the business with the opportunities to exploit and threats to avoid. However, other business functions and academic disciplines don't share this assumption and have been actively eroding the influence of marketing in the strategy dialogue.

The diminution of the strategic role of marketing began in the early eighties.[1] There are few signs that this slide will be reversed in the foreseeable future. The reasons are grounded in the fit of the issues, trends, and fashions in the strategic arena with the distinctive competencies of marketers. When the fit is close, then marketing gains influence by contributing superior insights. As the fit loosens or other disciplines and functions have competencies more attuned to the emerging issues, then marketing loses ground.

The judgment that the strategic role of marketing is declining – albeit from a high starting point – is both controversial and arguable since there is little or no empirical evidence directly relevant to the issue. Our approach will be to first offer some evidence of the present state of affairs. Next, we will review the major forces and trends that are shaping the contemporary strategy dialogue within leading multi-divisional firms in highly contested global markets. Some of these issues are supportive of a strong role for marketing, while others work against that role. Then, we will match these issues with the distinctive strategic competencies of marketing. This reveals a sizable gap between the possibilities for marketers to seize the opportunities for thought leadership, and lower probability that marketers will actually pursue the opportunity to regain a lead role.

What is the role of marketing in the strategy dialogue?   The answer depends on: (1) what is meant by marketing – whether it is viewed as a general management responsibility, an organizational orientation, or a distinct function, (2) the level of analysis – corporate business unit, or brand; and (3) the perspective used, with especially noticeable differences between practitioners and marketing academics on one hand and academics from other functions and disciplines on the other.

Among *practitioners* there is widespread interest in marketing as a general management responsibility (primarily at the business level), and general acceptance of the need to build a market orientation throughout their organization. The most forceful position was taken by Regis McKenna[2] when he proclaimed 'marketing is everything'. As he defines marketing, it is not a function, 'it is a way of doing business . . . (its job) is to integrate the customer into the design of the product and to design a systematic process for interaction that will create substance in the relationship' (p. 68). Most of the commentators on this article agreed with his argument, although some took exception to the title. After all, many CEOSs are on record as endorsing the need for a thoroughgoing market orientation (see, for example, Avishai and Taylor.[3]

Paradoxically, the deeper marketing is embedded within an organization and becomes the defining theme for shaping competitive strategies, the more likely is the role of marketing as a distinct function to be diminished. As Glazer[4] concluded, 'If the changing information environment succeeds in transforming business activity along the lines suggested here, marketing as a philosophy would appear to have triumphed even as its activities have become too important to be left to the marketing function' (p. 17). This blurring and obscuring of the functional role of marketing is also reflected in prescriptions about emerging organizations that are designed to cope with diverse, turbulent, and knowledge-rich environments (Achrol[5]). When 'marketing becomes too important to leave to marketers', as David Packard of Hewlett-Packard once observed, then the distinctive marketing activities and perspectives lose their dominant influence in the strategy dialogue. At the extreme, the marketing function could disappear as a distinct management function and specialty. Perhaps marketing and strategic planning will merge into a single core function responsible for keeping the firm focused on the changing marketplace.[6] In this scenario, the responsibility for understanding customers and making sure the firm delivers superior value to them will become part of everyone's job description.

Within *academic* circles, the contribution of marketing, as an applied management discipline, to the development, testing, and dissemination of strategic theories and concepts has been marginalized during the past decade. Academics outside of marketing pay little attention to marketing literature or theory. For example, studies of journal citation patterns in either management or strategic management do not include any marketing journals (although most organizational behaviour journals were included, as were several from economics and finance.)[7] Even the marketing concept has been largely ignored in other management fields. Thus, a review of 'all variables that have been proposed seriously as indices of organizational effectiveness'[8] failed to mention customer satisfaction. Similarly, the marketing concept is nowhere to be found in a discussion of competing principles of management presumed to be causally related to the effectiveness of organizations.[9]

In retrospect, the 1960s were the era of marketing's widest influence and brightest promise. The business policy field was largely concerned with corporate strategy and the integration of functional strategies – leaving the functions to define the strategic choices and especially the critical choice of product markets to serve. There was even the genesis of a theory of competitive advantage proposed by Alderson.[10] During the 1970s, marketers made important contributions to the development of the new generation of quantitative and prescriptive portfolio models, and the study of pooled business experience in the PIMS data base.[11]

Why has marketing lost influence in the academic discourse about strategy? One reason is the preemption of marketing frameworks, concepts, and methods by other fields of inquiry. The best example is industrial organization economics, which has employed such concepts as segmentation and positioning, life cycle analysis, and innovation and diffusion processes, and put them in a better package for general management usage. The work of Michael Porter[12,13] has been especially influential. Conversely, when marketers address strategic issues, there is a tendency to employ the theories and frameworks of other academic disciplines: transaction cost analyses, strategic typologies such as those Miles and Snow have developed, social interaction theory, organizational culture, game theory, and industry structural analysis come to mind. Such borrowing is appropriate for an applied discipline such as marketing, but does result in a lop-sided balance of trade in influential ideas.

Significant preemption was underway in the seventies and accelerated in the next decade as strategic management matured as a discipline. The defining event was the Pittsburgh Conference,[14] where the discipline was defined as 'a process that deals with the entrepreneurial work of the organization, with organizational renewal and growth, and more particularly with developing and utilizing the strategy which is to guide the organization's operation' (p. 11). In effect, a new field of inquiry had come into existence, built on the foundations of the previous business policy work on functional integration, with a liberal borrowing from related areas including marketing.

Meanwhile, marketing ceded some territory by shifting the balance of research activity further toward micro issues. Important advances were made in understanding consumer choice and influence processes and in teasing insights from scanner data, but inevitably this meant an over-emphasis on brand tactics for fast-moving consumer package goods. This is reminiscent of

Biggadike's[15] contention that, although marketers have the tools and concepts to tackle strategic management issues, they are unlikely to do so because their orientation is toward technological solutions to short-term problems at a brand or product level. Indeed, the question was posed whether 'marketers are interested in raising their level of aggregation to the business unit or industry level, and their time horizon to the long run. . . . [Consequently] it will be up to strategic management students to make the transfer of marketing concepts and methods to strategic issues.'

The final reason for the loss of influence is that marketers have been tardy in addressing some of the important issues of the past decade, and tend to stay too long with outmoded characterizations of strategy processes and issues. The purpose of the next section is to identify some of the opportunities that marketers might pursue with a long-run research and action agenda.

Shifting priorities in strategic management

Issues continually emerge and fade within the strategy field in response to environmental changes and cumulative knowledge development. Since strategic management researchers see their purpose as addressing the life and death issues of central interest to top management, new issues will emerge as fast as the environment of these managers changes. This makes it difficult to keep up with the current high priority topics within the field, and doubly difficult to forecast the issues of the future. Nonetheless, a reasonable snapshot of the present concerns of general managers comes from a recent survey of leading academics within the strategic management field.[16] The major drawback of this survey is that areas seen as having the most impact on strategic research in the next ten years (summarized in Table 1) have been filtered through the biases and preferences of the academics in the sample. Hopefully, they are reasonable gate-keepers and interpreters of the field, so their nomination of global strategies as the top issue demands our attention. This macro topic subsumes 'global strategic thinking', 'global competition' and 'globalization of markets'. Close behind in the rankings, with almost the same frequency of choice, were four distinct issues. One of the four reflected the continued contribution of economic frameworks and paradigms. Despite the perception of some that economic perspectives were assuming dominance, the other three topics derived from organizational behavior and structure issues. Marketers should pay attention to the interest in strategic cognition and decision-making, which is an area of inquiry with strong affinity to the information processing theories in consumer behavior research. Others in the top set of issues included the rather ill-defined area of organizational ecology.[17] Marketers are beginning to pay attention to this field because of its demonstrable relevance to the understanding of marketing and competitive structural changes over the course of the industry and product life cycle.[18]

Because the judgments in Table 1 were made on a forced choice basis – respondents could only nominate their three top areas – there is no sense of relative importance. Given the methodology, it is not surprising to find functional strategies low in the list of areas with impact.

Table 1 Areas Having the Most Impact on Strategic Research in the 1990s

Areas	Percentage of respondents picking as one of three areas
Multinational/global strategies	13.5
Industry and competitor analysis	11.2
Strategic cognition and decision-making	11.2
Strategy implementation	11.2
Organization theory, population ecology, transformations	10.2
Technology	7.9
Alliances and co-op strategies	6.7
Functional strategies	4.5
Methodological approaches	4.5
Mergers, acquisitions, diversification	4.5
Transaction costs, financial economics	3.4
Organizational learning	2.2
Entrepreneurship, intrapreneurship	2.2
Other	3.4
	100.0%

Source: Lyles (1990) (Ref. 15)

The content of these emerging issues is likely to be shaped by what has been learned in the past, as well as by prevailing fads and fashions among practitioners and consultants who are constantly seeking new tools and frameworks. Marketing academics are often slow to respond to changes in 'received wisdom' and are prone to work on outdated problems or advocate methods that have been dismissed by users. We can illustrate this tendency in three areas where markets have not kept up with the latest developments: the changing role of strategic planning concepts and methods, the emerging focus on the sources of advantage, and the consequences of changes in the boundaries of organizations.

The attack on strategic planning

Since the mid-eighties, the traditional top-down approaches to strategic planning favoured in marketing textbooks have been in disarray; line managers resent the intrusions or dismiss them as irrelevant to their competitive problems, the strategies often can't be implemented, and, consequently, large corporate planning groups are being dismantled.

The most damaging attacks have been directed at the absolutist assumptions that strategy making is the prerogative of the top corporate officers and the planning staff, and that the desired strategic directions could be forced downward. What seems to matter more is the understanding and acceptance of the strategy by those responsible for its implementation. Often the most effective strategies come from those closest to the market opportunities and technological possibilities who then champion an initiative.[19]

Managers also found that the simplistic prescriptions of such familiar planning tools as portfolio models, experience curves, and 'change the game' strategies were often misleading or wrong. Frequently the premises did not hold true. The largest market share did not always assure the most profitable position or the greatest market influence; the risks of high growth markets eroded their attractiveness; and portfolio position was not necessarily a guide to cash flow. Even the well-documented conclusions about the importance of timing of market entry[20] have been challenged by growing evidence that what matters is the ability to surmount barriers to imitation with innovations that permit entry into uncontested segments.

The overall consequences of all this revisionist thinking about the proper role of strategic planning are still unclear. Two results are coming into better focus. One is that such notions as distinct served markets that define defensible competitive spaces, and strategic business units as autonomous, discrete, and self-sufficient entries, are being supplanted by more holistic concepts that highlight the value of interdependencies in the competencies of business units and conceive of markets as spheres of technological influence. A second development is the increasing acceptance of a new yard-stick for judging market strategies according to their ability to enhance shareholder value.[21] This will inevitably force a closer integration of marketing and financial perspectives on strategy.

Focusing on the sources of advantage

A compressed history of scholarship and thinking in the strategy field would show three phases of development. In phase one, which roughly corresponded to the seventies, the focus was on the *outcomes* of strategy. Much was made of market share strategies, the relationship of market share to profitability was debated (and the debate continues, for example by Gale and Buzzell[22] and the experience curve relationship of costs and cumulative output was a major building block. Toward the end of this phase, industry structure analysis – epitomized by Porter's five forces model[12] – gained prominence. The second phase shifted attention to the *positional advantages* firms had created in order to achieve lower costs or superior value in the market. This phase peaked in the mid- to late eighties and led to active interest in strategic typologies, generic strategies, and the dimensions of advantage such as quality or channel relations. By the late eighties, a third phase emerged, as attention shifted to the *sources* of advantage in recognition of the fact that positional and performance superiority are derived from relative superiority in the skills and resources a business has to deploy. This was a belated recognition that what really matters is the specific actions that management takes to deploy resources to enhance quality, shorten time to market, and build strong customer and channel relationships. Notions of empowerment, team building, and closeness to the customer became increasingly fashionable.

Among the triggers for the transition to phase three were the recognition of the superiority of the Japanese in managing quick response systems, the steering effect of the Baldridge Quality Award, greater emphasis on managing processes, and a belated recognition of the importance of invisible assets[23] or core competencies.[24] These competencies are embodied in the superior skills of employees – the technologies they have mastered, what they have learned about their market, and the prevailing values and culture. Because these core competencies have been so difficult to identify, most of the attention has been directed to visible aspects such as knowing how to coordinate diverse production skills, harmonize streams of technology, and organize work processes. This is a very internal view of competencies. So far, the emerging stream of thinking in marketing about the contribution of the market orientation to performance[25,26] has not informed the discussions of core competencies.

Loosening the boundaries of the organization

It is sobering to consider the mismatch between the evolving, fluid character of contemporary business organizations and the large bureaucratic, hierarchically-structured, functional organization that is the implicit model encountered in most marketing texts. These large monolithic firms engage in a series of transactions with customers, using channel as conduits, and strive for scale economies to justify integrating as many activities as possible.[27] The challenges to this self-contained model of an organization are numerous and daunting:

- Relations with customers are being modified by a desire for collaborative relationships grounded in mutual trust. These relationships are being further tightened with electronic data interchange, which creates a continuous flow of information about requirements and usage patterns and enhances two-way communications.
- Relationships with channel members are being complicated as the tidy distinction between direct and indirect channels is being swamped by a complicated clutter of competing modes. The channels are also exercising their power as consolidation at this level of the business system lessens the number of members and information technology magnifies this power by giving them direct access to customer information.
- Relations with competitors are no longer simply defined by parallel striving and a zero-sum mentality, but may be supplanted by cooperative relationships[28] that reveal competitor inter-trading, joint activities up to and including joint ventures and participation in industry consortia.

These trends, when magnified and intensified by global competition, help to explain the trend toward more responsive forms of organization. These have been variously called networks, strategic partnerships, alliances, and shamrocks,[27] but all are characterized by an increasing focus and specialization of core activities and the use of partners to undertake other activities where the firm is not as well qualified. Indeed, Achrol[5] sees two emerging forms – the marketing exchange company and the marketing coalition company – that serve as the organizing hubs of complex networks of functionally specialized firms. Whatever organizational forms eventually evolve, we can be sure they will not be traditional. We can assert with equal confidence that the traditional marketing strategy frameworks and approaches are not adequate to deal with long-run buyer-seller relationships and strategic alliances. One forecast of these consequences has the role and purpose of marketing shifting from 'manipulation of the customer to genuine customer involvement; from telling and selling to communicating and sharing knowledge; from last-in-line function to corporate credibility champion.'[29] The question that remains is whether marketing as a field is going to actively participate in the strategy dialogue unleashed by these organizational challenges.

The strategic competencies of marketing

The field of marketing is qualified to make more significant contributions to the theory and practice of strategy. Whether these contributions are made – and have recognizable influence – depends on marketers seeing their relationship with other functions more clearly, and then mobilizing their competencies more effectively. One vehicle for encouraging this outcome is an explicit articulation of these competencies. This is a daunting task, with few empirical touch points to provide guidance, and highly susceptible to errors of both omission and commission.

A concept of marketing competencies that is more broadly specified and sharply articulated in strategic terms should also help overcome the prevailing view of marketing within strategic management as a narrowly engaged operating function. Consequently, marketing is looked to for guidance only in terms of its undeniable expertise in understanding customers and markets. Even within this domain there is a tendency to overlook such important aspects as the design and management of channels, the analysis of market responses to strategic moves, the use of environmental scanning to identify market opportunities, and the identification and development of new products.

Within this broadened view of marketing we can distinguish three levels of potential contributions:

1   *Distinctive competencies.* These are the aspects of strategy where marketing as a function or discipline is the unchallenged expert.

2 *Integrative competencies.* Here marketing takes the lead role in a multi-discipline or multi-function approach to an aspect of strategy content or process that is primarily integrative in nature.

3 *Supportive competencies.* These are aspects where marketing makes a useful contribution but does not provide the dominant perspective.

The choice of specific integrative competencies was guided by Jemison's[30] comparison of three paradigms of strategic management research emerging from industrial organization economics, marketing, and administrative behavior. Each represents a perspective from which cross-disciplinary research may be initiated. For our purposes the interesting comparisons are the unit of analysis, the type of problem addressed (whether content or process), and the dominant inference pattern within the paradigm. These are summarized in Table 2. His interpretation gives a lead role to marketing in matters of business definition and positions, choice of alternative growth paths, management of channel partners and relationships, and cooperative strategies for serving markets.[31]

Table 2 Comparison of Strategic Management Paradigms

Basis of comparison	Industrial organization economics	Marketing	Administrative behaviour
Unit of analysis	Industry and strategic group	Business, product and market	Firm, business and functions
Type of problem addressed	Content	Content	Process
Dominant inference patterns	Industry structure sets limits on firm performance	Managers manipulate product-market combinations to affect performance	Managers manipulate structure and process which affect performance

Source: Adapted from Jemison (1981) (Ref. 30)

The choice of supportive competencies was guided by the notion that the primary concern of strategic management should be the formulation and implementation of corporate strategic direction.[32] This comprises the organizational context of strategic decisions – including the management of interdependencies between business units, the strategic decision process – including the formal systems for planning, implementing, or controlling, and the acquisition and allocation of resources to existing businesses and renewal activities. Marketers can contribute to theory and practice within each of these areas, because the appropriate unit of analysis is often the individual product-market. A corporate or 'top down' perspective is inevitably only partially informed about the threats and opportunities at this level of competitive interaction. The strategic decision process requires a dialogue between corporate and business unit levels. Similarly, marketers can inform and influence the choice of organizational arrangement and controls, especially where it affects the ability of the organization to satisfy customers.

The eventual classification of competencies was further influenced by the Charnes *et al.*[33] argument that it is unwise to regard substantive theorizing as the only form or even the most important form of scientific progress. In their view theory with real empirical referents is not possible without concurrent data base developments and modelling of empirical and information system phenomena. They further argue that methodological developments, such as conjoint analysis, should be judged on responsiveness to management needs rather than satisfaction of the theoretical conditions of one or more sets of theories or axioms. This argument is sufficiently persuasive that the distinction between theories and managerial frameworks versus models and methods is used as the second dimension for classifying marketing's strategic competencies. The two dimensions of classification come together in Table 3, including our judgment as to representative competencies within each of the cells.

Table 3   The Strategic Competencies of Marketing

Competencies	Theories of Managerial Frameworks	Models and methods
A Distinctive	● Market segmentation and positioning ● Product market definition ● Marketing concept	● Marketing mix allocation models ● Market share attraction models ● Models of new product diffusion
B Integrative	● Managing vertical market structures and relationships with channel partners ● Market share strategies ● Models of market evolution (product life cycle analysis) ● Differentiation strategies (customer value analysis) ● Cross-cultural analysis for international markets ● New product development process	● Market response to market mix variables (decision support models) ● Demographic and life style analysis ● Conjoint (trade-off analysis) ● Market mapping methods ● Measurement of perceived quality and customer satisfaction
C Supportive	● Competitive response (game-theoretic models) ● Industry and competitor analysis ● Strategic group analysis ● Organizational design and planning processes ● Market-based sources of synergy (inter-dependencies) ● Strategic cognition and decision-making (behavioral decision theory) ● Organizational change processes ● Resource allocation and financial valuation approaches	● Market survey and experimentation ● Resource allocation models (e.g. portfolio analysis, analytical hierarchy process) ● Environmental scanning

Toward a distinctive marketing role in the strategy dialogue

There is no facile, straightforward answer to the question of how marketing will contribute to the strategy dialogue in the future. On the present evidence, a cautiously positive answer is warranted – especially when marketing is viewed as a general management function, for here a leadership role is widely endorsed by practitioners. One caution, however, is that this acceptance may lead to the eventual subordination of the marketing function to a supporting role within the flexible organization of the future where everyone is involved with marketing.

Whether marketing as an academic discipline will exercise thought leadership within the broad terrain of strategy is less certain. Some grounds for optimism are found in the convergence of the competencies of marketers with the strategic imperatives of the nineties. These trends will put an increasing premium on understanding and managing relationships in boundary-less organizations, understanding the processes by which superior customer value is created, and analyzing dynamic and fragmenting markets. These issues play to marketing's comparative advantages. Similarly, the growing emphasis on the sources of competitive advantage meshes well with the recent efforts by marketers to conceptualize and operationalize a market orientation.

Tempering this positive picture is the persistent inability of marketers to make a concerted attack on global management issues, address the structural consequences of industry and market dynamics, or seriously incorporate technological advances into their research agenda. There are significant exceptions to this generalization (see, for example, Capon and Glazer[34]) but their scarcity is telling. Meanwhile, information technology is reshaping the conduct of business, whereas many marketers have been preoccupied with the analytical possibilities opened up by the scanner data explosion. These efforts bring new power to tactical decisions, but deflect attention from the possibilities for new competitive strategies and improvements in management process. We still seem to have a long way to go to overcome the unbalance fixation with the brand as the unit of analysis and the related fascination with consumer choice processes in consumer package goods markets.

Marketers will only be able to assume a significant role in strategy if other functions and disciplines do not step forward first. The prognosis for marketing – based on the present trends and past behaviour of other disciplines – is not encouraging. However, there are mixed signals coming from the field of strategic management regarding its ability or willingness to tackle some of the issues. Some commentators have argued that:

> The ascendance and eventual dominance of economists in the field [of strategic management] seemed to totally eclipse those doing administratively-oriented research. . . . [T]he role of management was either ignored or accorded a passing

reference, as research on strategic groups, risk-return relationship, and diversification focused on the firm as an abstract entity rather than as a social institution with an economic purpose. (Bartlett and Ghoshal,[35] p. 8)

This is certainly an arguable proposition, but it does suggest that exclusionary paradigms are taking root in this field, leaving room for other innovative and insightful approaches to gain influence.

After surveying the tightly-woven web of emerging strategy issues to be addressed by increasingly fluid organizations with shifting and porous boundaries in response to unprecedented market and technological changes, the safest conclusion is that no single discipline or perspective can or should aspire to dominate the strategy dialogue. Complex issues will best be illuminated by multi-disciplinary research approaches and theoretical frame-works, and dealt with by multi-disciplinary teams of managers. Marketers can and will make productive contributions to this kind of dialogue once the possibilities for collaborative work are appreciated and old habits of insularity succumb to new realities.

References

1 Day, George S. and Robin Wensley (1983). 'Marketing Theory with a Strategic Orientation', *Journal of Marketing* 47 (Fall), 79-89.
2 McKenna, Regis (1991). 'Marketing is Everything.' *Harvard Business Review* 69 (January-February), 65-79.
3 Avishai, Bernard, and William Taylor (1989). 'Customers Drive a Technology-Driven Company: An interview with George Fisher.' *Harvard Business Review* 67 (November-December) 107-114.
4 Glazer, Rashi (1991). 'Marketing is an Information-Intensive Environment: Strategic Implications of Knowledge as an Asset.' *Journal of Marketing* 55 (October), 1-19.
5 Achrol, Ravi S. (1991). 'Evolution of the Marketing Organization: New Forms for Turbulent Environments.' *Journal of Marketing* 55 (October), 77-93.
6 Webster, Frederick E. (1991). 'The Changing Role of Marketing in the Corporation.' *Commentary*, Cambridge, MA: Marketing Science Institute (October), 91-127.
7 Franke, Richard H, Timothy W. Edlund, and Frederick Oster (1990). 'The Development of Strategic Management: Journal Quality and Article Impact.' *Strategic Management Journal* 11 (March-April), 243-253.
8 Campbell, John P. (1977). 'On the Nature of Organizational Effectiveness.' In *New Perspectives on Organizational Effectiveness*, edited by P.S. Goodman and J.M. Pennings, San Francisco, Jossey-Bass.
9 Lewin, Arie Y. and John W. Minton (1986). 'Determining Organizational Effectiveness: Another look and an Agenda for Research.' *Management Science* 32 (May), 514-538.
10 Alderson, Wroe (1965). *Dynamic Marketing Behaviour*, Homewood IL, Irwin.
11 Buzzell, Robert D. and Bradley T. Gale (1987). *The PIMS Principles: Linking Strategy to Performance*, New York, Free Press.
12 Porter, Michael (1980). *Competitive Strategy*, New York, Free Press.
13 Porter, Michael (1985). *Competitive Advantage: Creating and Sustaining Superior Performance*, New York, Free Press.
14 Schendel, Dan and Charles W. Hoger (1979). *Strategic Management: A New View of Business Policy and Planning*, Boston, Little Brown.
15 Biggadike, Ralph E. (1981). 'The Contributions of Marketing to Strategic Management', *Academy of Management Review* 6 (August), 621-632.

16 Lyles, Marjorie (1990). 'A Research Agenda for Strategic Management in the 1990s.' *Journal of Management Studies* 27 (July), 363-375.
17 Singh, Jitendra (1990). *Organisational Evolution: New Directions*, Newbury Park, CA, Sage Publications.
18 Lambin, Mary and George S. Day (1989). 'Evolutionary Processes in Competitive Markets: Beyond the Product Life Cycle.' *Journal of Marketing* (Summer), 1-17.
19 Mintzberg, Henry (1987). 'Crafting Strategy.' *Harvard Business Review* 69 (July-August), 66-79.
20 Robinson, William T. (1988). 'Sources of Market Pioneer Advantages: The Case of Industrial Goods Industries.' *Journal of Marketing Research* 14 (February), 87-94.
21 Rappaport, Alfred (1986). *Creating Shareholder Value: The New Standard for Business Performance*, New York, Free Press.
22 Gale, Bradley T. and Robert D. Buzzell (1990). 'Market Position and Competitive Strategy.' In *The Interface of Marketing and Strategy*, eds George S. Day, Barton Weitz and Robin Wensley, Greenwich, CT, JAI Press.
23 Itami, Hiroyuki (1987). *Mobilizing Invisible Assets*, Cambridge, MA, Harvard University Press.
24 Prahalad, C.K. and Gary Hamel (1990). 'The Core Competencies of the Corporation.' *Harvard Business Review* 68 (May-June), 79-91.
25 Kohli, Ajay K. and Bernard Jaworski (1990). 'Market orientation: The Construct, Research Propositions and Managerial Implications.' *Journal of Marketing* 54 (April), 1-18.
26 Narver, John C. and Stanley F. Slater (1990). 'The Effect of Market Orientation on Business Profitability.' *Journal of Marketing* 54 (October), 20-35.
27 Webster, Frederick E. (1991). 'The Changing Role of Marketing in the Corporation.' *Commentary*. Cambridge MA, Marketing Science Institute (October), 91-127.
28 Easton Geoffrey (1990). 'Relationships Among Competitors.' In *The Interface of Marketing and Strategy*, eds George S. Day, Barton Weitz and Robin Wensley, Greenwich, CT, JAI Press.
29 McKenna, Regis (1991). 'Marketing is Everything.' *Harvard Business Review* 69 (January-February), 65-79.
30 Jemison, David B. (1981). 'The Importance of an Integrative Approach to Strategic Management Research.' *Academy of Management Review* 6 (August), 601-608.
31 Day, George S. (1990). *Market-Driven Strategy: Processes for Creating Value*. New York, Free Press.
32 Day, George S. and Robin Wensley (1983). 'Marketing Theory with a Strategic Orientation.' *Journal of Marketing* 47 (Fall), 79-89.
33 Charnes, A., W.W. Cooper, D.B. Learner and F.Y. Phillips (1985). 'Management Science and Marketing Management.' *Journal of Marketing* 49 (Spring), 93-105.
34 Capon, Noel and Rashi Glazer (1987). 'Marketing and Technology: A Strategic Coalignment.' *Journal of Marketing* 51 (July), 1-14.
35 Bartlett, Christopher A. and Sumantra Ghosha (1991). 'Global Strategic Management: Impact on the New Frontiers of Strategy Research.' *Strategic Management Journal* 12 (Summer), 5-16.

3 An understanding of marketing strategy

Gordon E. Greenley

This article is concerned with an understanding of marketing strategy and with the differentiation and clarification of concepts used in conjunction with marketing strategy. The impetus for this research arose out of a major programme of research, which has been carried out by the writer, the results of which are separate to this article and which have already been published elsewhere.[1,2,3] The research highlighted that, although all the respondent companies claim to have a marketing strategy, the marketing executives responding all exhibited great difficulty in explaining this strategy, and definitions varied widely, with little commonality of response. Hence the impetus to develop an overall understanding of marketing strategy within the framework of a journal article.

In order to develop this understanding an exhaustive search of the literature has been completed. The outcome of this reference to the literature also exhibits wide variations in the understanding of marketing strategy by the writers concerned, with the utilization of many concepts and phrases, resulting in many varied explanations as to its nature. Therefore, confusion on the part of marketing executives is, perhaps, to be expected. Hence, further impetus to develop an understanding, within the framework of an article. However, the body of knowledge within the literature has been taken as being the source for developing this understanding, as it represents the development work of marketers within this area.

The understanding of marketing strategy developed in this article is through a process involving three different levels of treatment. The first two levels arise out of the overall strategic planning of the company and provide the framework out of which marketing strategy should be developed. However, as these two levels provide the framework for developing the actual marketing strategy, they are not considered to be part of it. The third level of the process is the actual marketing strategy, which is considered to be composed of five component parts. The article concludes that, in defining its marketing strategy, a company needs firstly to establish the two levels from the strategic planning framework, then from this define each of the marketing strategy component parts. It is also concluded that failure to follow this process leads to ineffective definition, implementation and effectiveness of marketing strategies.

The article is presented in four sections. The first discusses explanations of marketing strategy from the literature. The second section examines strategic planning as a basis for developing levels one and two of the process, whereas the third section explains the resultant understanding of marketing strategy. The last section summarizes the article and suggests consequential implications.

Explanations from the literature

Most writers on the subject of marketing strategy start with a broad encompassing statement of what they consider it to be. For example, Chang and Campo-Flores[4] refer to marketing strategy as being crucial and central issues to the use of the marketing function. Similarly, Baker[5] sees it as being a broad means of achieving given aims, Luck and Ferrell[6] as being fundamental means or schemes and Kotler[7] as being the grand design to achieve objectives. Similar broad statements were also given by the companies participating in the previously reported research. Several companies claimed that their marketing strategy was a long-term activity, others that it provided for the overall achievement of objectives and others that it provided a broad plan of action. Other comments were given as even wider statements, such as to sell as large a quantity as possible or to maximize profits.

Having made such a statement, most writers then move on to explain the detailed issues, means or schemes which they prescribe as constituting a marketing strategy. Here there are four major bases that are used in the literature to explain the detail of marketing strategy. These are the marketing mix, the product life cycle, market share and competition, and positioning. In addition, some writers also advocate special marketing strategies for both international and industrial markets. The remainder of this section is concerned with an explanation of these approaches.

The marketing mix base

A common approach in the literature is simply to link these issues to the elements of the marketing mix. Indeed, Foxall[8] defines marketing strategy as being an indication of how each element of the marketing mix will be used to achieve the marketing objectives. This definition gives a complete reliance on the mix and therefore the utilization of the elements is the strategy. This is, however, a very simplified and restricted approach to marketing strategy, as will be illustrated later in the article. Chang and Campo-Flores[4] also develop this theme, suggesting a range of marketing component strategies which constitute the total marketing strategy. These they give as product strategy, distribution strategy, sales promotion strategy and pricing strategy. This approach is also followed by Jain,[9] who gives the same breakdown, again following a simple approach of related marketing strategy to the mix elements. A modification of this approach is prescribed by Udell,[10] who splits the issues into price and non-price strategies. Yet another modification is that by Foster,[11] who puts an emphasis on the companies' product mix and, in particular, reducing product prolification.

The PLC base

Other writers extend this theme of the marketing mix to the concept of the product life cycle. For example, Kotler,[12] Baker[5] and Doyle[13] outline that the marketing strategy for a particular product needs to be modified as the product moves through the various stages of its PLC. This is based upon a change of the mix at the different stage, so that a change is made in the relative degree of reliance of each element, giving a different mix, and hence a different marketing strategy, at each stage. This treatment is extended by other writers, such as Scheuing,[14] who defines a specific strategy for each stage of the PLC, labelling them life cycle marketing strategies. However, there are two major problems associated with this approach. The first is that it is difficult for the company to be able, at a particular point in time, to identify the stage at which a product is within its life cycle. The other problem is that the specific strategies for each stage do not always allow for application to all products, given the wide variation experienced by companies in market and product conditions.

The market share base

Another approach used in the literature to explain the issues involved in marketing strategy is to link the latter to market share and competition. A major example here comes from the work of Bloom and Kotler.[15] Their approach is firstly to explain how a company can identify its optimal market share, given a particular set of conditions. Having identified this level the company needs a marketing strategy to achieve the optimum. The second stage is to select a strategy from a range of strategies that are designed to build, maintain or even reduce market share. However, within each of these share-linked marketing strategies they also advocate a range of further strategies, again based upon the elements of the marketing mix. A similar approach is also advocated by Buzzell, Gale and Sultan,[16] although they label the alternatives as being building, holding and harvesting strategies. Alternatively, strategies for companies with low market shares are given by Woo and Cooper.[17] Similarly, Doyle[18] also links marketing strategy to market share.

Here the approach is simply to equate one strategy as the pursuit of market share and another strategy as its non-pursuit. However, overall this approach of linking marketing strategy to market share appears to be merely the utilization of the elements of the marketing mix, linked with an objective or aim (and therefore not a strategy) which is concerned with a pre-determined level of achievement (being market share).

In addition to the market share link, competitive marketing strategies have also been described by Kotler,[12] with a revision in a later publication.[19] In the earlier work he prescribed a range of nine competitive marketing strategies, prescribing that the company chooses, at a particular point in time, that which relates directly to the activities of its competitors. In the later work he advocates an approach in which the company has a range of competitive marketing strategies from which to choose, depending upon which of four strategy ranges the company's market share dictates that it falls into. Here there is a liberal use of the word 'strategy'; there are strategies within strategies and application of the approach is perhaps not immediately apparent.

The positioning base

Another approach from the literature in the explanation of marketing strategy is to utilize the concept of positioning. The major overall problem here is the variation given in the literature as to the meaning of positioning. For example, Wind and Claycamp[20] explain a product's position as its overall situation in the market relative to its sales, market share and profitability. Cravens[21] sees positioning as being the selection of a marketing strategy from a range of alternatives, although the latter can be considered to be component parts of corporate strategy, as developed by Ansoff.[22] Yet another variation of the interpretation of product positioning is reflected in the articles of Alpert and Gatty[23] and Holmes.[24] Here a product's position is related to its customers, in that it explains the user profile and how they perceive the image of the product.

The concept of positioning can also be explained in terms of both market and product positions, as illustrated, for example, by Kotler.[7] Here the company investigates the segmentation of a particular market and then decides which segment or segments to participate in. This selection is referred to as market positioning. For each segment the company requires a product, or products, and the number of products developed, plus their overall nature, is referred to as product positioning. This is developed for a range of products in an article by Warwick and Sands[25] and the application of market segmentation in marketing strategy for UK Building Societies is illustrated by Doyle and Newbould.[26]

International markets

Although several references are made in the literature to international marketing strategies, these tend to relate to the elements of the marketing mix. The basic tenet here is that these need to be varied for different countries, based upon variations in market conditions in these countries. For example, Keegan[27] gives a range of five alternative marketing strategies for a particular overseas market, based upon the elements of the product and communications. This range allows for variation in the product and the communications mix, but is nevertheless based on the marketing mix. Similarly, Halfill,[28] in reporting the results of a survey, uses the phrase multinational marketing strategy, but again is basing this on the marketing mix, with the emphasis on advertising. In a survey to investigate the nature of international marketing strategies in American companies, Samli[29] also illustrates this emphasis on the marketing mix, but identifies an orientation of the mix towards competitors within each market.

Industrial markets

In the case of industrial marketing strategies which are described in the literature, a similar situation exists. Copulsky[30] describes industrial marketing strategies as also being based upon the marketing mix, but with an emphasis on the product and price. A similar emphasis was also reported by Cunningham and Hammouda,[31] from their investigations into a UK engineering company. Two other articles on industrial marketing strategy also emphasize the orientation to the marketing mix, but broaden their base to utilize the concept of positioning. In the article by Forbis and Mehta[32] the use of market segmentation is advocated and hence market positioning is included in their industrial marketing strategy. Similarly Corey[33] utilizes market segmentation, but advocates both market and product positioning within industrial marketing strategies.

This completes the discussion of the explanations of marketing strategy from the literature. The next section is concerned with a review of strategic planning, as a basis for developing levels one and two of the marketing strategy process.

A review of strategic planning

As levels one and two of the marketing strategy process developed in this article are from the company's strategic planning, a review of both the nature of, and stages involved in, strategic planning is necessary. This will provide a basis for developing levels one and two, being the framework for developing the actual marketing strategy as level three.

Corporate planning is a concept which represents the summation of the total planning to be carried out in a company and writers such as Taylor and Sparks[34] and Hussey[35] split corporate planning into strategic planning and operational planning. Strategic planning is seen by Hussey to be the process which defines the overall objectives of the company and the means by which these objectives are to be obtained. The emphasis given by Ackoff[36] is that strategic planning is differentiated from other planning in that its consequences have an enduring effect on the firm and are broad issues which relate to the long term. Due to the influence of the effects of strategic planning, Higgins[37] identifies the responsibility of strategic planning as lying with top management, as opposed to the functional managers. The various stages involved in strategic planning will be discussed later in this section.

Operational planning, however, is seen by Denning[38] to be a projection into the future of plans which cover existing company operations. Here the plans are the responsibility of functional managers, as the concern is seen to be the operation of these functions into the future. The marketing function is seen to predominate in this area of planning, as for example given by Higgins,[37] and therefore marketing planning is taken as being part of operational planning. Although strategic planning is seen by Ackoff[36] to be concerned with the long term, operational planning, due to its very nature, necessarily relates to the short term, in that it is based on the firm's present operational base of resources. However, looking into the long-term future necessitates not only the setting of objectives and strategies, but must also include, as suggested by the Society for Long-Range Planning,[39] 'translating strategy into detailed operational programmes', which is very much the responsibility of operational planning. Therefore, operational plans are also needed in the long-term situation, which leads Scott[40] to identify both strategic long-range plans and operational long-range plans. Short-term operational planning is also labelled tactical planning by many writers, such as Hussey,[35] although Higgins[37] sees operational planning and tactical planning as being synonymous. However, tactical planning is seen by Winkler[41] as being specific action and by Chang and Campo-Flores[4] as being specific action designed to executive strategies. In the context of this article, marketing strategy is seen as being part of the long-term operational planning of the marketing function. The relationship of marketing strategy to these forms of planning is illustrated in Figure 1.

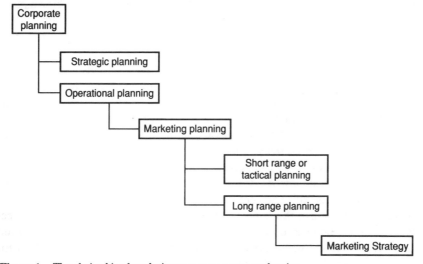

Figure 1   *The relationship of marketing strategy to corporate planning*

Review of the stages of strategic planning

Although writers within the literature give various stages within the strategic planning process, writers such as Taylor and Sparks,[34] Hussey[35] and Kollat *et al.*[42] tend to follow the stages given in Figure 2.

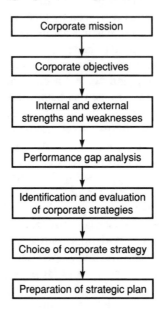

Figure 2   *The stages of strategic planning*

The approach starts with a specification of the overall direction which the firm wishes to pursue, given in the form of a corporate mission plus corporate objectives. The latter relate to certain levels of achievement or performance, refer to the total company and are applicable to the long run. After determining the strengths and weaknesses of both its internal and external environments, plus any gaps between its objectives and current base likely performance, the company moves on to consider its corporate strategy. This is seen by Hovell[43] as being the means of directing resources to achieve the objectives. The strategic planning process given advocates the identification and evaluation of alternative strategies, before the company chooses that to be pursued. Within these stages of strategic planning, level one of the marketing strategy process is seen as being the corporate mission and level two is seen as being the corporate strategy. Therefore, in order to develop these levels as being the overall framework for determining marketing strategy, further consideration will be given to both corporate mission and strategy.

Kollat *et al.*[42] explain the concept of corporate mission as being concerned with a long-term vision of what the business is, or is striving to become. Chang and Campo-Flores[4] describe it as being the scope and direction of business endeavours. The scope of business is taken to be defined in terms of customers, products and business areas. Therefore, the purpose of establishing a mission is to develop an encompassing understanding of the company's purpose and overall direction. In developing the mission, Drucker[44] suggests that a series of questions about the company need to be posed, such as; what is our business? what will be our business? what should our business be? The establishment of such a mission, in which these areas are defined, is seen by Kotler[45] as providing personnel with a shared sense of opportunity, direction, significance and achievement.

A major contribution to the understanding of corporate strategy is the well known work of Ansoff.[22] The view taken by Ansoff is that corporate strategy is made up of four component parts, from which it is possible to develop a range of alternative strategies. These four components are summarized as follows:

1 *Product–market scope:* this specifies the particular industries to which the firm is to restrict its business, defining the broad areas of product and market participation.
2 *Growth vector:* this relates to the alternatives available to the firm to achieve growth of sales and output, giving the alternatives of market penetration, market development, product development and diversification.
3 *Competitive advantages:* concerned with how the firm will be able to develop advantages over its competitors within these industries and vectors.
4 *Synergy:* in simple terms, this is concerned with evaluating how the firm's strengths and weaknesses will affect its market participation. In the words of Ansoff, 'it is concerned with the desired characteristics of fit between the firm and its products-markets.'

This section has reviewed strategic planning as a basis for developing levels one and two of the marketing strategy process and these levels have been identified as being corporate mission and corporate strategy.

The resultant understanding

As already mentioned, levels one and two of the understanding provide the framework for developing the marketing strategy which is given as level three.

As the corporate mission provides an encompassing understanding of the company's purpose and overall direction, it is considered as being level one of the process in developing a market strategy. Hence the mission provides the broad scope of the business in terms of customers, products and business areas, which is the starting point for making decisions on marketing strategy, in that the central issues of the total marketing operation must follow the company's central theme. Within this scope the framework is prescribed in the form of the classes of customers the firm wishes to serve, giving the scope for market positioning and examining suitability of variations in the marketing mix. Similarly the scope of products provides a framework for product positioning as well as giving ramifications within the marketing mix. The scope of business areas also gives a framework to market positioning, in that the supply of products to different areas (such as industrial, consumer, or international business areas) will each have different ramifications on the decisions to be made on marketing strategy. The theme of purpose also needs to be reflected in the marketing strategy. This may vary from company to company as it could be based upon the development of a particular technology, a particular raw material, a particular section of society, or indeed on any other similar theme. However, whatever the specification of the purpose, the components of the marketing strategy must support it. Finally, the direction of the company also has ramifications for marketing strategy. Directions aimed at growth, stability or contraction would each result in different decisions being made in the components of marketing strategy, as would a diversification direction as opposed to a non-diversification direction.

Level two of the understanding is the established corporate strategy, which is considered to be the second part of the marketing strategy framework. The product–market scope component of corporate strategy is itself an extension of the corporate mission as it gives more detail in specifying the scope of the business. Although this component is narrower in its definition of scope than the corporate mission it still allows for decision making within marketing strategy, in the selection of markets, market segments, product lines and individual products. However, the point is that the product–market scope component defines the framework for these decisions, giving the range to be pursued. The growth-vector component also provides a decision-making framework for marketing strategy. Here the selected alternatives for pursuing growth will each affect the marketing mix to be determined within the marketing strategy. Each growth alternative will also affect decisions on product positioning and the very nature of the market within each growth alternative will require a different approach to market positioning. The component of competitive advantage will dictate the approach to be taken in each element of the marketing mix and indeed will affect their interrelationship. Overall approaches to competitors may also necessitate making decisions on both market and product positioning. Finally, the corporate strategy component of synergy will affect marketing strategy in that identified company strengths and weaknesses, in relation to the approaches the company is to take towards these, may provide either restrictions to the development of marketing strategy, or, indeed, may provide an improvement to its effectiveness.

Level three of the understanding is the actual marketing strategy. The approach taken in this article is to specify marketing strategy as being composed of five component parts, three of which have been discussed in section one, and two of which have not yet been discussed. The first three components relate to market positioning, product positioning and the marketing mix, and are discussed further as follows.

Market positioning

This part of the strategy is concerned with deciding which approach to adopt relative to the segmentation of the market and the selection of the segments in which the company is to participate. Depending upon the range of product-market scopes, or strategic business units (SBUs) adopted, each scope may require a different approach to segmentation within the market. In selecting the segments for participation the company has the choice of pursuing all segments, only one segment, or several. This choice could well be affected by the rate of growth required, the nature of competitors within the segments and the corporate approach to them, plus the synergy developed by the relative strengths and weaknesses. This component is seen as being logically the first decision to be made in establishing a marketing strategy.

Product positioning

Having selected the market segments for each product-market scope, the number of products which the firm is to offer to each segment must be determined and their overall nature must be specified. Again this decision area can be affected by the corporate strategy components of growth, competition and synergy. However, the major considerations are obviously the market requirements within each segment. The understanding of these requirements obviously provides a basis for deciding whether each segment of participation requires one or several products, as well as determining the overall nature of each product. However, specific details of product specifications are not considered to be part of the marketing strategy, but are considered to be decisions relative to the tactical planning of marketing. This point will be pursued further in the summary.

Marketing mix

Having determined the range of segments in which they will participate, plus the nature and number of products to be offered, the next decision in formulating the marketing strategy is to determine the utilization of the individual elements of the mix, plus the relative degree of reliance to be placed upon each. Again the distinction needs to be made between the role of the marketing mix within marketing strategy and its role within marketing tactics. In the former, decisions are required to determine which of the elements given by McCarthy[46] are to be used in order to market the selected products, as well as deciding the relative degree of importance or reliance to be placed on each in order to satisfy the market requirements. However, the role of the marketing mix within marketing tactics is in the specification of details, such as product features, brand name and image, price structure, copy platform and selling techniques. Again the finalization of this component is affected by market requirements, so that the marketing strategy may need to vary with product market scope. In addition, the corporate approach to competitors may also affect decisions, as could the corporate approach to growth, plus effective synergy.

The two additional components not yet discussed are market entry and timing. These are discussed as follows.

Market entry

This component is concerned with how the company intends to enter, re-enter, position itself, or re-position itself within each of the selected market segments. Here Kotler[7] gives the alternatives of acquisition, collaboration and internal development. In the former the approach of acquiring an existing product(s) or company is well documented, as, for example, given by Fogg.[47] The selection of this strategy would be affected by the overall direction of the company as specified within the corporate mission. Also the corporate strategy components of growth, competitive advantage and synergy would also relate to such a decision. Collaboration with another company that can provide expertise in marketing, or indeed any other business area, can be similarly affected by corporate strategy. The purpose element of the corporate mission would provide the guideline for such a strategy, but the overall level of synergy within the company would give a major indication of the need to adopt a collaboration strategy. Finally, internal development means that the company does not need to involve other companies, so that the marketing operations are developed by the company through its own resources. Adoption of such a strategy would again be affected by the purpose element of the corporate mission, the level of synergy and also the stipulated rates of growth.

Timing

Here the component relates to the point in time at which the other components of the marketing strategy are to be implemented, plus the points in time when particular tactics within the marketing mix are to be implemented. One approach here is to link the strategy to competitors' activity, as, for example, outlined by Jain.[9] Here the strategy can be to be first to implement, or to be early but following the first company, or to take a laggard position, being one of the last companies to implement. Here the competitive advantage component of corporate strategy is likely to have a bearing, as is the purpose element of the corporate mission. Another approach of selecting times is to follow relevant indicators from the external environment. These can range from economic indicators, to industry trends, to seasonal trends, to trade exhibitions. Here there is probably less effect from the corporate mission and strategy, although the immediacy of required growth would need to be considered. The timing component of marketing strategy also relates to selecting the optimum time to exploit a particular market or market segment. Abell[48] has identified the importance of recognizing the time period associated with a particular opportunity within a market, which he labels the 'strategic window'. Here he offers an approach in the decision-making process, to determine when the particular implementation of strategy or tactics should take place. Here there can be consideration of the corporate strategy, in relation to the immediacy of required growth, the impact on such a strategic window of the corporate approach to competitors and the level of synergy within the company.

The rationale for finalizing marketing strategy as being composed of these five components is that they represent the central issues of the marketing operation. These vary from the specific activities to be carried out within each of the elements of the marketing mix, which, as previously discussed, represent the marketing tactics. The PLC base is rejected due to its inherent weaknesses, which make it unsuitable as a basis for strategy, although it is recognized that at the tactical level adjustments to the mix are valid relative to the PLC. The market share base is rejected as it is considered to be an objective at which to aim strategy performance, as opposed to being a marketing strategy basis itself. Also, particular attention to competitors as a marketing strategy base is rejected. This is because full consideration of competitors is, by necessity, given in the formulation of the five selected component parts. In addition, more direct consideration is taken of competitors in both the planning and implementation of marketing tactics. Finally, the international and industrial market bases are also rejected, as the principle established is that the five components of marketing strategy can be applied as a general rule. Therefore all can be applied in any market situation, regardless of the nature of the market profile and regardless of the particular market requirements. However, what is obviously important in formalizing the five components for any market situation is a full understanding of the total environment of the marketing operation. This includes both internal aspects, plus the external environment of not only the market conditions, but also the full macro-environment. This, therefore, gives the variation in the application of the five components within any specific market, as opposed to a stereotyped market *per se*.

In section two a split was identified between long-range operational planning and short-range operational planning. The five components of marketing strategy are considered to be enduring in nature and therefore are considered to be the marketing element of long-range operational planning. Market positioning can be considered to be enduring in that, once a company has selected market segments for participation, the consequential commitment to capital investment and other resources means that it is likely to be for a relatively long period of time. This also applies to product positioning, where both customer expectations and production commitment need to be catered for over a relatively long period of time. Also, once the reliance is established within each element of the marketing mix, then commitment to investment and the organizational structure mean a relatively long-term involvement. In the case of both market entry and timing, again there is an enduring effect. Once these decisions have been made, then again commitment is established for a relatively long period of time. Alternatively, marketing tactics are considered to be transient in nature and are therefore considered to be the marketing element of short-range operational planning. Hence the tactics relate to the annual marketing plan, within the framework of marketing strategy, and can be adjusted through the annual plan relative to market conditions. The outcome of such a classification is that the marketing tactics are the prime means of achieving the annual marketing objectives, even though they are developed within the framework of marketing strategy. However, the marketing strategy is seen as being a means of achieving the corporate objectives, with only a contribution to the marketing objectives by providing the framework for the marketing tactics. However, this does not mean to say that marketing strategy should be located within strategic planning, as tends to be suggested by writers such as Abel and Hammond.[49] Indeed, marketing strategy is seen as being very much the concern of the marketing function, in that, as already established, it constitutes the marketing element of long-range operational planning.

Summary and implications

The aim of this article was to develop an understanding of marketing strategy. The approach was to survey the literature on marketing strategy and then to review the strategic planning process. The latter provided a basis for developing levels one and two of the understanding, which were specified as being the corporate mission and the corporate objectives. These two levels provided the framework for the development of the third level of the understanding, which is the actual marketing strategy to be developed. This was specified as being composed of five component parts, being market positioning, product positioning, the marketing mix, market entry and timing. It was also argued that marketing strategy is the marketing element of long-range operational planning and relates directly to the attainment of the corporate objectives. Alternatively, marketing tactics are seen as being the marketing element of short-range operational planning, giving a direct contribution to the attainment of the marketing objectives.

Therefore the outcome of the understanding is that, in defining its marketing strategy, a company needs firstly to establish the two levels from the strategic planning framework, then from this define each of the marketing strategy component parts. Failure to follow this process must lead to ineffective definition, implementation and effectiveness of marketing strategies, as supported by the nature of the presented process.

Finally, two observations from the literature which relate to the utilization of marketing strategy need to be emphasized. The first has been reported by writers such as Hayes and Abernathy,[50] Anderson[51] and Piercy.[52] These writers report that the marketing emphasis in companies in recent times has been orientated towards short-term gains in revenue and profits. Therefore the emphasis is being placed on the marketing tactics of short-range operational planning. Although the latter is obviously important, full consideration of marketing strategy is of equal importance, not only to contribute to future performance and success, but also to provide a framework for the operation of the annual marketing plan. The final observation comes from the work by Carroll.[53] This observation is that the word strategy has been abused by many writers, having become 'a grandiose synonym for the word important'. Hence the word strategy has been unjustifiably included in the title of many articles and books in an attempt to improve their importance and academic respectability. To a certain extent this trend appears to be in the opposite direction to the first observation. However, the danger is that, as reflected by Carroll, a true understanding and application of strategy within marketing (or indeed within any other business function), can become confused by the very body of knowledge which is attempting to clarify it.

References

1   Greenley, G.E., 'An Overview of Marketing Planning in U.K. Manufacturing Companies', *European Journal of Marketing*, Vol. 16 No. 7, 1982, pp. 3-16.
2   Greenley, G.E., 'Where Marketing Planning Fails', *Long Range Planning*, Vol. 16 No. 1, February 1983, pp. 106-15.
3   Greenley, G.E., 'Effectiveness in Marketing Planning', *Strategic Management Journal*, Vol. 4 No. 1, March 1983; 'An overview of Marketing Planning in U.K. Service Companies', *Marketing Intelligence and Planning*, Vol. 1 No. 3, 1983, pp. 55-68.
4   Chang, Y.N. and Campo-Flores, F., *Business Policy and Strategy*, Santa Monica, Goodyear Publishing, 1980.
5   Baker, M.J., 'Limited Options for Marketing Strategists', *Marketing*, June 1978, pp. 23-27.
6   Luck, D.J. and Ferrell, O.C., *Marketing Strategy and Plans*, Englewood Cliffs, Prentice-Hall, 1979.
7   Kotler, P., *Marketing Management: Analysis, Planning and Control*, 3rd edition, Englewood Cliffs, Prentice-Hall, 1976.
8   Foxall, G.R., *Strategic Marketing Management*, London, Croom Helm, 1981.
9   Jain, S.C., *Marketing Planning and Strategy*, Cincinnati, South-Western Publishing, 1981.
10 Udell, J.G., 'The Perceived Importance of the Elements of Strategy', *Journal of Marketing*, Vol. 32, January 1968, pp. 34-40.
11 Foster, D.W., 'Product-Market Strategy', *Long Range Planning*, Vol. 3, March 1970, pp. 70-77.
12 Kotler, P., 'Competitive Strategies for New Product Marketing over the Life Cycle', *Management Science*, Vol. 12 No. 4, December 1965, pp. 104-119.
13 Doyle, P., 'The Realities of the Product Life Cycle', *Quarterly Review of Marketing*, Summer 1976, pp. 1-6.

14   Scheuing, E.E., 'The Product Life Cycle as an Aid in Strategy Decisions', *Management International Review*, Vol. 4 No. 5, 1969, pp. 111-125.

15   Bloom, P.N. and Kotler, P., 'Strategies for High Market-Share Companies', *Harvard Business Review*, Vol. 53 No. 6, November-December 1975, pp. 63-72.

16   Buzzell, R.D., Gale, B.T. and Sultan, R.G.M., 'Market Share – a Key to Profitability', *Harvard Business Review*, Vol. 53 No. 1, January-February 1975, pp. 97-106.

17   Woo, C.Y.Y. and Cooper, A.C., 'Strategies of Effective Low Share Businesses', *Strategic Management Journal*, Vol. 2 No. 3, July/ September 1981, pp. 301-318.

18   Doyle, P., 'Market Share and Marketing Strategy', *Quarterly Review of Marketing*, Autumn 1975, pp. 1-3.

19   Kotler, P., *Marketing Management: Analysis, Planning and Control*, 4th edition, Englewood Cliffs, Prentice-Hall, 1980.

20   Wind, Y. and Claycamp, H.J., 'Planning Product Line Strategy: A Matrix Approach', *Journal of Marketing*, Vol. 40, January 1976, pp. 2-9.

21   Cravens, D.W., 'Marketing Strategy Positioning', *Business Horizons*, December 1975, pp. 53-61.

22   Ansoff, H.I., *Corporate Strategy*, New York, McGraw-Hill, 1968.

23   Alpert, L. and Gatty, R., 'Product Positioning by Behavioural Life-Styles', *Journal of Marketing*, Vol. 33, April 1969, pp. 65-69.

24   Holmes, J.H., 'Profitable Product Positioning', *MSU Business Topics*, Spring 1973, pp. 27-32.

25   Warwick, K.M. and Sands, S., 'Product Positioning: Problems and Promises', *University of Michigan Business Review*, November 1975, pp. 17-20.

26   Doyle, P. and Newbould, G.D., 'Marketing Strategies of Building Societies', *Management Decision*, Vol. 13 No. 1, 1975, pp. 41-50.

27   Keegan, W.J., 'Multinational Product Planning: Strategic Alternatives', *Journal of Marketing*, Vol. 33, January 1969, pp. 58-62.

28   Halfill, D.S., 'Multinational Marketing Strategy: Implications of Attitudes Towards Country of Origin', *Management International Review*, Vol. 20 No. 4, 1980, pp. 26-29.

29   Samli, A.C., 'International Marketing Strategy Decisions and the Growth Rate of Major American Firms', *European Journal of Marketing*, Vol. 8 No. 2, 1974, pp. 108-118.

30   Copulsky, W., 'Strategies in Industrial Marketing', *Industrial Marketing Management*, Vol. 5, 1976, pp. 23-27.

31   Cunningham, M.T. and Hammouda, M.A.A., 'Product Strategy for Industrial Goods', *Journal of Management Studies*, Vol. 6 No. 2, May 1969, pp. 223-242.

32   Forbis, J.L. and Mehta, T., 'Value-Based Strategies for Industrial Products', *Business Horizons*, Vol. 24 No. 3, May/June 1981, pp. 32- 42.

33   Corey, E.R., 'Key Options in Market Selection and Product Planning', *Harvard Business Review*, Vol. 53 No. 5, September/October 1975, pp. 119-128.

34   Taylor, B. and Sparks, J.R., *Corporate Strategy and Planning*, London, Heinemann, 1979.

35   Hussey, D.E., *Corporate Planning*, Oxford, Pergamon, 1979.

36   Ackoff, R.L., *A Concept of Corporate Planning*, New York, Wiley, 1970.

37   Higgins, J.C., *Strategic and Operational Planning Systems*, London, Prentice-Hall, 1980.

38   Denning, B.W., *Introduction to Corporate Planning: Selected Concepts*, London, McGraw-Hill, 1971.

39   Society for Long-Range Planning, 'Editorial Definition', *Long-Range Planning*, Vol. 14 No. 1, 1981.

40   Scott, B.W., *Long-Range Planning in American Industry*, American Management Association, 1965.

41   Winkler, J., *Winkler on Marketing Planning*, London, Associated Business Programmes/Cassell, 1972.

42   Kollat, D.T., Blackwell, R.D. and Robeson, J.F., *Strategic Marketing*, New York, Holt, Rinehart and Winston, 1972.

43   Hovell, P.J., 'The Marketing Concept and Corporate Strategy', *Management Decision*, Vol. 17 No. 2, 1979, pp. 157-167.

44   Drucker, P., *Management: Tasks, Responsibilities, Practices*, New York, Harper and Row, 1973.

45 Kotler, P., 'Strategic Planning and the Marketing Process', *Business*, Vol. 30 No. 3, May-June 1980, pp. 2-9.
46 McCarthy, E.J., *Basic Marketing*, seventh edition, USA, Richard Irwin, 1981.
47 Fogg, C.D., 'New Business Planning: the Acquisition Process', *Industrial Marketing Management*, Vol. 5, 1976, pp. 95-113.
48 Abell, D.F., 'Strategic Windows', *Journal of Marketing*, Vol. 42 No. 3, July 1978, pp. 21-26.
49 Abell, D.F. and Hammond, J.S., *Strategic Market Planning*, Englewood Cliffs, Prentice-Hall, 1979.
50 Hayes, R.H. and Abernathy, W.J., 'Managing Our Way to Economic Decline', *Harvard Business Review*, Vol. 58, July-August 1980, pp. 67-77.
51 Anderson. P.F., 'Marketing Strategic Planning and the Theory of the Firm', *Journal of Marketing*, Vol. 46, Spring 1982, pp. 15-26.
52 Piercy, N., 'Cost and Profit Myopia', *Quarterly Review of Marketing*, Vol. 7 No. 4, July 1982, pp. 1-12.
53 Carroll. P.J., 'The Link between Performance and Strategy', *The Journal of Business Strategy*, Vol. 2 No. 4, Spring 1982, pp. 3-20.

Reproduced from Greenley, G. (1993). An understanding of marketing strategy. *European Journal of Marketing*, **23** [8], 45–58, by permission of MCB University Press.

4 Strategic windows

Derek F. Abell

Strategic market planning involves the management of any business unit in the dual tasks of *anticipating* and *responding* to changes which affect the marketplace for their products. This article discusses both of these tasks. Anticipation of change and its impact can be substantially improved if an organizing framework can be used to identify sources and directions of change in a systematic fashion. Appropriate responses to change require a clear understanding of the alternative strategic options available to management as a market evolves and change takes place.

Dynamic analysis

When changes in the market are only incremental, firms may successfully adapt themselves to the new situation by modifying current marketing or other functional programs. Frequently, however, market changes are so far reaching that the competence of the firm to continue to compete effectively is called into question. And it is in such situations that the concept of 'strategic windows' is applicable.

The term 'strategic window' is used here to focus attention on the fact that there are only limited periods during which the 'fit' between the key requirements of a market and the particular competencies of a firm competing in that market is at an optimum. Investment in a product line or market area should be timed to coincide with periods in which such a strategic window is open. Conversely, disinvestment should be contemplated if what was once a good fit has been eroded – i.e., if changes in market requirements outstrip the firm's capability to adapt itself to them.

Among the most frequent questions which management has to deal with in this respect are:

- Should funds be committed to a proposed new market entry? Now? Later? Or not at all? If a commitment is to be made, how large should it be?

- Should expenditure of funds of plant and equipment or marketing to support existing product lines be expanded, continued at historical levels, or diminished?
- When should a decision be made to quit and throw in the towel for an unprofitable produce line or business area?

Resource allocation decisions of this nature all require a careful assessment of the future evolution of the market involved and an accurate appraisal of the firm's capability to successfully meet key market requirements. The strategic window concept encourages the analysis of these questions in a dynamic rather than a static framework, and forces marketing planners to be as specific as they can about these future patterns of market evolution and the firm's capability to adapt to them.

It is unfortunate that the heightened interest in product portfolio analysis evident in the last decade has failed to adequately encompass these issues. Many managers routinely classify their various activities as 'cows', 'dogs', 'stars', or 'question marks' based on a *static* analysis of the *current* position of the firm and its market environment.

Of key interest, however, is the question not only of where the firm is today, but of how well equipped it is to deal with *tomorrow*. Such a *dynamic* analysis may foretell non-incremental changes in the market which work to disqualify market leaders, provide opportunities for currently low share competitors, and sometimes even usher in a completely new cast of competitors into the marketplace. Familiar contemporary examples of this latter phenomenon include such products as digital watches, women's pantyhose, calculators, charter air travel, office copiers, and scientific instrumentation.

In all these cases existing competitors have been displaced by new contenders as these markets have evolved. In each case changing market requirements have resulted in a *closing* strategic window for incumbent competitors and an *opening* window for new entrants.

Market evolution

The evolution of a market usually embodies more far reaching changes than the relatively systematic changes in customer behavior and marketing mix due to individual product life cycles. Four major categories of change stand out:

1 The development of new primary demand opportunities whose marketing requirements differ radically from those of existing market segments.
2 The advent of new competing technologies which cannibalize the existing ones.
3 Market redefinition caused by changes in the definition of the product itself and/or changes in the product market strategies of competing firms.
4 Channel changes.

There may be other categories of change or variants in particular industries. That doesn't matter; understanding of how such changes may qualify or disqualify different types of competitors can still be derived from a closer look at examples within each of the four categories above.

New primary demand

In a primary demand growth phase, decisions have to be reached by existing competitors about whether to spend the majority of the resources fighting to protect and fortify market positions that have already been established, or whether to seek new development opportunities.

In some cases, it is an original entrant who ploughs new territory – adjusting his approach to the emergent needs of the marketplace; in other cases it is a new entrant who, maybe basing his entry on expertise developed elsewhere, sees a 'strategic window' and leapfrogs over the original market leader to take advantage of the new growth opportunity. Paradoxically, pioneering competitors who narrowly focus their activities in the early stages of growth may have the most difficulty in making the transition to new primary demand growth opportunities later. Emery Air Freight provides an example of a company that did face up to a challenge in such a situation.

Emery Air Freight.   This pioneer in the air freight forwarding business developed many of the early applications of air freight in the United States. In particular, Emery's efforts were focused on servicing the 'emergency' segment of the market, which initially accounted for a substantial portion of all air freight business. Emery served this market via an extensive organization of regional and district offices. Among Emery's major assets in this market was a unique nationwide, and later worldwide, communications network; and the special competence of personnel located in the district offices in using scheduled carriers in the most efficient possible way to expedite deliveries.

As the market evolved, however, many new applications for air freight emerged. These included regular planned shipments of high value-low weight merchandise, shipments of perishables; 'off-line' service to hard-to-reach locations, and what became known as the TCC (Total Cost Concept) market. Each of these new applications required a somewhat different approach than that demanded by the original emergency business.

TCC applications, for example, required detailed logistics planning to assess the savings and benefits to be obtained via lower inventories, quicker deliveries and fewer lost sales through the use of air freight. Customer decisions about whether or not to use air freight required substantially more analysis than had been the case for 'emergency' use; furthermore, decisions which had originally been made by traffic managers now involved marketing personnel and often top management.

A decision to seek this kind of business thus implied a radical change in Emery's organization – the addition of capability to analyze complex logistics systems and to deal with upper echelons of management.

New competing technologies

When a fundamental change takes place in the basic technology of an industry, it again raises questions of the adaptability to new circumstances of existing firms using obsolete technology.

In many cases established competitors in an industry are challenged, not by another member of the same industry, but by a company which bases its approach on a technology developed outside that industry. Sometimes this results from forward integration of a firm that is eager to develop applications for a new component or raw material. Texas Instrument's entry into a wide variety of consumer electronic products from a base of semi-conductor manufacture, is a case in point. Sometimes it results from the application by firms of a technology developed in one market to opportunities in another. Or sometimes a breakthrough in either product or process technology may remove traditional barriers to entry in an industry and attract a completely new set of competitors. Consider the following examples:

- Watchmakers have recently found that a new class of competitor is challenging their industry leadership – namely electronic firms who are seeking end market applications for their semi-conductors, as well as a new breed of assemblers manufacturing digital watches.
- Manufacturers of mechanical adjustable speed drive equipment found their markets eroded by electrical speed drives in the early 1900s. Electrical drives were based on rotating motor-generator sets and electronic controls. In the late 1950's, the advent of solid state electronics, in turn, virtually obsoleted rotating equipment. New independent competitors, basing their approach on the assembly of electronic components, joined the large electrical equipment manufacturers in the speed drive market. Today, yet another change is taking place, namely the advent of large computer controlled drive systems. This is ushering yet another class of competitors into the market – namely, companies whose basic competence is in computers.

In each of these cases, recurrent waves of new technology fundamentally changed the nature of the market and usually ushered in an entirely new class of competitors. Many firms in most markets have a limited capability to master all the technologies which might ultimately cannibalize their business. The nature of technological innovation and diffusion is such that most *major* innovations will originate outside a particular industry and not within it.

In many cases, the upheaval is not only technological; indeed the nature of competition may also change dramatically as technology changes. The advent of solid state electronics in the speed drive industry, for example, ushered in a number of small, low overhead, independent assemblers who based their approach primarily on low price. Prior to that, the market had been dominated by the large electrical equipment manufacturers basing their approach largely on applications engineering coupled with high prices and high margins.

The 'strategic window' concept does not preclude adaption when it appears feasible, but rather suggests that certain firms may be better suited to compete in certain technological waves than in others. Often the cost and the difficulty of acquiring the new technology, as well as the sunk-cost commitment to the old, argue against adaption.

Market redefinition

Frequently, as markets evolve, the fundamental definition of the market changes in ways which increasingly disqualify some competitors while providing opportunities for others. The trend towards marketing 'systems' of products as opposed to individual pieces of equipment provides many examples of this phenomenon. The situation of Docutel illustrates this point.

Docutel.   This manufacturer of automatic teller machines (ATMs) supplied virtually all the ATMs in use up to late 1974. In early 1975, Docutel found itself losing market share to large computer companies such as Burroughs, Honeywell, and IBM as these manufacturers began to look at the banks' total EFTS (Electronic Funds Transfer System) needs. They offered the bank a package of equipment representing a complete system of which the ATM was only one component. In essence their success may be attributed to the fact that they redefined the market in a way which increasingly appeared to disqualify Docutel as a potential supplier.

Market redefinition is not limited to the banking industry; similar trends are underway in scientific instrumentation, process control equipment, the machine tool industry, office equipment, and electric control gear, to name but a few. In each case, manufacturers basing their approach on the marketing of individual hardware items are seeing their 'strategic window' closing as computer systems producers move in to take advantage of emerging opportunities.

Channel changes

Changes in the channels of distribution for both consumer and industrial goods can have far reaching consequences for existing competitors and would-be entrants.

Changes take place in part because of product life cycle phenomena – the shift as the market matures to more intensive distribution, increasing convenience, and often lower levels of channel service. Changes also frequently take place as a result of new institutional development in the channels themselves. Few sectors of American industry have changed as fast as retail and wholesale distribution, with the result that completely new types of outlets may be employed by suppliers seeking to develop competitive advantage.

Whatever the origin of the change, the effect may be to provide an opportunity for a new entrant and to raise questions about the viability of existing competitors. Gillette's contemplated entry into the blank cassette tape market is a case in point.

Gillette. As the market for cassettes evolved due to increased penetration and new uses of equipment for automotive, study, business, letter writing, and home entertainment, so did distribution channels broaden into an increasing number of drug chains, variety stores, and large discount stores.

Presumably it was recognition of a possible 'strategic window' for Gillette that encouraged executives in the Safety Razor Division to look carefully at ways in which Gillette might exploit the cassette market at this particular stage in its evolution. The question was whether Gillette's skill in marketing low-priced, frequently purchased package goods, along with its distribution channel resources, could be applied to marketing blank cassettes. Was there a place for a competitor in this market to offer a quality, branded product, broadly distributed and supported by heavy media advertising in much the same way that Gillette marketed razor blades?

Actually, Gillette decided against entry, apparently not because a 'strategic window' did not exist, but because profit prospects were not favorable. They did, however, enter the cigarette lighter business based on similar analysis and reportedly have had considerable success with their *Cricket* brand.

Problems and opportunities

What do all these examples indicate? First, they suggest that the 'resource requirements' for success in a business – whether these be financial requirements, marketing requirements, engineering requirements, or whatever – may change radically with market evolution. Second, they appear to suggest that, by contrast, the firm's resources and key competencies often cannot be so easily adjusted. The result is a *predictable* change in the fit of the firm to its market – leading to defined periods during which a 'strategic window' exists and can be exploited.

The 'strategic window' concept can be useful to incumbent competitors as well as to would-be entrants into a market. For the former, it provides a way of relating future strategic moves to market evolution and of assessing how resources should be allocated to existing activities. For the latter, it provides a framework for diversification and growth.

Existing businesses

Confronted with changes in the marketplace which potentially disqualify the firm from continued successful participation, several strategic options are available:

1 An attempt can be made to assemble the resources needed to close the gap between the new critical marketing requirements and the firm's competences.
2 The firm may shift its efforts to selected segments, where the 'fit' between requirements and resources is still acceptable.
3 The firm may shift to a 'low profile' approach – cutting back severely on all further allocation of capital and deliberately 'milking' the business for short-run profit.
4 A decision may be taken to exit from that particular market either through liquidation or through sale.

All too frequently, however, because the 'strategic window' phenomenon is not clearly recognized, these strategic choices are not clearly articulated. Instead, 'old' approaches are continued long after the market has changed with the result that market position is lost and financial losses pile up. Or, often only half-hearted attempts are made to assemble the new resources required to compete effectively; or management is simply deluded into believing that it can adapt itself to the new situation even where this is actually out of the question.

The four basic strategic choices outlined above may be viewed hierarchically in terms of *resource commitment*, with No. 1 representing the highest level of commitment. Only the company itself can decide which position on the hierarchy it should adopt in particular situations, but the following guideline questions may be helpful:

● To what extent do the changes call for skills and resources completely outside the traditional competence of the firm? A careful analysis has to be made of the gap which may emerge between the evolving requirements of the market and the firm's profile.
● To what extent can changes be anticipated? Often it is easier to adapt through a series of minor adjustments – a stepping stone approach to change – than it is to be confronted with a major and unexpected discontinuity in approach.
● How rapid are the changes which are taking place? Is there enough time to adjust without forfeiting a major share of the market which later may be difficult to regain?
● How long will realignment of the functional activities of the firm take? Is the need limited to only some functions, or are all the basic resources of

the firm affected – e.g., technology, engineering, manufacturing, marketing, sales, and organization policies?

- What existing commitments – e.g., technical skills, distribution channels, manufacturing approaches, etc. – constrain adaption?

- Can the new resources and new approaches be developed internally or must they be acquired?

- Will the changes completely obsolete existing ways of doing business or will there be a chance for coexistence? In the case of new technologies intruding from outside industry, the decision often has to be made to 'join-em rather than fight-em'. Not to do so is to risk complete obsolescence. In other cases, coexistence may be possible.

- Are there segments of the market where the firm's existing resources can be effectively concentrated?

- How large is the firm's stake in the business? To the extent that the business represents a major source of revenues and profit, a greater commitment will probably need to be made to adapt to the changing circumstances.

- Will corporate management, in the event that this is a business unit within a multi-business corporation, be willing to accept different goals for the business in the future than it has in the past? A decision not to adapt to changes may result in high short-run returns from that particular business. Looking at the problem from the position of corporate planners interested in the welfare of the total corporation, a periodic market-by-market analysis in the terms described above would appear to be imperative prior to setting goals, agreeing on strategies, and allocating resources.

New entrants

The 'strategic window' concept has been used implicitly by many new entrants to judge the direction, timing, and scale of new entry activities. Gillette's entry into cigarette lighters, major computer manufacturers entry into ATMs, and Procter & Gamble's entry into many consumer markets *after* pioneers have laid the groundwork for a large scale, mass market approach to the specific product areas, all are familiar examples.

Such approaches to strategic market planning require two distinctly different types of analysis:

1 Careful assessment has to be made of the firm's strengths and weaknesses. This should include audits of all the key resources of the company as well as its various existing programs of activity.
2 Attention should be directed away from the narrow focus of familiar products and markets to a search for opportunities to put unique competencies to work. This requires a broader appreciation of overall

environmental, technical and market forces and knowledge of many more markets, than is encountered in many firms today. It puts a particular burden on marketing managers, general managers, and business planners used to thinking in terms of existing activities.

Analysis of patterns of market evolution and diagnosis of critical market requirements in the future can also be of use to incumbent competitors as a forewarning of potential new entry. In such cases, adjustments in strategy can sometimes be made in advance, which will ultimately deter would-be new competitors. Even where this is not the case, resource commitments may be adjusted to reflect the future changes in structure of industrial supply.

Conclusion

The 'strategic window' concept suggests that fundamental changes are needed in marketing management practice, and in particular in strategic market planning activities. At the heart of these changes is the need to base marketing planning around predictions of future patterns of market evolution and to make assessments of the firm's capabilities to deal with change. Such analyses require considerably greater strategic orientation than the sales forecasting activities which underpin much marketing planning today. Users of product portfolio chart analysis, in particular, should consider the dynamic as opposed to the static implications in designating a particular business.

Entry and exit from markets is likely to occur with greater rapidity than is often the case today, as firms search for opportunities where their resources can be deployed with maximum effectiveness. Short of entry and exit, the allocation of funds to markets should be timed to coincide with the period when the fit between the firm and the market is at its optimum. Entering a market in its early stages and evolving with it until maturity may, on closer analysis, turn out to be a serious management error.

It has been said that while the life of the product is limited, a market has greater longevity and as such can provide a business with a steady and growing stream of revenue and profit if management can avoid being myopic about change. This article suggests that as far as any one firm is concerned, a market also is a temporary vehicle for growth, a vehicle which should be used and abandoned as circumstances dictate – the reason being that the firm is often slower to evolve and change than is the market in which it competes.

Bibliography

1 Ben M. Enis, Raymond LaGarce and Arthur E. Prell, 'Extending the Product Life Cycle,' *Business Horizons*, June 1977, p. 46.
2 Nelson N. Foote, 'Market Segmentation as a Competitive Strategy,' presented at the Consumer Market Segmentation Conference, American Marketing Association, Chicago, February 24, 1967.

3 The Product Portfolio, Boston Consulting Group Perspective; see also, 'A Note on the Boston Consulting Group Concept of Competitive Analysis and Corporate Strategy,' Intercollegiate Case Clearing House No. 9-175-175; and George S, Day, 'Diagnosing the Product Portfolio,' *Journal of Marketing*, Vol. 41 No. 2 (April 1977), p. 29.

4 See the following cases: Emery Air Freight Corporation (B); Gillette Safety Razor Division: The Blank Cassette Project; and Docutel Corporation; Intercollegiate Case Clearing House Nos. 9-511-044, 9-574-058 and 9- 578-073 respectively.

5 A.C. Cooper, E. DeMuzzio, K. Hatten, D.J. Hicks and D. Tock, 'Strategic Responses to Technological Threats,' Proceedings of the Business Policy and Planning Division of the Academy of Management, Paper #2, Boston, Academy of Management, August 1974.

6 Derek F. Abell, 'Competitive Marketing Strategies: Some Generalizations and Hypotheses,' Marketing Science Institute, April 1975, Report No. 75-107.

7 Derek F. Abell, 'Business Definition as an Element of the Strategic Decision,' presented at the American Marketing Association/Marketing Science Institute Conference on Product and Market Planning, Pittsburgh, November 1977.

8 William E. Rothschild, *Putting It All Together: A Guide to Strategic Thinking* (New York, Amacom, 1976), pp. 103-121.

9 Theodore Levitt, 'Marketing Myopia,' *Harvard Business Review*, September-October 1975, p. 26.

Reproduced from Abell, D.F. (1978). Strategic windows. *Journal of Marketing*, **42**(3), 22-25 by permission of the American Marketing Association.

5 Marketing warfare in the 1980s

Philip Kotler and Ravi Singh

Marketing is merely a civilized form of warfare in which most battles are won with words, ideas, and disciplined thinking.

Albert W. Emery

As the 1980s get under way, numerous signs point to an era of slower economic growth. Scarce resources, proliferation of technological resources across nations, sharply rising costs of energy, economic slow downs, trade barriers, political tensions, levelling off of population growth in the developed world, and other factors suggest that company prospects for prosperity and growth will become tougher in the years ahead.

Companies will have to pursue their profitability at the expense of other companies, through market share gains rather than market growth gains. The scene will move from normal marketing competition to marketing warfare. Successful marketing will require devising competition-centred strategies, not just customer-centred and distribution-centred strategies.

The purpose of this article is to show how military strategy ideas can help business firms formulate effective marketing strategies for the 1980s. Too many business firms sound tough and act tough but fail to be subtle enough in thinking through their marketing attack and defense options. The use of brute force against competition is usually the least effective way to win a battle or war. We will consider the following questions:

- How close is business competition to military warfare?
- What business objectives make sense in a confrontation situation?
- What military strategies are available for market attack, and what are their respective strengths and weaknesses?
- What military strategies are available for market defense, and what are their respective strengths and weaknesses?

Military science and marketing competition

The increased need of businesses to develop competitor-centred strategies to win market share will lead managers to turn increasingly to the subject of military science. The classic works of Clausewitz, Liddell Hart, and other military theorists are being increasingly combed for ideas, just as economic theory and consumer behaviour theory were combed in the last two decades for their potential applications to improve market performance.[1]

Several signs of this stepped-up interest in the military metaphor have already appeared. One of the leading management-education firms, Advanced Management Research, has sponsored several successful one-day seminars, bearing such titles as 'Marketing Warfare' and 'Attacking the Competition'. These seminars featured topics such as 'pre-battle preparation', 'marketing weapons', 'guerrilla warfare', and 'attack formation'. The seminar brochure reads, 'Perhaps the best book on marketing ever published is *On War* by the famous Prussian general and military theorist, Carl von Clausewitz.' The well-known advertising agency of Ries Cappiello Colwell, Inc., which pioneered 'position' thinking in marketing in the 1970s, is now making presentations to various companies on marketing warfare, and articles dealing with competitive strategy are on the increase.[2]

Business people frequently use military talk to describe their situations. There are price 'wars', 'border clashes', and 'skirmishes' among the major computer manufacturers; an 'escalating arms race' among cigarette manufacturers; 'market invasion' and 'guerrilla warfare' in the coffee market. A company's advertising is its 'propaganda arm', its salesmen are its 'shock troops', and its marketing research is its 'intelligence'. There is talk about 'confrontation', 'brinkmanship', 'super-weapons', 'reprisals', and 'psychological warfare'.

The real question is whether the use of 'warfare' language in business is just descriptive or whether it really aids in thinking and planning competitive strategy. We believe it does. We will show how principles drawn from military strategy apply in three critical business decisions areas - namely, determining objectives, developing attack strategies, and developing defense strategies.

The meaning of war

Is the objective of war the same as the objective of competition? It turns out that military theorists differ among themselves as to the objective of war. Clausewitz, the nineteenth century's greatest military theorist, saw war as a necessary means to pursue national self-interest. 'War is a mere continuation of policy by other means.' The object of war is to vanquish the enemy by achieving an unconditional surrender. This is accomplished by breaking the enemy's will to resist, which generally requires overwhelming the enemy on the battlefield. 'The destruction of the enemy's main forces on the battlefield constitutes the only true aim in war.' Although Clausewitz had a more subtle concept of war, this dictum, along with other loosely dropped phrases such as 'Blood is the price of victory,' influenced the conduct of war for over a century before World War II. They led his less profound disciples, such as Marshall Foch, to confuse the means with the end.[3]

The twentieth century's greatest military theorist, Captain Basil H. Liddell Hart, sets the contemporary position - 'The "object" in war is a better state of peace, even if only from your own point of view.'[4] Liddell Hart was severely critical of Clausewitz: '[T]he universal adoption of the theory of unlimited war has gone far to wreck civilization. The teachings of Clausewitz, taken without understanding, largely influenced both the causation and character of World War I. Thereby it led on, all too logically, to World War II.'[5]

Cutthroat competition can lead to ultimate defeat

Modern competitors rarely adopt the Clausewitzian objective of 'total annihilation of the enemy.' This is not to deny that competitors have the capacity to conduct themselves this way. Any large well-resourced company can destroy any small company by lowering its prices substantially and causing losses both to its competitor and itself until the competitor is forced out of business. And two large companies could slug it out until one of them surrenders or retreats. 'Cutthroat competition' is the name given to this extreme state of business warfare, which has characterized business competition in certain periods in certain industries (such as the oil industry and the rubber industry). Cutthroat competition à la Clausewitz would be much more prevalent were it not for the antitrust laws starting with the Sherman Act (1890) and continuing later with the Clayton Act (1914). The legal sentiment has been that 'unfair methods of competition in commerce are unlawful,' 'where the effect . . . may be to substantially lessen competition or tend to create a monopoly in any line of commerce.' Indeed, were it not for the antitrust laws, it could be argued that war, not peace, is the natural state of business.

A company, in fact, has to be very careful not to take actions whose purpose appears to be to weaken or destroy a competitor. The company can take normal steps to woo consumer preference for its products (improve product quality and service, improve communication and promotion, lower prices in a reasonable way in relation to costs, increase distribution, and so on) even when this hurts a competitor, as long as it does not hurt competition. That Miller beer's aggressive marketing hurt Schlitz and that Texas Instruments' aggressive marketing hurt Rockwell were the consequences and not the aims of the policies that these aggressive companies adopted.

Besides running afoul of antitrust legislation, companies that compete on the basis of wiping out competition will find in their very victory the seeds of ultimate defeat. While a unique advantage at a given time may afford it the brute force of wiping out competition, it is difficult to conceive of a single company differentiating its product line sufficiently to meet all segment variations. 'Thinly spread' over the market, and complacent in its commanding position, it would offer an ideal target for the next clever and forceful competitor to come along and shatter its foundations.

Attaining a better state of peace

Liddell Hart's doctrine that 'the object in war is a better state of peace' may be a more appropriate guiding objective for business. When a company undertakes warlike manoeuvres toward another firm - when Bic attacks Gillette and Kodak attacks Polaroid - the objective is not to annihilate the other but to attain a better state of peace. Bic is under no illusion that it will destroy Gillette. Rather, it is conducting limited warfare with a limited objective - attaining a certain substantial and durable share of the razor market. 'When a government appreciates that the enemy has the military superiority, either in general or in a particular theatre, it may wisely enjoin a strategy of limited aim.'[6] The issue is largely what distribution of shares (or territory) the two will agree to settle on. When Kodak introduced its own version of the instant camera, it may have aimed to achieve the dominant share, but Polaroid fought back and managed to contain Kodak's share at about 25 per cent and now both of them seem to be accepting this compromise share. This is not to say that Kodak may not mount another attack in the future to raise its share, say to 50 per cent.

There is another interpretation of business seeking 'a better state of peace'. Each business seeks to groove itself in some part of the market where it has a natural and comparative advantage, enough to discourage other firms with less advantage from attacking it. As a result, the market is occupied by several firms practising peaceful coexistence, because each is safe and supreme in its own territory. When war breaks out, it does so because some competitor is doing a poor job of serving its niched market segment, because some competitor is trying to bring some new advantage to that market segment, or because environmental change is causing major shifts in the composition of segments.

Defining strategic objectives

Each competitor must define its strategic objectives in each of its markets. The military 'principle of objective' holds that 'every military operation must be directed toward a clearly defined, decisive, and attainable objective.'

Choosing the enemy

Deciding on the business objective, whether it is to crush the competitor, reduce its share, or freeze its share, interacts with the question of who the competitor is. Unlike war, where the enemy is 'given' the business firm in most cases is able to choose its enemy. All markets are occupied by one or more firms that enjoy different competitive positions, strengths, and weaknesses. One firm is the market leader, having the largest market share. One or more other firms are market challengers in that they are large and willing to fight one another and the leader for territory. Still other firms are large but play the role of market followers, being content with their current positions in the market and wishing not to rock the boat. Finally, several smaller firms are market nichers that serve small market segments which usually do not attract the interest or actions of the larger firms.

Basically, an aggressor can choose to attack one of three types of firms:

- It can attack the market leader. This is a high-risk but potentially high-pay-off strategy and makes good sense if the leader is not a 'true leader' and is not serving the market well. The 'terrain' to examine closely is consumer satisfaction. If a substantial area is unserved, it offers a great strategic target. Miller's campaign in the beer market was so successful because it pivoted initially on discovering the 'light' beer segment. The alternative strategy is to out-innovate the leader across the whole segment. Thus Xerox took the copy market away from 3M by developing a better copying process (dry copying instead of wet copying).
- The aggressor could attack firms of similar size who are not doing the job and whose resources are not formidable. Both consumer satisfaction and innovation potential need to be examined minutely. It is even possible to conceive of a frontal attack strategy of just snowing the enemy under, should its resources be limited.
- The aggressor could define its enemies as the smaller firms that have fewer resources and are often not doing a very economic job. Several of the major beer companies grew to their present size not by stealing one another's customers so much as by gobbling up the 'small fry', namely, local and regional brewers (also called a 'guppy strategy').

Thus, the issue of choosing the enemy and choosing the objective interact. If the attacking company goes after the market leader, its objective may be to attain or maintain a certain share. If it goes after a small local company, its objective may be to drive that company out of existence. The important principle remains: 'Every military operation must be directed toward a clearly defined, decisive, and attainable objective.'

Waging war: selecting the right attack strategy

Given clear objectives, how do military strategists view their major options in attacking an enemy? The starting point is known as the 'principle of mass', which holds that 'superior combat power must be concentrated at the critical time and place for a decisive purpose.' We can make progress by imagining a competitor who occupies a certain market territory. We can distinguish five possible strategies of attack:

- Frontal attack
- Flanking attack
- Encirclement attack
- Bypass attack
- Guerrilla attack.

They are illustrated in Figure 1 and discussed below.

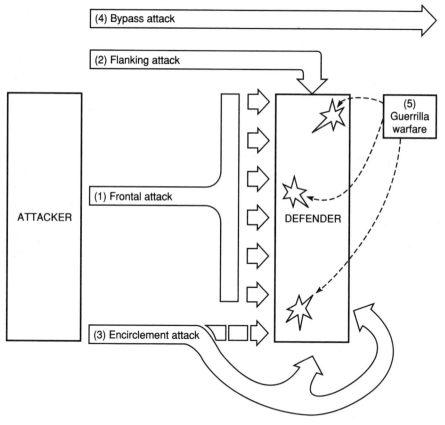

Figure 1 *Attack strategies*

Frontal attack

An aggressor is said to launch a frontal (or 'head-on') attack when it masses its forces right up against those of its opponent. It attacks the opponent's strengths rather than its weaknesses. The outcome depends on who has the greater strength and endurance. In a pure frontal attack, the attacker matches product for product, advertising for advertising, price for price, and so on. Recently, the second-placed razor blade manufacturer in Brazil decided to go after Gillette, the market leader. Management was asked if it was offering the consumer a better blade. 'No,' was the reply. 'A lower price?' 'No.' 'Better allowances to the trade?' 'No.' 'Then how do you expect to take share away from Gillette?' it was asked. 'Sheer determination' was the reply. Needless to say, its offensive failed.

For a pure frontal ttack to succeed, the aggressor needs a strength advantage over the competitor. The 'principle of force' says that the side with the greater manpower (resources) will win the engagement. This is modified if the defender has greater firing efficiency through enjoying a terrain advantage (such as holding a mountain top). The military dogma is that for a frontal attack to be successful against a well-entrenched opponent or one controlling the 'high ground', the attacking forces must deploy a 3:1 advantage in combat firepower to be successful. If the aggressor has a smaller force or poor firepower than the defender, a frontal attack amounts to a suicide mission and makes no sense. RCA, GE and Xerox learned this the hard way when they launched frontal attacks on IBM, overlooking its superior defensive position.[7]

As an example of a successful pure frontal attack and the resources it required, consider S.C. Johnson & Sons' entry into the shampoo market with its new 'Agree' brand.[8] In 1977, with what *Forbes* describes as 'almost Japanese-like thoroughness', S.C. Johnson first raided Colgate and others for experienced executives. Then it blitzed the market with a $14 million promotion that included 30 million sample bottles of its new hair conditioner, Agree. That about equalled the industry's total promotion on hair conditioners. It grabbed 15 per cent of the market in its first year, wrested from such giants as Gillette's Toni, Breck and Clairol (by 1979, its share was 20 per cent). Then, in 1978, it invaded the shampoo market, reportedly spending $30 million in marketing costs in the summer of that year. It ended up with a 6 per cent share of that market.

As an alternative to a pure frontal attack, the aggressor may launch a modified frontal attack, the most common being to cut its prices *vis-à-vis* the opponent's. Such attacks can take two forms. The more usual ploy is to match the leader's offer on other counts and beat it on price. This can work if:

● The market leader does not retaliate by cutting price, too; and
● The competitor convinces the market (1) that its product is equal to the competitor's or (2) that, at a lower price, it is real value.

The rapid proliferation of 'generic brands' in canned foods and basic household goods provides an excellent example of a competitor's convincing the market that, at a lower price, its product is a real value. Helene Curtis is a master practitioner of the somewhat risky strategy of convincing the market that its product is equal to the competitor's.[9] Curtis makes no bones about its approach - making budget imitations of leading high-priced brands and promoting them with blatant comparative advertising campaigns: 'We do what theirs does for less than half the price,' is the message. In 1972, Curtis had a meagre one per cent share of the shampoo market for its five Suave shampoos. Its new strategy was launched in 1973. By 1976, it had overtaken Procter & Gamble's Head & Shoulders and Johnson & Johnson's Baby Shampoo to lead the market in volume. Its share hit 16 per cent in 1979.

The other form of price-aggressive strategy is one in which the attacker invests heavily in research to achieve lower production costs and then attacks competitors on a price basis. Texas Instruments has been brilliantly successful in using the price weapon strategically. It invests heavily in R&D and moves very rapidly down the experience curve. The Japanese, too, launch frontal attacks on the basis of cost-related price cutting, and this is one of the most viable bases upon which a sustained frontal attack strategy can be founded.

Flanking attack

An army on a battlefield is deployed to be strongest where it expects to attack or be attacked. It is necessarily less secure in its flanks and rear. Its weak spots (blind sides), therefore, are natural points of attack for the enemy. The major principle of modern offensive warfare is concentration of strength against weakness.[10] The aggressor will act as if he will attack the strong side to tie up the defender's troops, but launch the real attack at the side or rear. This 'turning' manoeuvre catches the defending army off guard. Flanking attacks always make sense, and are particularly attractive to the aggressor possessing fewer resources than the opponent. If he cannot overwhelm the defender with brute strength, he can out-manoeuvre him with subterfuge.

A flanking attack can be directed against a competitor along two strategic dimensions – geographical and segmental. A geographical attack consists of the aggressor's spotting areas in the country or the world in which the opponent is not performing at high levels. For example, some of IBM's rivals chose to set up strong branches in medium- and smaller-sized cities which are relatively neglected by IBM. According to a Honeywell field sales manager:

> Out in the rural areas, we are relatively better off than in the cities. We have been quite successful in these areas because our sales force does not meet the ten plus to one ratio it hits in the cities where IBM concentrates its people. Thus, ours must be a concentration game.[11]

The other, and potentially more powerful, flanking strategy is to spot uncovered market needs not being served by the leaders:

● German and Japanese auto-makers chose not to compete with American auto-makers by producing large, flashy, gas-guzzling automobiles, even though these were supposedly the preference of American buyers.

Instead, they recognized an unserved consumer segment who wanted small, fuel-efficient cars. They moved vigorously to fill this hole in the market and to their satisfaction and Detroit's surprise, American taste for smaller, fuel-efficient cars grew to be a substantial part of the market.

- 'Discovering' so to speak, the 'light' beer segment, Miller Brewing Company pivoted on this unserved gap in the market and vigorously developed it into a huge breach across the whole industry's front and propelled itself from seventh place in the industry to a very close second in five years.

A flanking strategy is another name for identifying shifts in market segments - which are causing gaps to develop that are not being served by the industry's product profile - and rushing in to fill the gaps and develop them into strong segments. Instead of a bloody battle between two or more companies trying to serve the same market, flanking leads to a fuller coverage of the varied needs of the whole market. Flanking is the best tradition of the modern marketing philosophy which holds that the purpose of marketing is to 'discover needs and serve them.' Flanking attacks have a higher probability of being successful than frontal attacks. This is also borne out in military history. In his penetrating analysis of the thirty most important conflicts of the world from the Greek wars up to World War I (which embraced more than 280 campaigns), Liddell Hart concluded that in only six campaigns did decisive results follow strategies of direct head-on assault.[12] The strategy of indirect approach has overwhelming support from history as the most effective and economic form of strategy.

Encirclement

The pure flanking manoeuvre was defined as pivoting on a gap in the existing market coverage of the enemy. The encirclement manoeuvre, on the other hand, is seen as an attempt to disperse this coverage so that the enemy's segment differentiation (and therefore brand loyalty) is diluted and a more fluid front is created that can be pierced at a number of points and enveloped into new segments. Encirclement (also called envelopment) involves launching a grand offensive against the enemy on several fronts so that the enemy must protect his front, sides, and rear simultaneously. The aggressor may offer the market everything the opponent offers and more, so that the offer is unrefusable. Encirclement makes sense as a strategy under circumstances where the aggressor has, or is able to muster, resources superior to those of the opponent and believes that the encirclement will be complete and swift enough to break the opponent's will to resist.

Seiko's attack on the watch market illustrates an encirclement strategy.[13] For several years, Seiko has been acquiring distribution in every major watch outlet and overwhelmed its competitors and consumers with an enormous variety of constantly changing models. In the United States, it offers some 400 models, but its marketing clout is backed by the some 2,300 models it makes and sells worldwide. 'They hit the mark on fashion, features, user preferences, and everything else that might motivate the consumer,' says an admiring vice-president of a US competitor.

An encirclement attack does not always work, as Hunt's found out when it tried to blitz Heinz's brand of catsup in a grab for increased market share. In 1963, Hunt's, with a 19 per cent share of the catsup market, launched a major encirclement attack on Heinz to go after Heinz's 27 per cent market share. Hunt's rolled out a number of marketing attacks simultaneously. It introduced two new flavours of capsup (pizza and hickory) to disrupt the consumer's traditional taste preference for Heinz and also to capture more retail shelf space. It lowered its price to 70 per cent of Heinz's price. It offered heavy trade allowances to the retailers. It raised its advertising budget to over twice the level of Heinz's. This marketing programme meant that Hunt's would lose money while the battle raged but would make it up if it attracted enough brand switchers. The strategy failed to work. The Heinz brand continued to enjoy consumer preference, and as a result, not enough Heinz users tried the Hunt's brand and most of those who did returned to the Heinz brand. By the mid-1970s, Heinz had increased its share to over 40 per cent through heavy advertising.

Hunt's debacle underscores our core proposition that segmentation opportunity is fundamental to choosing the axis for an indirect approach. If empty niches do not exist, or cannot be created by segment diffusion tactics, then what is a flank attack in the mind of the aggressor peters out into a plain front attack in the marketplace. As such, it would require the 3:1 advantage in combat firepower to succeed.

Bypass attack

The bypass is the most indirect of assault strategies and eschews any belligerent move directed against the enemy's existing segment span. Conceptually, the bypass hinges on a much more global, or at least macro, conception of competition than enemy A and his territory Z. It is analogous to peacetime political warfare ('cold war') in which allied pacts, so to speak, are created against the prospect of future hostilities in the core confrontation zone. For a company, it means bypassing the arch enemy and attacking easier markets to broaden one's resources base. This offers two lines of approach: diversifying into unrelated products and diversifying into new geographical markets for existing products.

Consider, for example, Colgate's impressive turnaround.[14] In the United States, Colgate has always struggled in Procter & Gamble's shadow. In the heavy duty detergents, P&G's Tide routed Colgate's Fab by almost 5:1. In dishwashing liquids, P&G had almost twice Colgate's share. In soaps, too,

Colgate trailed far behind. When David Foster took over as CEO in 1971, despite its $1/3 billion in sales, Colgate still had the reputation of a stodgy marketer of soap and detergent. By 1979, Foster had transformed the company into a $4.3 billion conglomerate, capable of challenging P&G if necessary.

Foster's real achievement was in recognizing that any head-on battle with P&G was futile. 'They outgunned us 3 to 1 at the store level,' said Foster, 'and had three research people to our one.' Foster's strategy was simple - maintain Colgate's lead abroad and bypass P&G at home by diversifying into markets sans P&G. A string of acquisitions followed in textiles and hospital products, cosmetics and a range of sporting goods and food products. The outcome: in 1971, Colgate was underdog to P&G in about half of its business. By 1976, in three-fourths of its business it was either comfortably placed against P&G or didn't face it at all.

Guerrilla warfare

Guerrilla warfare is another option available to a market aggressor. Guerrilla warfare consists of making small, intermittent attacks on different territories of the opponent, with the aim of harassing and demoralizing the opponent and eventually securing concessions. The military rationale was stated by Liddell Hart:

> The more usual reason for adopting a strategy of limited aim is that of awaiting a change in the balance of force - a change often sought and achieved by draining the enemy's force, weakening him by pricks instead of risking blows. The essential condition of such a strategy is that the drain on him should be disproportionately greater than on oneself. The object may be sought by raiding his supplies; by local attacks which annihilate or inflict disproportionate loss on parts of his force; by bringing him into unprofitable attacks; by causing an excessively wide distribution of his force; and, not least, by exhausting his moral and physical energy.[15]

The guerrilla attacker will use both conventional and unconventional means to harass the opponent. In the business world, these would include selective price cuts, supply interferences, executive raids, intense promotional bursts, and assorted legal actions against the opponent. The last, legal action, is becoming one of the most effective ways to harass the other side. Many firms find it worthwhile to search the opponent's legal conduct for possible violations of antitrust law, trademark infringement, and deceptive trade practices.

As an example, a Seattle-based beer distributor who had been supplying beer to Alaska by ship was upset when the Oetker Group of West Germany obtained a 75 per cent tax credit for ten years from the Alaska legislature to establish beer production in Alaska. The Seattle distributor slapped a lawsuit on Oetker, charging the tax incentive was unconstitutional. Oetker eventually won in the courts, but four years of delay crippled its hope of capitalizing on the oil pipeline construction boom. After operating just thirty months, Oetker closed its Anchorage brewery.[16]

Normally guerrilla warfare is practised by a smaller firm against a larger one. Not able to mount a frontal or even an effective flanking attack, the smaller firm launches a barrage of short promotional and price attacks in random corners of the larger opponent's market in a manner calculated to gradually weaken the opponent's market power. Even here, the attacker has to decide between launching a few major attacks or a continual stream of minor attacks. Military dogma holds that a continual stream of minor attacks usually creates more cumulative impact, disorganization, and confusion in the enemy than a few major ones. In line with this, the attacker would find it more effective to attack small, isolated, weakly defended markets rather than major stronghold markets like New York, Chicago, and Los Angeles, where the defender is better entrenched and more willing to retaliate quickly and decisively.

It would be a mistake to think of a guerrilla campaign as only a 'low resource' strategy alternative available to financially weak challengers. Conducting a continual guerrilla campaign can be expensive, although admittedly less expensive than a frontal, encirclement, or even flanking attack. Furthermore, guerrilla war is more a preparation for war than a war itself. Ultimately it must be backed by a stronger attack if the aggressor hopes to 'beat' the opponent. Hence, in terms of resources, guerrilla warfare is not necessarily a cheap operation.

Picking the right defense strategy

We have seen that attack strategies in business can be clarified through considering the classic offenses available in military engagements. Are models of military defensive action also pertinent to corporate engagements? The answer is yes, although the strategic issues may often appear as reflections of offense employed in other directions.

There are six models of defensive deployment that can provide useful insight. They are illustrated in Figure 2 and discussed in the following paragraphs.

Position defense ('The fortified front line')

The traditional concept of defense is closely tied to a psychology of 'fortification'. The French Maginot Line, the German Siegfried Line, and most recently the Israeli Barley Line on the Suez are twentieth-century versions of the 'fort' of the middle ages. Like almost all the great forts of history, these extensive, supposedly impregnable, fortified front lines all failed in the hour of peril. Static fortlike defense, like frontal attack, is apparently one of the riskiest strategies in the military theatre.

How do we interpret static defense in the business world? The appropriate analogy is that of marketing myopia. The marketing concept for many years now has sought to demolish the myth of the invincible product. Certainly, Henry Ford's myopia about his Model T brought an enviably healthy company with $1 billion in cash reserves at its zenith to the brink of financial ruin. Even such death-defying brands as Coca-Cola and Bayer Aspirin cannot be relied upon by their companies as the main sources of future growth and profitability. Coca-Cola today, in spite of producing nearly half the soft drinks of the world, has aggressively moved into the wine market, has acquired fruit drink companies, and has diversified into desalinization equipment and plastics.[17] Clearly, leaders under attack would be foolish to base their defense on putting all their resources into building fortifications around their current product.

Reasonable broadening, however, makes sense. Armstrong Cork exemplified a successful market-broadening strategy by redefining its domain from 'floor covering' to 'decorative room covering' (including walls and ceilings). By recognizing the customer's need to create a pleasant interior through various covering materials, Armstrong Cork expanded into neighbouring businesses that were synergistically balanced for growth and defense.

The other alternative to generating 'strategic depth' is diversification into unrelated technologies. The multi-division corporation is such a common feature today that it seems almost the only route to growth and competitive strength. In a strategic sense, market diversification is the defense analogue to the bypass attack. Thus, Colgate and Levers not only bypassed P&G in their offensive postures but simultaneously built a defensive depth from which to draw resources in future counter attacks or challenges that they may need to launch in the confrontation zone with P&G.

Mobile defense ('Defense in depth')

Far superior to position defense is mobile defense, in which the firm attempts to stretch its domain over new territories that can serve as future centres for defense of counter attack. It spreads to these new territories not so much through normal brand proliferation as through innovation activity on two fronts, namely, market broadening and market diversification. These moves generate 'strategic depth' for the firm which enables it to weather continual attacks and to launch retaliatory strikes.

Market broadening is the 'defense-in-depth' solution advocated by Theodore Levitt in his widely acclaimed 'Marketing Myopia'.[18] Levitt calls upon a company to shift its focus from the current product to the underlying generic need and to get involved in R&D across the whole range of technology associated with that need. Thus, 'petroleum' companies are asked to recast themselves into 'energy' companies. Implicitly, this demands dipping their research fingers into the oil, coal, nuclear, hydroelectric, and chemical industries. But this market-broadening strategy should not be carried too far. In a strategic sense, it faults two fundamental principles - the principle of the objective ('clearly defined and attainable') and the principle of mass. The objective of being in the energy business is too broad. The energy business is not a single need but a whole range of needs (heating, lighting, propelling, and so on). That leaves very little in the world that is not potentially the energy business. Furthermore, too much broadening would dilute the company's mass in the competitive theatre today, and survival today surely must take precedence over the grand battles imagined for some tomorrow. The error of marketing myopia would be replaced by marketing hyperopia, a condition where vision is better for distant than for near objects.

Preemptive defense ('Offensive defense')

Offense as a form of preemptive defense assumes that prevention is better than cure. It assumes that war and not peace is the natural state of business. Preemptive defense includes all the attack strategies considered earlier.

For example, a company could launch a flank or envelopmental attack against a competitor whose market share is approaching some criterion mark. When Chrysler's market share began rising from 12 to 18 per cent some years ago, one rival marketing executive was overheard to say, 'If they [Chrysler] go to 20 per cent, it will be over our dead bodies.'[19]

Or a company could practice a sort of sustained guerrilla action across the market - hitting one competitor here, another there - and keep everyone off balance at the tactical theatre. Or the offensive defense could assume the proportions of a brand market envelopment, as practised by Seiko, or the sustained frontal barrage of the Texas Instruments' type. Sustained high-pressure strategies aim at retaining the initiative at all times and keeping the competition always on the defensive.

Companies fortunate enough to enjoy high levels of market assets - high brand loyalty, technological leadership, and so on - would probably find it disadvantageous to pursue too broad a preemptive strategy. They have the capacity to weather some punishment and may even prefer to entice the opponents into expensive and costly attacks that will not pay off (they hope) in the long run. Heinz let Hunt's carry out its massive attack in the catsup market without much counter-offensive; and in the end this proved very costly to Hunt's. Standing firm in the face of an attack, however, calls for great confidence in the ultimate superiority of the company's market offer.

'Flank-positioning' defense

The flanking 'position' is established by a defender as a hedge against some probable but uncertain eventuality, or as a defensive corner overlooking a weak front. As in the military theatre, a flanking position is of little value if it is so lightly held that an enemy could pin it down with a small force while its main formations swing past unmolested. A careful assessment of any potential threat must be made and, if indicated, a relatively serious commitment made to flanking the threat.

Many instances of flank positions are to be found in the business world. The defensive stance taken by Chicago-based Jewel Food Stores is instructive of flank positions in some markets coupled with a head-on counter-offensive in others. The company believes that the supermarket will continue to remain a dominant force and its counter-offense consists of strengthening its assortments 'fit' *vis-à-vis* changing lifestyle parameters of its consumer segment. The fast-food boom has been met by offering a wide assortment of instant and frozen meals, the discount food challenge by promoting generic lines, and Jewel's various supermarkets are being tailored to suit local demands for assortments such as fresh baker products and ethnic foods. However, the company is taking no chances with some institution developments in other fields. It has set up the Jew-T division, which is a network of 'box' discount stores patterned after pioneer Aldi. Watching a sudden turnaround in the competitive position of 'independent' in 1977, Jewel's Star Market division in New England promptly began moving into franchising the following year. To hedge the 'combo' store challenge, it integrated a large number of its supermarkets with its Osco Drug stores, using both side-by-side and fully integrated designs.

The 'counter-offensive' in defense

A defender can respond to an attack by mobilizing his reserves and counter-attacking the opponent. He has the strategic choice of meeting the attacker spearhead on, manoeuvring against the flank of the attacker, or launching a pincer movement threatening to cut off the attacking formations from their base of operation.

When Oxy-5 blitzed the acne medications market with an extremely powerful promotional attack, the market leader, Clearasil, retaliated with a stepped-up counter-promotion of its own. Sometimes erosion of market share is so rapid that such a head-on counter-stroke may be necessitated. But a defender enjoying some strategic depth can often weather the initial attack and repose effectively at the opportune moment. In many situations, it may be worth some minor setbacks to allow the offensive to develop fully (and be understood) before countering. This may seem a dangerous strategy of 'wait and see', but there are sound reasons for not barrelling into a counter-offensive.

A better retort to an offensive is for the defender to pause and identify a chink in the attacker's armour, namely, a segment gap in which a viable counter-offensive can be launched. Cadillac designed its Seville as an alternative to the Mercedes and pinned its hope on offering a smoother ride and more creature comforts than Mercedes was willing to design.

An example of pincering out the opponent's attack is Heublein's strategy in defending its Smirnoff vodka against an attack from Wolfschmidt in the 1960s. Wolfschmidt priced at a dollar less a bottle and claimed to be of the same quality. After considering all frontal counter-offensive alternatives, Heublein rejected these as detrimental to its profits and came up with a brilliant pincering manoeuvre. It raised the price of Smirnoff by one dollar (effectively preventing segment diffusion) and introduced two new brands to meet Wolfschmidt head-on (same price) and on the other flank (lower price).

'Hedgehog' defense ('Strategic withdrawal')

Strategic withdrawal is a move to consolidate one's competitive strength in the market, and concentrate mass at pivotal positions for counterattack. The hedgehog pattern of withdrawing into consolidated positions along the front line fits the marketing operation of counter-segmentation.[20] In the slow-growth 1980s, an increasing opportunity seemed to be emerging for profitable strategy in either eliminating or fusing these fragmented segments. This opinion is shared by seventy chief marketing executives of Fortune's 500 who responded to a questionnaire. Westinghouse's refrigerator models have been cut from forty to the thirty that accounted for 85 per cent of sales. General Motors has standardized its auto engines and now offers fewer options. Campbell's Soup, Heinz, General Mills, Del Monte, Georgia-Pacific, Studebaker-Worthington, Gable Industries, and APL Corporation are among those that have significantly pruned their product lines in recent years. Once again we find the underlying principle is concentration of mass if the desegmentation opportunity permits.

Conclusion

During the prosperous 1950s and 1960s, rapid economic growth allowed companies to focus their attention on the character of demand rather than the character of competition. The emerging 'market concept' held that companies would succeed if they finely analyzed consumer needs and wants and met them with appropriate products, prices, distribution, and promotion. Successful companies would be those practising a consumer orientation, and the plans of competitors would at best be incidental.

The 1970s might be loosely described as the decade of distribution orientation. Mass merchandising retailers and other distributors grew in power, and manufacturers found themselves selling to fewer but larger marketing intermediaries. It was a decade when manufacturers focused their attention increasingly on the problems of skilful manoeuvring in the 'power' politics of distribution.

The 1980s is not about repudiating a deep consumer and distribution orientation but rather about adding a deep competition orientation.

Companies now have to choose markets whose needs they can satisfy and whose competitors they can handle. Companies must know each competitor's plans and resources in selecting their own target markets and objectives.

Military principles and stratagems are not the whole answer to competitive strategy but they do provide insight into what it takes for a company to succeed in attacking another company or in defending itself against an aggressor. Company managements have always talked loosely about 'going to battle', 'invading markets', 'returning fire with fire', and so on.

But management has rarely appreciated the full array of possible attack and defense strategies and their relative requirements and merits. This article has emphasized the foolishness of 'head-on' attacks and 'fortification' defenses in the light of the availability of more subtle confrontation strategies.

As market share and rank become more obsessive concerns in the executive suite,[21] management must deepen its understanding of military strategy doctrines. A military consciousness, however, must not replace the more basic marketing consciousness. The company must still be good at 'finding needs and filling them', but now it must also know how to out-manoeuvre its competitors in the same task.

Notes

1   See Carl von Clausewitz, *On War* (London: Routledge & Kegan Paul); B.H. Liddell Hart, *Strategy* (New York: Praeger, 1967); and J.F.C. Fuller, *The Conduct of War, 1789-1961* (London: Eyre & Spottiswoode, 1961).
2   See Michael E. Porter, 'How Competitive Forces Shape Strategy,' *Harvard Business Review*, March-April 1979, pp. 137-145; Richard G. Hamermesh and Steven B. Silk, 'How to Compete in Stagnant Industries,' *Harvard Business Review*, September-October, 1979, pp. 161-168.
3   Marshall Ferdinand Foch was primarily responsible for indoctrinating the French Army to the dogmatic philosophy *l'offensive brutale et a outrance*. As a consequence, World War I witnesses the senseless and bloody dissipation of French infantry in futile frontal charges against entrenched German machine guns and barbed wire. The Russians, even today, include 'annihilation' as one of their nine fundamental principles of strategy.
4   Liddell Hart, note 1 *supra*, at 351.
5   *Id.* at 357.
6   *Id.* at 334.
7   See 'RCA Goes Head-to-Head with IBM,' *Fortune*, Oct. 1970; 'The 250 Million Dollar Disaster That Hit RCA,' *Business Week*, Sept. 25, 1971.
8   See 'Stopping the Greasies,' *Forbes*, July 9, 1979, p. 121.
9   'A "Me-Too" Strategy That Paid off,' *Fortune*, Aug. 27, 1979, p. 86.
10 Liddell Hart, note 1 *supra*, at 347.
11 Quote in 'Honeywell Information Systems' (case available from the Intercollegiate Case Clearing House, Soldiers Field, Boston, 1975), pp. 7-8.
12 Liddell Hart, note 1 *supra*, at 161.
13 See 'Seiko's Smash,' *Business Week*, June 5, 1978, p. 89.
14 See 'The Changing of the Guard,' *Fortune*, Sept. 24, 1979; 'How to be Happy Though No. Two,' *Forbes*, July 15, 1976, p. 36.
15 Liddell Hart, note 1 *supra*, at 335.
16 'Alaska Chills a German Beer,' *Business Week*, April 23, 1979, p. 42.

17 'The Strategy That Refreshes?' *Forbes*, Nov. 27, 1978, p. 81.
18 See Theodore Levitt, 'Marketing Myopia,' *Harvard Business Review*, July-August, 1960, pp. 45-56.
19 'If the Big Three's A Crowd, Blame Chrysler,' *Newsweek*, May 20, 1968, p. 84.
20 See Alan J. Resnik, Peter B.B. Turney, and J. Barry Mason, 'Marketers Turn to Counter-Segmentation,' *Harvard Business Review*, September- October 1979, p. 100.
21 See Robert D. Buzzell, Bradley T. Gale and Ralph G.M. Sultan, 'Market Share - A Key to Profitability,' *Harvard Business Review*, January-February 1975, p. 97; 'Corporate Strategists Giving New Emphasis to Market Share, Rank,' *Wall Street Journal*, Feb. 3, 1978.

Reproduced from Kotler, P. and Singh, R. (1980). Marketing warfare in the 1980s. *Journal of Business Strategy*, **1**(3), 30–41, by permission of Faulkner & Gray Publishers, New York.

Part Two
Environmental Analysis

One conclusion emerging unanimously from the articles in Part One is that research in the area of marketing has important implications for other fields of management which overlap with marketing. Part Two focuses on perhaps the most important of these 'synergies', that of environmental analysis, which is equally important to the understanding of issues in strategy formation and development as it is to marketing issues. This contribution is also accepted as being increasingly important to organizations as the environment is perceived to become more competitive, more complex, less easily analysed, and generally more changeable.[1] Indeed, it is often argued[2] that the management of change is now the central problem of strategic management. For example, in recently launching the *Journal of Strategic Change*, Ansoff described strategic management as being

> concerned with the adaptation of business firms, and other environment-serving organizations, to turbulent environments, which is precisely the problem of managing discontinuous strategic change. (Ansoff, 1992, p. 7)

This reflects a view of the environment which is summarized by Ansoff:

> since the 1940s the environment of many business firms has progressively become more and more turbulent, unpredictable and surpriseful . . . [because of] the acceleration of the speed of change in the environment which has occurred during the past 30 years. (Ansoff, 1984, p. 455)

The term 'environment', when used in the context of marketing strategy, generally refers to the mix of variables external to an organization which might affect the performance of an organization in its markets. In marketing textbooks these variables are typically clustered under the labels of *technological, economic, political* and *social* factors.

Other labels are sometimes added and each cluster of variables could be subdivided further according to the specific circumstances of each particular sector, market and organization, resulting in what Sanderson and Luffman (1988 – Chapter 6, this section) refer to as the 'almost infinite number of [external] environmental variables' including competition, suppliers, customers and stakeholders (Porter, 1979 – Chapter 7, this section), all of which clearly have an influence on the organization's environment.

It is important to recognize that it makes little sense to distinguish unambiguously between an organization's **internal** environment (its culture, structure and socio-political processes) and its **external** environment since there will generally be some confusion as to which variables are most appropriately conceived as predominantly external or internal to an organization. For example, predominantly internal variables (such as personnel, corporate culture, incentive systems, staff expertise) must inevitably affect the external performance of an organization in its markets. Nor is it necessarily the case that managers have full 'control' over the internal environment (where organizational culture can be very awkward to 'manage') and none over the external environment (where, for example, political lobbying by industry groups can be very influential).

Some of the literature on strategic decision-making reinforces this overlap between internal and external environments by pointing out that a manager's perception of external variables such as competitive response and market demand is fundamentally coloured by internal factors such as organizational culture and political interaction between managers (Piercy and Giles, 1989). It may well be the case that the distinction between 'external' and 'internal' variables is based on outmoded concepts of organizational 'boundaries' and managerial control which are now increasingly being superseded by notions of organizations as constituted by relationships and networks (Hirschhorn and Gilmore, 1992; Gummesson, 1987).

The three articles in Part Two address the problems of environment analysis from three perspectives – Sanderson and Luffman (1988) consider the environment from both the macro and the micro levels, while Porter (1979) focuses on the competitive environment, and Day and Wensley (1988) concentrate on individual competitive relationships.

In the first of these articles, Sanderson and Luffman discuss the increasing importance and complexity of environmental analysis as perhaps the chief task of strategic planning. They adopt the conventional structure of the environment suggested by Kotler (1985) distinguishing between the *macro-environment*, comprising economic, social, technological, and political variables which are largely beyond the direct influence of the organization; and the *micro-environment*, comprising the variables which an organization can influence (e.g. pricing, product development, service levels, quality) and through which an organization makes its competitive response to developments in the macro-environment. Sanderson and Luffman also give additional attention to the international environment because of the significant effect of national and cultural differences on environmental variables.

Many writers have addressed the problems of environmental complexity and perception noted by Sanderson and Luffman, though discussion has often been limited to issues of access to the appropriate environmental information, as though analysis, interpretation, communication and response were simply automatic outcomes, routinely dependent on data inputs. Sanderson and Luffman, in the article reprinted here, take a different perspective, identifying several 'problems and shortcomings' in the analysis process by which organizations perceive and respond to their environments, including: the innate personal style of managers (e.g. optimism/pessimism); managers' perception of their role within the organization (e.g. 'idea generator', 'process manager', 'cost controller'); organizational culture (e.g. entrepreneurial, managerial, production oriented, technological, risk-averse) and the level of crisis facing the organization which may render environmental analysis a superfluous luxury because of the time it takes. This list might also be extended by reference to further variables such as organizational sub-cultures (Sackmann, 1992), managers' career expectations and age (Grimm and Smith, 1991), managers' skill and competence (Cockerill, 1989), or the level of resource invested by the organization in its marketing and planning support functions. In a later work Piercy and Giles explain the importance of these managerial perceptual filters clearly, though without clear suggestions as to how to redress the inherent problems of bias or how to access systematically the potential benefits of managerial exprience:

> constructed from past experiences, attitudes and predispositions, and the culture which tells managers what to give attention and what to ignore . . . this perception of the world is highly imperfect, subjective and biased, but represents *reality* to the people concerned. It is impossible to ignore or avoid this influence on executives' perceptions and we take it as implicitly the initial base-point in planning. (Piercy and Giles, 1989, p. 25)

Further insight into the significance of managerial perception in environmental analysis is offered by Gronhaug and Haukedal's (1988) study of how two rival firms perceived opportunities and threats in an 'extremely volatile environment' (international freight shipping services). Of the two organizations, one did very little strategic planning or environmental scanning, acting instead on the largely uncoordinated intuition of individual managers within a relatively inflexible outlook. The second organization had a clear commitment to change, engaged in extensive environmental scanning, recruited highly educated managers from outside the industry, used frequent internal meetings to coordinate action and exchange ideas, and so was able to maintain a much more flexible outlook. The latter organization perceived the environment as being very much more volatile and problematic than did the former. This study provides a convincing view of how an organization's perception of its environment affects its strategy development processes. Gronhaug and Haukedal point out that environments have to be perceived and interpreted to be meaningful, and that managers do this through a process of information selection and prioritization which is mediated through their inherently conservative cognitive schemata (or 'mind-set'). They list other internal factors influencing the organization's perception of the environment as: organizational structure, the design of the organization's information processing system, the organization's perception of its previous and future roles, its management systems, its culture, and its current operations. Through these various factors an organization and its individual managers form a perception of the new environment, especially of its threats and opportunities, which will be manifested in 'images of the future which in turn will affect organizational [strategic] actions' (p. 6). The authors conclude that

> the importance of perceiving environmental change and the ability to create images about future opportunities [i.e. make predictions] can hardly be overstated. (Gronhaug and Haukedal, 1988, p. 16)

A number of writers recommend scenario development (Dittrich, 1988; Whipple, 1989) and environmental scanning for the analysis of volatile environments. For example, Sanderson and Luffman argue that: 'firms in volatile, hostile environments will tend to direct more resources to scanning than those in stable, friendly environments.' Porter and Millar (1985) describe enthusiastically the potential of IT systems to support this scanning activity through collecting and analysing data, and through marketing decision support systems which, they argue, will allow organizations to cope competitively with volatile environments. An important implication of this approach is that environmental volatility is eased by information and that IT allows organizations to manage information in great quantity and at sufficient speed to deliver prompt analyses of fast-changing environments as a guide to strategic action. The same assumptions are evident in the work of many writers in the fields of strategy and marketing, while the recognition that information management is the essence particularly of the marketing function dates at least from the work of Alderson (1965).

Others have criticized this approach (Lenz and Lyles, 1985; Mowen and Gaeth, 1992), pointing out the practical difficulties of information management in marketing, including the problems of too much as well as too little information and analysis, and the inherent limitations of computerized marketing information systems (MkIS).[3] For example, Mowen and Gaeth point out that marketing decision support systems based on computerized information management and processing 'are essentially algorithms that integrate data in a consistent and mathematically correct manner' (Mowen and Gaeth, 1992, p. 177) whereas the balance of research suggests strongly that managers do not make decisions in this way (Mintzberg, 1973; Stewart, 1963).

Clearly, information cannot be regarded as value-neutral as sometimes seems to be the case in analyses originating from the field of industrial economics (Porter, 1980; 1985; Porter and Millar, 1985) and marketing (McDonald, 1989 – Chapter 21, Part Four of this book), any more than MkIS can adequately capture:

> that often controversial and unorganized mess of managerial experience . . . belief and knowledge – this is, after all, the fabric of the company that differentiates it from its competitors. (Piercy and Giles, 1989, p. 27).

The second article of Part Two (Porter, 1979) focuses on what is for most managers probably the most immediate aspect of the strategic environment – the competitive environment – laying the groundwork for Porter's subsequent impressive book on competitive analysis (Porter, 1980). In doing so Porter expands the traditional concept of competition as 'direct industry rivalry' to include competition (or 'bargaining power') within the value chain both upstream (i.e. between an organization and its suppliers) and downstream (i.e. between an organization and its customers). Porter's analysis extends also to the foreseeable future by including the competitive threat of new entrants to the industry as well as competitive threats arising from substitute products and services. These five competitive forces are mapped in Porter's well-known *five force model* of industry competition. Porter argues that competition (more accurately the 'perception' of competition) is the spur to strategy formation and that strategy is therefore shaped by competitive analysis.

The five force model provides a structure for competitive analysis which is fundamentally dependent on the related concept of *mobility barriers* (Caves and Porter, 1977). It is suggested that mobility barriers limit the ability of organizations to enter or to exit from industry sectors, while also limiting the ability of established competitors to move from one market to another within a sector. For example, typical mobility barriers within a sector might include geographical location (markets may be too distant to service profitably), or technological requirements (some markets are more technologically advanced than others), or price/brand sensitivity (some segments are more sensitive to price or to brands than others).

Accepting that organizations vary in their ability to influence or antici- pate their competitive environment, Porter briefly discusses the strategic options implied by his model in three categories: *defensive strategies* for organizations not able, or wishing, to adjust the competitive structure of their industry; *offensive strategies* for more proactive and influential competitors; and *exploitative strategies* for those capable of analysing the competitive dynamics of their industry and so more able to anticipate developments.

Porter's approach emphasizes the dynamic character of competition which cannot be assessed adequately except in a longitudinal frame, and also the multifaceted requirements of effective competitive analysis where a firm's competitive position is dependent upon a wide range of external, internal, historic and latent factors. A major problem facing strategy theorists in the 1990s, he suggests (Porter, 1991), is how to combine an understanding of the causes of competitive superiority at any given moment (identified through competitive analysis) with an understanding of how competitive positions change over time – what Porter refers to as a dynamic theory of strategy (Porter, 1991).

Porter has made important contributions to competitive analysis and to understanding the principles of industry structure. However, as with so much of management theory, practice often fails to live up to the ideals of 'theory' raising important questions about the nature of theory in management. For example, Porter recommends that strategy decision-makers and analysts consider a wide range of contingent circumstances in an intellectual process of assessment, prioritization, extrapolation and selection (Porter, 1980, 1985). This approach assumes that information, analysis, intellectual processes and objectives are widely available and susceptible to only one perception, interpreta- tion and conclusion – or at least that such differences as do arise will be resolvable through rational discussion. Many researchers (e.g. Pennings, 1985) have found that the nature of decision-making in organizations is fundamentally incompatible with these assumptions, that there can be significant differences of view as to, for example, what are appropriate organizational objectives, which markets the organization is addressing, who are the organization's competitors, what are the organization's relative strengths and weaknesses, what priority to place on the various factors, what measures are meaningful, what conclusions to draw and so on. Even in the fanciful case of organizations which are equally matched in terms of resources, market strength, product range, customer focus and the like, the differences in managerial experience, intuition, perception, capability, professional skill and in organizational culture and management processes would surely be sufficient to provide for a wide variety of strategic decision-making outcomes.

Whereas Porter's article develops an approach towards identifying competitors and competitive threats, the third article of Part Two (Day and Wensley, 1988) takes the process a step further by developing an approach to assessing the relative competitiveness of rivals once they have been identified. Day and Wensley point out that organizations tend to adopt either a competitor focus or a customer focus in their assessment. It is suggested that this is a complexity-reduction technique because it is simply too complex to attempt assessment from both perspectives. Clearly, a balanced approach would be more desirable and this is what Day and Wensley attempt to develop.

They offer a model linking superior skills and resources[4] to consequent positional advantages[5] with an emphasis on performance measures which relate to competitive realities rather than to statistical convenience. Day and Wensley are not alone in warning of the weakness of traditional measures of competitive position such as market share and profitability. *Market share* depends on the unlikely assumption that rivals share precisely the same view of the market, while *profitability* is driven by accounting conventions rather than competitive pressures, and both measures reflect historic situations rather than future possibilities. Nevertheless, these measures can be useful when taken as part of a package of measures, especially perhaps in more mature and stable markets where sector 'norms' are published by independent analysts, though stability seems less typical of contemporary competitive environments than may once have been the case (Whipp *et al.*, 1989).

Day and Wensley criticize several approaches to strategic measurement and modelling arguing that no individual measure of strategic position is without important flaws of theory and/or practice. It is this critical examination of available measures which is certainly one of the chief contributions of this article. They conclude that the optimal approach is one involving a number of measures and where management judgement remains informed but independent. For example, 'first-mover advantages' arise from the willingness of managers to invest in new markets or fresh technologies (where there is usually insufficient data for statistical measures to be applied) and would never arise unless pioneering managers were prepared to act independently of measures. The authors also stress that managerial judgement is subject to problems of 'myopia', partial recollection, selective perception, over-simplification, and often seems to favour 'hard' statistically-oriented data rather than informal 'soft' assessments. This last issue – preference for 'hard' data – may be deceptive to some extent because of the probable tendency for individuals (consciously or otherwise) to seek 'hard' data to support their 'soft' intuition (or what Mintzberg (1987) refers to as 'wisdom' – see Chapter 19, Part Four of this book). What may be more at issue is the perceived greater legitimacy of 'hard' information sources *per se* over 'soft' sources. The persuasive power of 'soft' sources amongst customers (such as word-of-mouth endorsements) should alert analysts to the underlying problem – that of finding ways to develop and analyse 'soft' sources more rigorously (Miles, 1979).

In volatile environments, however, it may often be difficult to analyse emerging opportunities and threats adequately in terms of previous knowledge and experience, underlining the importance of imagination and continual innovation in responding to volatile environments. In similar contexts other writers have emphasized the need for *strategic flexibility* (Harrigan, 1985; Ansoff, 1991), *adaptiveness* (Toffler, 1985; McKee *et al.*, 1989), or *strategic opportunism* (Isenberg, 1987; Stacey, 1990) in responding to rapidly changing environments.

How 'strategic flexibility' can be achieved is not so easily established and probably depends on the 'flexibility' of individual managers faced with novel situations. In researching how managers cope with novel situations, Mowen and Gaeth (1992) analysed the heuristics used by managers in marketing decision-making. They concluded that managers were significantly influenced by any similarities they observed between emerging events and their own experience; that managers tended to deal with multifaceted situations by engaging with one facet (the most familiar) and then adapting incrementally to each additional facet as it became manifest; and that managers tended to judge outcomes subjectively. This research largely confirmed earlier work by Tuler (1988) in management areas more generally while questioning the widespread assumption that when faced with volatile environments, organizations should respond by focusing on the fundamental models and techniques of marketing planning supported by investment in information technology (Hedley, 1976; Lysonski and Pecotich, 1992).

A wide array of other studies has come to similar conclusions about how organizations should respond to volatile environments, especially with respect to: the inappropriateness of a simple or prescriptive approach to competitive success (Boynton and Victor, 1991); the importance of a ready access to a range of potentially useful expertise (Gronhaug and Haukedal, 1988); the value of generating internal innovativeness (Loveridge, 1990); the necessity of flatter, more flexible organizational structures with efficient internal channels of communication (Peters and Waterman, 1982); the willingness to delegate responsibility for strategy development within a context of 'strategic control' and under the guidance of a generalized statement of organizational objectives or 'mission' (Campbell *et al.*, 1990); the openness to organizational learning and willingness to adopt the resultant 'lessons' (Bahlmann, 1990); and the importance of maintaining close relationships with a range of customers, suppliers and potential collaborators (Goldhar and Lei, 1991; Gummesson, 1987). At the risk of over-simplification, these studies seem to advocate a view of strategy development in volatile environments as a process of cautious experimentation which avoids taking things for granted and maintains an alert monitoring of the competitive environment.

On the other hand, no organization is capable of constant change. Periods of continuity and consolidation are required to 'internalize' change, as has been noted by many writers in the fields of strategy (Johnson, 1986; Mintzberg, 1987), organizational behaviour (Child, 1977; Handy, 1982), and administrative systems (Kamenka, 1989; Beer, 1979). As Mintzberg notes:

> change takes place in spurts, each followed by a period of continuity . . . [reflecting] the interplay between a dynamic environment and bureaucratic momentum with leadership mediating between the two forces. (Mintzberg, 1978, pp. 943, 934)

The multiple difficulties of environmental analysis will remain an important focus for future research in marketing and strategy formation but strategic decisions for specific businesses will also depend crucially on business analysis, the focus of Part Three. The contents of Parts Two and Three are therefore closely related and will provide readers with a basis for making interesting comparisons of theory and analytical technique.

References

Alderson, W. (1965), *Dynamic Marketing Behavior*, Richard D. Irwin, Homewood, IL.

Ansoff, H.I., (1984), *Implanting Strategic Management*, Prentice-Hall International, Englewood Cliffs, NJ.

Ansoff, H.I. (1991), 'Strategic Management in a Historical Perspective', in Hussey, D.E. (ed.), *International Review of Strategic Management*, volume 2.2, Wiley, Chichester.

Ansoff, H.I. (1992), 'Welcome to the Journal of Strategic Change', *Journal of Strategic Change*, vol. 1, no. 1, 7-9.

Bahlmann, T. (1990), 'The Learning Organization in a Turbulent Environment', *Human Systems Management*, vol. 9, no. 4, 249-256.

Beer, S. (1979), *The Heart of Enterprise*, Wiley, NY.

Boynton, A.C. and Victor, B. (1991), 'Beyond Flexibility: Building and Managing the Dynamically Stable Organization', *California Management Review*, vol. 34, no. 1, Fall 1991, pp. 53-66.

Campbell, A., Devine, M. and Young, D. (1990), *A Sense of Mission*, The Economist Books, Hutchinson, London.

Caves, R.E. and Porter, M.E. (1977), 'From Entry Barriers to Mobility Barriers, Conjectural Decisions and Contrived Deterrence to New Competition', *Quarterly Journal of Economics*, vol. 91, May, 241-261.

Child, J. (1977), *Organization: a Guide to Problems and Practice*, Harper & Row, London.

Cockerill, A. (1989), 'The Kind of Competence for Rapid Change', *Personnel Management*, vol. 21, no. 9, September, 52-56.

Day, G.S. and Wensley, R. (1988), 'Assessing Advantage: a Framework for Diagnosing Competitive Superiority', *Journal of Marketing*, volume 52, April, 1-20.

Dittrich, J.E. (1988), *The General Manager and Strategy Formulation: Objectives, Missions, Strategies, Policies*, Wiley, NY.

Goldhar, J.D. and Lei, D. (1991), 'The Shape of Twenty-First Century Global Manufacturing', *Journal of Business Strategy*, vol. 12, no. 2, March/ April, 37-41.

Grimm, C.M. and Smith, K.G. (1991), 'Management and Organizational Change: A Note on the Railroad Industry', *Strategic Management Journal*, vol. 12, no. 7, October, 557-562.

Gronhaug, K. and Haukedal, W. (1988), 'Environmental Imagery and Strategic Actions', *Scandinavian Journal of Management*, vol. 4, no. 1/2, 5-17.

Gummesson, E. (1987), 'The New Marketing: Developing Long-Term Interactive Relationships', *Long Range Planning*, vol. 20, no. 4, Aug. 10-20.

Handy, C.B. (1982), *Understanding Organizations*, Third edition, Penguin Books, Harmondsworth.

Harrigan, K.R. (1985), *Strategic Flexibility*, D.C. Heath & Co., Lexington.

Hedley, B. (1976), 'A Fundamental Approach to Strategy Development', *Long Range Planning*, vol. 9, December, 2-11.

Hirschhorn, L. and Gilmore, T. (1992), 'The New Boundaries of the "Boundaryless" Company', *Harvard Business Review*, vol. 70, no. 3, May-June, 104-115.

Isenberg, D.J. (1987), 'The Tactics of Strategic Opportunism', *Harvard Business Review*, March/April, 92-97.

Johnson, G. (1986), 'Managing Strategic Change – the Role of Strategic Formulae', in McGee, J. and Thomas, H. (eds) *Strategic Management Research: a European Perspective*, Wiley, Chichester. pp. 71-87.

Kamenka, E. (1989), *Bureaucracy*, Basil Blackwell, Oxford.

Kotler, P. (1985), *Marketing Management: Analysis, Planning, Implementation and Control*, Fifth edition, Prentice-Hall International, Englewood Cliffs, NJ.

Lenz, R.T. and Lyles, M.A. (1985), 'Paralysis by Analysis: is Your Planning System Becoming too Radical?', *Long Range Planning*, 18 (4), 64-72.

Loveridge, R. (1990), 'Incremental Innovation and Appropriate Learning Styles in Direct

Services', in Loveridge, R. and Pitt, M. (eds), *The Strategic Management of Technological Innovation*, Wiley, Chichester.

Lysonski, S. and Pecotich, A. (1992), 'Strategic Marketing Planning, Environmental Uncertainty and Performance', *International Journal of Research in Marketing*, vol. 9, 247-255.

McDonald, M.H.B. (1989), 'Ten Barriers to Marketing Planning', *Journal of Marketing Management*, vol. 5, no. 1, Summer 1-18.

McKee, D.O., Varadarjan, P.R. and Pride, W.M. (1989), 'Strategic Adaptability and Firm Performance: a Market Contingent Perspective', *Journal of Marketing*, vol. 53, no. 3, 21-35.

Miles, M.B. (1979), 'Qualitative Data as an Attractive Nuisance: the Problem of Analysis', *Administrative Science Quarterly*, vol. 24, December (special edition edited by John Van Maanen), 590-601.

Mintzberg, H. (1973), *The Nature of Managerial Work*, Harper & Row, New York.

Mintzberg, H. (1978), 'Patterns in Strategy Formation', *Management Science*, vol. 24, no. 9, May, 934-948.

Mintzberg, H. (1987), 'Crafting Strategy', *Harvard Business Review*, vol. 65, July/August.

Mintzberg, H. (1991), 'Learning 1, Planning 0: Reply to Igor Ansoff', *Strategic Management Journal*, vol. 12, 463-466.

Mowen, J.C. and Gaeth, G.J. (1992), 'The Evaluation Stage in Marketing Decision Making', *Journal of the Academy of Marketing Science*, vol. 20, no. 2, 177-187.

Pennings, J.M. (1985), 'On the Nature and Theory of Strategic Decisions', in Pennings, J.M. (ed), *Organizational Strategy and Change: New Views on Formulating and Implementing Strategic Decisions*, Jossey-Bass, San Francisco. 1-34.

Peters, T.J. and Waterman, R.H. Jnr. (1982), *In Search of Excellence*, Harper & Row, London.

Piercy, N.F. and Giles, W. (1989), 'The Logic of Being Illogical in Strategic Marketing Planning', *Journal of Marketing Management*, vol. 5, no. 1, Summer, 19-31.

Porter, M.E. (1979), 'How Competitive Forces Shape Strategy', *Harvard Business Review*, vol. 57, March-April, 137-145.

Porter, M.E. (1980), *Competitive Strategy: Techniques for Analysing Industries & Competitors*, Free Press, New York.

Porter, M.E. (1985), *Competitive Advantage: Creating & Sustaining Superior Performance*, Free Press, New York.

Porter, M.E. (1991), 'Towards a Dynamic Theory of Strategy', *Strategic Management Journal*, vol. 12, Winter, 95-117.

Porter, M.E. and Millar, V.E. (1985), 'How Information Gives You Competitive Advantage', *Harvard Business Review*, vol. 63, no. 4, July/ August, 149-160.

Sackmann, S.A. (1992), 'Culture and Subcultures: An Analysis of Organizational Knowledge', *Administrative Science Quarterly*, vol. 37, no. 1, March, 140-161.

Sanderson, S.M. and Luffman, G.A. (1988), 'Strategic Planning and Environmental Analysis', *European Journal of Marketing*, vol. 22, no. 2, 14-27.

Stacey, R.D. (1990), *Dynamic Strategic Management for the 1990s: Balancing Opportunism & Business Planning*, Kogan Page, London.

Stewart, R. (1963), *The Reality of Management*, Heinemann, London.

Toffler, A. (1985), *The Adaptive Corporation*, McGraw-Hill, New York.

Tuler, S. (1988), 'Individual, Group and Organisational Decision Making in Technological Emergencies: a Review of Research', *Industrial Crisis Quarterly*, vol. 2, 109-138.

Whipp, R., Rosenfeld, R. and Pettigrew, A.M. (1989), 'Culture and Competitiveness: Evidence from Two Mature UK Industries', *Journal of Management Studies*, vol. 26, no. 6, 561-585.

Whipple, W., III (1989), 'Evaluating Alternative Strategies Using Scenarios', *Long Range Planning*, vol. 22, no. 3, June, 82-86.

Notes

1 Note that this perception is difficult to demonstrate through statistical measures and has been challenged by some writers with a greater sensitivity to historical comparison (e.g. Mintzberg, 1991).

2 See, for example: Calori, R. and Lawrence, P. (eds) (1991), *The Business of Europe: Managing Change*, Sage Publications, London; Pettigrew, A.M. and Whipp, R. (1992), *Managing Change for Competitive Success*, Basil Blackwell, Oxford.

3 For a realistic view of the advantages and disadvantages of IT systems in marketing see Proctor, R.A. (1991), 'Marketing Information Systems', *Management Decision*, vol. 29, no. 4, 55-60.

4 *Superior skills* and *superior resources*, in combination, might be thought of as comparable to the *distinctive competencies* discussed by several other writers (see Prahalad, C.K. and Hamel, G. (1990), 'The Core Competence of the Corporation', *Harvard Business Review*, May/June, 79-91 – Chapter 10, Part Three of this book.

5 *Positional advantages* are closely related to Porter's generic competitive strategies (Porter, 1980).

6 Strategic planning and environmental analysis

S. M. Sanderson and G. A. Luffman

All is flux, nothing stays still

– Heracleitus, 6th Century BC

Introduction

In a recent speech Sir John Harvey Jones, the chairman of Imperial Chemical Industries, asserted that, of all forms of human creativity, the business organization is perhaps the most ephemeral. The history of enterprise is littered with household names which have gone out of existence. Amongst the reasons for such a phenomenon, of prime importance is a form of corporate Darwinism in which firms have failed to adapt to changes in the environment.

Strategic planning includes amongst its chief concerns the understanding and diagnosis of the environment. Indeed any strategy is a tangible manifestation of how well the firm has understood and responded to the environment that it faces. The task is not easy for there are no simple models or algorithms that ensure success; there are an almost infinite number of environmental variables, and, further, there is a close relationship between what a firm wants to look at, how it does it and the strategy that it wishes to pursue. Yet, the fact remains that, at the limit, if you get it wrong, you go out of business, but that getting it right does not ensure success, although there is some evidence to suggest that firms which have well-developed systems of environmental analysis perform better in some domains than others.[1]

The environment consists of a large number of non-controllable variables which, together, pose both threats and opportunities for companies in pursuit of their objectives. Such threats and opportunities are both current and in the future, but as the essence of strategy is that it has a future orientation, the emphasis of threats and opportunities analysis should be on the future shape of the environment. The process is essentially two-fold: first, environmental analysis which identifies and monitors potential threats and opportunities, and, secondly, diagnosis which, through a process of decision making, assesses the significance to the company of such threats and opportunities. In terms of a marketing strategy, the analysis of the environment will be against current product/market strategies and predictions of variance, whilst the diagnosis stage will concern itself with the significance of environmental change in terms of improvements to existing strategies, new products and/or markets. Thus, environmental appraisal, although not peculiar to marketing strategy, is an integral part of the strategic planning process.

A model of the environment

Although comprising a large number of variables or forces, the environment may be described by aggregating many of the variables into sub-environments as shown in Figure 1.

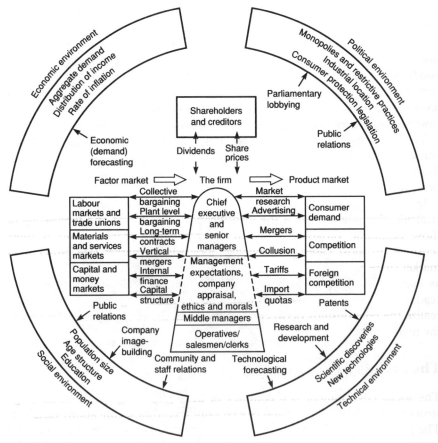

Figure 1   *The firm and its environment – a descriptive model*

The effects of the state and dynamics of the environment are felt by all major areas of an organization, and thus environmental analysis is part of strategic decision making for the major functions of a company. Generally, most functions will deal with that part of the environment with which they closely interact as part of a general corporate planning function. Marketing strategy, however, because it has the responsibility for managing demand which itself is a function of environmental change, needs to be sensitive to changes in the wider environment, not just the proximate marketplace. Changes in all of the environments shown in Figure 1 can have a significant effect on both what a firm markets and how it does it. For the purpose of illustration, major environmental variables and their effects on marketing strategy are discussed.

The economic environment

The economic environment consists of the current and future state of key economic variables used to describe wealth, purchasing power, savings and consumption, together with government economic policy deployed to affect those variables. For many products, economic variables, such as GNP or disposable income, are key determinants of demand, particularly in capital goods or industrial products. The distribution of income in society provides opportunities for firms to differentiate product or service offerings in terms of level of disposable income. The rate of inflation and government policy towards it can greatly affect consumers' attitudes to credit.

The relationship between strategy and the economic environment is not simply that when the economy improves all firms can do better. In periods of downturn, although seemingly posing a threat, opportunities may exist for firms to market lower-priced substitutes.

In terms of strategic marketing tasks, of prime importance as part of the strategic planning process is the identification, monitoring and forecasting of those economic variables to which the company's market effort is most sensitive. In most cases, this involves forecasts of market size rather than market share, as the latter is more often a function of marketing effort, as well as exogenous variables such as GNP. Fortunately, economic forecasts are readily available in the financial press. The key marketing task is to attempt to realize the relationships between movements in the economy and changes in the marketplace.

The social environment

The social environment is a complex of demographic (population size, age structure, location) and cultural (social values, attitudes, education) variables. The pace of change in the social environment may be slow, but its effects are inexorable. Demography is a prime component of demand and changes in the demographic structure can have lasting effects on marketing strategy. A threat to many companies has been the general ageing of the population. Thus companies specializing in baby and infant products have had to search for new markets or products. Opportunities presented by the growing older sector of the population have been somewhat limited due to income constraints, but, with more people retiring with occupational pensions, the spending power of this segment will increase for certain products and services.

Cultural variables, as they affect values and attitudes, although seemingly slow moving, can have profound effects on marketing strategy, providing both threats and opportunities. For example, equal opportunity is beginning to result in women moving into higher paid, more demanding occupations, which has presented opportunities for specialist retailers of women's wear. Social values regarding health have had a threatening effect on tobacco companies. Nor is the effect limited to consumer goods. Manufacturers have been affected, as can be seen in the current debate about nuclear energy generation. Some of the effects of social change can result in rapid change, for example, fashion, but, generally, the strategist has time to evaluate the corporate response to such changes.

Marketing strategy has a two-fold response to social change: first, to monitor and evaluate its impact in terms of product offerings and marketing methods, but, secondly, a more proactive role of building company image within society via what has been termed the company's publics. Social attitudes to companies can translate themselves into competitive advantage or disadvantage in a number of social domains, or publics, as can be seen in Figure 2. Social acceptance is, for many companies in hostile environments, a key area of marketing strategy.

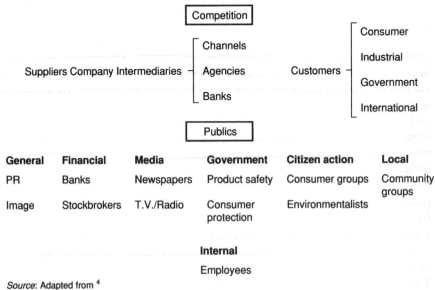

Source: Adapted from [4]

Figure 2

The technological environment

The technological environment is compounded of the impact of science and technology in product and process innovation. Thus, its effects can be felt by a company from raw material through to final goods marketing. In terms of marketing strategy, technological change offers the opportunity to purchase cheaper/better raw materials, improve product quality through process improvements, and the potential to alter the marketing of products and services in order to gain competitive advantage. The major threats are to product obsolescence, a general shortening of product and service life cycles and the ability of technology to alter methods of marketing such that the individual firm cannot afford to compete. An example of this latter phenomenon is in the financial services industry where computerization of financial services has led to a proliferation of automatic telling machines (ATMs). The cost of such systems means that only the large institutions can afford to deploy them, which has led to consortia being formed by competing companies in order to keep up with the growth in customer service. Thus, companies in competition have been forced into strategies of co-operation.

The major task for marketing management is to monitor the effects of technological change as it affects competitive advantage, but, as can be seen, the effects are not limited to the final goods market or simply new product innovation, but can affect processes and marketing methods. Similarly, there has to be an interface with R&D functions in the company in order to give research a market orientation.

The political environment

Government at both national and local levels can affect companies not only on a day-to-day basis through law, policies and its authority, but also at a strategic level by creating opportunities and threats. Specifically, these arise because, at a competitive level, government can determine industry structure via monopoly, and restrictive trade practices legislation further. By legislating it can thus encourage competition. Companies can be beneficiaries of fiscal and trade benefits through regional development programmes and industrial regeneration policies, which, in turn, can bestow cost benefits. Protection of infant industries and indigenous companies can render market penetration difficult, particularly overseas. Finally, Government, of itself, is a large consumer and producer of products and services; thus, government purchasing power and buying methods are of importance to many companies. In terms of politics rather than government, different political ideologies can greatly affect the mood of enterprise by privatization and nationalization.

As can be seen, the effect on marketing strategy goes well beyond the effects of the government's role as protector of consumers through consumer law. The nature of competition can be affected by government, either as a result of structural or procedural change; for example, the recent Financial Services

Act that has resulted in a far more open market for personal financial services allowing building societies to embark on new product development from which hitherto they were barred by legal status.

The strategic response by firms to the effects of government ranges from close monitoring of government by those firms who are closely affected to a more proactive response of lobbying and public relations aimed at government, as well as traditional methods such as financial support of political parties. For many companies, such as defence contractors, educational suppliers, manufacturers of hospital products, etc, the actions and mood of government are vital inputs to the strategic planning process.

The marketing environment

As can be seen in Figure 1, the four foregoing environments are seen as important influences on companies. In terms of marketing strategy, it can be seen that some areas of the environment are prime components of demand (population, wealth, etc.) and that others are of themselves the components of a marketing system (suppliers, competition, customers), but that all of them are instrumental in creating and influencing markets. Recent authorities[3] have pointed to the need for firms to attempt to create a *gestalt* of environmental change rather than focus on independent variables. Whilst it is not impossible for single environmental effects to pose threats and opportunities for companies, generally the effects are felt because of the dynamics of a number of variables. For example, the dramatic rise in supermarket shopping since the war arises from changes in wealth and car ownership, the rise in importance of the weekend as a leisure maximizing time, which, in turn, was assisted by changes in office hours, such that Saturday working disappeared, changes in technology which allow for food to last longer, ownership of refrigerators, the availability of media to advertise products, changes in the law regarding shop opening hours and, finally, changes in the attitudes of customers to shopping. Although the supermarket may now have become something of a retail institution, the dynamics of the environment which created it are currently shaping it in different directions via competition which is tending to concentrate the industry, technology which is creating new forms of payment systems, and the potential for home shopping and customer expectations which are leading to a widening of the product base and new forms of retailing. Concentration on any one of these variables would show a partial picture, whereas the whole effect is probably more than the sum of the parts.

Kotler[4] has suggested that a firm's total environment can be usefully subdivided into the micro and macro environments. Essentially a firm's micro environment consists of those elements of the wider environment with which the firm interacts in order to fulfil the marketing function together with the competitive environment and what he terms a set of publics. Such an environment is shown in Figure 2. The behaviour of the micro environment is to a large degree a function of the macro environment. The utility of the distinction is that it focuses the attention of managers on the important aspects of environment appraisal, in that marketing management knows that part of the wider environment which it has to monitor most closely in terms of its function whilst being aware of movements in the wider environment but where monitoring is either not as important in the shorter term or is done by some other part of the organization. The importance, however, should not be understressed, as most surveys of executives[5] show that the competitive environment is perceived as the most important to monitor.

The competitive environment

One of the major reasons for this sensitivity may well be that the environment is composed of actors whose prime role is to pose threats for any company. The nature of the competitive process has gained much comment, particularly since the work of Porter,[6] but of prime concern to the marketing strategist are the current strategies of competitors, the potential of new competition to enter the market, the behaviour of suppliers and buyers, and the availability of substitute products. The competitive environment is where the marketing function in a company has to live on a daily basis, and its effects are thus so proximate to a firm that it becomes a major user of resources in environment appraisal. Changes in competitors' strategies can present both threats and opportunities. Examples of the latter may be the exit of a major competitor, opportunities for new product development as substitutes or successful realization of market opportunities in advance of competition.

The nature of competition in a given market is to a large extent a function of its structure. Economists have for some time pointed to the degree of concentration as being a prime determinant of competitive behaviour. This has led firms to concentrate a market positively in order to gain advantage through price leverage or economies of scale.

The supplier or factor environment

The factor market comprises the supply of raw material, labour and capital which are endemic to business. The major effects of this environment on strategy are seen in terms of price and availability. Whilst these two areas may be a function of physical supply, often the negotiating powers of the supplier and buyer can affect both. This has important implications for marketing strategy as the price of raw materials can greatly affect competitiveness in the market. There is now a general realization that the factor market and its dynamic forms an important area of influence in marketing strategy. This effect becomes greater the higher the proportion of turnover which is accounted for by externally sourced inputs.

Buyers

Buyers are created and influenced by changes in other environments, but, where buying is done for the purpose of resale, as in retailing, there are other strategic consequences of their behaviour. Large buyers, particularly in concentrated markets, have power. This power increases the greater the concentration of the buying market, as compared with the supplying industry. Power can manifest itself to the strategic detriment of the supplier by having prices and qualities squeezed by buyers. The strategic consequences of marketing to large powerful buyers involves balancing the potential for market share against the exercise of power by retailers. This has resulted in some companies embarking on a policy of avoiding large customers or attempting to balance the customer portfolio with both large and small. In the longer term, it is an integral part of environment appraisal to monitor the structural variables of the marketplace.

The international environment

Although the model of environmental appraisal presented above is perfectly capable of being used in any country, appraisal of international markets is different, as some of the environmental factors may be difficult to quantify and may assume a greater importance. As Glueck and Jauch[7] have pointed out, environmental appraisal of overseas markets often promotes the importance of the socio-economic, government and competitor sectors. A number of techniques have been assembled in order to evaluate potential and risk in overseas environments, what they all share in common as the identification of key environment variables, weighting them in order to arrive at a benchmark score for a foreign economy. Brooke[8] offers a complete list of such variables which may then be aggregated into an index of country risk. The complete list is shown in Table 1.

Table 1

1 The national economy
    1.1   Gross domestic product per head
    1.2   Personal savings/gross domestic product
    1.3   Average annual percentage increase in consumer price index over the last five years for which figures are available
    1.4   Energy consumption per head
    1.5   National budget priorities
    1.6   National credit position
    1.7   Income distribution
    1.8   Balance of payments
    1.9   Exchange rates
    1.10 Industry-specific items

2   The social facts
  2.1   Total population
  2.2   Population density (people per square kilometer)
  2.3   Life expectancy at birth
  2.4   Average annual increase in population over last five years
  2.5   Inhabitants per doctor
  2.6   Existence of culture clash and other potential for disturbance
  2.7   Availability of managers
  2.8   Problems over foreign managers or workers
  2.9   Industry-specific items

3   The political conditions
  3.1   Membership of a treaty organization (score according to the effect of the regulations on the business: if none weight zero)
  3.2   Membership of a development organization
  3.3   Stability of central government
  3.4   Stability of civil service
  3.5   Years since independence
  3.6   Loans from the International Monetary Fund or other such bodies – their availability
  3.7   Incidence of riots or war
  3.8   Options available for company formation
  3.9   Availability of suitable collaborators
  3.10   Industry-specific items

4   The economic policies
  4.1   National industrial ambitions
  4.2   Nationalization
  4.3   Indigenization
  4.4   Other policies related to foreign ownership
  4.5   Tariffs
  4.6   Local content or assembly required
  4.7   Corporate taxation
  4.8   Personal taxation
  4.9   Corruption
  4.10   Industry-specific items

5   Geographical and cultural
  5.1   Position on trade route
  5.2   External postal and telegraph links
  5.3   Internal postal and telegraph communications
  5.4   Land area
  5.5   Climate
  5.6   Distance from home base
  5.7   Transport system
  5.8   Distance from home culture
  5.9   Literacy rate
  5.10   Industry-specific items

6   Production and supply
  6.1   Supply centre potential
  6.2   Availability of raw materials and components
  6.3   Storage facilities
  6.4   Legal constraints
  6.5   Patent laws
  6.6   Degree of industrialization
  6.7   Technology transfer
  6.8   Research and development potential
  6.9   Other location considerations
  6.10   Industry-specific items

7 Marketing factors
   7.1 How well established is the local industry
   7.2 The strength of the competition
   7.3 Customer position
   7.4 Consumer protection
   7.5 Competition policies
   7.6 Advertising regulations
   7.7 Acceptability of products
   7.8 Distribution channels
   7.9 Availability of research services
   7.10 Industry-specific items

8 Company factors
   8.1 Existing markets
   8.2 Existing agent/licensee unsatisfactory (this rates high when investment is under consideration)
   8.3 Capital available
   8.4 Satisfactory return on investment forecasts
   8.5 Staff available
   8.6 Proposal fits with existing investment
   8.7 Servicing other markets
   8.8 Logistic factors

Source: [8]

He then suggests that the analyst scores each of the factors and weights them to arrive at an index which can be aggregated to arrive at a country index. Further, the scores can be estimated for current and past performance as well as a five-year view of their dynamic. Kern[9] suggests that, for many aspects of international trade, five years is too short a time period and recommends a period of 20-25 years, particularly in terms of international indebtedness. Risk, it is suggested, arises out of:

- *Financial factors*
  - Outstanding debt as a percentage of GNP
  - Interest payments
  - Growth in debt
  - Reserves and balance of payments and
  - Imports in relation to foreign currency reserves.
- *Structural/economic factors*
  - Commodity reliance in exports, and
  - Economic management.
- *Political factors*
  - Political vulnerability and stability
  - Internal conflict, and
  - Cultural differences.

As with many models, each of the variables is scored to arrive at a risk potential. All of these models have a degree of artificiality associated with using numerical values for each factor, but they offer a preliminary guide to the potential of a country based on environmental variables.

Environmental analysis and strategy formulation

The impact of environmental change on marketing strategy formulation involves a process of decision making regarding the significance of environmental forces. As has been suggested, the total process of environmental appraisal involves choice and, thus decision. To monitor the total environment comprehensively would necessitate inordinate resource commitment. Thus firms have to focus their scanning on those variables to which they are most sensitive. Such focusing is the result of organizational learning which is bounded by values, objectives, strategies and performance. In essence, the strategic decision maker has to balance the environmental force with its probable impact on the company. This is shown in Figure 3 where such a system will begin to establish priorities for monitoring.

		High	Medium	Low
Probability of occurrence	High	High priority	High priority	Medium priority
	Medium	High priority	Medium priority	Low priority
	Low	Medium priority	Low priority	Low priority
		High	Medium	Low

Source [10]

Probable impact on corporation

Figure 3 *Issues priority matrix*

Further, as environmental appraisal takes place continuously through time, the general state of the environment will influence what is scanned. Glueck[11] has shown that, in differing time periods with altered states of the economy, firms will tend to promote different aspects of the environment for appraisal. For many companies, a guide to appraisal stems from the state of their own environment. For example, firms in volatile, hostile environments will tend to direct more resources to scanning than those in stable, friendly environments.

For many organizations, environmental appraisal has become a regular part of the strategic planning system. Such a process begins with search activity for environmental information. This can be done formally, via surveys, or informally by simply talking to key actors in the system, such as customers, distribution, consultants or competitors. There is much evidence to support the view that much search behaviour is informal and verbal in nature. Normally, such search behaviour will be conducted in terms of the current product/market mix. Having described what is, the next step is to plot its dynamic in order to show what the effects have been over time and then to extrapolate to show future effects. These forecasts should then be aggregated or reconciled in order to show a complete picture, as any marketing strategy, like demand analysis, is the result of a system of independent variables.

With a picture of the likely environment, the key task is to assess impact in terms of marketing strategy. At this stage, firms will be influenced by the varying degrees of hostility, reliability and friendliness when deciding how to respond. Further, the degree of risk and attitudes to risk are important. The results of environmental appraisal feed directly into the objective-setting process, in that a set of threats and opportunities will allow the company to fine-tune its objectives and create a time frame around the strategy selected. As an example of environmental appraisal, Figure 4 shows a possible generic model of an environmental scanning system.

Problems and shortcomings

Although several authors have established a relationship between environmental appraisal and corporate success, there appears to be some inherent shortcomings and potential problems associated with the process. These arise in a number of areas:

Stage	Task	Variables	Activity
Analysis	Environmental Review	*Economic* GNP disposable income, savings levels, monetary fiscal policies	Forecasts of key variables City opinion
		Social Population size, distribution, family size, household formation	Description and forecasts of variables
		Technological R&D spend, sources of ideas, patents	Technological forecasting
		Political Consumer protection, location, product safety, structural policies	Political and environmental scanning via media legal department
		Marketing Changes in supplier market Changes in channels, market dynamics	Interrogation of marketing information system Forecasts of markets and market share
Diagnosis	Decision making about impact and risk	As above	Scenario Generation focus Changes to objectives and current strategy

Figure 4 *Environmental scanning system*

- *Personal attitudes to risk and uncertainty* Differing managers will bring their own attitudes to risk to bear on the process of environmental diagnosis. Optimists will interpret environmental forces in a different manner from pessimists. This can arise either because of some innate personal style or as a function of role perception within the organization. Miller and Friesen[12] found archetypes of companies which were successful and unsuccessful at meeting the challenges of the environment where a good deal of the success or failure can be attributed to the attitudes of top management.
- *Corporate attitudes to planning* Planning is a cerebral response to the environment which requires the acceptance of a 'thinking' attitude. This is often at odds with a 'doing' culture and leads to phrases such as 'paralysis by analysis'. There has to be some trade-off between thinking and doing normally achieved by the former making the latter easier to do. However, the attitudes of entrepreneurs as an example may be against the notion of planning a strategic response to the environment.

Strategic response

There appears to be two schools of thought regarding what companies actually do with the results of environmental diagnosis. Some authors see the organization as being shaped by the environment, whilst others see managers taking a more proactive role in attempting to influence the environment. Jauch, Osborn and Glueck[13] found little evidence that organizations with similar environments reacted in the same way. It appears that organizations have many strategies available for dealing with a given environment. Paine and Anderson[14] suggest that strategy is not just a function of the environment, but also includes internal perceptions of the need for change. Thus, the view of a causation effect between environment and strategy may not be strictly accurate. There is little doubt that the actions of organizations can affect the environment through takeovers, mergers, aggressive strategies and exit, and that such actions can be taken in order to further the objectives of any one organization. As Cooper and Schendel[15] have shown, such behaviour may well be to resist or ignore change, or to give the organization time to react.

Corporate health

For organizations in crisis, environmental scanning is somewhat of a luxury. Alternatively, for those in a strong position, there may be more time and resources available to accomplish the task. The financial state of a company can affect attitudes to planning, particularly in terms of short vs. long-term considerations. Thus, there may be a strong correlation between the perception of tasks needed to correct a situation and the willingness to indulge in planning.

Summary

Change and its management is the essence of successful management. The model of analysis and diagnosis is essentially a simple one; however, the effects of its use are complex. There is now significant doubt regarding the degree of dependence existing between a firm and its environment. External appraisal depends to a large degree on internal factors, such that appraisal may be a result of what a firm wants to look at, and this affects how it searches and responds. For marketing strategies, the effects of the environment are endemic to the creation of successful strategies, they provide market opportunity for growth and pose threats to products and markets, as well as the elements of a marketing strategy. Incorporation of the results of environmental analysis can affect corporate and marketing objectives, as well as methods of attaining these objectives.

The task, however, is bounded by certain constraints, not least of which are researching the process, attitudes to risk, the state of the organization and the degree of felt need for change; but perhaps the major area of concern is that environmental appraisal is of itself a part of the strategic process, such that its results depend, to a large extent, on what the firm wants to look at. Thus, at worst, it can become a self-fulfilling prophecy which has little impact on strategic thinking.

References

1   Miller, D. and Friesen, P., 'Strategy Making in Context: Ten Empirical Archetypes', *Journal of Management Studies*, Vol. 14 No. 3, 1977, pp. 253-80; Grinyer, P.H. and Norburn, D., 'Planning for Existing Markets: Perceptions of Executives and Financial Performance', *Journal of Royal Statistical Society*, Vol. 138, 1975; Grinyer, P.H. and Norburn, D., 'Planning for Existing Markets: An Empirical Study', *International Studies in Management and Organisation*, Vol. 7 No. 3-4, 1977/78.

2   Lowes, B. and Sparkes, J.R., *Modern Managerial Economics*, Heinemann, London, 1974.

3   Miller, D. and Mintzberg, H., 'The Case for Configuration', working paper, McGill University, November 1980. Abstracted in Glueck, W.F. and Jauch, L.R., *Business Policy and Strategic Management*, 4th ed., McGraw-Hill, New York, 1984.

4   Kotler, P., *Marketing Management*, 5th ed., Prentice-Hall, 1985.

5   See, for example, Aguilar, F., *Scanning the Business Environment*, Macmillan, London, 1967; Wall, S.L., 'What the Competition is Doing: You Need to Know', *Harvard Business Review*, November-December 1974, p. 22.

6   Porter, M.E., *Competitive Strategy*, Free Press, New York, 1980.

7   Glueck, N.F. and Jausch, L.R., Business Policy and Strategic Management, op cit.

8   Brooke, M.Z. and Buckley, P.D. (eds.), *Handbook of International Trade*, Kluwer, London, 1982.

9   Kern, D., 'The Evaluation of Company Risk and Economic Potential', *Long Range Planning*, Vol. 18, 1985, pp. 17-25.

10 Lederman, L.L., 'Foresight Activities in the USA: Time for a Reassessment', *Long Range Planning*, Vol. 17, June 1984, p. 46.

11 Glueck, N.F. and Jausch, L.R., *Business Policy and Strategic Management*, op. cit.

12 Miller, D. and Frieson, P., 'Strategy Making in Context: Ten Empirical Archetypes', *Journal of Management Studies*, Vol. 14 No. 3, October 1977, pp. 253-80.

13 Jauch, L.R., Osborn, R.N. and Glueck, N.F., 'Short-term Financial Success in Large Business Organisations – The Environment-strategy Connection', *Strategic Management Journal*, Vol. 1, January-March 1980, pp. 49-64.
14 Paine, F. and Anderson, C., 'Contingencies Affecting Strategy Formulation and Effectiveness: An Empirical Study', *Journal of Management Studies*, Vol. 14 No. 2, 1977, pp. 147-58.
15 Cooper, A. and Schendel, D., 'Strategic Responses to Technological Threats', *Business Horizons*, February 1976, pp. 61-9.

Reproduced from Sanderson, S.M. and Luffman, G.A. (1988). Strategic planning and environmental analysis. *European Journal of Marketing*, 22(2), 14-27, by permission of MCB University Press.

7 How competitive forces shape strategy

Michael E. Porter

The essence of strategy formulation is coping with competition. Yet it is easy to view competition too narrowly and too pessimistically. While one sometimes hears executives complaining to the contrary, intense competition in an industry is neither coincidence nor bad luck.

Moreover, in the fight for market share, competition is not manifested only in the other players. Rather, competition in an industry is rooted in its underlying economics, and competitive forces exist that go well beyond the established combatants in a particular industry. Customers, suppliers, potential entrants, and substitute products are all competitors that may be more or less prominent or active depending on the industry.

The state of competition in an industry depends on five basic forces, which are diagrammed in Figure 1. The collective strength of these forces determines the ultimate profit potential of an industry. It ranges from *intense* in industries like tires, metal cans, and steel, where no company earns spectacular returns on investment, to *mild* in industries like oil field services and equipment, soft drinks, and toiletries, where there is room for quite high returns.

In the economists' 'perfectly competitive' industry, jockeying for position is unbridled and entry to the industry very easy. This kind of industry structure, of course, offers the worst prospect for long-run profitability. The weaker the forces collectively, however, the greater the opportunity for superior performance.

Whatever their collective strength, the corporate strategist's goal is to find a position in the industry where his or her company can best defend itself against these forces or can influence them in its favor. The collective strength of the forces may be painfully apparent to all the antagonists; but to cope with them, the strategist must delve below the surface and analyze the sources of each. For example, what makes the industry vulnerable to entry? What determines the bargaining power of suppliers?

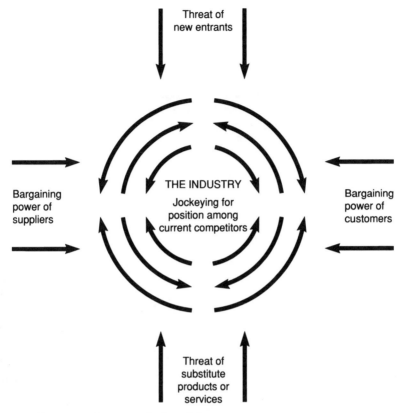

Figure 1 *Forces governing competition in an industry*

Knowledge of these underlying sources of competitive pressure provides the groundwork for a strategic agenda of action. They highlight the critical strengths and weaknesses of the company, animate the positioning of the company in its industry, clarify the areas where strategic changes may yield the greatest payoff, and highlight the places where industry trends promise to hold the greatest significance as either opportunities or threats. Understanding these sources also proves to be of help in considering areas for diversification.

Contending forces

The strongest competitive force or forces determine the profitability of an industry and so are of greatest importance in strategy formulation. For example, even a company with a strong position in an industry unthreatened by potential entrants will earn low returns if it faces a superior or a lower-cost substitute product – as the leading manufacturers of vacuum tubes and coffee percolators have learned to their sorrow. In such a situation, coping with the substitute product becomes the number one strategic priority.

Different forces take on prominence, of course, in shaping competition in each industry. In the ocean-going tanker industry the key force is probably the buyers (the major oil companies), while in tires it is powerful OEM buyers coupled with tough competitors. In the steel industry the key forces are foreign competitors and substitute materials.

Every industry has an underlying structure, or a set of fundamental economic and technical characteristics, that gives rise to these competitive forces. The strategist, wanting to position his company to cope best with its industry environment or to influence that environment in the company's favor, must learn what makes the environment tick.

This view of competition pertains equally to industries dealing in services and to those selling products. To avoid monotony in this article, I refer to both products and services as 'products'. The same general principles apply to all types of business.

A few characteristics are critical to the strength of each competitive force. I shall discuss them in this section.

Threat of entry

New entrants to an industry bring new capacity, the desire to gain market share, and often substantial resources. Companies diversifying through acquisition into the industry from other markets often leverage their resources to cause a shake-up, as Philip Morris did with Miller beer.

The seriousness of the threat of entry depends on the barriers present and on the reaction from existing competitors that the entrant can expect. If barriers to entry are high and a newcomer can expect sharp retaliation from the entrenched competitors, obviously he will not pose a serious threat of entering.

There are six major sources of barriers to entry:

1 *Economies of scale* These economies deter entry by forcing the aspirant either to come in on a large scale or to accept a cost disadvantage. Scale economies in production, research, marketing, and service are probably the key barriers to entry in the mainframe computer industry, as Xerox and GE sadly discovered. Economies of scale can also act as hurdles in distribution, utilization of the sales force, financing, and nearly any other part of a business.
2 *Product differentiation* Brand identification creates a barrier by forcing entrants to spend heavily to overcome customer loyalty. Advertising, customer service, being first in the industry, and product differences are among the factors fostering brand identification. It is perhaps the most important entry barrier in soft drinks, over-the-counter drugs, cosmetics, investment banking, and public accounting. To create high fences around their businesses, brewers couple brand identification with economies of scale in production, distribution, and marketing.

3 *Capital requirements* The need to invest large financial resources in order to compete creates a barrier to entry, particularly if the capital is required for unrecoverable expenditures in up-front advertising or R&D. Capital is necessary not only for fixed facilities but also for customer credit, inventories, and absorbing start-up losses. While major corporations have the financial resources to invade almost any industry, the huge capital requirements in certain fields, such as computer manufacturing and mineral extraction, limit the pool of likely entrants.

4 *Cost disadvantages independent of size* Entrenched companies may have cost advantages not available to potential rivals, no matter what their size and attainable economies of scale. These advantages can stem from the effects of the learning curve (and of its first cousin, the experience curve), proprietary technology, access to the best raw materials sources, assets purchased at preinflation prices, government subsidies, or favorable locations. Sometimes cost advantages are legally enforceable, as they are through patents. (For an analysis of the much-discussed experience curve as a barrier to entry, see the appendix to this article.)

5 *Access to distribution channels* The new boy on the block must, of course, secure distribution of his product or service. A new food product, for example, must displace others from the supermarket shelf via price breaks, promotions, intense selling efforts, or some other means. The more limited the wholesale or retail channels are and the more that existing competitors have these tied up, obviously the tougher that entry into the industry will be. Sometimes this barrier is so high that, to surmount it, a new contestant must create its own distribution channels, as Timex did in the watch industry in the 1950s.

6 *Government policy* The government can limit or even foreclose entry to industries with such controls as license requirements and limits on access to raw materials. Regulated industries like trucking, liquor retailing, and freight forwarding are noticeable examples; more subtle government restrictions operate in fields like ski-area development and coal mining. The government also can play a major indirect role by affecting entry barriers through controls such as air and water pollution standards and safety regulations.

The potential rival's expectations about the reaction of existing competitors also will influence its decision on whether to enter. The company is likely to have second thoughts if incumbents have previously lashed out at new entrants or if:

● The incumbents possess substantial resources to fight back, including excess cash and unused borrowing power, productive capacity, or clout with distribution channels and customers

● The incumbents seem likely to cut prices because of a desire to keep market shares or because of industrywide excess capacity

● Industry growth is slow, affecting its ability to absorb the new arrival and probably causing the financial performance of all the parties involved to decline.

Changing conditions. From a strategic standpoint there are two important additional points to note about the threat of entry.

First, it changes, of course, as these conditions change. The expiration of Polaroid's basic patents on instant photography, for instance, greatly reduced its absolute cost entry barrier built by proprietary technology. It is not surprising that Kodak plunged into the market. Product differentiation in printing has all but disappeared. Conversely, in the auto industry economies of scale increased enormously with post-World War II automation and vertical integration – virtually stopping successful new entry.

Second, strategic decisions involving a large segment of an industry can have a major impact on the conditions determining the threat of entry. For example, the actions of many U.S. wine producers in the 1960s to step up product introductions, raise advertising levels, and expand distribution nationally surely strengthened the entry roadblocks by raising economies of scale and making access to distribution channels more difficult. Similarly, decisions by members of the recreational vehicle industry to vertically integrate in order to lower costs have greatly increased the economies of scale and raised the capital cost barriers.

Powerful suppliers and buyers

Suppliers can exert bargaining power on participants in an industry by raising prices or reducing the quality of purchased goods and services. Powerful suppliers can thereby squeeze profitability out of an industry unable to recover cost increases in its own prices. By raising their prices, soft drink concentrate producers have contributed to the erosion of profitability of bottling companies because the bottlers, facing intense competition from powdered mixes, fruit drinks, and other beverages, have limited freedom to raise *their* prices accordingly. Customers likewise can force down prices, demand higher quality or more service, and play competitors against each other – all at the expense of industry profits.

The power of each important supplier or buyer group depends on a number of characteristics of its market situation and on the relative importance of its sales or purchases to the industry compared with its overall business.

A *supplier* group is powerful if:

● It is dominated by a few companies and is more concentrated than the industry it sells to.
● Its product is unique or at least differentiated, or if it has built up switching costs. Switching costs are fixed costs buyers face in changing

suppliers. These arise because, among other things, a buyer's product specifications tie it to particular suppliers, it has invested heavily in specialized ancillary equipment or in learning how to operate a supplier's equipment (as in computer software), or its production lines are connected to the supplier's manufacturing facilities (as in some manufacture of beverage containers).

- It is not obliged to contend with other products for sale to the industry. For instance, the competition between the steel companies and the aluminum companies to sell to the can industry checks the power of each supplier.
- It poses a credible threat of integrating forward into the industry's business. This provides a check against the industry's ability to improve the terms on which it purchases.
- The industry is not an important customer of the supplier group. If the industry *is* an important customer, suppliers' fortunes will be closely tied to the industry, and they will want to protect the industry through reasonable pricing and assistance in activities like R&D and lobbying.

A *buyer* group is powerful if:

- It is concentrated or purchases in large volumes. Large-volume buyers are particularly potent forces if heavy fixed costs characterize the industry – as they do in metal containers, corn refining, and bulk chemicals, for example – which raise the stakes to keep capacity filled.
- The products it purchases from the industry are standard or undifferentiated. The buyers, sure that they can always find alternative suppliers, may play one company against another, as they do in aluminum extrusion.
- The products it purchases from the industry form a component of its product and represent a significant fraction of its cost. The buyers are likely to shop for a favorable price and purchase selectively. Where the product sold by the industry in question is a small fraction of buyers' costs, buyers are usually much less price sensitive.
- It earns low profits, which create great incentive to lower its purchasing costs. Highly profitable buyers, however, are generally less price sensitive (that is, of course, if the item does not represent a large fraction of their costs).
- The industry's product is unimportant to the quality of the buyers' products or services. Where the quality of the buyers' products is very much affected by the industry's product, buyers are generally less price sensitive. Industries which this situation pertains to include oil field equipment, where a malfunction can lead to large losses, and enclosures for electronic medical and test instruments, where the quality of the enclosure can influence the user's impression about the quality of the equipment inside.

- The industry's product does not save the buyer money. Where the industry's product or service can pay for itself many times over, the buyer is rarely price sensitive; rather, he is interested in quality. This is true in services like investment banking and public accounting, where errors in judgment can be costly and embarrassing, and in businesses like the logging of oil wells, where an accurate survey can save thousands of dollars in drilling costs.
- The buyers pose a credible threat of integrating backward to make the industry's product. The Big Three auto producers and major buyers of cars have often used the threat of self-manufacture as a bargaining lever. But sometimes an industry engenders a threat to buyers that its members may integrate forward.

Most of these sources of buyer power can be attributed to consumers as a group as well as to industrial and commercial buyers; only a modification of the frame of reference is necessary. Consumers tend to be more price sensitive if they are purchasing products that are undifferentiated, expensive relative to their incomes, and of a sort where quality is not particularly important.

The buying power of retailers is determined by the same rules, with one important addition. Retailers can gain significant bargaining power over manufacturers when they can influence consumers' purchasing decisions, as they do in audio components, jewelry, appliances, sporting goods, and other goods.

Strategic action. A company's choice of suppliers to buy from or buyer groups to sell to should be viewed as a crucial strategic decision. A company can improve its strategic posture by finding suppliers or buyers who possess the least power to influence it adversely.

Most common is the situation of a company being able to choose whom it will sell to – in other words, buyer selection. Rarely do all the buyer groups a company sells to enjoy equal power. Even if a company sells to a single industry, segments usually exist within that industry that exercise less power (and that are therefore less price sensitive) than others. For example, the replacement market for most products is less price sensitive than the overall market.

As a rule, a company can sell to powerful buyers and still come away with above-average profitability only if it is a low-cost producer in its industry or if its product enjoys some unusual, if not unique, features. In supplying large customers with electric motors, Emerson Electric earns high returns because its low-cost position permits the company to meet or undercut competitors' prices.

If the company lacks a low cost position or a unique product, selling to everyone is self-defeating because the more sales it achieves, the more vulnerable it becomes. The company may have to muster the courage to turn away business and sell only to less potent customers.

Buyer selection has been a key to the success of National Can and Crown Cork & Seal. They focus on the segments of the can industry where they can create product differentiation, minimize the threat of backward integration, and otherwise mitigate the awesome power of their customers. Of course, some industries do not enjoy the luxury of selecting 'good' buyers.

As the factors creating supplier and buyer power change with time or as a result of a company's strategic decisions, naturally the power of these groups rises or declines. In the ready-to-wear clothing industry, as the buyers (department stores and clothing stores) have become more concentrated and control has passed to large chains, the industry has come under increasing pressure and suffered falling margins. The industry has been unable to differentiate its product or engender switching costs that lock in its buyers enough to neutralize these trends.

Substitute products

By placing a ceiling on prices it can charge, substitute products or services limit the potential of an industry. Unless it can upgrade the quality of the product or differentiate it somehow (as via marketing), the industry will suffer in earnings and possibly in growth.

Manifestly, the more attractive the price-performance trade-off offered by substitute products, the firmer the lid placed on the industry's profit potential. Sugar producers confronted with the large-scale commercialization of high-fructose corn syrup, a sugar substitute, are learning this lesson today.

Substitutes not only limit profits in normal times; they also reduce the bonanza an industry can reap in boom times. In 1978 the producers of fiberglass insulation enjoyed unprecedented demand as a result of high energy costs and severe winter weather. But the industry's ability to raise prices was tempered by the plethora of insulation substitutes, including cellulose, rock wool, and styrofoam. These substitutes are bound to become an even stronger force once the current round of plant additions by fiberglass insulation producers has boosted capacity enough to meet demand (and then some).

Substitute products that deserve the most attention strategically are those that (a) are subject to trends improving their price-performance trade-off with the industry's product, or (b) are produced by industries earning high profits. Substitutes often come rapidly into play if some development increases competition in their industries and causes price reduction or performance improvement.

Jockeying for position

Rivalry among existing competitors takes the familiar form of jockeying for position – using tactics like price competition, product introduction, and advertising slugfests. Intense rivalry is related to the presence of a number of factors:

- Competitors are numerous or are roughly equal in size and power. In many U.S. industries in recent years foreign contenders, of course, have become part of the competitive picture.
- Industry growth is slow, precipitating fights for market share that involve expansion-minded members.
- The product or service lacks differentiation or switching costs, which lock in buyers and protect one combatant from raids on its customers by another.
- Fixed costs are high or the product is perishable, creating strong temptation to cut prices. Many basic materials businesses, like paper and aluminum, suffer from this problem when demand slackens.
- Capacity is normally augmented in large increments. Such additions, as in the chlorine and vinyl chloride businesses, disrupt the industry's supply-demand balance and often lead to periods of over-capacity and price cutting.
- Exit barriers are high. Exit barriers, like very specialized assets or management's loyalty to a particular business, keep companies competing even though they may be earning low or even negative returns on investment. Excess capacity remains functioning, and the profitability of the healthy competitors suffers as the sick ones hang on.[1] If the entire industry suffers from overcapacity, it may seek government help – particularly if foreign competition is present.
- The rivals are diverse in strategies, origins, and 'personalities.' They have different ideas about how to compete and continually run head-on into each other in the process.

As an industry matures, its growth rate changes, resulting in declining profits and (often) a shakeout. In the booming recreational vehicle industry of the early 1970s, nearly every producer did well; but slow growth since then has eliminated the high returns, except for the strongest members, not to mention many of the weaker companies. The same profit story has been played out in industry after industry – snowmobiles, aerosol packaging, and sports equipment are just a few examples.

An acquisition can introduce a very different personality to an industry, as has been the case with Black & Decker's takeover of McCullough, the producer of chain saws. Technological innovation can boost the level of fixed costs in the production process, as it did in the shift from batch to continuous-line photo finishing in the 1960s.

While a company must live with many of these factors – because they are built into industry economics – it may have some latitude for improving matters through strategic shifts. For example, it may try to raise buyers' switching costs or increase product differentiation. A focus on selling efforts in the fastest-growing segments of the industry or on market areas with the lowest fixed costs can reduce the impact of industry rivalry. If it is feasible, a company can try to avoid confrontation with competitors having high exit barriers and can thus side-step involvement in bitter price cutting.

Formulation of strategy

Once the corporate strategist has assessed the forces affecting competition in his industry and their underlying causes, he can identify his company's strengths and weaknesses. The crucial strengths and weaknesses from a strategic standpoint are the company's posture *vis-a-vis* the underlying causes of each force. Where does it stand against substitutes? Against the sources of entry barriers?

Then the strategist can devise a plan of action that may include (1) positioning the company so that its capabilities provide the best defense against the competitive force; and/or (2) influencing the balance of the forces through strategic moves, thereby improving the company's position; and/or (3) anticipating shifts in the factors underlying the forces and responding to them, with the hope of exploiting change by choosing a strategy appropriate for the new competitive balance before opponents recognize it. I shall consider each strategic approach in turn.

Positioning the company

The first approach takes the structure of the industry as given and matches the company's strengths and weaknesses to it. Strategy can be viewed as building defenses against the competitive forces or as finding positions in the industry where the forces are weakest.

Knowledge of the company's capabilities and of the causes of the competitive forces will highlight the areas where the company should confront competition and where avoid it. If the company is a low-cost producer, it may choose to confront powerful buyers while it takes care to sell them only products not vulnerable to competition from substitutes.

The success of Dr Pepper in the soft drink industry illustrates the coupling of realistic knowledge of corporate strengths with sound industry analysis to yield a superior strategy. Coca-Cola and Pepsi-Cola dominate Dr Pepper's industry, where many small concentrate producers compete for a piece of the action. Dr Pepper chose a strategy of avoiding the largest-selling drink segment, maintaining a narrow flavor line, forgoing the development of a captive bottler network, and marketing heavily. The company positioned itself so as to be least vulnerable to its competitive forces while it exploited its small size.

In the $11.5 billion soft drink industry, barriers to entry in the form of brand identification, large-scale marketing, and access to a bottler network are enormous. Rather than accept the formidable costs and scale economies in having its own bottler network – that is, following the lead of the Big Two and of Seven-Up – Dr Pepper took advantage of the different flavor of its drink to 'piggyback' on Coke and Pepsi bottlers who wanted a full line to sell to customers. Dr Pepper coped with the power of these buyers through extraordinary service and other efforts to distinguish its treatment of them from that of Coke and Pepsi.

Many small companies in the soft drink business offer cola drinks that thrust them into head-to-head competition against the majors. Dr Pepper, however, maximized product differentiation by maintaining a narrow line of beverages built around an unusual flavor.

Finally, Dr Pepper met Coke and Pepsi with an advertising onslaught emphasizing the alleged uniqueness of its single flavor. This campaign built strong brand identification and great customer loyalty. Helping its efforts was the fact that Dr Pepper's formula involved lower raw materials cost, which gave the company an absolute advantage over its major competitors.

There are no economies of scale in soft drink concentrate production, so Dr Pepper could prosper despite its small share of the business (6%). Thus Dr Pepper confronted competition in marketing but avoided it in product line and in distribution. This artful positioning combined with good implementation has led to an enviable record in earnings and in the stock market.

Influencing the balance

When dealing with the forces that drive industry competition, a company can devise a strategy that takes the offensive. This posture is designed to do more than merely cope with the forces themselves; it is meant to alter their causes.

Innovations in marketing can raise brand identification or otherwise differentiate the product. Capital investments in large-scale facilities or vertical integration affect entry barriers. The balance of forces is partly a result of external factors and partly in the company's control.

Exploiting industry change

Industry evolution is important strategically because evolution, of course, brings with it changes in the sources of competition I have identified. In the familiar product life-cycle pattern, for example, growth rates change, product differentiation is said to decline as the business becomes more mature, and the companies tend to integrate vertically.

These trends are not so important in themselves; what is critical is whether they affect the sources of competition. Consider vertical integration. In the maturing minicomputer industry, extensive vertical integration, both in manufacturing and in software development, is taking place. This very significant trend is greatly raising economies of scale as well as the amount of capital necessary to compete in the industry. This in turn is raising barriers to entry and may drive some smaller competitors out of the industry once growth levels off.

Obviously, the trends carrying the highest priority from a strategic standpoint are those that affect the most important sources of competition in the industry and those that elevate new causes to the forefront. In contract aerosol packaging, for example, the trend toward less product differentiation is now dominant. It has increased buyers' power, lowered the barriers to entry, and intensified competition.

The framework for analyzing competition that I have described can also be used to predict the eventual profitability of an industry. In long-range planning the task is to examine each competitive force, forecast the magnitude of each underlying cause, and then construct a composite picture of the likely profit potential of the industry.

The outcome of such an exercise may differ a great deal from the existing industry structure. Today, for example, the solar heating business is populated by dozens and perhaps hundreds of companies, none with a major market position. Entry is easy, and competitors are battling to establish solar heating as a superior substitute for conventional methods.

The potential of this industry will depend largely on the shape of future barriers to entry, the improvement of the industry's position relative to substitutes, the ultimate intensity of competition, and the power captured by buyers and suppliers. These characteristics will in turn be influenced by such factors as the establishment of brand identities, significant economies of scale or experience curves in equipment manufacture wrought by technological change, the ultimate capital costs to compete, and the extent of overhead in production facilities.

The framework for analyzing industry competition has direct benefits in setting diversification strategy. It provides a road map for answering the extremely difficult question inherent in diversification decisions: 'What is the potential of this business?' Combining the framework with judgment in its application, a company may be able to spot an industry with a good future before this good future is reflected in the prices of acquisition candidates.

Multifaceted rivalry

Corporate managers have directed a great deal of attention to defining their businesses as a crucial step in strategy formulation. Theodore Levitt, in his classic 1960 article in HBR, argued strongly for avoiding the myopia of narrow, product-oriented industry definition.[2] Numerous other authorities have also stressed the need to look beyond product to function in defining a business, beyond national boundaries to potential international competition, and beyond the ranks of one's competitors today to those that may become competitors tomorrow. As a result of these urgings, the proper definition of a company's industry or industries has become an endlessly debated subject.

One motive behind this debate is the desire to exploit new markets. Another, perhaps more important motive is the fear of overlooking latent sources of competition that someday may threaten the industry. Many managers concentrate so single-mindedly on their direct antagonists in the fight for market share that they fail to realize that they are also competing with their customers and their suppliers for bargaining power. Meanwhile, they also neglect to keep a wary eye out for new entrants to the contest or fail to recognize the subtle threat of substitute products.

The key to growth – even survival – is to stake out a position that is less vulnerable to attack from head-to-head opponents, whether established or new, and less vulnerable to erosion from the direction of buyers, suppliers, and substitute goods. Establishing such a position can take many forms – solidifying relationships with favorable customers, differentiating the product either substantively or psychologically through marketing, integrating forward or backward, establishing technological leadership.

Appendix: The experience curve as an entry barrier

In recent years, the experience curve has become widely discussed as a key element of industry structure. According to this concept, unit costs in many manufacturing industries (some dogmatic adherents say in *all* manufacturing industries) as well as in some service industries decline with 'experience', or a particular company's cumulative volume of production. (The experience curve, which encompasses many factors, is a broader concept than the better-known learning curve, which refers to the efficiency achieved over a period of time by workers through much repetition.)

The causes of the decline in unit costs are a combination of elements, including economies of scale, the learning curve for labor, and capital-labor substitution. The cost decline creates a barrier to entry because new competitors with no 'experience' face higher costs than established ones, particularly the producer with the largest market share, and have difficulty catching up with the entrenched competitors.

Adherents of the experience curve concept stress the importance of achieving market leadership to maximize this barrier to entry, and they recommend aggressive action to achieve it, such as price cutting in anticipation of falling costs in order to build volume. For the combatant that cannot achieve a healthy market share, the prescription is usually, 'Get out.'

Is the experience curve an entry barrier on which strategies should be built?

The answer is: not in every industry. In fact, in some industries, building a strategy on the experience curve can be potentially disastrous. That costs decline with experience in some industries is not new to corporate executives. The significance of the experience curve for strategy depends on what factors are causing the decline.

If costs are falling because a growing company can reap economies of scale through more efficient, automated facilities and vertical integration, then the cumulative volume of production is unimportant to its relative cost position. Here the lowest-cost producer is the one with the largest, most efficient facilities.

A new entrant may well be more efficient than the more experienced competitors; if it has built the newest plant, it will face no disadvantage in having to catch up. The strategic prescription, 'You must have the largest, most efficient plant,' is a lot different from, 'You must produce the greatest cumulative output of the item to get your costs down.'

Whether a drop in costs with cumulative (not absolute) volume erects an entry barrier also depends on the sources of the decline. If costs go down because of technical advances known generally in the industry or because of the development of improved equipment that can be copied or purchased from equipment suppliers, the experience curve is no entry barrier at all – in fact, new or less experienced competitors may actually enjoy a cost *advantage* over the leaders. Free of the legacy of heavy past investments, the newcomer or less experienced competitor can purchase or copy the newest and lowest-cost equipment and technology.

If, however, experience can be kept proprietary, the leaders will maintain a cost advantage. But new entrants may require less experience to reduce their costs than the leaders needed. All this suggests that the experience curve can be a shaky entry barrier on which to build a strategy.

While space does not permit a complete treatment here, I want to mention a few other crucial elements in determining the appropriateness of a strategy built on the entry barrier provided by the experience curve:

- The height of the barrier depends on how important costs are to competition compared with other areas like marketing, selling, and innovation.
- The barrier can be nullified by product or process innovations leading to a substantially new technology and thereby creating an entirely new experience curve.* New entrants can leapfrog the industry leaders and alight on the new experience curve, to which those leaders may be poorly positioned to jump.
- If more than one strong company is building its strategy on the experience curve, the consequences can be nearly fatal. By the time only one rival is left pursuing such a strategy, industry growth may have stopped and the prospects of reaping the spoils of victory long since evaporated.

Notes

1 For a more complete discussion of exit barriers and their implications for strategy, see Michael L. Porter, 'Please Note Location of Nearest Exit,' *California Management Review*, Winter 1976, p. 21.
2 Theodore Levitt, 'Marketing Myopia,' reprinted as a *Harvard Business Review* Classic, September-October 1975, p. 26.

*For an example drawn from the history of the automobile industry, see William J. Abernathy and Kenneth Wayne, 'Limits of the Learning Curve', *Harvard Business Review*, March-April 1979, p. 166.

8 Assessing advantage: a framework for diagnosing competitive superiority

George S. Day and Robin Wensley

Strategy is about seeking new edges in a market while slowing the erosion of present advantages. Effective strategy moves are grounded in valid and insightful monitoring of the current position coupled with evidence that reveals the skills and resources affording the most leverage on future cost and differentiation advantages. Too often the available measures and methods do not satisfy these requirements. Only a limited set of measures may be used, depending on whether the business starts with the market and uses a customer-focused approach or alternatively adopts a competitor-centred perspective. To overcome possible myopia, the evidence of advantage should illuminate the sources of advantage as well as the manifestations of superior customer value and cost superiority, and should be based on a balance of customer and competitor perspectives.

The notion that superior performance requires a business to gain and hold an advantage over competitors is central to contemporary strategic thinking. Businesses seeking advantage are exhorted to develop distinctive competencies and manage for lowest delivered cost or differentiation through superior customer value. The promised payoff is market share dominance and profitability above average for the industry.

This advice is sound, but usually difficult to follow. Management first must understand the reasons for the current advantages or deficiencies of the business and the vulnerability of the advantages to copying or leap-frogging by competitors. Without a proper diagnosis, managers cannot choose the best moves to defend or enhance the current position. For many reasons the prevailing approaches to understanding competitive advantages are unlikely to yield valid and insightful diagnoses. We therefore evaluate the current approaches and methods within an organizing framework that clarifies the nature of competitive advantage. Our primary objective, however, is to use this framework to propose a process that can be used to ensure a thorough and balanced assessment of the reasons for the competitive position of a business.

Perspectives on competitive position. Little is known about how managers decide what advantages distinguish their business and how those advantages were gained. Two distinct approaches have been identified; one starts with the market and is customer-focused and the other is primarily competitor-centred.

Competitor-centred assessments are based on direct management comparisons with a few target competitors. This approach often is seen in stalemated industries where the emphasis is on 'beat the competition'. The key question is, 'How do our capabilities and offerings compare with those of competitors?' These businesses watch costs closely, quickly match the marketing initiatives of competitors, and look for their sustainable edge in technology. Managers keep a close watch on market share and contracts won or lost to detect changes in competitive position.

Customer-focused assessments start with detailed analyses of customer benefits within end-use segments and work backward from the customer to the company to identify the actions needed to improve performance. This 'market back' orientation is found in service-intensive industries such as investment banking where new services are easily imitated, cost of funds is the same, and entry is easy.[1]

Relatively little attention is given to competitors' capabilities and performance – the emphasis is on the quality of customer relationships. Evidence of continuing customer satisfaction and loyalty is more meaningful than market share.

Why should it matter how managers view the arena in which they compete? The reason is that market environments are not unambiguous realities. They are given meaning in the minds of managers through processes of selective attention and simplification.[2] Otherwise managers could not possibly cope with the myriad of trends and events that must be organized, analysed for patterns, and acted upon. Managers therefore adopt a customer-focused or competitor-centred perspective to help simplify their environment and decide what information is to be gathered and how it is to be screened and interpreted.

Simplification comes at a cost, which is the risk that only a partial and biased picture of reality is created. A competitor-centred perspective leads to a preoccupation with costs and controllable activities that can be compared directly with corresponding activities of close rivals. Customer-focused approaches have the advantage of examining the full range of competitive choices in light of the customers' needs and perceptions of superiority, but lack an obvious connection to activities and variables that are controlled by management. Clearly a balance of the two characteristic perspectives is needed. In practice most businesses tilt – in some cases very sharply – toward one or the other.

A significant complication in the search for a balanced perspective is the confusing welter of overlapping meanings of 'competitive advantage'. Because there is no agreement on what elements to include or how they are related, information gaps cannot be identified. We address this problem with an organizing framework that distinguishes the sources of advantage from their consequences for relative competitive position and performance superiority. We then use this framework to guide an evaluation of the many ways in which competitive advantages have been measured. For example, we examine the merits of management judgements of strengths and weaknesses and how they compare with measures of market share, comparisons of the relative size of resource commitments, and customer comparisons of competitors on their purchase criteria. Eleven distinct measurement approaches are evaluated for (1) *conceptual validity* (is the measure compatible with the framework?), (2) *measurement feasibility* (does the measure employ readily available inputs that are likely to provide reliable and unbiased information?), and (3) *diagnostic insights* (will the measure yield information that can guide strategic choices to enhance the long-run value of the business?). Finally, we propose steps that can be taken to reorient marketing research to offer a balanced view of present and prospective advantages. The payoff for management is better insights into the actions that promise the greatest effect on the competitive position of a business.

The concept of competitive advantage

There is no common meaning for 'competitive advantage' in practice or in the marketing strategy literature. Sometimes the term is used interchangeably with 'distinctive competence' to mean relative superiority in skills and resources. Another widespread meaning refers to what we observe in the market – positional superiority, based on the provision of superior customer value or the achievement of lower relative costs, and the resulting market share and profitability performances.

Neither of these meanings gives a complete picture, but taken together they describe both the state of advantage and how it was gained.[3] This integrated view is based on positional and performance superiority being a consequence of relative superiority in the skills and resources a business deploys. These skills and resources reflect the pattern of past investments to enhance competitive position. The sustainability of this positional advantage requires that the business set up barriers that make imitation difficult. Because these barriers to imitation are continually eroding, the firm must continue investing to sustain or improve the advantage. Thus, the creation and sustenance of a competitive advantage are the outcome of a long-run feedback or cyclical process (Figure 1).

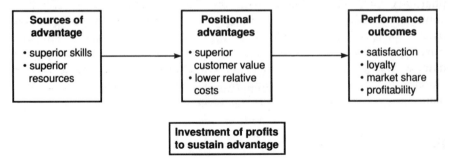

Figure 1 *The elements of competitive advantage*

Underlying the simple, sequential determinism of the source-position-performance framework is a complex environment fraught with uncertainty and distorted by feedbacks, lags, and structural rigidities. Before introducing these complexities, we describe each of the primary elements of the framework.

Sources of advantage

Superior skills and resources, taken together, represent the ability of a business to do more or do better (or both) than its competitors.

Superior skills are the distinctive capabilities of personnel that set them apart from the personnel of competing firms. Some of the benefits of superior skills arise from the ability to perform individual functions more effectively than other firms. For example, superior engineering or technical skills may lead to greater precision or reliability in the finished product. Other skills are derived from the systems and organization structure that enable a firm to adapt more responsively and faster to changes in market requirements.

Superior resources are more tangible requirements for advantage that enable a firm to exercise its capabilities. They may reside in the scale of the manufacturing facility, the location, the breadth of salesforce and distribution coverage, the availability of automated assembly lines, or the family brand name.

The distinction between the antecedent *sources* of advantage and the *positional* advantages that result when they are deployed adroitly is seen readily in successful turnaround strategies such as that of Foremost-McKesson in drug retailing. The management recognized that their skills – derived from an in-depth knowledge of their suppliers' and customers' businesses and the myriad of products they handle – could be parleyed into something more than a delivery and billing service. By enhancing these skills with heavy investments in data processing hardware and systems resources, the firm sharply reduced the costs of the many activities between the suppliers; finished goods and the pharmacy shelf. These actions made the firm so efficient that its suppliers could not possibly do as well on their own. The resulting information was used to offer unique value-added services to both suppliers and customers. Foremost now can help manufacturers manage inventories, analyse market data, and plan new product development efforts. Retailers are tied more closely through leases of electronic ordering equipment, shelf management plans, and even the provision of price labels.

Positions of advantage

The positional advantages of a business are directly analogous to competitive mobility barriers that could deter a firm from shifting its strategic position. They are understood best within the value chain or business system framework attributed to McKinsey and Co., but largely developed into a management tool by Porter.[4] A value chain first classifies the activities of the firm into the discrete steps performed to design, produce, market, deliver, and service a product. Supporting these specific value-creation activities are firmwide activities such as procurement, human resource management, and technology development as well as the infrastructure of systems and management that ties the value chain together. Only activities with a great impact on differentiation, that account for a large or growing proportion of costs, need be considered.

Lowest delivered cost positions   An overall cost edge is gained by performing most activities at a lower cost than competitors while offering a parity product. NUCOR, for example, has achieved an enviable sell cost position by making extensive use of scrap metal instead of iron ore and producing all its steel by the efficient continuous-casting method, which eliminates the intermediate step of making ingots. This strategy also can be focused on a distinct market segment. For example Fort Howard Paper uses only recycled pulp, rather than the more expensive virgin pulp, to make toilet paper and other products. The quality, however, is acceptable only to the away-from-home market (office buildings, hotels, and restaurants), so the company does not try to sell to the home market through grocery stores.

Differentiated positions   A business is differentiated when some value-adding activities are performed in a way that leads to perceived superiority along dimensions that are valued by customers. For these activities to be profitable, the customers must be willing to pay a price premium for the benfits and the premium must exceed the added costs of superior performance. A business or its products can be distinguished favourably in a myriad of ways: providing superior service, using a strong brand name, offering innovative features, and providing superior product quality are some of the favoured routes. Thus Procter & Gamble is regaining lost share in the disposable diaper market with a new super-absorbent contoured model; Salomon has gained a dominant position in the ski bindings market with a stream of innovations such as set-in bindings that meet the needs of average rather than expert skiers; Digital Equipment has enhanced its position in the minicomputer market with an artificial intelligence system that dramatically reduces the time required to fill orders and increases accuracy. This view of differentiation as perceived superiority – and possibly uniqueness – on some attributes that are important to customers is consistent with the position taken by Dickson and Ginter.[5] It goes beyond physical product attributes to embrace all activities and linkages of the business, including the kind of comprehensive support that Salomon provides its dealers to ensure they actively promote the superior features of its boots and bindings.

Performance outcomes

The most popular indicators of marketing effectiveness and competitive advantage are market share and profitability. Is this popularity due to their ready availability, strong track record, or conceptually superior insights? Alternative measures such as customer satisfaction and the value of the customer franchise are little used, even though they afford the considerable benefit of reflecting customer responses to positional advantages and thus should precede the market share and profitability outcomes.

Market share   The premise of this measure is that we can distinguish winners from losers by the market shares they achieve, just as the outcome of a horse race is given by the final standings. This view of competition is simplistic; in reality competition is played out over many time periods with evolving markets. There is a strong temptation to extend the use of market share from a measure of past performance to a reliable indicator of future advantages. Is this a reasonable extension? Though there are few markets in which current share does not have a strong relationship to future share, we seldom find an exact mapping of current market shares onto future shares. Instead a significant 'regression toward the mean' effect has been found in the analysis of market share changes in the PIMS database.[6-8] This phenomenon raises some fundamental questions about the interpretation of market shares.

Market share and profitability   There are several compelling reasons why the usual causal explanation is partially or completely wrong. Possibly the direction of causality is from profit to share: businesses that are lucky or uniquely endowed select initially defensible and profitable positions, then reinvest the profits so they can grow faster than their less fortunate rivals. The most persuasive explanation is that both causal mechanisms are operating over time to yield the association of share and profit observed at any point in time.

Early in the evolution of the market, first-mover advantages dominate. As the market matures, the question is whether management can capitalize on the initially strong position and build new skills and resources to keep abreast of changes in technology and market requirements. This multiple-mechanism view has support from several studies of changes in the PIMS database,[9,10]

What does this emerging view of market share, as largely an outcome of strategic moves to secure cost and differentiation advantages,[11] imply for the relevance of market share as an indicator of advantage? If it is to serve as more than simply an outcome measure we need to be sure that the observed share

- Was gained in a way that competitors will have difficulty imitating, and
- Refers to a market with relatively stable boundaries. A dominant share of a market in which competitive forces are evolving rapidly affords little assurance of future advantage.

The last caveat points up a further difficulty with market share measures due to the ambiguity of market definitions. The answer to the question 'share of what market?' often forces difficult compromises.[12] A useful market definition should reflect the strategic choices of the business. To be a valid measure of competitive forces, however, it also should relate to ways the competitors define the market and should reflect emerging commonalities and differences in market segment behaviour. A single market share measure is unlikely to satisfy these requirements.

Profitability Current profitability is the reward from past advantages after the current outlays needed to sustain or enhance future advantages have been paid. Because profitability is influenced by actions taken in many previous time frames, it is unlikely to be a complete reflection of current advantage. When the environment is turbulent it may be a misleading indication. Consequently, the same arguments used to conclude that market share should be interpreted as an outcome can be applied to profitability.

The interpretation of profitability is complicated further by limitations in the prevailing modes of valuation. The cost-based approaches that underlie most accounting results are fundamentally different from approaches that estimate financial value from the stream of future benefits.[13,14] Accounting conventions oriented to allocating historic and current costs to satisfy tax requirements are ill-suited to the valuation of the sources of advantage. The consequences of the accounting mindset are most evident in the treatment of intangibles. Goodwill becomes an arithmetic necessity rather than a genuine commercial asset with future value. Similarly, investments in the skill and knowledge base are treated as current overhead, without consideration of their contribution to long-run performance. However, the future value of an asset depends critically on how it is used and whether the stream of benefits can be protected from competitive forces. Thus we return full circle to the question of how investments in sources of advantage yield positional advantages and superior performance outcomes.

Converting skills and resources into superior positions and outcomes

Information on the relative standing of a business on the sources, positions, and performance dimensions of its competitive advantage is only a means to an end. What managers really want to know is how to get the greatest improvement in performance for the least expenditure. To do so requires identification of the skills and resources that exert the most leverage on positional advantages and future performance, then selective allocation of resources toward those high leverage sources. These are the key success factors of the business that 'must be applied or controlled for the business to be successful'.[15] They are tailored closely to the type of business; the key success factors for machine tools do not apply to college book publishing, as we see in Table 1.

Table 1 The Nature of Key Success Factors[a]

Market	*Skill and resource factors that create value or lower costs*	*Important aspects of value to the customer*
College book publishing	Relationships with quality authors Strong editorial capabilities Publisher strength in discipline Backlist depth Sales per title	Quality of published books Publisher reputation Fit with other published works
Machine tools	Design and manufacturing quality Simplification of parts variability Instant response from central depots Raw material stock	Tool quality Parts availability

[a]Adapted from MacAvoy (1987)

The conversion of sources of advantage into payoffs has been addressed only in a piecemeal way. The strategy literature generally asks how superior skills and resources are converted into positional advantages. These are the structural determinants or 'drivers' of cost or differentiation advantages.[4] In contrast, marketers – as represented by those building decision calculus and market share attraction models – generally skip the intervening positional stage. The modelling is confined to the relationship of the input sources of advantage (relative advertising, sales, and promotion expenditures, for example) with the performance outcomes of market share or profit. Neither the marketing nor strategy approach gives much attention to the conversion of positional advantages into superior outcomes. This is a serious gap, for the intervening stage does much to mediate the relationship of inputs to outputs. The remainder of this section examines the conversion steps in detail.

Converting sources into positions of advantage

The drivers of positional advantages are the high leverage skills and resources that do the most to lower costs or create value to customers. Each activity in a firm's value chain is influenced by the combined effect of these drivers.[4]

Cost drivers are the structural determinants of the cost of each activity that are largely under a firm's control. The primary drivers are (1) the scale economies or diseconomies for each activity, (2) learning that improves knowledge and processes independently of scale, (3) the patterns of capacity utilization, and (4) the linkages that are present when the way one activity is performed affects another activity. Linkages act as cost drivers when, for example, higher quality material and more costly product designs are used to reduce service costs.

Drivers of differentiation are analogues to cost drivers but represent the underlying reasons why an activity is executed in a unique or superior way. They correspond directly to the sources of advantage that reside in superior skills or resources when mobilized by an effective strategy. The principal drivers are (1) policy choices about what activities to perform and how intensely to perform them, including features, performance, level of advertising spending, extent of services provided, and the skills and experience of personnel employed in the activity, (2) linkages within the value chain, such as coordination between sales and service to improve the speed of order handling or with suppliers and distributors, and (3) timing that gains first-mover advantages. Other drivers include location, interrelationships with other businesses, learning, and scale that permits an activity to be performed in a unique way not possible at smaller volumes. Different combinations of drivers interact to determine the extent to which an activity is unique or superior to that of competitors.

The usefulness of the notion of drivers is difficult to assess. At best it is a descriptive tool, lacking any theory to clarify how drivers work or even how they can be isolated. It is not even apparent that they all mean the same thing. For example, some drivers of differentiation correspond directly to sources of advantage such as location, scale, or level of integration. However, 'policy choices', the most prominent driver of differentiation, are discretionary decisions about activities to perform and how to perform them. Though such decisions are critical, they are not sources of advantage. Instead they are mediating events that determine the degree of leverage an investment in a particular skill or resource has on cost or differentiation.

Converting sources directly to performance

The characteristic work on this conversion has been done by marketers with models that are variants on the 'fundamental theorem of market share determination'. The theorem holds that the market shares of various competitors are proportional to their shares of total marketing effort.[16] This relationship is a pivotal feature of the so-called market share attraction models[17] and has been integrated into the STRATPORT portfolio model by Larreche and Srinivasan.[18] The basic notion also has been applied directly to a game-theoretic analysis of monopolistic competition assessing a firm's competitive strength as the product of its functional expenditures and competencies.[19] A recent effort[20] to classify strategic variables into success producers or failure preventers (where an increased level of effort above a threshold level will not increase performance) also relies on the notion that relative effort levels roughly correspond to competitive advantages.

The most extensive application of the theorem is by Cook[21] in the 'new paradigm of marketing strategies'. In this model, a firm has an advantage when its capacity to supply products is greater than the market demand for its output. The resulting slack can be applied to exploiting opportunities to gain share. The size of this advantage is estimated by subtracting the firm's share of strategic investments from its share of units sold. The central premise is that an equilibrium is reached when the firm's share of spending on conventional mix investments is the same as the market share. If the share of strategic marketing investment falls below the current share of units sold, share of units eventually will decline in search of a new balance in consumer preferences.

Though the structure of the Cook model can be faulted on many grounds,[22] the flaws in the valuation mechanism are potentially more damaging. The basic valuation model proposed by Cook – and implicitly endorsed in many marketing models – presumes the *current* level of investment in terms of annual cash outlays is the proper basis for assessing the level of market share a business can sustain. The resulting market share has a net present value that relates current outlays to the discounted value of the future revenue stream.[23] In reality this model provides only a partial picture of the potential value of past and current strategic investments. A complete picture must reflect (1) the link between today's investments and opportunities to execute tomorrow's options, (2) the value of first-mover advantages, and (3) the strategic choice of when and how the profit potential of a positional advantage will be realized.

Valuing options to be exercised in the future Why do firms invest in manifestly unprofitable projects to establish a toehold in a potentially attractive technology?[24] In effect they are buying an option to make a later move, because the first move does not commit them to proceed further.[25] If the first stage fails or the market sours, the firm can stop after the initial investment and cut its losses. However, especially in the case of new technologies, the first investment often is a necessary condition to learning enough to be in a position to make further investments. Options of this kind are intangible assets and in growth markets may account for a large fraction of the value of a business. Conventional discounted cash flow analysis is unable to value such options properly.[26]

First-mover advantages are derived from the opportunity pioneers have to shape the rules of subsequent competition to their advantage. These advantages are achieved through pre-emption of competition, access to scarce resources, proprietary experience effects, the image of leadership that is not available to followers, and customer loyalty that is gained when switching costs are high.

Why should relative timing enhance or detract from the value of a marketing investment? The fundamental reason is an irreducible ambiguity as to which combination of factors was responsible for superior or inferior performance, which acts as a powerful inhibitor to direct imitation.[27] In the presence of uncertainty, the performance that prospective imitators can expect to achieve varies greatly. If a large nonrecoverable cost also is associated with such a move, prospective entrants are further deterred from imitating the best firm in the market. Instead they are forced to develop different market positions or appeals, or leap-frog with new technologies, if they are to achieve acceptable returns. Strong evidence supports the notion that pioneering consumer brands gain long-run market share rewards as a result of the difficulty of emulating their success.[28] Similarly, a recent study of mature industrial businesses found the average market share at maturity was 30% for the pioneers that survived, 21% for followers, and only 15% for late entrants.[29]

The payoff from positional advantages

A differentiation or cost advantage eventually should be rewarded with share and/or profitability superior to those of competitors. The size and duration of the superior payoff will depend on

- Whether the value perceived by the customer and the resulting price premiums are greater than the extra cost of the activities that create differentiation.
- The objectives of the business in terms of the tradeoff between higher immediate profit (realized by taking the maximum feasible price premium) and increased market share gained with a penetration price.
- the difficulty the competitors will have in matching or leap-frogging the advantage. Not all industries afford equal opportunities to sustain an advantage. Those with durable, irreversible, and market-specific assets and a slow pace of technological change are much more likely to promise enduring profitability.

These considerations usually are overlooked in marketing models based on simple response functions that relate a change in marketing expenditures to a change in share or sales. The message is clear: to understand how a competitive advantage is created and sustained we must understand the intermediate stage of positional advantages. Otherwise the exercise is devoid of diagnostic value.

Toward an integrated concept of competitive advantage

The various extensions to the basic source-position-performance framework that are needed to portray better the realities of competitive strategy formulation are summarized in Figure 2.

MANAGEMENT JUDGMENTS

	Analysis of strengths and weaknesses	Comparison of value chains of firms versus target competitor; configuration and total costs	
COMPETITOR CENTRED	Relative size of resources		**POINTS OF SUPERIORITY**
	Value chain		
	Customer choice criteria	Comparison of attribute ratings of firm versus competitors	
CUSTOMER FOCUSED	Segment differences in benefits		**POINTS OF SUPERIORITY**

CUSTOMER JUDGMENTS

Figure 2 *A framework for assessing advantage*

- Superior skills and resources are not automatically converted into positional advantages, nor is there a certain performance payoff from superior cost or differentiation positions. Both conversions are mediated jointly by strategic choices, including objectives and entry timing and the quality of tactics and implementation.
- The managerial usefulness of any effort to assess advantage comes from the accurate identification of the handful of skills and resources that have the greatest leverage on position and performance. These are the key success factors that must be managed obsessively to ensure long-run competitive effectiveness.

- This framework describes the performance of a business in relation to that of its competitors. The absolute performance also depends on the attractiveness of the overall market as determined by competitive structure and behaviour.

The next issue is the ability of the available methods to yield valid and insightful measures of the competitive standing of a business as required by each of the constructs in the framework.

Methods for assessing advantage

The possible measurement methods are classified in Table 2 by their place in the conceptual framework and whether they take the vantage point of customers or competitors. The immediate message of this table is that each of the many methods for assessing advantage has a specific and limited role that gives only a partial picture of the complete framework. Thus customers have little to say about how a business has gained an advantage they value (e.g., which skills and resources created and sustained superior customer service). Conversely, analyses of competitive superiority in skills and resources are made by people within the firm using competitors as the standard of comparison. The findings do not tell whether the firm will be distinguished favourably in the eyes of customers or end users. A comprehensive diagnosis can be gained only with a combination of methods. The purpose of the following sections is to guide the selection of the appropriate methods.

Table 2   Methods of Assessing Advantage

Competitive-centred	Customer-focused
A Assessing sources (distinctive competencies)	
1 Management judgements of strengths and weaknesses	
2 Comparison of resource commitments and capabilities	
3 Marketing skills audit	
B Indicators of positional advantage	
4 Competitive cost and activity comparisons	5 Customer comparisons of
(a) Value chain comparisons of relative costs	attributes of firm vs. competitors
(b) Cross-section experience curves	(a) Choice models
	(b) Conjoint analysis
	(c) Market maps
C Identifying key success factors	
6 Comparison of winning vs. losing competitors	
7 Identifying high leverage phenomena	
(a) Management estimates of market share elasticities	
D Measure of performance	
10 (a) Market share	8 Customer satisfaction surveys
11 Relative profitability (return on sales and return	9 Loyalty (customer franchise)
on assets)	10 (b) Relative share of end-user
	segments

Competitor-centred methods

The essence of these methods is a direct comparison with target competitors. Because the departure point for this comparison is the business, the frame of reference usually is confined to direct rivals. Hence the emphasis is on relative skills and resources and the resulting cost position. The search is directed toward finding those activities the firm does better than its competitors.

The most competitor-centred method is judgemental identification of distinctive competencies, which are based on 'unique levels and patterns of both skills and resources, deployed in ways that cannot be duplicated by others'.[31] However, a firm can have a distinctive competence without gaining a competitive advantage if what it does best is relatively unimportant to customers or competitors. Key success factors therefore have an important role in disciplining the competitive analysis process, for they direct attention to high leverage competencies. Several methods such as value chain analysis can be adapted to help identify key success factors.

Identifying distinctive competencies

Neither planning practice nor the strategic management literature has advanced much beyond *ad hoc* judgements of strengths and weaknesses for this purpose. The present state of the art reflects the original formulations of the distinctive competencies notion by Selznick[32] and Learned *et al.*[33] Current discussions, such as those of Glueck and Jauch[34] and Hitt and Ireland,[35] add little other than longer lists of factors to consider.

Judgemental analyses of strengths and weaknesses (Table 2, A1) The virtues of this general framework are also its drawback. It is deliberately broad and generalized to encompass an almost limitless array of potentially influential factors, which means it can be used in most situations. Conversely, it gives no guidance on how to avoid simply creating an indiscriminate listing of competencies that does not isolate those few that are especially important.

There are several reasons why the usual enumeration of strengths and weaknesses provides little guidance. First, the judgements commonly are made without an explicit reference point (are distinctive competencies relative to competitors or relative to other lesser capabilities of the business?). Second, there is often no distinction between what the business does well that is valued by customers and what it does well that is unimportant to customers. Too often the identification of competencies is based solely on internal considerations. Third, the judgements tend to be based on historical data or simple trend extrapolations. Because they primarily reflect past successes they are unlikely to produce insights into future possibilities for advantage. One way to overcome these problems is to employ a participative process involving taskforces to set priorities.[36] This process will not be effective unless it is guided by a conceptual framework to facilitate strategic thinking. The Porter[37] model of the five forces that determine industry profitability often is used for this purpose.

Direct comparisons of resource commitments and capabilities (Table 2, A2)
Disproportionate weight tends to be given to 'hard' data about competitors because it is accessible and in a format that invites direct comparison. Such tangible and visible factors as size of salesforce, number of dealers, and plant capacity generally are used to estimate the relative size of resource commitments. These data may be analysed in terms of share of marketing effort and strategic investments as proposed by Cook[21] in the model described before. Not only is this model limited, but this type of data gives a narrow view of the relative size of competitive capabilities and commitments. A complete assessment would also consider:

● Functional capabilities as reflected in such measures as the number of new products successfully developed, speed of response to service calls, the flexibility of processing equipment, and the union situation.
● Forecasts of competitors' investment priorities and patterns of spending[38] as an indication of the capacity to grow
● Capability to respond quickly to moves by others, as determined by uncommitted cash reserves, excess plant capacity, and new products on the shelf
● Ability to adapt to change, as a consequence of exit barriers, cost of unused capacity, and the structure of fixed versus variable costs.

Assessing superiority in skills: the role of the marketing skills audit (Table 2, A3)
An old adage in planning circles holds that hard numbers drive out soft impressions. Skills are 'the most distinctive encapsulation of the organization's way of doing business',[39] but may be simply too subtle to measure. Distinctive skills may be what really matters in the long run for they are the essence of adaptive organizations,[40,41] but how is one to identify competitive superiority on each of the following three skill sets that Peters[39] identifies as essential?

1 A focus on total customer satisfaction
2 A focus on continuous innovation
3 A widespread commitment from all levels of the organization to the first two orientations.

For these skills to make an enduring difference, they must pervade all activities of the business. Unless they are nurtured continually they come to be taken for granted and performance erodes. However, it is very difficult to detect slippage in the exercise of these skills before superiority is lost. Even IBM – a paragon of excellence – recently has admitted that it got out of touch with its customers.[42] According to the chairman, John Akers, IBM persisted in trying to sell its products rather than solutions to the problems of integrating computer systems, wringing out productivity gains, and using information systems for competitive advantage. One vehicle for assessing such a 'slippery' skill as a focus on total customer satisfaction is the most generic of all forms of assessment – the marketing audit. It is a 'comprehensive, systematic, independent and periodic examination of a business unit's marketing environment, objectives, strategies and activities . . .'.[43] Depending on who does it, for what reasons, and with which data sources, such audits might reveal this skill factor. None of the available literature, however, identifies a customer orientation or focus on customer satisfaction as an overriding theme in guiding an audit or offers guidance on how to identify this package of skills. In principle, an audit does have the breadth of concern and capacity to address these issues. We suspect that few audits give adequate attention to such manifestations of customer orientation as the integration of management functions toward serving customer needs and the willingness to invest in and act on customer research or reward employees on the basis of customer satisfaction. Such information, coupled with evidence of competitors' performance on these dimensions, would give a powerful insight into the ability of the business to respond to changing market requirements.

Biases in management judgements   In the absence of objective and comparative measure of subtle skills, the only recourse is to the knowledge of the business unit managers. However, their assessments often are subverted by myopia. Subjective judgements are readily biased by selective perceptions and dominated by facts and opinions that are easy to retrieve. Often 'hard' evidence of the past or current success of a strategy is given more weight than 'soft' assessments of future threats.[44,45] This problem is particularly insidious with performance measures such as share and profitability, which reflect the payoff from past competitive advantages. Further bias stems from differences across organizational levels in the perceptions of which skill and resource factors are important. The problem has received little consideration, despite one study that found senior managers emphasized personnel and financial capabilities whereas middle managers based their judgements of strengths and weaknesses on technical and marketing attributes.[46] This study also found a persistent pattern of unwarranted optimism at higher levels in the organization. Such divergent opinions are difficult to reconcile without external points of reference for validation.

Some progress has been made by marketing researchers in understanding[47] and overcoming the problems of managerial bias in judgements.[48] This work has concentrated on improving managerial estimates of the parameters of decision calculus models. Better overall judgements result when an external measure of expertise can be used confidently to pick the best expert for an issue. The results are even better than those of the Delphi method often proposed as a solution. Unfortunately even the 'best' expert is not immune to the biasing effects of selective perception.

Indicators of positional advantages

Competitor-centred approaches to identifying positional superiority help managers to answer the question, 'How do we compare with our competitors?' The answers usually are framed in terms of observable differences in value chains, including (1) the choice of activities undertaken, (2) the way the activities are performed, and (3) consequences for the cost of each activity as well as total cost. Because it is difficult to say without recourse to customer judgements whether an activity is being performed better by a competitor, the emphasis of competitor-centred methods is inevitably on cost differences. The nature of the available methods also reinforces this cost emphasis.

Value chain comparisons of relative costs (Table 2, B4a)   A firm's cost position depends on the configuration of the activities in its value chain versus that of competitors and its relative location on the cost drivers of each activity. A cost advantage is gained when the cumulative cost of performing all the activities is lower than the competitors' costs. The first step in determining the relative cost position is the identification of each competitor's value chain. Ideally, costs and assets then should be assigned to each of these activities. In practice this step is extremely difficult because the business does not have direct information on the costs of the competitors' value activities. Some costs can be estimated from public data or interviews with suppliers and distributors, whereas others can be derived by reverse engineering and similar techniques. For example, it is usually possible to determine the size of a competitor's salesforce and its expense and compensation arrangements. The result is a partial picture based on accurate data that can be filled out with informed judgement.

Cross-sectional experience curves (Table 2, B4b)   provide a comparison of the current total cost positions of the competitors in a market according to their cumulative experience base.[49] With such a curve it is possible to estimate the relative profitability of each competitor at the prevailing price. These comparisons are appropriate only when all significant competitors are similar in scope, strategy, and value chain configuration. Outside these restrictive circumstance the slope of the curve is too difficult to estimate with confidence, so it is better to resort to direct estimates of costs.

Identifying key success factors

Numerous methods have been proposed for identifying key success factors.[50] Most involve *ad hoc* judgements of industry experts and management. Though the results may be very insightful, testing their validity is usually difficult and they lack obvious action implications. For example, how useful is it to know that the key success factors in the food processing industry are new product development, good distribution, and effective advertising? For ice cream two very different factors have been identified: the ability to control seasonal variations and the ability to ensure economic refrigeration capacity throughout the distribution process.[15] Though these factors seem plausible, it is not clear that there are big differences in them among competitors or that changes in them will have a significant impact on either costs or perceived value.

More defensible insights come from explicitly relating current *sources* of advantage to the achievement of advantageous competitive *positions* or superior *performance*. To do so requires a feedback of information about the outcomes of the competitive advantage process back to the antecedents of advantage. Two adaptations of this approach have been proposed in the strategy literature: (1) discover what distinguishes winning companies from losers and (2) look for high leverage phenomena. Unfortunately, there is no evidence of the validity of either of these methods, nor have they been subjected to comparative tests. Some progress has been reported in applying these methods to specific functional areas such as information systems.[51]

Comparisons of winning versus losing competitors (Table 2, C6)   Key success factors are inferred from an analysis of differences in performance among competitors. For this approach to yield useful insights, three difficult questions must be answered. First, which competitors should be included in the comparison set? Second, what criteria should be used to distinguish the winners from the losers (e.g. profitability, growth, market share, creation of new markets)? Third, what are the reasons for the differences in performance? Rothschild[38] identifies four categories of reasons: uniqueness of the vision or strategy, the resources possessed, differences in assumptions about the environment, and fortuitous factors such as good timing or location. There is no evidence that these reasons are either mutually exclusive or exhaustive, so their contribution to insight is speculative.

Overall, this procedure is a worthwhile starting place. For example, comparisons of firms that have succeeded in the deregulating transportation and communications markets with their weaker rivals that are being bought up show that ownership of a large facilities network – gives a larger than expected cost advantage. This advantage results from economies of flow or density, which behave like economies of scale in that average costs decline as network traffic increases. What is worrisome to many observers is that these advantages will be difficult to contest in the future, so the prognosis is for continued high levels of industry concentration.

Identifying high leverage phenomena (Table 2, C7) Carroll[52] argues that the typical key success factors are too superficial to be actionable because they identify 'things' such as customer service and access to resources, rather than relationships between desired outcomes and controllable inputs. Better insights come from thorough knowledge of the 'strategic phenomena' of the business.[52,53] Ideally these are causal relationships describing how controllable variables such as plant scale, production run length, and salesforce density affect desirable outcomes such as manufacturing and sales costs per unit. A representative relationship is between distance shipped and distribution cost per unit. The reported relationships suggest a bias toward cost-based advantages, though some have very indirect impacts on costs (e.g. the relationship of brand purchases per period and brand loyalty).

The analysis task is formidable, for a myriad of potential relationships must be examined but only a few will be found to have significant leverage. Then the current position of each leading competitor is located for each significant relationship and an estimate is made of how these competitors will change their positions. No guidelines are offered on how to find the key relationships, other than to use line management to hypothesize a number of possibilities and then test them with data. The reliance on situational knowledge does not ensure either completeness or validity.

Management estimates of market share elasticities (Table 2, C7a) The problems of finding high leverage phenomena are seemingly no worse than the difficulties inherent in the elasticity analysis proposed by Hofer and Schendel[31] for a similar purpose. The analysis measures the degree to which the total revenues of a business will be increased or decreased by changes in marketing activities such as pricing, sales effort, and service levels. A variant of this approach has a long and successful history in decision calculus models[54] applied at the brand or product line level. It is unclear whether the concept of elasticities or response coefficients can be generalized meaningfully to the business level in the absence of any reported applications. Such applications would be susceptible to the usual problems of estimation of response coefficients by means of time series data or management judgement.

Drivers of activities on the value chain (Table 2, C7b) are analogous to strategic phenomena. The difference is that drivers are estimated for each relevant activity in the value chain. Because this is a more systematic procedure, important strategic relationships between sources and outcomes are less likely to be overlooked. Even so, the procedure is better suited to cost drivers than to differentiation drivers, because the former are based on relationships that can be identified largely from internal data obtained by:

- Examining the basic economics of the business, for example, the effect of local market share on salesforce costs
- Analysing the performance consequences of past fluctuations in costs
- Asking 'what if' questions of line managers on the effects of changing a parameter such as line speed on yield
- Comparisons of the firm's costs with competitors' cost for each activity.

Regrettably, the notion of drivers has the same problems as other methods of identifying key success factors. All are better at cataloguing the possibilities than isolating the few areas where superior execution or increased investment will have the greatest impact. In short, much progress must be made before the notion of key success factors fulfils its promise.

Customer-focused measures

A customer perspective means the comparison of competitors is made by customers rather than by the management team, as summarized in Figure 3. Emphasis is shifted from the cost factors and the internal value chain activities addressed in the competitor-centred approaches to segment differences and differentiation advantages.

Perspectives on positional advantages

Choice models (Table 2, B5a) Most methods that use customer judgements are variations on the basic multiattribute choice model. All ask the same question – 'Why are competitive alternatives selected from a consideration set?' – and employ the same model structure to answer the question. A customer's beliefs about the performance of each supplier on the attributes that correspond to their purchase criteria are multiplied by the relative importance of each attribute, then summed to obtain an overall attitude score.

The most common version is the linear compensatory model,[55] so called because good performance on one attribute can offset or compensate for poor performance on another attribute.

Diagnostic insights are gained from the importance weights. Perceived differences between alternatives on the important attributes provide direct evidence of advantage. The importance weights can be measured directly (by using a constant sum scale, for example) or derived by regressing the attribute ratings against an overall preference judgement for each alternative. The estimated regression weights then serve as proxies for importance. The first stage of analysis is often a grid plot of the importance rating of each attribute against the comparative performance rating for the business.[56] Attention is directed to important attributes on which the business is judged not to be performing well.

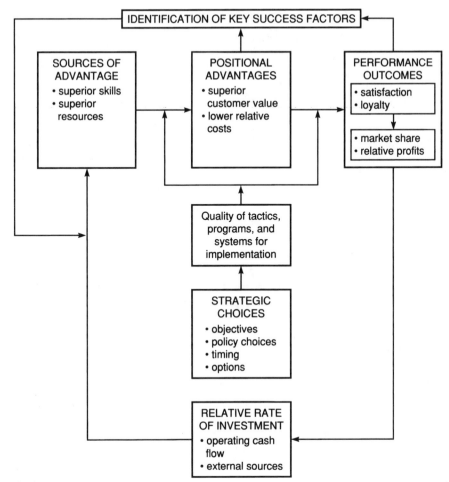

Figure 3   *Comparing competitors*

Though this approach to assessing advantage has long been used by consumer goods companies, it is equally relevant to industrial and service markets. DuPont has undertaken dozens of such studies to good effect.[57] The company has found the overall ratings of competitive standing correlate well with market share, so managers have confidence in the approach. The payoff comes from the attribute-by-attribute comparisons between DuPont's performance and that of specific competitors in specific market segments. To counteract the belief of DuPont managers that they already know the most important attributes, the researchers ask all members of the business team to list and rank the attributes. The internal list is invariably incomplete. More significant is the wide variation in importance rankings found within the team. The salesforce has one view, whereas operations and R&D often hold very different views.

All successful (reported) applications of customer-judgement methods share two features. First, they specify the attributes precisely (e.g. does better service mean repair capability, response time, or delivery time?). Specificity comes at a cost, as the attributes are often highly correlated, but the diagnostic insights are certainly superior.

The second feature of effective applications is customer or product segmentation based on similarities in attribute judgements. Gensch[58] used this criterion to identify segments of the market of a heavy electric equipment manufacturer according to their degree of relative preference and loyalty.[59] This information was used to target 'switchable' customers for whom the firm was the second choice by only a narrow margin. Doyle and Saunders[60] clustered all products in a highly differentiated specialty chemical market according to similarity of purchase attributes. The strategic insights came from evaluation of the attractiveness of each product segment in terms of size, growth, strength of competition, and fit with the firm's capabilities. The results dissuaded management from the risks of the 'majority fallacy' by showing that niches away from the middle of the market were less competitive as target segments for a late entrant.

The full payoff from choice models will come when they can incorporate the effect of controllable marketing variables as well as product attributes on the choice among competitive alternatives. Progress in this direction has been reported by Carpenter and Lehmann.[61] They formulated a multinominal logit model to explain brand switching probabilities as a function of each competitor's marketing mix, product features, and their interactions. The output of the model reveals groups of competing brands based on their features and the impact of marketing mix elements on these groupings.

Conjoint analysis (Table 2, B5b)   Most choice models lack a mechanism for recognizing trade-offs among levels of attributes, and seldom is it possible to calculate the value of satisfying each choice criterion by estimating how it affects buyers' cost or performance. As a result the relative importance weights do not necessarily reflect the amount of buyer value that accrues from improvements in performance on each attribute. On the surface, conjoint analysis appears to overcome these problems. The procedure has the capacity to decompose an overall preference or value for money measure into utility scores, or part worths, for each level of each attribute.[62,63] However, it is apparently little used for assessing competitive advantage.[64] Among the barriers to usage are burdensome and specialized data collection procedures,[65] which sharply limit the number of attributes that can be analysed. Also, the models yield unreliable estimates of past worths if the choice alternatives are so close in performance that fine distinctions among alternatives are obscured. In mature markets where differentiation advantages have been eroded to very thin edges, the ability to tease out subtle perceived differences is an essential feature of any useful method.

Market mapping (Table 2, B5c)   The maps compress the information from customer judgements about related attributes to a few composite dimensions. Their relationships among competitors from the customers' point of view. They serve the same function as the 'war board' used by military strategists to understand the geographic location and type of enemy emplacements, as well as targets of opportunity.[66] Market maps are very helpful for revealing the general pattern of perceived competitive differences and also for identifying submarket boundaries. Thus they provide a useful context for undertaking fine-grained analyses of the specific reasons why customers prefer one competitor over another. Such analyses must be done separately, for the compression of attribute data into a few dimensions obscures the details of individual attributes and the action implications are lost.

Customer evidence of relative performance

Three performance measures require direct customer input because the insights they provide cannot be inferred from historical evidence of market share, sales volume or profitability.

Customer satisfaction (Table 2, D8)   High on the list of strategic priorities is the achievement of long-run customer satisfaction. Few firms routinely monitor satisfaction, however, and when they do the information usually lacks relevance to issues of competitive advantage. One exception is IBM, where all marketing activities (including service, sales, and software support) as well as equipment performance are directly evaluated and compensated on the basis of measures of satisfaction collected in blind surveys.

   Why has the potential of this measure not been realized? Obviously, commitment to the concept is a problem, but the limitations of the usual survey measures are also an impediment. Satisfaction surveys typically are limited to assessing overall satisfaction and intentions to repurchase to reveal problems experienced by recent buyers. The measures are seldom comparative, as they focus only on the brand or product most recently purchased, and may not isolate the contribution of each product or service attribute to overall satisfaction. These are correctable problems that should be addressed in the light of research on the determinants of satisfaction.[67] Satisfaction once was believed to derive from a disconfirmation process; if performance as experienced measured up to prior expectations, satisfaction ensued. This view is too simplistic. Actual product performance relative to the perceived performance of the competitive options appears to have a greater influence on satisfaction.

Customer loyalty (Table 2, D9)   Many measures of competitive advantage are attempts to quantify the depth and quality of the customer franchise of the firm's products. Strong brand loyalty is the most common indicator of a valuable customer franchise, but how is such a measure to be intepreted? Economists assert that there is loyalty when the costs a consumer would incur in searching for further information exceed the benefits from the search.[68] Though this model may be correct, it is not very revealing because it does not indicate how perceptions are formed or changed. Behavioural measures such as share of purchase requirements satisfied by a brand[69] are equally flawed. These measures overlook the crucial aspect of loyalty as a tendency or bias toward a particular brand that may or may not be evidenced by actual purchase behaviour. A customer who has a loyalty bias toward brand A may encounter a purchase decision in which brand B is heavily price-promoted and therefore may choose brand B. In effect, the perceived superiority of the preferred brand is not sufficient to offset the price disadvantage. To understand loyalty in this setting, one must supplement the purchase behaviour measure with knowledge of intermediate attitudes.

Relative share of end-user segments (Table 2, D10b) A single market share measure obscures as much as it reveals. A 20% share could reveal either a strong competitive position (e.g. if no other competitor has more than a 10% share) or a weak position (e.g. if the dominant competitor has 50% of the market). Hence it is always better to use a measure of relative market share, obtained by dividing the share of the firm by the share of the top three competitors.[70]

Further diagnostic insights result from examining the variability in relative market share across end-user segments within the served market. If a business has the same share in every possible segment, it probably does not have a differentiated position. No brand can be equally competitive across segments that reflect very different patterns of benefits sought unless it lacks a distinct need-satisfying capability. Conversely, a business with considerable variability of shares across end-use segments or customer groups is sharply positioned to satisfy a distinct pattern of needs in one or two segments. Moran[71] has evidence that well-positioned consumer brands are more profitable because they face a lower demand elasticity within their target segments that can be converted into higher prices. Additional incremental profit comes from marketing efficiencies due to higher repeat purchase rates and customer loyalty.

The validity of the diagnostic insights from segment share differentials rests on the assumption that a more sharply focused brand or business can compete more effectively than a less focused one. Whether this assumption is true depends on the overall balance between the cost savings from economies of scope, achieved by breadth of participation in many adjacent segments,[72] and the enhanced profitability from focus on a few market segments. The choice of scope verses focus will depend in turn on the degree of segmentation in the market, for minor differences between segments will not impede larger firms from eventually entering as the 'niche' grows and becomes more attractive.

Summary and implications

An effective competitive strategy begins with the timely and actionable diagnosis of the current and prospective advantages of the business within the served market. How do managers know whether the available assessments are aiding the search for advantage or hindering it with misleading and partial information? The answer depends on how well the evidence of advantage satisfies the following requirements.

1 There is adequate illumination of the sources of advantage, as well as their manifestations of superior customer value or lowest delivered cost and superior performance.
2 There is a balance of customer-focused and competitor-centred methods so the risk of myopia due to selective attention and simplification is minimized.
3 The results have credibility while being more than a simple confirmation of prior prejudice and industry conventional wisdom. Proprietary information about the sources that exert the most leverage on positional advantages and future performance is itself a competitive advantage.

Taken together, these requirements are the basis for a process for assessing the effectiveness and quality of the performance analysis in a business.

The nature of advantage: the SPP framework

Any attempt to understand a specific competitive situation must account for three defining features of the concept of competitive advantage. First, competitive advantage is a high level notion that is inherently ambiguous until it is separated into its component parts: the sources, positions, and performance outcomes (SPP). None of these elements can serve in the place of the others. Thus, an integrative multiple measures perspective is required before a full picture can be drawn.

Second, though advantages reside in superior skills and resources, they are revealed in competitive product markets. A point of advantage can be exploited profitably only when it offers significant benefits that are perceived and valued by customers and are difficult for competitors to emulate. The appropriate unit of analysis to reveal such an advantage is a market segment characterized by a distinct profile of benefits.

Third, superior skills and resources are not automatically converted into positional advantages – nor is there a certain performance payoff from superior cost or differentiation positions. Both these conversions are mediated jointly by strategic choices, including the tradeoffs among objectives and the timing of entry and the quality of implementation.

Seeking diagnostic insights: information as advantage

The usual test of a measurement approach is whether the results are credible (believable) and add insights beyond the confirmation of past beliefs. What this test overlooks is a possibility that the new and valid insights may be unavailable to or unappreciated by managers in competing firms. Early information about the emergence of a new market segment, the side effects of a new technology, or the limitations of a new material becomes a potent competitive advantage for the first mover able to capitalize on the implications.

The notion of symmetries in insights about how to compete for future advantage requires managers in competing firms to hold significantly different perceptions and beliefs. However, individual firms appear to share the same assumptions about their market environment. In fact, an informal but often crucial validity test is whether a diagnostic insight conforms to a consensual 'industry' understanding. This conformity is a plausible explanation for why new entrants, unencumbered by conventional wisdom, can 'change the rules of the competitive game' even when they can be seen to have been acting on widely available information.

There is likely to be an inverse relationship between the ready availability of a particular measure and its capacity to generate new and valuable insights. The widespread familiarity with such proxy measures of competitive advantage as market share and return on sales means they already have been incorporated into managerial perceptions of advantage within most competitors. They have become explanations without diagnostic power and as such virtual tautologies: 'IBM has a competitive advantage because it has the highest worldwide market share'. Hence they become merely descriptive rather than diagnostic.

In practice, the readily available evidence of advantage is likely to be not only descriptive, but also historical, distorted, and incomplete. The evidence is *historical* because of the convenience of using readily available measures being collected on a routine basis to monitor past performance and serve other needs. It is *distorted* because most available measures are linked to the control and reward system, and the alternative measures tend to rely on management judgements of relative competence and positional advantages of their business, which are biased by selective perceptions and recall of past successes. Finally, the available measures are usually *incomplete* because they are derived from inappropriate conceptual frameworks.

Balancing customer and competitor perspectives

Lack of completeness is a result of a reactive posture toward the assessment of advantage. By simply relying on evidence that is available or customary in the industry, firms may evolve passively towards an unbalanced reliance on either customer-focused or competitor-centred measures, to the possible neglect of the other perspective.

Limits to competitor-centring When market demand is predictable, the competitive structure is concentrated and stable, and there are a few powerful customers, the emphasis is necessarily on competitors. Even in this setting, solely competitor-centred measures have drawbacks. The preoccupation with costs and internal activities may obscure opportunities for differentiation through creative linkages of seller, distributor, and buyer value chains. Such a perspective also deflects attention from changes in market segment structures or customer requirements that might shift attribute judgements. Further, the competitors are assumed to be doing a proper marketing job. Managers with this mindset are more likely simply to emulate their competitors when they select strategies. Such an approach reduces the likelihood of experiments with innovative strategies to alter the basis of competition. This situation is unfortunate, for strategies that 'change the frame' with new types of service, new delivery systems, or new production systems are the surest way to gain a sustainable edge.

Managerial or other 'expert' judgement is needed in all competitor-centred methods to specify the competitors to watch and to judge the relative performance of the business and its competitors. Even seemingly firm measures of market share are a matter for judgement and debate about the appropriate served market. The susceptibility of these judgements to bias should be minimized by validation from market sources and triangulation with other ways of measuring the same variable.

Limits of customer-focusing In dynamic markets with shifting mobility barriers, many competitors, and highly segmented end-user markets, a tilt toward a customer focus is mandatory. Unfortunately, most of the customer-focused measures are remote from the activities of the business. It is seldom apparent how the attributes that are important to the customer are influenced by activities in the value chain. A perception of superior service gained by faster delivery of orders can be influenced by manufacturing processes, the choice of technology, shipping methods, or order-handling activities. These relationships are not available from customer-focused measures, nor are there any clues as to the sustainability of the advantages. Are competitors willing and able to match the strategic move? In short, neither perspective on advantage gives a complete picture to decision makers.

Appraising the measurement system

The specific measures of competitive advantage a business should use depend on the situation. The measures appropriate or even feasible for a semiconductor or auto parts manufacturer differ from those suited to a retail banker or apparel manufacturer. This fact does not exempt the monitoring system – comprising the measures used and the composite picture they give of the competitive position – from having to meet the basic requirements of any attempt to assess advantages. These requirements are posed as the critical questions in Table 3 that form the basis of an appraisal audit.

First, an explicit effort must be made to achieve a degree of balance and interaction between the customer-focused and competitor-centred perspectives. Though one domain of measurement may be emphasized over the other, there must be a mechanism for comparing the results of the different perspectives. Seldom are marketing research data or available methods used as effectively as possible. In practice, most marketing research is descriptive (what is the potential of this market?), tactical (what is the sales impact of this quarter's couponing programme?), or motivated by curiosity about the complexities of consumer behaviour or market structures. Generally the research is not directed toward understanding fundamental relationships between the sources of advantage and the resulting positional advantage and performance. As a result, the linkage between the variable marketing researchers measure and the factors managers control and manipulate is poor. To overcome this problem, researchers must give more attention to measuring customer value explicitly and must undertake clinical studies of the impact of the firm's activities on buyer costs and performance.

Table 3   Appraising the Measurement System

Relationship between competitor-focused and customer-centred approaches

– Is there an appropriate balance between the two?
– Is market research data being used effectively?

Source-position-performance framework
– Are measures being used from different 'stages'?
– Are these measures being compared and contrasted?

Nature of individual measures
– Have the potential errors and biases in the measure been recognized?
– Is it possible to look at trends in the measure as well as current levels?

Overall process
– Is the process evolving in the light of changes in our markets and among our competitors?
– Is the process adequately linked to strategy formulation, resource allocation, and tactical planning?

Second, we must audit the coverage the specific measures give of the source-position-performance framework. We would look for the use of measures at different stages as well as explicit attempts to compare and contrast them. In practice, it is critical to know whether the judged superiority in skills and resources can continue to support the observed positional superiority in the market. If it cannot, how long can a positional advantage be sustained and what needs to be done to stop the erosion? To attack these questions with any confidence we must test for inconsistencies between individual measures and also between elements of advantage. For instance, it is useful to compare managers' judgements of attribute importance with customer judgements.

Third, we must look more closely at the way each specific measure is obtained. How well does it satisfy the criteria of validity, feasibility, and diagnostic value? Further, the fact that all measures depend on some degree of judgement is no excuse for not challenging the assumptions, particularly historic ones, incorporated in the measurement approach. In many cases, performance aspects such as market share are measured in terms of historic market structures with inadequate recognition of emerging competitors and channels.

Finally, we must look critically at the overall measurement process and its development and impact within the organization. Are we learning and developing as the situation changes? How is the system designed to recognize the need for change? What potentially contradictory measures are being used to ensure the current system is adequate? Finally, any measurement system will be of commercial value only if it is linked adequately to the strategy formulation, resource allocation, and tactical planning processes of the firm.

Notes and references

1   Bhide (1986).
2   Pfeffer and Salancik (1978).
3   Though our focus is on understanding how to compete better in a chosen product-market arena, this can be achieved only if the context is properly defined. The choice of product-market arena is partly a matter of strategic choice, reflecting the definition of the business (Abell, 1980) and the capabilities of the business, and partly an empirical question of whether the competing alternatives are perceived to be substitutes (Day *et al.*, 1979). It is possible that the choice of where to compete actually follows assessment of how to compete.
4   Porter, M.E. (1985), *Competitive Advantage: Creative and Sustaining Superior Performance*, New York: The Free Press.
5   Dickson, Peter R. and James L. Ginter (1987), 'Market Segmentations, Product Differentiation and Marketing Strategy', *Journal of Marketing*, 51 (Spring), 1-10.
6   Buzzell, Robert D. (1981), 'Are There "Natural" Market Structures?' *Journal of Marketing*, 45 (Winter), 42-51.
7   Wagner, Harvey M. (1984), 'Profit Wonders; Investment Blunders', *Harvard Business Review*, 62 (September-October), 121-35.
8   In more technical terms, this is merely the problem of distinguishing between random walk behaviour and a more complex causal structure. Some analysts who have looked at market share data have argued a strong and pure random walk interpretation (Mancke, 1974). In so doing they have had to assume some complete form of capital market failure so that the firms failing (relatively speaking) in earlier rounds have no access to additional funds (even though they face exactly the same opportunity set as their competitor). Others have attempted to isolate the random walk component either by inference (Caves *et al.*, 1977) or the application of more tightly specified models (Rumelt and Wensley, 1981). The fact remains that the mere auto-correlation between current and past market share is in itself equally consistent with a pure random walk model.
9   Jacobson, Robert and David A. Aaker (1985), 'Is Market Share All That It's Cracked Up to Be?' *Journal of Marketing*, 49 (Fall), 11-22.
10 Rumelt, R.P. and J.R.C. Wensley (1981), 'Market Share and the Rate of Return: Testing the Stochastic Hypothesis', Working Paper MGL-03, University of California, Los Angeles.
11 Gale, Bradley T. and Robert D. Buzzell (1988), 'Market Position and Competitive Strategy', in *The Interfaces of Marketing and Strategy*, George S. Day, Barton Weitz, and Robin Wensley (eds), Greenwich, CT: JAI Pres, Inc.

12   Day (1981).
13   Alberts, William W. and James M. McTaggart (1984), 'Value-Based Strategic Investment Planning' *Interfaces*, 14 (January-February), 138-51.
14   Rappaport, Alfred (1981), 'Selecting Strategies that Create Shareholder Value', *Harvard Business Review*, 59 (May/June), 139-49.
15   Ohmae, Kenichi (1982), *The Mind of the Strategist*. New York: McGraw-Hill Book Company.
16   Kotler, Philip (1984), *Marketing Management: Analysis, Planning and Control*, 5th ed. Englewood Cliffs, NH: Prentice-Hall, Inc.
17   Little, John D.C., David E. Bell and Ralph E. Keeney (1975), 'A Market Share Theorem', *Journal of Marketing Research*, 12 (May), 136-41.
18   Larreche, Jean-Claude and V. Srinivasan (1982), 'STRATPORT: A Model for the Formulation of Business Portfolio Strategies', *Management Science*, 28 (September), 979-1001).
19   Karnani, Aneel (1982), 'Equilibrium Market Share – A Measure of Competitive Strength', *Strategic Management Journal*, 3 (January-March), 43-51.
20   Varadarajan, V.R. (1985), 'A Two-Factor Classification of Competitive Strategy Variables', *Strategic Management Journal*, 6 (October-December), 357-76.
21   Cook Victor J., Jr. (1983), 'Marketing Strategy and Differential Advantage', *Journal of Marketing*, 47 (Spring), 68-75.
22   The fundamental theorem as applied by Cook has numerous restrictive assumptions. Relaxing them renders the theorem virtually unmanageable for diagnostic or prescriptive purposes. To be fully specified, a model based on this theorem should incorporate (1) differences between firms in their ability to spend marketing dollars effectively, (2) the likelihood of diminishing returns to additional investments, (3) the carryover effects of past investments, and (4) synergistic effects of the marketing mix variables. None of these considerations are included in the Cook model. Further problems stem from the assumptions about the function relating market share responsiveness to changes in share of investments (Chattopadhyay, *et al.*, 1985).
23   Cook, Victor J., Jr. (1985), 'The Net Present Value of Market Share', *Journal of Marketing*, 49 (Summer), 49-63.
24   Ohmae, Kenichi (1985), *Triad Power*, New York: McGraw-Hill Book Company.
25   Wensley, Robin, Patrick Barwise, and Paul Marsh (1984), 'Strategic Investment Decisions', *Research in Marketing*, 8.
26   Meyers, Stewart C. (1984), 'Finance Theory and Financial Strategy', *Interfaces*, 14 (January-February), 126-37.
27   Lippman and Rumelt (1982) have developed a theory of 'uncertain imitability' to explain how initial advantages can be sustained when competitors are faced with this uncertainty.
28   Urban, Clen L., Theresa Carter, and Zofia Mucha (1985), 'Market Share Rewards to Pioneering Brands: An Exploratory Empirical Analysis', in *Strategic Marketing and Management*, H. Thomas and D. Gardner (eds), New York: John Wiley & Sons, Inc. 239-52.
29   Robinson, William T. (1984), 'Market Pioneering and Sustainable Market Share Advantages in Industrial Goods Manufacturing Companies,' Krannert School, Purdue University (November).
30   Ghemawat, Pakaj (1986), 'Sustainable Advantage', *Harvard Business Review*, 64 (September-October), 55-8.
31   Hofer, Charles W. and Dan Schendel (1978), *Strategy Formulation: Analytical Concepts*, Minneapolis: West Publishing Co.
32   Selznick, Philip (1957), *Leadership in Administration*, New York: Harper & Row Publishers Inc.
33   Learned, E.P., C.R. Christensen, K.R. Andrews, and W.D. Guth (1969), *Business Policy: Text and Cases*, Homewood, IL: Richard D. Irwin, Inc.
34   Glueck, William F. and Lawrence R. Jauch (1984), *Strategic Management and Business Policy*, 2nd ed., New York: McGraw-Hill Book Company.
35   Hitt, Michael A. and R. Duane Ireland (1985), 'Corporate Distinctive Competence, Strategy, Industry and Performance', *Strategy Management Journal*, 6 (July/September), 273-93.

36 King, William R. (1983), 'Integrating Strength-Weakness Analysis into Strategic Planning', *Journal of Business Strategy*, 4 (Spring), 475-87.

37 Porter, Michael E. (1980), *Competitive Strategy*, New York: The Free Press.

38 Rothschild, William E. (1984), *How to Gain (and Maintain) the Competitive Advantage*, New York: McGraw-Hill Book Company.

39 Peters, Thomas J. (1984), 'Strategy Follows Structure: Developing Distinctive Skills', *California Management Review*, 26 (Spring), 111-25.

40 Mintzberg, Henry (1978), 'Patterns in Strategy Formulation', *Management Science*, 24, 934-48.

41 Quinn, James Brian (1980), *Strategies for Change: Logical Incrementalism*. Homewood, IL: Richard D. Irwin, Inc.

42 Loomis, Carol J. (1987), 'IBM's Big Blues: A Legend Tries to Remake Itself', *Fortune* (January 10), 34-54.

43 Kotler, Philip, William Gregor, and William Rodgers (1977), The Marketing Audit Comes of Age', *Sloan Management Review*, 18 (Winter), 25-43.

44 Barnes, J.H. (1984), 'Cognitive Biases and Their Impact on Strategic Planning', *Strategic Management Journal*, 5 (April-June), 129-38.

45 Hogarth, Robin M. and Spyros Makridakis (1981), 'Forecasting and Planning: An Evaluation', *Management Science*, 27 (February), 115-38.

46 Stevenson, Howard H. (1976), 'Defining Strengths and Weaknesses', *Sloan Management Review*, 17 (Spring), 51-68.

47 Chakravarti, Dipankar, Andrew Mitchell and Richard Staelin (1981), 'Judgement Based Marketing Decision Models: Problems and Possible Solutions', *Journal of Marketing*, 45 (Fall), 13-23.

48 Larreche, Jean-Claude and Reza Moinpour (1983), 'Management Judgement in Marketing: The Concept of Expertise', *Journal of Marketing Research*, 20 (May), 110-21.

49 Day, George S. and David B. Montgomery (1983), 'Diagnosing the Experience Curve', *Journal of Marketing*, 47 (Spring), 44-58.

50 Leidecker, Joel K. and Albert V. Bruno (1984), 'Identifying and Using Critical Success Factors', *Long Range Planning*, 17 (February), 23-32.

51 Boynton, Andrew C. and Robert W. Zmud (1984), 'An Assessment of Critical Success Factors', *Sloan Management Review*, 25 (Summer), 17-27.

52 Carroll, Peter J. (1982), 'The Link Between Performance and Strategy', *Journal of Business Strategy*, 2 (Spring), 3-20.

53 MacAvoy, Robert E. (1983), 'Corporate Strategy and the Power of Competitive Analysis', *Management Review* (July), 9-19.

54 Little (1979).

55 Wilkie, William L. and Edgar A. Pessemier (1973), 'Issues in Marketing's Use of Multiattribute Attitude Models', *Journal of Marketing Research*, 10 (November), 428-41.

56 Martilla, John A. and John C. James (1977), 'Importance-Performance- Analysis', *Journal of Marketing*, 51 (January), 77-9.

57 Root, H. Paul (1986), 'Industrial Market Intelligence Systems: A Source of Competitive Advantage', presentation to the Business-to-Business Marketing Conference, American Marketing Association, New Orleans (April).

58 Gensch, Dennis H. (1984), 'Targeting the Switchable Industrial Customer', *Marketing Science*, 3 (Winter), 41-54.

59 A multivariate logit model was used to translate the customer's judgements of the relative *importance* of nine product and service attributes (such as price, warranty, quality, energy losses, financial strengths, and ability to meet delivery dates) and the *perceived value* ratings of each supplier on these attributes (on good to poor scale) into a prediction of the probability of each supplier's being chosen. This model is noteworthy because it incorporates the notions of thresholds, diminishing returns to scale, and saturation levels (Rao and Winter, 1978). Individual respondents were grouped into homogeneous segments prior to the estimation of the logit coefficients. These segments had very different weightings of the attributes in their preference functions.

60 Doyle, Peter and John Saunders (1985), 'Market Segmentation and Positioning in Specialised Industrial Markets', *Journal of Marketing*, 49 (Spring), 24-32.

61   Carpenter, Gregory S. and Donald R. Lehmann (1985), 'A Model of Marketing Mix, Brand Switching, and Competition', *Journal of Marketing Research*, 22 (August), 318-29.

62   Green, Paul E. and V. Srinivasan (1978), 'Conjoint Analysis in Consumer Research: Issues and Outlook', *Journal of Consumer Research*, 5 (September), 103-23.

63   Green, Paul E. and Yoram Wind (1975), 'New Way to Measure Consumers' Judgements', *Harvard Business Review*, 53 (July-August), 107-17.

64   Cattin, Philippe and Dick R. Wittink (1982), 'Commercial Use of Conjoint Analysis: A Survey', *Journal of Marketing*, 46 (Summer), 44- 53.

65   Urban, Glen L. and John R. Hauser (1980), *Design and Marketing of New Products*, Englewood Cliffs, NJ: Prentice-Hall, Inc.

66   Shocker, Allan D. and David W. Stewart (1983), 'Mapping Competitive Relationships: Practices, Problems and Promise', Working Paper 83-115, Vanderbilt University (September).

67   Churchill, Gilbert A., Jr., and Carol Surprenant (1982), 'An Investigation into the Determinants of Customer Satisfaction', *Journal of Marketing Research*, 19 (November), 491-504.

68   In fact, Porter (1976) goes further to characterize a detailed process of evaluation depending not only on the nature of the information itself, but also on the relevant source. Though the model presented remains plausible, it is important to recognize that little empirical evidence (and no first-hand evidence) is provided to support the model itself.

69   Johnson, Tod (1984), 'The Myth of Declining Brand Loyalty', *Journal of Advertising Research*, 24 (February/March), 9-17.

70   Capon, Noel and Joan Robertson Spogli (1976), 'Strategic Market Planning: A Comparison and Critical Examination of Two Contemporary Approaches', in *Educators' Proceedings*, Chicago: American Marketing Association, 219-23.

71   Moran, William T. (1984), 'Research on Discreet Consumption Markets Can Guide Resource Shifts', *Marketing News* (May 15), 4.

72   Teece, David J. (1980), 'Economies of Scope and the Scope of the Enterprise', *Journal of Economic Behaviour and Organisation*, 223-47.

Part Three

Organizational Analysis

At the heart of competitiveness is ensuring a sustained organizational advantage over rivals, this in turn highlighting the need for continual assessment of an organization's relative performance. Strategic development should naturally be led by the drive to ensure that such organizational advantages are maintained or, where eroded, replaced by equally durable advantages. It is likely to be influenced or directed by an organization's experience, such as its acquaintance with particular customers, technologies and markets, as well as its access to resources and the expectations of its major stakeholders. It is likely that its growth aspirations will be channelled towards perceived opportunities that satisfy these criteria. In general, the extent to which decision makers feel 'comfortable' with strategic alternatives may be a deciding factor. Overall, it would appear intuitively reasonable that the most appropriate means of organizational development should be built on prevalent strengths – what an organization knows and does well – while seeking to overcome quite obvious weaknesses.

It is natural, then, that a significant component of the process of strategic planning as traditionally proposed should involve some form of organizational assessment: an internal 'audit' of 'strengths and weaknesses'. Because of the importance of market related factors it can be expected that marketing, if one adopts a traditional functional stance on organizational structure, will have an active role in this organizational evaluation. This internal assessment can obviously be undertaken at several levels, such as: organizational; strategic business unit (SBU); functional; product group; and individual product.

The analysis at an organizational or SBU level will tend to focus on overall performance, often with regard to competitors. It may, for example, be concerned with comparisons of profitability that in turn point to generic strategic moves, such as more aggressive growth. There may also be consideration of competitive positioning, say, with regard to image and strategic profile, on which actions may have to be taken.

In the case of both organizational and SBU analyses, it is generally argued that there will be a functional analysis of the strengths and weaknesses of areas such as R&D, Marketing and Manufacturing; or an assessment of selected key capabilities and operations of the organization, such as technological strength, efficiency and effectiveness of product development, the resilience of the customer franchise, the image of brands, the nature of the relationships with suppliers and such like. The major aim is to identify those organizational features which can be advantageously exploited further; as against deficiencies or vulnerabilities which in some way have to be reduced or overcome. An organization may consider some of the areas outlined in Table 1.

Table One

Organizational area	*Consideration*
Technology	Competitive position – e.g. technology leadership or laggard
	Vulnerability of the organization's key technologies
	Involvement in or access to the science underpinning major technologies
	Compatibility with existing or emerging technological standards
Product development	Speed of development
	Success rate
	Relative cost of development
Customer base	Range
	Levels of customer satisfaction relative to rivals
	Discretionary spending power of key customers
	Degree of opinion leadership
	Support from major customers (in the case of organizational marketing)
Supplier relationships	Technological capability and innovativeness of suppliers
	Loyalty of suppliers
	Support from suppliers
Production	Efficiency
	Cost
	Quality of output
Marketing	Product range
	Brand visibility
	Market intelligence systems
	Sales management efficiency and effectiveness
Distribution	Relationships with distributors
	Management of inventory
	Channel structure(s)
Organizational structure and culture	Morale and commitment of personnel
	Flexibility of structure ('flat' organizations, 'empowerment', ...)

It is increasingly emphasized that it is important for organizations to compare their own performance against best practice, either from within or outside the industry, for key particular operations, such as new product development. This is commonly referred to as 'benchmarking' which Shetty (1993) succinctly summarizes in his paper included here. Although the term has easily entered everyday managerial parlance, its practical application may be hampered by difficulties in gaining access to performance data, especially of course on competitors' practices. However, there have arisen benchmarking 'clubs' where participants share information, although the benchmark being established in this way may not meet Shetty's criterion of being 'best practice'. In general, there is the risk that the comparative analysis is unduly restricted, especially unfortunate if those organizations used as models are not those which excel; and that benchmarking may lead to aping others rather than to developing innovative methodologies which establish as yet unachieved benchmarks.

Others have suggested a somewhat different perspective to the accepted approaches to internal analysis and have argued that the organization should identify the key capabilities or, as Prahalad and Hamel (1990) in the second article of Part Three term them, 'core competencies' and exploit and integrate them where appropriate to construct new businesses suited to the challenges of a dynamic environment. These 'core competencies' are the 'collective learning in the organization, especially how to coordinate diverse production skills and integrate multiple streams of technologies' as well as how work is organized and value created. An example of such a core competence would be, according to Prahalad and Hamel, Sony's ability to miniaturize. The exploitation of core competencies may involve the adoption of a holistic perspective of the organization: not, for example, regarding the diversified firm as several businesses, but rather attempting to exploit the relationships between businesses and extend capabilities of one to other areas of the organization. In essence, their approach may mean little more than identifying what the organization is good at and what design and production skills it needs to have in order to develop or maintain leadership in a primary product functionality, such as, for example, display technology.

Prahalad and Hamel stress the importance of protecting competencies, continuing to develop them and combining them where possible to produce differentiated and innovative offerings. However, it is equally important to pinpoint the competencies that are likely to be significant in the future and to ensure that the organization has access to these. It is not surprising, then, that strategic alliancing has assumed such a prominent position on management's agenda (Littler *et al.*, 1993).

Even if organizations adopt a comprehensive analytical stance, it is still necessary to assess the performance at a specific product group, individual product or market level. Here it can be expected that attention will be directed at analysing market shares; gross margins and other indicators of profitability; complaints; stock levels; competitive activity; and consumer perceptions. Static observations are unlikely to provide meaningful indications of performance. Rather, it should be expected that the aim will be to examine trends in these indicators, and explore the reasons for any changes, however subtle. Detailed analysis at this level can highlight future potential difficulties and opportunities, as well as assisting in developing an impression of the future financial and competitive positions of the organization.

Where organizations consist of several businesses or products, the attractiveness of each for future investment will, according to Hedley (1977) in the third article of Part Three, be dependent on relative market share and the growth in demand for the product(s). Businesses or products can then be categorized as 'stars' (high market share, high growth); 'cash cows' (high market share, low growth); 'question marks' (low market share, high growth markets); or 'dogs' (low market share, low growth). Such simplistic terminology has no doubt become familiar to many practitioners. According to Hedley, the major objective is to obtain a balanced portfolio of businesses or products. This means that in order to maintain and generally increase revenue there is an adequate flow of cash from the 'cash cows' to support the conversion of an appropriate number of 'question marks' to 'star' status, to ensure that the business has sufficient stars that will become the 'cash cows' of the future. It is generally assumed that the 'dogs will be deleted or sold.

Many criticisms can be levelled at this approach. There may be problems in defining 'market' and therefore 'market share'; the ranges covered by 'high' and 'low' are clearly susceptible to manipulation; the possibilities of external financing are excluded from the analysis; and the impact of non-price influences on demand is ignored. Moreover, the approach is deterministic, and acceptance of its prescriptions could lead to sub-optimum and even significantly inappropriate decisions. For example, so-called 'dog' businesses might have positive relationships with others, and to abandon them, as this 'model' suggests, could have adverse consequences for businesses and products at present in more attractive quadrants.

In general, the analysis rests on the assumption that products have a life cycle, of which, in particular, the 'mature' stage is of sufficient duration to enable the company to reap the benefits of its previous investment in what are termed 'cash cows'. The industry may however witness the introduction of a new technology which might give a 'groin kick' to the technology of the 'star' come 'cash cow', and thereby severely undermine its market position. Finally, the emphasis on 'market share' (which acts as a surrogate measure of cumulative 'experience') can blinker decision-makers to such possibilities and perhaps further the dependence of a vulnerable industry, while rivals may leapfrog the firm by acquiring 'experience' through the purchase of plant and equipment embodying 'state-of-the-art' technology.

It is also clear that companies that persist in product markets that are experiencing declines in overall demand can reap above average returns, often significantly so (Harrigan 1980).

The use of market growth as one of the criteria has also been seriously questioned. As Wensley (1981) points out in the fourth article of Part Three, the model is based on the premise that growth markets are more attractive, yet

. . . the current limited state of empirical knowledge about the costs and benefits of investing in market share shifts does not support the contention that, on average, the payoff is better from investing cash in gaining market share in rapid growth markets.

'Dynamic' markets may be extremely risky, particularly those experiencing rapid rates of technological change (Littler and Leverick, 1994). Moreover, markets which are identified as 'growth' also tend to attract other participants on to the bandwagon. Competition can often be intense, especially so if the original generally favourable forecasts of the market's prospects are not realized.

The Directional Policy Matrix summarized by Robinson *et al.* (1978), in the fifth and last article of Part Three employs a much more multidimensional approach. For example, market growth is part of a composite indicator termed 'market attractiveness', while 'relative market share' is a component of a more comprehensive indicator of competitive position. It might be a useful means of representing an organization's portfolio of business/product activities, so that asymmetries can be clearly detected. It does, however, lead to unsurprising and limited conclusions.

Are, however, the qualities and vulnerabilities of an organization so clearly and unambiguously obvious? Would different individuals or groups of managers undertaking such analyses of an organization independently arrive at similar conclusions? Is there some form of objective space inside which individual perceptions, prejudices and political ambitions are abandoned? Moreover, there is clear evidence that organizations develop their own culture which can in itself define the manner in which, for instance, general intelligence, external events and such like are perceived and interpreted. Unfortunate downturns in profitability can be viewed as temporary blips; the maintenance of existing strategies can be rationalized in terms of a 'strategic recipe' that has proved itself successful in the past; unpalatable events may be disregarded; and where there is continued underperformance the response may be based on incremental alterations to an existing formula (Johnson, 1988) until the inappropriateness of this becomes so stark that more dramatic changes in strategy are hurriedly imposed on the organization.

References

Harrigan, K.R. (1980), *Strategies for Declining Businesses*, Lexington Books, Lexington.

Hedley, B. (1977), 'Strategy and the "Business Portfolio" ', *Long Range Planning*, Vol. 10, February, 9-15.

Johnson, G. (1988) 'Rethinking Incrementalism', *Strategic Management Journal*, Vol. 9, No. 1, Jan-Feb, 75-91.

Littler, D.A. and Leverick, F. (1994), 'Marketing Planning in New Technology Sectors', in Saunders J. (ed.) *The Marketing Initiative*, Prentice Hall, Englewood Cliffs, NH.

Littler, D.A. *et al*, (1993), 'Collaboration in New Technology Based Product Markets', *Technology Analysis and Strategic Management*, Vol. 5, No. 3, 211-233.

Prahalad, C.K. and Hamel, G. (1990), 'The Core Competence of the Corporation', *Harvard Business Review*, May/June, 79-91.

Robinson, S.J.Q., Hichens, R.E. and Wade, D.P. (1978), 'The Directional Policy Matrix – Tool for Strategic Planning', *Long Range Planning*, Vol. 11, June, 8-15.

Shetty, Y.K. (1993), 'Aiming High: Competitive Benchmarking for Superior Performance', *Long Range Planning*, 26, No. 1, 39-44.

Wensley, R. (1981), 'Strategic Marketing: Betas, Boxes, or Basics', *Journal of Marketing* Vol. 45, Summer, 173-182.

9 Aiming high: competitive benchmarking for superior performance

Y. K. Shetty

In competitive benchmarking a firm's performance is measured against that of 'best-in-class companies' to determine how to achieve performance levels. Business functions are analysed as processes which produce a product or customer service, and benchmarking can be applied to strategy, operations or management support functions. Customers are the primary source for market and competitive intelligence. Benchmarking should be a continuous process and should aim not just to match but to beat the competition. The article describes the process at Xerox Corporation.

Corporate America faces more competition in global markets and often fails to meet the challenge, as is evident in trade deficits, slow productivity growth, stagnant real wages, and declining share of world markets, even for high technology products. Many firms' declining competitiveness is reflected in decreasing market shares and poorer business performance.

To address this challenge, many major US corporations have launched a variety of initiatives to improve their strategic and operational performance. One such strategic management technique is 'benchmarking'.[1] This paper discusses the evolution of benchmarking and emphasizes process, potentials, and limitations of the technique.

The concept

Forms of benchmarking have been employed for many years. Walter Chrysler used to tear apart a new model of Oldsmobile to determine what went into the car, how much it cost, and how it was made, an early example of 'reverse engineering'. This information helped Chrysler understand his competitors. Many companies employ this benchmarking in marketing, production, and research and development, either formally or informally. Financial performance is regularly benchmarked against the competitors and the industry. However, benchmarking techniques have been refined and applied to a wider range of products, practices and performance. Xerox is reputed to be the first company to systematically implement company-wide benchmarking. Japanese companies have long been recognized for their utilization of information about competitors' products, which they used to identify American companies' weaknesses and to achieve formidable positions in industries ranging from steel, automobiles, semiconductors and consumer electronics.[2] More American companies are following in their footsteps, including Ford, Eastman Kodak, GTE, General Motors, Motorola, AT & T, Du Pont, Corning, and NYNEX.[3]

Benchmarking is 'the continuous process of measuring products, services and practices against the toughest competitors or those companies recognized as industry leaders'.[4] Benchmarking must be practised continuously to identify the best industry practices. The products, services, practices and performance, both of the company and its competitors are evaluated to identify weaknesses and strengths. A firm's performance is measured against that of best-in-class companies to determine how to achieve those performance levels. Information is used to establish company goals and strategies. Benchmarking can be applied to virtually any or all areas of organizations, manufacturing and marketing as well as support functions including human resources, accounting and management information systems. Most business functions are analysed as processes, which produce a product, whether the product is a good, a process, or a service. The technique reveals the best industry practices and how these practices are employed. The best practices of the industry need not always involve direct competitors. Non-competitors can provide information about the best practices in an industry.

Striving for superiority

Benchmarking involves more than simple emulation; it is a mechanism to search for best practices to improve strategic and operational performance. Emulation will not always be successful because firms do not have the same resources, technological expertise, distinctive skills and corporate culture. Furthermore, emulation may help a company meet competitors' performance, but it is unlikely to reveal practices to beat them. Benchmarking provides only one important source of data. An official with General Motors once summed up the car-marker's strategy: 'It was not necessary to lead in technical design or run the risk of untried experiments, provided that our cars were at least equal in design to the best of our competitors.'[5] GM's reactive competitive strategy failed. Japanese car manufacturers use the benchmarking data in a proactive manner. They study their competition and also constantly determine what makes people buy cars and use the information to develop innovative products. Mazda Chairman Yamamoto calls this 'Kansei engineering', which he defines as 'absolute awareness of both reason and emotion'. Using benchmarking only for emulation will result in endless games of strategic leap-frog. Successful firms use benchmarking to be creative, not reactive. These companies learn what competitors are doing but also formulate a vision of what customers want, a critical factor in the formulation of a competitive strategy. Clearly both perspectives are needed.[6] Information on customer needs coupled with industry best practices would enhance the ability of the firm to respond to market conditions.

Motives

Chinese General Sun Tzu wrote, 'If you know your enemy and know yourself, you need not fear the result of a hundred battles.' This aphorism also applies to the business world where firms battle for market leadership against competitors, both domestic and global. To gain a superior competitive position, US companies must reduce costs, improve productivity, enhance quality, provide better customer service, and become more innovative. Developing new products, introducing new technologies and more effective marketing strategies are all essential components of a successful competitive strategy. Benchmarking, if properly implemented, can identify competitors' strategies, strengths and weaknesses, determine the key factors of success and utilize this information to surpass the competition. The development of innovative business strategies will help a firm surpass the best in class.

Types of benchmarking

There are three basic types of benchmarking: (1) strategic benchmarking, (2) operational benchmarking, and (3) management benchmarking.[7] *Strategic benchmarking* involves the comparison of different business strategies to identify key elements in a successful strategy. *Operational benchmarking* focuses on relative cost position or ways to increase product differentiation. The functional areas to be benchmarked depend on the function analysed. For engineering functions, analysis may concern design efficiency. Manufacturing, distribution and sales operation may focus on cost effectiveness. Nevertheless, operational benchmarking generally involves one or both of two variables: competitive cost and competitive differentiation. *Management benchmarking* involves an analysis of support functions. Virtually any support function can be benchmarked, involving human resource management, market planning, management information systems, logistics and order processing.

The process

Benchmarking is comprised of five basic steps: (1) identification of the function to be benchmarked, (2) selection of the superior performers, (3) collection and analysis of data, (4) establishing performance goals, and (5) implementing plans, and monitoring results.[8]

Identify the function to be benchmarked

Functions that can be benchmarked include unit cost, inventory turns, service calls, customer satisfaction, or any other product of a particular function. Every function of the business delivers some 'product', either a physical good, an order or a service. Benchmarking can be applied to all these products. Xerox initiated benchmarking in its manufacturing operations and examined unit manufacturing costs.[9]

Selected product features and operating capabilities were compared against those of competition, called product quality and feature comparisons. Xerox then looked at competitors' processes and compared transportation, warehousing and inventory management with those of the competition. Xerox found that managers initially tended to concentrate on comparative costs. As managers became more familiar with benchmarking, they emphasized practices, processes, and methods factors which determine whether the benchmark costs can be achieved. The experiences of Xerox and other companies suggest that practically all business functions can be benchmarked. In general, activities important in providing a competitive advantage should be selected. For example, a company interested in production costs should benchmark activities that represent a significant or growing proportion of cost. Methods such as Porter's value chain analysis can be adapted to help to identify key activities.[10]

Select the superior performers

The competitor or the industry leaders (business-to-business, direct product or service competitors) are certainly prime candidates to benchmark, although benchmarking can also be conducted against leadership companies or organizations regardless of industry. For example, when Xerox Business Systems' Logistic and Distribution function sought ways to further increase productivity, it benchmarked L.L. Bean, the catalogue sales company known for its effective and efficient warehousing and distribution. It also used other non-competitors to benchmark collection procedures and automated inventory control. In general, firms should be identified that best perform the benchmarked functions.

Data collection and analysis

There are many ways to collect data on competitors.[11] Identifying sources of information about rival firms or industry leaders can be a formidable task.

Fortunately, many managers will find they already have considerable amounts of information. Company employees are an excellent source of competitor intelligence through their professional and personal associations. Customers can provide information about competitors' products, service, pricing, and other attributes. According to several studies, customers are the primary source for market and competitor intelligence.[12] Suppliers and distributors are also useful sources. Newspapers, trade journals, magazines, government publications, corporate annual reports, company publications, consultants and presentations at professional meetings can also provide valuable information.

Xerox, for example, used public sources, consultants, personal contacts with leading firms, the insights of company employers and surveys conducted by students of graduate business schools. It also sent a team of employees to L.L. Bean's operations. Companies must select that method or combination of methods which best meet their needs.

Analysis should be based on a full understanding of the company's current processes as well as those of the benchmarked firms. The data should focus on the processes and practices rather than just the results. Comparing company functions against those of firms that perform the function best will identify any performance gap. If the analysis shows that the company performs better than the benchmarked firm, the goal will be to identify ways to sustain that superiority.

Set performance goals Establishing operational goals for improvement involves careful planning to incorporate new processes and practices. Findings must be clearly communicated to all organizational levels. Allow sufficient time for employees to evaluate benchmark findings and to agree on the performance levels and the practices and processes used to reach these goals. Performance goals and the selection of best practices must be incorporated into functional, business and operating plans. Performance goals should be designed to surpass the best-in-class.

Implementation and measurement The benchmarking should be viewed as a means to improve performance to gain superiority. Implementation should involve periodic measurement and assessment of attempts to reach stated goals. Take corrective action if performance does not meet goals. To incorporate changes in the competitive environment, there must also be a built-in provision for recalibration and to update customers' perceptions. Such a proactive strategy balances the focus on competitors and customers, reducing the risk of selective attention and simplification. Progress toward goals must be reported to encourage feedback needed to help implement the plan. Additionally, this feedback also helps establish new performance targets.

The process shown in Figure 1 is deceptively simple. Benchmarking requires several iterations and is a judgemental process. It may be difficult to identify functions and firms to be benchmarked until some preliminary studies have been made. Note the feedback loops to provide data for setting new performance goals.

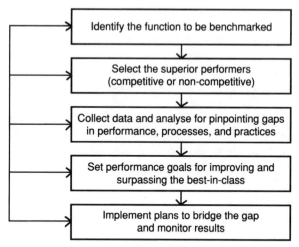

Figure 1   *Process of benchmarking*

Benchmarking in practice

In 1979, Xerox, which dominated the market for high technology copying machines, found that its market share had shrunk from 49 per cent to 22 per cent within a few years, due largely to high-quality, lower priced Japanese copiers. Top managers were determined to meet this challenge and initiated several ambitious quality and productivity programmes, one of which was competitive benchmarking. Xerox sought superiority in quality and cost. It first conducted comprehensive surveys to monitor customer satisfaction and compare customers' reactions to products. Product quality, services, and practices of Xerox were compared to those of the leading firms. Xerox employees toured Japanese factories and R&D facilities and reverse engineered competitors' products. Xerox then determined if and why their competitors' products were superior, and how these differences might be corrected. The results convinced Xerox that many changes from product design to sales, service and employee involvement were needed. Xerox set performance goals for these areas and implemented plans to achieve these goals.

Xerox reduced manufacturing costs by 50 per cent, reduced product development cycles by 25 per cent, and increased revenue per employee by 20 per cent. Xerox suppliers went from a 92 per cent defect-free rate to a 99.95 per cent defect-free rate. Xerox also started to regain market shares. An industry source subsequently ranked Xerox first in reliability and quality in four out of six categories of copiers and duplicators. The results prompted top management to adopt benchmarking as a corporate-wide effort and directed all units and cost centres to implement the procedure. The variety of firms used for benchmarking, various products and processes is shown in Figure 2. At the 1983 annual meeting of shareholders, Xerox President David Kearns announced that the firm's leading priority was to achieve leadership in the marketplace.

Xerox achieved impressive results and received the prestigious Malcolm Baldridge National Quality Award in 1989, which is equivalent to one of Japan's greatest honours, the Deming Prize. Xerox strongly believes that competitor benchmarking and employee involvement are the key to achieving quality and competitive success. Xerox now requires that strategic and operational plans include benchmarking analyses.

Value of benchmarking

Benchmarking helps companies strive for superiority and offers many tangible and intangible benefits.[13] It helps identify and compare elements of competitors' strategies, many of which may contain invaluable information for assessing the competition. The process also incorporates the best practices from an industry to improve internal processes and to establish performance targets. Traditionally, firms evaluate the performance of an organizational unit by comparing it with other units in the company. This comparison often reinforces complacency. Benchmarking incorporates market and competitive forces in goal-setting. Better knowledge of competitors' capabilities and of the reasons underlying superiority will identify alternative sources of competitive advantage. Benchmarking firms outside the industry identify the best practices and can incorporate technological advances that are not recognized in an industry, e.g., bar coding, which originated in the grocery industry but has since been applied in many industries. Benchmarking can also elucidate a competitor's interpretation of customer requirements and detect deficiencies in a company's interpretation of customer requirements. Findings can stimulate and motivate employees to become 'the best of the best' in the industry.

Benchmarking legitimizes a company's goals by linking them with external markets. It is a proactive way to effect change. It establishes standards for customer requirements and encourages employees to think competitively. It often increases employees' awareness of company costs and performance in products and services. The process encourages an organization to look outside the firm for solutions to a problem and to compare performance against other firms, thus fostering competitive self-renewal.

Figure 2.   Companies benchmarked by Xerox – products, processes, and practices

Areas of benchmarking	*Benchmark companies*
Manufacturing Operations Quality Management	Fuji-Xerox Toyota Komatsu
Billing and Collection	American Express
Research and Product Development	American Telephone and Telegraph Hewlett-Packard
Automated Inventory Control	American Hospital Supply
Distribution	L.L. Bean Inc. Hershey Foods Mary Kay Cosmetics
Employee Suggestions	Milliken Carpet
Factory Floor Layout	Ford Motor Company Cummins Engine
Marketing Participate Management Employee Involvement	Proctor and Gamble
Quality Improvement	Florida Power and Light
Strategy Implementation	Texas Instruments
Computer Operations	Deere and Company

Source: Company documents.

Limitations

Benchmarking has limitations. If employed simply to meet the competitor's performance, it will not lead to superiority and it may discourage action by innovative employees. It can be difficult to obtain useful information about competitors. Competitors may be uncooperative and some firms may be tempted to resort to questionable practices. Gathering competitive intelligence requires considerable time, effort, and money. Even though service operations can be broken down into their components to estimate costs, it is more difficult to benchmark service operations than to benchmark products. Services often involve skills and timeliness factors that are difficult to quantify. Benchmarking used simply to emulate competitors will result in only a short-lived competitive advantage. Further, there can be ethical and legal questions about some 'intelligence' activities, such as paying a competitor's employees for information, stealing company plans, and recording conversations, but these issues are beyond the scope of this article.[14]

The major limitations primarily concern the difficulties of conceiving and implementing a viable programme. Companies should have reasonable expectations. For example, coupling benchmark studies with customers' expectations will lead to superior products and services. It may be more feasible to study non-competitors, who may be more willing to share information on a quid pro quo basis, particularly when both firms perceive that the study is open and beneficial.[15] Professionals in non-competing firms are often eager to share more information. Xerox also found that many competing firms are willing to share information on a quid pro quo basis.

It is important to determine how much resources will be devoted to the process. Xerox and Ford spent millions of dollars while other companies have benefited from more limited efforts. Firms can derive substantial benefits from analysing their own operations and the 'best-in-class' firms, so failing to collect all desired data will not nullify the value of such a study. Further, the costs of benchmark studies will be less of an issue as companies become more knowledgeable about the process. Companies are developing guidelines to discourage unethical and questionable practices associated with intelligence gathering. Reasonable attempts to gather information are portrayed positively in the business press.[16]

Conclusion

Intense international competition and declining profitability are encouraging US firms to improve their competitive performance. One of the long-term initiatives that they employ to improve performance is competitive benchmarking. Benchmarking is the continuous measuring of a firm's products, services, processes, and practices against those of the best competitors or those companies recognized as industry leaders. It helps managers compare performance function by function, and to determine why performance differs, and to establish performance goals to become the best in the industry.

Maximum and sustainable benefits require the integration of benchmarking with the setting of the objectives, operating plans and overall management. Increasing evidence suggests that the best measure of performance involves a consideration of customers and competitive firms. Benchmarking can help companies accurately measure market requirements. By forcing companies to measure their performance against that of the best companies to identify strategies to improve performance, benchmarking shows considerable potential for improving competitive performance.

Notes and references

1 Lawrence S, Pryor, 'Benchmarking: A self-improvement strategy', *The Journal of Business Strategy*, 10 (6), 28-32 (1989).
2 Allen K, Engel, 'Number one in competitor intelligence', *Across the Board*, 24 (12) 43-47 (1987).
3 Lawrence S. Pryor, *op. cit.* p. 29.
4 David T. Kearns, 'Leadership through quality', *Academy of Management Executive*, 4 (2), 87 (1990). See also C. Kennedy, 'Xerox charts a new strategic direction', *Long Range Planning*, 22 (1).
5 'Create and service'. *The Economist*, December 1, 1990, p. 77.
6 George S. Day and Robin Wensley, 'Assessing advantage: A framework for diagnosing competitive superiority', *Journal of Marketing*, 52, 1-20, April (1988).
7 Lawrence S. Pryor, *op. cit.* p. 29. For further examples of the scope of applications, see G. Press, 'Assessing competitors' business philosophies', *Long Range Planning*, October (1990) and J. Murphy, 'Assessing the value of brands', *Long Range Planning*, June (1990).
8 Adapted from Robert Camp, 'Benchmarking: The search for industry best practices that lead to superior performance', *Quality Progress*, 22 (2), 70-75, February (1989).
9 The discussion of Xerox Corporation is based on the following sources: 'Competitive Benchmarking: What Is It and What It Can Do For You', Stamford, Con. Xerox Corporation, May 1987; Frances Gaither Tucker, Seymor M. Zivan and Robert C. Camp, 'How to measure yourself against the best', *Harvard Business Review*, 67 (1), 70-75, January-February (1987).
10 For a fuller discussion of the Value Chain, see Michael E. Porter, *Competitive Advantage*, The Free Press, New York, pp. 98-99 (1985).
11 David B. Montgomery and Charles B. Weinberg, 'Toward strategic intelligence systems', *Journal of Marketing* 43, 46 Fall (1979); Michael Porter, *Competitive Strategy*, The Free Press, New York, pp. 71-74.
12 Benjamin Gilad and Tamar Gilad, *Business Intelligence Systems*, American Management Associations, New York, p. 95 (1988).
13 Lawrence S. Pryor, *op. cit.* pp. 28-32; 'Competitive Benchmarking: The Path to Leadership', Xerox Corporation, Stamford, Con. (1986).
14 See J.E. Prescott (ed.) 'Advances in Competitive Intelligence' (1989) and 'Competitive Intelligence Review', Society of Competitive Intelligence Professionals, Washington, D.C.
15 Frances Gaither Tucker, Seymor M. Zivan and Robert C. Camp, 'How to Measure Yourself Against the Best', pp. 70-75; Robert C. Camp, *Benchmarking*, ASQC Quality Press, Milwaukee, Wisconsin (1989).
16 Larry L. Wall, 'What the competitor is doing: You need to know', *Harvard Business Review*, 52 (6), 1-12, November-December (1974); Lawrence S. Pryor, *op. cit.* p. 31.

10 The core competence of the corporation

C. K. Prahalad and Gary Hamel

The most powerful way to prevail in global competition is still invisible to many companies. During the 1980s, top executives were judged on their ability to restructure, declutter, and delayer their corporations. In the 1990s, they'll be judged on their ability to identify, cultivate, and exploit the core competencies that make growth possible – indeed, they'll have to rethink the concept of the corporation itself.

Consider the last ten years of GTE and NEC. In the early 1980s, GTE was well positioned to become a major player in the evolving information technology industry. It was active in telecommunications. Its operations spanned a variety of businesses including telephones, switching and transmission systems, digital PABX, semiconductors, packet switching, satellites, defense systems, and lighting products. And GTE's Entertainment Products Group, which produced Sylvania color TVs, had a position in related display technologies. In 1980, GTE's sales were $9.98 billion, and net cash flow was $1.73 billion. NEC, in contrast, was much smaller, at $3.8 billion in sales. It had a comparable technological base and computer businesses, but it had no experience as an operating telecommunications company.

Yet look at the positions of GTE and NEC in 1988. GTE's 1988 sales were $16.46 billion, and NEC's sales were considerably higher at $21.89 billion. GTE has, in effect, become a telephone operating company with a position in defense and lighting products. GTE's other businesses are small in global terms. GTE has divested Sylvania TV and Telenet, put switching, transmission, and digital PABX into joint ventures, and closed down semiconductors. As a result, the international position of GTE has eroded. Non-U.S. revenue as a percent of total revenue dropped from 20% to 15% between 1980 and 1988.

NEC has emerged as the world leader in semiconductors and as a first-tier player in telecommunications products and computers. It has consolidated its position in mainframe computers. It has moved beyond public switching and transmission to include such lifestyle products as mobile telephones, facsimile machines, and laptop computers – bridging the gap betwen telecommunications and office automation. NEC is the only company in the world to be in the top five in revenue in telecommunications, semiconductors, and mainframes. Why did these two companies, starting with comparable business portfolios, perform so differently? Largely because NEC conceived of itself in terms of 'core competencies', and GTE did not.

Rethinking the corporation

Once, the diversified corporation could simply point its business units at particular end product markets and admonish them to become world leaders. But with market boundaries changing ever more quickly, targets are elusive and capture is at best temporary. A few companies have proven themselves adept at inventing new markets, quickly entering emerging markets, and dramatically shifting patterns of customer choice in established markets. These are the ones to emulate. The critical task for management is to create an organization capable of infusing products with irresistible functionality or, better yet, creating products that customers need but have not yet even imagined.

This is a deceptively difficult task. Ultimately, it requires radical change in the management of major companies. It means, first of all, that top managements of Western companies must assume responsibility for competitive decline. Everyone knows about high interest rates, Japanese protectionism, outdated antitrust laws, obstreperous unions, and impatient investors. What is harder to see, or harder to acknowledge, is how little added momentum companies actually get from political or macroeconomic 'relief'. Both the theory and practice of Western management have created a drag on our forward motion. It is the principles of management that are in need of reform.

NEC versus GTE, again, is instructive and only one of many such comparative cases we analyzed to understand the changing basis for global leadership. Early in the 1970s, NEC articulated a strategic intent to exploit the convergence of computing and communications, what it called 'C&C'.[1] Success, top management reckoned, would hinge on acquiring *competencies*, particularly in semiconductors. Management adopted an appropriate 'strategic architecture', summarized by C&C, and then communicated its intent to the whole organization and the outside world during the mid-1970s.

NEC constituted a 'C&C Committee' of top managers to oversee the development of core products and core competencies. NEC put in place coordination groups and committees that cut across the interests of individual businesses. Consistent with its strategic architecture, NEC shifted enormous resources to strengthen its position in components and central processors. By using collaborative arrangements to multiply internal resources, NEC was able to accumulate a broad array of core competencies.

NEC carefully identified three interrelated streams of technological and market evolution. Top management determined that computing would evolve from large mainframes to distributed processing, components from simple Ics to VLSI, and communications from mechanical cross-bar exchange to complex digital systems we now call ISDN. As things evolved further, NEC reasoned, the computing, communications, and components businesses would so overlap that it would be very hard to distinguish among them, and that there would be enormous opportunities for any company that had built the competencies needed to serve all three markets.

NEC top management determined that semiconductors would be the company's most important 'core product'. It entered into myriad strategic alliances – over 100 as of 1987 – aimed at building competencies rapidly and at low cost. In mainframe computers, its most noted relationship was with Honeywell and Bull. Almost all the collaborative arrangements in the semiconductor-component field were oriented toward technology access. As they entered collaborative arrangements, NEC's operating managers understood the rationale for these alliances and the goal of internalizing partner skills. NEC's director of research summed up its competence acquisition during the 1970s and 1980s this way: 'From an investment standpoint, it was much quicker and cheaper to use foreign technology. There wasn't a need for us to develop new ideas.'

No such clarity of strategic intent and strategic architecture appeared to exist at GTE. Although senior executives discussed the implications of the evolving information technology industry, no commonly accepted view of which competencies would be required to compete in that industry were communicated widely. While significant staff work was done to identify key technologies, senior line managers continued to act as if they were managing independent business units. Decentralization made it difficult to focus on core competencies. Instead, individual businesses became increasingly dependent on outsiders for critical skills, and collaboration became a route to staged exits. Today, with a new management team in place, GTE has repositioned itself to apply its competencies to emerging markets in telecommunications service.

The roots of competitive advantage

The distinction we observed in the way NEC and GTE conceived of themselves – a portfolio of competencies versus a portfolio of businesses – was repeated across many industries. From 1980 to 1988, Canon grew by 264%, Honda by 200%. Compare that with Xerox and Chrysler. And if Western managers were once anxious about the low cost and high quality of Japanese imports, they are now overwhelmed by the pace at which Japanese rivals are inventing new markets, creating new products, and enhancing them. Canon has given us personal copiers; Honda has moved from motorcycles to four-wheel off-road buggies. Sony developed the 8 mm camcorder, Yamaha, a digital piano. Komatsu developed an underwater remote-controlled bulldozer, while Casio's latest gambit is a small-screen color LCD television. Who would have anticipated the evolution of these vanguard markets?

In more established markets, the Japanese challenge has been just as disquieting, Japanese companies are generating a blizzard of features and functional enhancements that bring technological sophistication to everyday products. Japanese car producers have been pioneering four-wheel steering, four-valve-per-cylinder engines, in-car navigation systems, and sophisticated electronic engine-management systems. On the strength of its product features, Canon is now a player in facsimile transmission machines, desktop laser printers, even semiconductor manufacturing equipment.

In the short run, a company's competitiveness derives from the price/performance attributes of current products. But the survivors of the first wave of global competition, Western and Japanese alike, are all converging on similar and formidable standards for product cost and quality – minimum hurdles for continued competition, but less and less important as sources of differential advantage. In the long run, competitiveness derives from an ability to build, at lower cost and more speedily than competitors, the core competencies that spawn unanticipated products. The real sources of advantage are to be found in management's ability to consolidate corporate-wide technologies and production skills into competencies that empower individual businesses to adapt quickly to changing opportunities.

Senior executives who claim that they cannot build core competencies either because they feel the autonomy of business units is sacrosanct or because their feet are held to the quarterly budget fire should think again. The problem in many Western companies is not that their senior executives are any less capable than those in Japan nor that Japanese companies possess greater technical capabilities. Instead, it is their adherence to a concept of the corporation that unnecessarily limits the ability of individual businesses to fully exploit the deep reservoir of technological capability that many American and European companies possess.

The diversified corporation is a large tree. The trunk and major limbs are core products, the smaller branches are business units; the leaves, flowers, and fruit are end products. The root system that provides nourishment, sustenance, and stability is the core competence. You can miss the strength of competitors by looking only at their end products, in the same way you miss the strength of a tree if you look only at its leaves (Figure 1).

Core competencies are the collective learning in the organization, especially how to coordinate diverse production skills and integrate multiple streams of technologies. Consider Sony's capacity to miniaturize or Philips's optical-media expertise. The theoretical knowledge to put a radio on a chip does not in itself assure a company the skill to produce a miniature radio no bigger than a business card. To bring off this feat, Casio must harmonize know-how in miniaturization, microprocessor design, material science, and ultrathin precision casing – the same skills it applies in its miniature card calculators, pocket TVs, and digital watches.

Competencies: The roots of competitivness

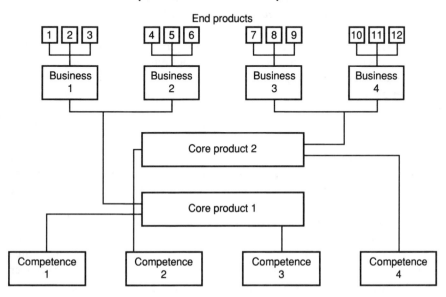

Figure 1 *The corporation, like a tree, grows from its roots. Core products are nourished by competencies and engender business units, whose fruit are end products*

If core competence is about harmonizing streams of technology, it is also about the organization of work and the delivery of value. Among Sony's competencies is miniaturization. To bring miniaturization to its products, Sony must ensure that technologists, engineers, and marketers have a shared understanding of customer needs and of technological possibilities. The force of core competence is felt as decisively in services as in manufacturing. Citicorp was ahead of others investing in an operating system that allowed it to participate in world markets 24 hours a day. Its competence in systems has provided the company the means to differentiate itself from many financial service institutions.

Core competence is communication, involvement, and a deep commitment to working across organizational boundaries. It involves many levels of people and all functions. World-class research in, for example, lasers or ceramics can take place in corporate laboratories without having an impact on any of the businesses of the company. The skills that together constitute core competence must coalesce around individuals whose efforts are not so narrowly focused that they cannot recognize the opportunities for blending their functional expertise with those of others in new and interesting ways.

Core competence does not diminish with use. Unlike physical assets, which do deteriorate over time, competencies are enhanced as they are applied and shared. But competencies still need to be nurtured and protected; knowledge fades if it is not used. Competencies are the glue that binds existing businesses. They are also the engine for new business development. Patterns of diversification and market entry may be guided by them, not just by the attractiveness of markets.

Consider 3M's competence with sticky tape. In dreaming up businesses as diverse as 'Post-it' notes, magnetic tape, photographic film, pressure-sensitive tapes, and coated abrasives, the company has brought to bear widely shared competencies in substrates, coatings, and adhesives and devised various ways to combine them. Indeed, 3M has invested consistently in them. What seems to be an extremely diversified portfolio of businesses belies a few shared core competencies.

In contrast, there are major companies that have had the potential to build core competencies but failed to do so because top management was unable to conceive of the company as anything other than a collection of discrete businesses. GE sold much of its consumer electronics business to Thomson of France, arguing that it was becoming increasingly difficult to maintain its competitiveness in this sector. That was undoubtedly so, but it is ironic that it sold several key businesses to competitors who were already competence leaders – Black & Decker in small electrical motors, and Thomson, which was eager to build its competence in microelectronics and had learned from the Japanese that a position in consumer electronics was vital to this challenge.

Management trapped in the strategic business unit (SBU) mind-set almost inevitably finds its individual businesses dependent on external sources for critical components, such as motors or compressors. But these are not just components. They are core products that contribute to the competitiveness of a wide range of end products. They are the physical embodiments of core competencies.

How not to think of competence

Since companies are in a race to build the competencies that determine global leadership, successful companies have stopped imagining themselves as bundles of businesses making products. Canon, Honda, Casio, or NEC may seem to preside over portfolios of businesses unrelated in terms of customers, distribution channels, and merchandising strategy. Indeed, they have portfolios that may seem idiosyncratic at times: NEC is the only global company to be among leaders in computing, telecommunications, and semiconductors *and* to have a thriving consumer electronics business.

But looks are deceiving. In NEC, digital technology, especially VLSI and systems integration skills, is fundamental. In the core competencies underlying them, disparate businesses become coherent. It is Honda's core competence in engines and power trains that gives it a distinctive advantage in car, motorcycle, lawn mower and generator businesses. Canon's core competencies in optics, imaging, and microprocessor controls have enabled it to enter, even dominate, markets as seemingly diverse as copiers, laser printers, cameras, and image scanners. Philips worked for more than 15 years to perfect its optical-media (laser disc) competence, as did JVC in building a leading position in video recording. Other examples of core competencies might include mechantronics (the ability to marry mechanical and electronic engineering), video displays, bioengineering, and microelectronics. In the early stages of its competence building, Philips could not have imagined all the products that would be spawned by its optical-media competence, nor could JVC have anticipated miniature camcorders when it first began exploring videotape technologies.

Unlike the battle for global brand dominance, which is visible in the world's broadcast and print media and is aimed at building global 'share of mind', the battle to build world-class competencies is invisible to people who aren't deliberately looking for it. Top management often tracks the cost and quality of competitors' products, yet how many managers untangle the web of alliances their Japanese competitors have constructed to acquire competencies at low cost? In how many Western boardrooms is there an explicit, shared understanding of the competencies the company must build for world leadership? Indeed, how many senior executives discuss the crucial distinction between competitive strategy at the level of a business and competitive strategy at the level of an entire company?

Let us be clear. Cultivating core competence does *not* mean outspending rivals on research and development. In 1983, when Canon surpassed Xerox in worldwide unit market share in the copier business, its R&D budget in reprographics was but a small fraction of Xerox's. Over the past 20 years, NEC has spent less on R&D as a percentage of sales than almost all of its American and European competitors.

Nor does core competence mean shared costs, as when two or more SBUs use a common facility – a plant, service facility, or sales force – or share a common component. The gains of sharing may be substantial, but the search for shared costs is typically a post hoc effort to rationalize production across existing businesses, not a premeditated effort to build the competencies out of which the businesses themselves grow.

Building core competencies is more ambitious and different than integrating vertically, moreover. Managers deciding whether to make or buy will start with end products and look upstream to the efficiencies of the supply chain and downstream toward distribution and customers. They do not take inventory of skills and look forward to applying them in nontraditional ways. (Of course, decisions about competencies *do* provide a logic for vertical integration. Canon is not particularly integrated in its copier business, except in those aspects of the vertical chain that support the competencies it regards as critical.)

Identifying core competencies – and losing them

At least three tests can be applied to identify core competencies in a company. First, a core competence provides potential access to a wide variety of markets. Competence in display systems, for example, enables a company to participate in such diverse businesses as calculators, miniature TV sets, monitors for laptop computers, and automotive dashboards – which is why Casio's entry into the hand-held TV market was predictable. Second, a core competence should make a significant contribution to the perceived customer benefits of the end product. Clearly, Honda's engine expertise fills this bill.

Finally, a core competence should be difficult for competitors to imitate. And it *will* be difficult if it is a complex harmonization of individual technologies and production skills. A rival might acquire some of the technologies that comprise the core competence, but it will find it more difficult to duplicate the more or less comprehensive pattern of internal coordination and learning. JVC's decision in the early 1960s to pursue the development of a videotape competence passed the three tests outlined here. RCA's decision in the late 1970s to develop a stylus-based video turntable system did not.

Few companies are likely to build world leadership in more than five or six fundamental competencies. A company that compiles a list of 20 to 30 capabilities has probably not produced a list of core competencies. Still, it is probably a good discipline to generate a list of this sort and to see aggregate capabilities as building blocks. This tends to prompt the search for licensing deals and alliances through which the company may acquire, at low cost, the missing pieces.

Most Western companies hardly think about competitiveness in these terms at all. It is time to take a tough-minded look at the risks they are running. Companies that judge competitiveness, their own and their competitors', primarily in terms of the price/performance of end products are courting the erosion of core competencies – or making too little effort to enhance them. The embedded skills that give rise to the next generation of competitive products cannot be 'rented in' by outsourcing and OEM-supply relationships. In our view, too many companies have unwittingly surrendered core competencies when they cut internal investment in what they mistakenly thought were just 'cost centers' in favor of outside suppliers.

Consider Chrysler. Unlike Honda, it has tended to view engines and power trains as simply one more component. Chrysler is becoming increasingly dependent on Mitsubishi and Hyundai: between 1985 and 1987, the number of outsourced engines went from 252,000 to 382,000. It is difficult to imagine Honda yielding manufacturing responsibility, much less design, of so critical a part of a car's function to an outside company – which is why Honda has made such an enormous commitment to Formula One auto racing. Honda has been able to pool its engine-related technologies; it has parlayed these into a corporatewide competency from which it develops world-beating products, despite R&D budgets smaller than those of GM and Toyota.

Of course, it is perfectly possible for a company to have a competitive product line up but be a laggard in developing core competencies – at least for a while. If a company wanted to enter the copier business today, it would find a dozen Japanese companies more than willing to supply copiers on the basis of OEM private label. But when fundamental technologies changed or if its supplier decided to enter the market directly and become a competitor, that company's product line, along with all of its investments in marketing and distribution, could be vulnerable. Outsourcing can provide a shortcut to a more competitive product, but it typically contributes little to building the people-embodied skills that are needed to sustain product leadership.

Nor is it possible for a company to have an intelligent alliance or sourcing strategy if it has not made a choice about where it will build competence leadership. Clearly, Japanese companies have benefited from alliances. They've used them to learn from Western partners who were not fully committed to preserving core competencies of their own. As we've argued in these pages before, learning within an alliance takes a positive commitment of resources – travel, a pool of dedicated people, test-bed facilities, time to internalize and test what has been learned.[2] A company may not make this effort if it doesn't have clear goals for competence building.

Another way of losing is forgoing opportunities to establish competencies that are evolving in existing businesses. In the 1970s and 1980s, many American and European companies – like GE, Motorola, GTE, Thorn, and GEC – chose to exit the color television business, which they regarded as mature. If by 'mature' they meant that they had run out of new product ideas at precisely the moment global rivals had targeted the TV business for entry, then yes, the industry was mature. But it certainly wasn't mature in the sense that all opportunities to enhance and apply video-based competencies had been exhausted.

In ridding themselves of their television businesses, these companies failed to distinguish between divesting the business and destroying their video media-based competencies. They not only got out of the TV business but they also closed the door on a whole stream of future opportunities reliant on video-based competencies. The television industry, considered by many U.S. companies in the 1970s to be unattractive, is today the focus of a fierce public policy debate about the inability of U.S. corporations to benefit from the $20-billion-a-year opportunity that HDTV will represent in the mid- to late 1990s.

Ironically, the U.S. government is being asked to fund a massive research project – in effect, to compensate U.S. companies for their failure to preserve critical core competencies when they had the chance.

In contrast, one can see a company like Sony reducing its emphasis on VCRs (where it has not been very successful and where Korean companies now threaten), without reducing its commitment to video-related competencies. Sony's Betamax led to a debacle. But it emerged with its videotape recording competencies intact and is currently challenging Matsushita in the 8 mm camcorder market.

There are two clear lessons here. First, the costs of losing a core competence can be only partly calculated in advance. The baby may be thrown out with the bath water in divestment decisions. Second, since core competencies are built through a process of continuous improvement and enhancement that may span a decade or longer, a company that has failed to invest in core competence building will find it very difficult to enter an emerging market, unless, of course, it will be content simply to serve as a distribution channel.

American semiconductor companies like Motorola learned this painful lesson when they elected to forgo direct participation in the 256k generation of DRAM chips. Having skipped this round, Motorola, like most of its American competitors, needed a large infusion of technical help from Japanese partners to rejoin the battle in the 1-megabyte generation. When it comes to core competencies, it is difficult to get off the train, walk to the next station, and then reboard.

From core competencies to core products

The tangible link between identified core competencies and end products is what we call the core products – the physical embodiments of one or more core competencies. Honda's engines, for example, are core products, linchpins between design and development skills that ultimately lead to a proliferation of end products. Core products are the components or subassemblies that actually contribute to the value of the end products. Thinking in terms of core products forces a company to distinguish between the brand share it achieves in end product markets (for example, 40% of the U.S. refrigerator market) and the manufacturing share it achieves in any particular core product (for example, 5% of the world share of compressor output).

Canon is reputed to have an 84% world manufacturing share in desktop laser printer 'engines', even though its brand share in the laser printer business is minuscule. Similarly, Matsushita has a world manufacturing share of about 45% in key VCR components, far in excess of its brand share (Panasonic, JVC, and others) of 20%. And Matsushita has a commanding core product share in compressors worldwide, estimated at 40%, even though its brand share in both the air-conditioning and refrigerator businesses is quite small.

It is essential to make this distinction between core competencies, core products, and end products because global competition is played out by different rules and for different stakes at each level. To build or defend leadership over the long term, a corporation will probably be a winner at each level. At the level of core competence, the goal is to build world leadership in the design and development of a particular class of product functionality – be it compact data storage and retrieval, as with Philips's optical-media competence, or compactness and ease of use, as with Sony's micromotors and microprocessor controls.

To sustain leadership in their chosen core competence areas, these companies *seek to maximize their world manufacturing share in core products*. The manufacture of core products for a wide variety of external (and internal) customers yields the revenue and market feedback that, at least partly, determines the pace at which core competencies can be enhanced and extended. This thinking was behind JVC's decision in the mid-1970s to establish VCR supply relationships with leading national consumer electronics companies in Europe and the United States. In supplying Thomson, Thorn, and Telefunken (all independent companies at that time) as well as U.S. partners, JVC was able to gain the cash and the diversity of market experience that ultimately enabled it to outpace Philips and Sony. (Philips developed videotape competencies in parallel with JVC, but it failed to build a worldwide network of OEM relationships that would have allowed it to accelerate the refinement of its videotape competence through the sale of core products.)

JVC's success has not been lost on Korean companies like Goldstar, Sam Sung, Kia, and Daewoo, who are building core product leadership in areas as diverse as displays, semiconductors, and automotive engines through their OEM-supply contracts with Western companies. Their avowed goal is to capture investment initiative away from potential competitors, often U.S. companies. In doing so, they accelerate their competence-building efforts while 'hollowing out' their competitors. By focusing on competence and embedding it in core products, Asian competitors have built up advantages in component markets first and have then leveraged off their superior products to move downstream to build brand share. And they are not likely to remain the low-cost suppliers forever. As their reputation for brand leadership is consolidated, they may well gain price leadership. Honda has proven this with its Acura line, and other Japanese car makers are following suit.

Control over core products is critical for other reasons. A dominant position in core products allows a company to shape the evolution of applications and end markets. Such compact audio disc-related core products as data drives and lasers have enabled Sony and Philips to influence the evolution of the computer-peripheral business in optical-media storage. As a company multiplies the number of application arenas for its core products, it can consistently reduce the cost, time, and risk in new product development. In short, well-targeted core products can lead to economies of scale *and* scope.

The tyranny of the SBU

The new terms of competitive engagement cannot be understood using analytical tools devised to manage the diversified corporation of 20 years ago, when competition was primarily domestic (GE versus Westinghouse, General Motors versus Ford) and all the key players were speaking the language of the same business schools and consultancies. Old prescriptions have potentially toxic side effects. The need for new principles is most obvious in companies organized exclusively according to the logic of SBUs. The implications of the two alternate concepts of the corporation are summarized in Figure 2.

Two concepts of the corporation: SBU or core competence

	SBU	*Core competence*
Basis for competition	Competitiveness of today's products	Interfirm competition to build competencies
Corporate structure	Portfolio of businesses related in product-market terms	Portfolio of competencies, core products, and businesses
Status of the business unit	Autonomy is sacrosanct; the SBU 'owns' all resources other than cash	SBU is a potential reservoir of core competencies
Resource allocation	Discrete businesses are the unit of analysis; capital is allocated business by business	Businesses and competencies are the unit of analysis: top management allocates capital and talent
Value added of top management	Optimizing corporate returns through capital allocation trade-offs among businesses	Enunciating strategic architecture and building competencies to secure the future

Figure 2

Obviously, diversified corporations have a portfolio of products and a portfolio of businesses. But we believe in a view of the company as a portfolio of competencies as well. U.S. companies do not lack the technical resources to build competencies, but their top management often lacks the vision to build them and the administrative means for assembling resources spread across multiple businesses. A shift in commitment will inevitably influence patterns of diversification, skill deployment, resource allocation priorities, and approaches to alliances and outsourcing.

We have described the three different planes on which battles for global leadership are waged: core competence, core products, and end products. A corporation has to know whether it is winning or losing on each plane. By sheer weight of investment, a company might be able to beat its rivals to blue-sky technologies yet still lose the race to build core competence leadership. If a company is winning the race to build core competencies (as opposed to building leadership in a few technologies), it will almost certainly outpace rivals in new business development. If a company is winning the race to capture world manufacturing share in core products, it will probably outpace rivals in improving product features and the price/performance ratio.

Determining whether one is winning or losing end product battles is more difficult because measures of product market share do not necessarily reflect various companies' underlying competitiveness. Indeed, companies that attempt to build market share by relying on the competitiveness of others, rather than investing in core competencies and world core-product leadership, may be treading on quicksand. In the race for global brand dominance, companies like 3M, Black & Decker, Canon, Honda, NEC, and Citicorp have built global brand umbrellas by proliferating products out of their core competencies. This has allowed their individual businesses to build image, customer loyalty, and access to distribution channels.

When you think about this reconceptualization of the corporation, the primacy of the SBU – an organizational dogma for a generation – is now clearly an anachronism. Where the SBU is an article of faith, resistance to the seductions of decentralization can seem heretical. In many companies, the SBU prism means that only one plane of the global competitive battle, the battle to put competitive products on the shelf *today*, is visible to top management. What are the costs of this distortion?

Underinvestment in developing core competencies and core products   When the organization is conceived of as a multiplicity of SBUs, no single business may feel responsible for maintaining a viable position in core products nor be able to justify the investment required to build world leadership in some core competence. In the absence of a more comprehensive view imposed by corporate management, SBU managers will tend to underinvest. Recently, companies such as Kodak and Philips have recognized this as a potential problem and have begun searching for new organizational forms that will allow them to develop and manufacture core products for both internal and external customers.

SBU managers have traditionally conceived of competitors in the same way they've seen themselves. On the whole, they've failed to note the emphasis Asian competitors were placing on building leadership in core products or to understand the critical linkage between world manufacturing leadership and the ability to sustain development pace in core competence. They've failed to pursue OEM-supply opportunities or to look across their various product divisions in an attempt to identify opportunities for coordinated initiatives.

Imprisoned resources   As an SBU evolves, it often develops unique competencies. Typically, the people who embody this competence are seen as the sole property of the business in which they grew up. The manager of another SBU who asks to borrow talented people is likely to get a cold rebuff. SBU managers are not only unwilling to lend their competence carriers but they may actually hide talent to prevent its redeployment in the pursuit of new opportunities. This may be compared to residents of an underdeveloped country hiding most of their cash under their mattresses. The benefits of competencies, like the benefits of the money supply, depend on the velocity of their circulation as well as on the size of the stock the company holds.

Western companies have traditionally had an advantage in the stock of skills they possess. But have they been able to reconfigure them quickly to respond to new opportunities? Canon, NEC, and Honda have had a lesser stock of the people and technologies that compose core competencies but could move them much quicker from one business unit to another. Corporate R&D spending at Canon is not fully indicative of the size of Canon's core competence stock and tells the casual observer nothing about the velocity with which Canon is able to move core competencies to exploit opportunities.

When competencies become imprisoned, the people who carry the competencies do not get assigned to the most exciting opportunities, and their skills begin to atrophy. Only by fully leveraging core competencies can small companies like Canon afford to compete with industry giants like Xerox. How strange that SBU managers, who are perfectly willing to compete for cash in the capital budgeting process, are unwilling to compete for people – the company's most precious asset. We find it ironic that top management devotes so much attention to the capital budgeting process yet typically has no comparable mechanism for allocating the human skills that embody core competencies. Top managers are seldom able to look four or five levels down into the organization, identify the people who embody critical competencies, and move them across organizational boundaries.

Bounded innovation   If core competencies are not recognized, individual SBUs will pursue only those innovation opportunities that are close at hand – marginal product-line extensions or geographic expansions. Hybrid opportunities like fax machines, laptop computers, hand-held televisions, or portable music keyboards will emerge only when managers take off their SBU blinkers. Remember, Canon appeared to be in the camera business at the time it was preparing to become a world leader in copiers. Conceiving of the corporation in terms of core competencies widens the domain of innovation.

Developing strategic architecture

The fragmentation of core competencies becomes inevitable when a diversified company's information systems, patterns of communication, career paths, managerial rewards, and processes of strategy development do not transcend SBU lines. We believe that senior management should spend a significant amount of its time developing a corporatewide strategic architecture that establishes objectives for competence building. A strategic architecture is a road map of the future that identifies which core competencies to build and their constituent technologies.

By providing an impetus for learning from alliances and a focus for internal development efforts, a strategic architecture like NEC's C&C can dramatically reduce the investment needed to secure future market leadership. How can a company make partnerships intelligently without a clear understanding of the core competencies it is trying to build and those it is attempting to prevent from being unintentionally transferred?

Of course, all of this begs the question of what a strategic architecture should look like. The answer will be different for every company. But it is helpful to think again of that tree, of the corporation organized around core products and, ultimately, core competencies. To sink sufficiently strong roots, a company must answer some fundamental questions: How long could we preserve our competitiveness in this business if we did not control this particular core competence? How central is this core competence to perceived customer benefits? What future opportunities would be foreclosed if we were to lose this particular competence?

The architecture provides a logic for product and market diversification, moreover. An SBU manager would be asked: Does the new market opportunity add to the overall goal of becoming the best player in the world? Does it exploit it or add to the core competence? At Vickers, for example, diversification options have been judged in the context of becoming the best power and motion control company in the world (see Appendix 'Vickers learns the value of strategic architecture').

The strategic architecture should make resource allocation priorities transparent to the entire organization. It provides a template for allocation decisions by top management. It helps lower level managers understand the logic of allocation priorities and discliplines senior management to maintain consistency. In short, it yields a definition of the company and the markets it serves. 3M, Vickers, NEC, Canon, and Honda all qualify on this score. Honda *knew* it was exploiting what it had learned from motorcycles – how to make high-revving, smooth-running, lightweight engines – when it entered the car business. The task of creating a strategic architecture forces the organization to identify and commit to the technical and production linkages across SBUs that will provide a distinct competitive advantage.

It is consistency of resource allocation and the development of an administrative infrastructure appropriate to it that breathes life into a strategic architecture and creates a managerial culture, team-work, a capacity to change, and a willingness to share resources, to protect priorietary skills, and to think long term. That is also the reason the specific architecture cannot be copied easily or overnight by competitors. Strategic architecture is a tool for communicating with customers and other external constituents. It reveals the broad direction without giving away every step.

Redeploying to exploit competencies

If the company's core competencies are its critical resource and if top management must ensure that competence carriers are not held hostage by some particular business, then it follows that SBUs should bid for core competencies in the same way they bid for capital. We've made this point glancingly. It is important enough to consider more deeply.

Once top management (with the help of divisional and SBU managers) has identified overarching competencies, it must ask businesses to identify the projects and people closely connected with them. Corporate officers should direct an audit of the location, number, and quality of the people who embody competence.

This sends an important signal to middle management: core competencies are *corporate* resources and may be reallocated by corporate management. An individual business doesn't own anybody. SBUs are entitled to the services of individual employees so long as SBU management can demonstrate that the opportunity it is pursuing yields the highest possible pay-off on the investment in their skills. This message is further underlined if each year in the strategic planning or budgeting process, unit managers must justify their hold on the people who carry the company's core competencies.

Elements of Canon's core competence in optics are spread across businesses as diverse as cameras, copiers, and semiconductor lithographic equipment and are shown in Figure 3. When Canon identified an opportunity in digital laser printers, it gave SBU managers the right to raid other SBUs to pull together the required pool of talent. When Canon's reprographics products division undertook to develop microprocessor-controlled copiers, it turned to the photo products group, which had developed the world's first microprocessor-controlled camera.

Also, reward systems that focus only on product-line results and career paths that seldom cross SBU boundaries engender patterns of behavior among unit managers that are destructively competitive. At NEC, divisional managers come together to identify next-generation competencies. Together they decide how much investment needs to be made to build up each future competency and the contribution in capital and staff support that each division will need to make. There is also a sense of equitable exchange. One division may make a disproportionate contribution or may benefit less from the progress made, but such short-term inequalities will balance out over the long term.

Incidentally, the positive contribution of the SBU manager should be made visible across the company. An SBU manager is unlikely to surrender key people if only the other business (or the general manager of that business who may be a competitor for promotion) is going to benefit from the redeployment. Cooperative SBU managers should be celebrated as team players. Where priorities are clear, transfers are less likely to be seen as idiosyncratic and politically motivated.

Core competencies at Canon

	Precision mechanics	Fine optics	Micro-electronics
Basic camera	■	■	
Compact fashion camera	■	■	
Electronic camera	■	■	
EOS autofocus camera	■	■	■
Video still camera	■	■	■
Laser beam printer	■	■	■
Color video printer	■		■
Bubble jet printer	■		■
Basic fax	■		■
Laser fax	■		■
Calculator			■
Plain paper copier	■	■	■
Battery PPC	■	■	■
Color copier	■	■	■
Laser copier	■	■	■
Color laser copier	■	■	■
NAVI	■	■	■
Still video system	■	■	■
Laser imager	■	■	■
Cell analyzer	■	■	■
Mask aligners	■		■
Stepper aligners	■		■
Excimer laser aligners	■	■	■

Figure 3   *Every Canon product is the result of at least one core competency*

Transfers for the sake of building core competence must be recorded and appreciated in the corporate memory. It is reasonable to expect a business that has surrendered core skills on behalf of corporate opportunities in other areas to lose, for a time, some of its competitiveness. If these losses in performance bring immediate censure, SBUs will be unlikely to assent to skills transfer next time.

Finally, there are ways to wean key employees off the idea that they belong in perpetuity to any particular business. Early in their careers, people may be exposed to a variety of businesses through a carefully planned rotation program. At Canon, critical people move regularly between the camera business and the copier business and between the copier business and the professional optical-products business. In mid-career, periodic assignments to cross-divisional project teams may be necessary, both for diffusing core competencies and for loosening the bonds that might tie an individual to one business even when brighter opportunities beckon elsewhere. Those who embody critical core competencies should know that their careers are tracked and guided by corporate human resource professionals. In the early 1980s at Canon, all engineers under 30 were invited to apply for membership on a seven-person committee that was to spend two years plotting Canon's future direction, including its strategic architecture.

Competence carriers should be regularly brought together from across the corporation to trade notes and ideas. The goal is to build a strong feeling of community among these people. To a great extent, their loyalty should be to the integrity of the core competence area they represent and not just to particular businesses. In traveling regularly, talking frequently to customers, and meeting with peers, competence carriers may be encouraged to discover new market opportunities.

Core competencies are the wellspring of new business development. They should constitute the focus for strategy at the corporate level. Managers have to win manufacturing leadership in core products and capture global share through brand-building programs aimed at exploiting economies of scope. Only if the company is conceived of as a hierarchy of core competencies, core products, and market-focused business units will it be fit to fight.

Nor can top management be just another layer of accounting consolidation, which it often is in a regime of radical decentralization. Top management must add value by enunciating the strategic architecture that guides the competence acquisition process. We believe an obsession with competence building will characterize the global winners of the 1990s. With the decade underway, the time for rethinking the concept of the corporation is already overdue.

Appendix   Vickers learns the value of strategic architecture

The idea that top management should develop a corporate strategy for acquiring and deploying core competencies is relatively new in most U.S. companies. There are a few exceptions. An early convert was Trinova (previously Libbey Owens Ford), a Toledo-based corporation, which enjoys a worldwide position in power and motion controls and engineered plastics. One of its major divisions is Vickers, a premier supplier of hydraulics components like valves, pumps, actuators, and filtration devices to aerospace, marine, defense, automotive, earth-moving, and industrial markets.

Vickers saw the potential for a transformation of its traditional business with the application of electronics disciplines in combination with its traditional technologies. The goal was 'to ensure that change in technology does not displace Vickers from its customers'. This, to be sure, was initially a defensive move: Vickers recognized that unless it acquired new skills, it could not protect existing markets or capitalize on new growth opportunities. Managers at Vickers attempted to conceptualize the likely evolution of (a) technologies relevant to the power and motion control business, (b) functionalities that would satisfy emerging customer needs, and (c) new competencies needed to creatively manage the marriage of technology and customer needs.

Despite pressure for short-term earnings, top management looked to a 10- to 15-year time horizon in developing a map of emerging customer needs, changing technologies, and the core competencies that would be necessary to bridge the gap between the two. Its slogan was 'Into the 21st Century'. (A simplified version of the overall architecture developed is shown in Figure 4.) Vickers is currently in fluid-power components. The architecture identifies two additional competencies, electric-power components and electronic controls. A systems integration capability that would unite hardware, software, and service was also targeted for development.

The strategic architecture, as illustrated by the Vickers example, is not a forecast of specific products or specific technologies but a broad map of the evolving linkages between customer functionality requirements, potential technologies, and core competencies. It assumes that products and systems cannot be defined with certainty for the future but that preempting competitors in the development of new markets requires an early start to building core

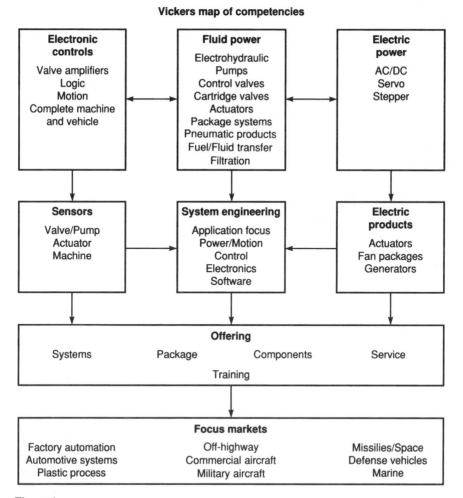

Vickers map of competencies

Electronic controls	Fluid power	Electric power
Valve amplifiers Logic Motion Complete machine and vehicle	Electrohydraulic Pumps Control valves Cartridge valves Actuators Package systems Pneumatic products Fuel/Fluid transfer Filtration	AC/DC Servo Stepper

Sensors	System engineering	Electric products
Valve/Pump Actuator Machine	Application focus Power/Motion Control Electronics Software	Actuators Fan packages Generators

Offering

Systems   Package   Components   Service

Training

Focus markets

| Factory automation
Automotive systems
Plastic process | Off-highway
Commercial aircraft
Military aircraft | Missilies/Space
Defense vehicles
Marine |

Figure 4

competencies. The strategic architecture developed by Vickers, while describing the future in competence terms, also provides the basis for making 'here and now' decisions about product priorities, acquisitions, alliances, and recruitment.

Since 1986, Vickers has made more than ten clearly targeted acquisitions, each one focused on a specific component or technology gap identified in the overall architecture. The architecture is also the basis for internal development of new competencies. Vickers has undertaken, in parallel, a reorganization to enable the integration of electronics and electrical capabilities with mechanical-based competencies. We believe that it will take another two to three years before Vickers reaps the total benefits from developing the strategic architecture, communicating it widely to all its employees, customers, and investors, and building administrative systems consistent with the architecture.

Notes

1 For a fuller discussion, see our article, 'Strategic Intent', *Harvard Business Review*, May-June 1989, p. 63.
2 'Collaborate with Your Competitors and Win', *Harvard Business Review*, January-February 1989, p. 133, with Yves L. Doz.

11 Strategy and the 'business portfolio'

Barry Hedley

All except the smallest and simplest companies comprise more than one business. Even when a company operates within a single broad business area, analysis normally reveals that it is, in practice, involved in a number of product-market segments which are distinct economically. These must be considered separately for purposes of strategy development.

It has been shown that the fundamental determinant of strategy success for each individual business segment is relative competitive position. As a result of the experience curve effect the competitor with high market share in the segment relative to competition should be able to develop the lowest cost position and hence the highest and most stable profits. This will be true regardless of changes in the economic environment. Hence relative competition position in the appropriately defined business segment forms a simple but sound strategic goal. Focusing on this goal provides a basis for effective long range planning even in the face of considerable environmental uncertainty.

Almost invariably, any company which reviews its various businesses carefully in this light will discover that they occupy widely differing relative competitive positions. Some businesses will be competitively strong already, and may appear to present no strategic problem; others will be weak, and the company must face the question of whether it would be worthwhile to attempt to improve their position, making whatever investments might be required to achieve this; if this is not done, the company can only expect poor performance from the business and the best option economically will be divestment.

Even in quite small companies, the total number of possible combinations of individual business strategies can be extremely large. The difficulty of making a firm final choice on strategy for each business is normally compounded by the fact that most companies must operate within constraints established by limited resources, particularly cash resources. This is an especially vital concern in times of high inflation or recession such as have been experienced in recent years.

An effective solution to this problem requires the development of a framework enabling the selection of the optimum combination of individual business strategies from the spectrum of possible alternatives and opportunities open to the company, whilst at the same time remaining within the boundaries set by the company's overall constraints. The purpose of this article is to discuss an approach to doing this which has evolved considerably in the course of its regular application in consulting assignments. The approach hinges on the integration of the implications of the experience curve effect for profit performance at the individual business level with an understanding of the nature of the strategy alternatives open to each business as a function of its overall growth rate. Final decisions on strategy for each business are then taken within the context of the company viewed explicitly as a portfolio of individual businesses. Hence the approach has come to be termed the product or *business portfolio* concept. This approach is superficially quite well known today.[1] However, there seems to be some confusion in practice as to exactly what it is and how it is meant to be applied. It is hoped that this article will help clarify the nature of the approach and its power as an aid to effective strategy development.

The business portfolio concept

The effect and value of growth

At its most basic, the importance of growth in shaping strategy choice is twofold. First, the growth of a business is a major factor influencing the likely ease – and hence cost – of gaining market share. In low growth businesses, any market share gained will tend to require an actual volume reduction in competitors' sales. This will be very obvious to the competitors and they are likely to fight to prevent the throughput in their plants dropping. In high growth businesses, on the other hand, market share can be gained steadily merely by securing the largest share of the *growth* in the business: expanding capacity earlier than the competitors, ensuring product availability and effective selling support despite the strains imposed by the growth, and so forth. Meanwhile competitors may even be unaware of their share loss because their actual volume of throughput has been well maintained. Even if aware of their loss of share, the competitors may be unconcerned by it given that their plants are still well loaded. This is particularly true of competitors who do not understand the strategic importance of market share for long term profitability resulting from the experience curve effect.

---

[1] A number of discussions of the business portfolio concept have appeared previously at various times in publications by The Boston Consulting Group. These include: *Perspectives*, The Product Portfolio (1970); *Commentary*, Growth and Financial Strategies (1971); and *Perspectives*, The Growth Share Matrix (1973).

An unfortunate example of this is given by the history of the British motorcycle industry. British market share was allowed to erode in motorcycles worldwide for more than a decade, throughout which the British factories were still fairly full: British motorcycle production volumes held up at around 80,000 units per year throughout the sixties; in sharp contrast, Japanese export volumes leapt from only about 60,000 in 1960 to 2.5 million in 1973; their total production volumes roughly tripled in the same period. The long term effect was that while Japanese real costs were falling rapidly British costs were not: somewhat oversimplified, this is why the British motorcycle industry faced bankruptcy in the early seventies.[2]

The second important factor concerning growth is the opportunity it provides for investment. Growth businesses provide the ideal vehicles for investment, for ploughing cash into a business in order to see it compound and return even larger amounts of cash at a later point in time. Of course this opportunity is also a need: the faster a business grows, the more investment it will require just to maintain market share. Yet the experience curve effect means that this is essential if its profitability is not to decline over time.

Importance of relative competitive position for cash generation

Whilst these growth considerations affect the rate at which a business will *use* cash, the relative competitive position of the business will determine the rate at which the business will *generate* cash: the stronger the company's position relative to its competitors the higher its margins should be, as a result of the experience curve effect. The simplest measure of relative competitive position is, of course, relative market share. A company's relative market share in a business can be defined as its market share in the business divided by that of the largest other competitor. Thus only the biggest competitor has a relative market share greater than one. All the other competitors should enjoy lower profitability and cash generation than the leader.

The growth-share matrix

Individual businesses can have very different financial characteristics and face different strategic options depending on how they are placed in terms of growth and relative competitive position. Businesses can basically fall into any one of four broad strategic categories, as depicted schematically in the growth-share matrix in Figure 1.

---

[2] The Boston Consulting Group Ltd., *Strategy Alternatives for the British Motorcycle Industry*, A Report prepared for the Secretary of State for Industry, HMSO (1975).

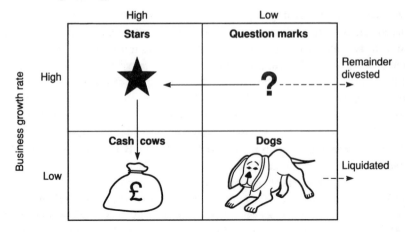

Figure 1   *The business portfolio or growth-share matrix*

Stars – high growth, high share – are in the upper left quadrant. Growing rapidly, they use large amounts of cash to maintain position. They are also leaders in the business, however, and should generate large amounts of cash. As a result, *star* businesses are frequently roughly in balance on net cash flow, and can be self-sustaining in growth terms. They represent probably the best profit growth and investment opportunities available to the company, and every effort should therefore be made to maintain and consolidate their competitive position. This will sometimes require heavy investment beyond their own generation capabilities and low margins may be essential at times to deter competition, but this is almost invariably worthwhile for the longer term: when the growth slows, as it ultimately does in all businesses, very large cash returns will be obtained if share has been maintained so that the business drops into the lower left quadrant of the matrix, becoming a *cash cow*. If *star* businesses fail to hold share, which frequently happens if the attempt is made to net large amounts of cash from them in the short and medium term (e.g. by cutting back on investment and raising prices, creating an 'umbrella' for competitors), they will ultimately become *dogs* (lower right quadrant). These are certain losers.

Cash cows – low growth, high share – should have an entrenched superior market position and low costs. Hence profits and cash generation should be high, and because of the low growth reinvestment needs should be light. Thus large cash surpluses should be generated by these businesses. *Cash cows* pay the dividends and interest, provide the debt capacity, pay for the company overhead *and* provide the cash for investment elsewhere in the company's portfolio of businesses. They are the foundation on which the company rests.

Dogs – low growth, low share – represent a tremendous contrast. Their poor competitive position condemns them to poor profits. Because the growth is low, there is little potential for gaining sufficient share to achieve a viable cost position at anything approaching a reasonable cost. Unfortunately, the cash required for investment in the business just to maintain competitive position, though low, frequently exceeds that generated, especially under conditions of high inflation. The business therefore becomes a 'cash trap' likely to absorb cash *perpetually* unless further investment in the business is rigorously avoided. The colloquial term *dog* describing these businesses, though undoubtedly pejorative, is thus rather apt. A company should take every precaution to minimize the proportion of its assets that remain in this category.

Question marks – high growth, low share – have the worst cash characteristics of all. In the upper right quadrant, their cash needs are high because of their growth, but their cash generation is small because of their low share. If nothing is done to change its market share, the *question mark* will simply absorb large amounts of cash in the short term and later, as the growth slows, become a *dog*. Following this sort of strategy, the *question mark* is a cash loser throughout its existence. Managed this way, a *question mark* becomes the ultimate 'cash trap'.

In fact there is a clear choice between only two strategy alternatives for a *question mark*, hence the name. Because growth is high, it should be easier and less costly to gain share here than it would be in a lower growth business. One strategy is therefore to make whatever investments are necessary to gain share, to try to fund the business to dominance so that it can become a *star* and, ultimately a *cash cow* when the business matures. This strategy will be very costly in the short term – growth rates will be even higher than if share were merely being maintained, and additional marketing and other investments will be required to make the share actually change hands – but it offers the only way of developing a sound business from the *question mark* over the long term. The only logical alternative is divestment. Outright sale is preferable; but if this is not possible, then a firm decision must be taken not to invest further in the business and it must be allowed simply to generate whatever cash it can while none is reinvested. The business will then decline, possibly quite rapidly if market growth is high, and will have to be shut down at some point. But it will produce cash in the short term and this is greatly preferable to the error of sinking cash into it perpetually without improving its competitive position.

Some examples

These then, are the four basic categories to which businesses can belong. Some companies tend to fit almost entirely into a single quadrant. General Motors and English China Clays are examples of predominantly *cash cow* companies. Chrysler, by comparison, is a *dog* which compounded its fundamental problem of low share in its domestic U.S. market by acquiring further mature low share competitors in other countries (e.g. Rootes which became Chrysler U.K.). IBM in computers, Xerox in photocopiers, BSR in low cost record autochangers, are all examples of predominantly *star* businesses. Xerox's computer operation, XDS, was clearly a *question mark*, however, and it is not surprising that Xerox recently effectively gave it away free to Honeywell, and considered itself lucky to escape at that price! When RCA closed down its computer operation, it had to sustain a write-off of about $490m. *Question marks* are costly.

Portfolio strategy

Most companies have their portfolio businesses scattered through all four quadrants of the matrix. It is possible to outline quite briefly and simply what the appropriate overall portfolio strategy for such a company should be. The first goal should be to maintain position in the *cash cows*, but to guard against the frequent temptation to reinvest in them excessively. The cash generated by the *cash cows* should be used as a first priority to maintain or consolidate position in those *stars* which are not self sustaining. Any surplus remaining can be used to fund a *selected* number of *question marks* to dominance. Most companies will find they have inadequate cash generation to finance market share-gaining strategies in all their *question mark*s. Those which are not funded should be divested either by sale or liquidation over time.

Finally, virtually all companies have at least some dog businesses. There is nothing reprehensible about this, indeed on the contrary, an absence of *dogs* probably indicates that the company has not been sufficiently adventurous in the past. It is essential, however, that the fundamentally weak strategic position of the *dog* be recognized for what it is. Occasionally it is possible to restore a *dog* to viability by a creative business segmentation strategy, rationalizing and specializing the business into a small niche which it can dominate. If this is impossible, however, the only thing which could rescue the *dog* would be an increase in share taking it to a position comparable to the leading competitors in the segment. This is likely to be unreasonably costly in a mature business, and therefore the only prospect for obtaining a return from a *dog* is to manage it for cash, cutting off all investment in the business. Management should be particularly wary of expensive 'turn around' plans developed for a *dog* if these do not involve a significant change in fundamental competitive position. Without this, the *dog* is a sure loser. An indictment of many corporate managements is not the fact that their companies have *dogs* in the portfolio, but rather that these *dogs* are not managed according to logical strategies. The decision to liquidate a business is usually even harder to take than that of entering a new business. It is essential, however, for the long term vitality and performance of the company overall that it be prepared to do *both* as the need arises.

Thus the appropriate strategy for a multibusiness company involves striking a balance in the portfolio such that the cash generated by the *cash cows*, and by those *question marks* and *dogs* which are being liquidated, is sufficient to support the company's *stars* and to fund the selected *question marks* through to dominance. This pattern of strategies is indicated by the arrows in Figure 1. Understanding this pattern conceptually is, however, a far cry from being able to implement it in practice. What any company should do with its own specific businesses is of course a function of the precise shape of the company's portfolio, and the particular opportunities and problems it presents. But how can a clear picture of the company's portfolio be developed?

The matrix quantified

Based on careful analysis and research it is normally possible to divide a company into its various business segments appropriately defined for purposes of strategy development. Following this critical first step, it is usually relatively straightforward to determine the overall growth rate of each individual business (i.e. the growth of the *market*, not the growth of the company within the market), and the company's size (in terms of turnover or assets) and relative competitive position (market share) within the business.[3]

Armed with these data it is possible to develop a precise overall picture of the company's portfolio of businesses graphically. This can greatly facilitate the identification and resolution of the key strategic issues facing the company. It is a particularly useful approach where companies are large, comprising many separate businesses. Such complex portfolios often defy description in more conventional ways.

The nature of the graphical portfolio display is illustrated by the example in Figure 2. In this chart, growth rate and relative competitive position are plotted on continuous scales. Each circle in the display represents a single business or business segment, appropriately defined. To convey an impression of the relative significance of each business, size is indicated by the area of the circle, which can be made proportional to either turnover or assets employed. Relative competitive position is plotted on a logarithmic scale, in order to be consistent with the experience curve effect, which implies that profit margin

[3]Frequently the ratio of the market share of the company in the business relative to that of the largest competitor can be used for the latter measure. In some business segments with more complex economics, different cost elements may have differing experience curve bases for cost reduction. In such cases a simple measure of overall relative competitive position is given by the weighted average of the company's relative position in each of these separate experience curve bases. The weights to be used in computing the average are the proportion of the total cost or value added accounted for by the cost element related to each experience base. The average relative share thus still represents an experience curve based proxy for relative cost position in this complex situation, just as it does in the simpler case where all costs in the business segment are simply a reflection of accumulated experience in that segment alone.

or rate of cash generation differences between competitors will tend to be related to the *ratio* of their relative competitive positions (market shares). A linear axis is used for growth, for which the most generally useful measure is *volume* growth of the business concerned, as in general rates of cash use should be directly proportional to growth.

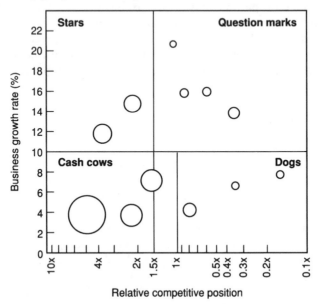

Figure 2 *Graphical representation of the portfolio (note: circle area is proportional to size of business concerned e.g. turnover or assets).*

The lines dividing the portfolio into four quadrants are inevitably somewhat arbitrary. 'High growth', for example, is taken to include all businesses growing in excess of 10 per cent per annum in volume terms. Certainly, above this growth rate market share tends to become fairly fluid and can be made to change hands quite readily. In addition many companies have traditionally employed a figure of 10 per cent for their discount rate in times of low inflation, and so this also tends to be the growth rate above which investment in market share becomes particularly attractive financially.[4]

The line separating areas of high and low relative competitive position is set at 1.5 times. Experience in using this display has been that in high growth businesses relative strengths of this magnitude or greater are necessary in order to ensure a sufficiently dominant position that the business will have the characteristic of a *star* in practice. On the other hand, in low growth businesses acceptable cash generation characteristics are occasionally, but not always

---

[4]It is an interesting mathematical fact that if the market were expected to grow in excess of the discount rate forever, the discounted present value of increased market share would actually be infinite`!

observed at relative strengths as low as 1 times; hence the addition of a second separating line at 1 times in the low growth area, to reflect this. These lines should, of course, be taken only as approximate guides in characterizing businesses in the portfolio as *dogs* and *question marks, cash cows* and *stars*. In actuality, businesses cover a smooth spectrum across both axes of the matrix. There is obviously no 'magic' which transforms a *star* into a *cash cow* as its growth declines from 10.5 to 9.5 per cent. It is undeniably useful, however, to have some device for broadly indicating where the transition points occur within the matrix, and the lines suggested here have worked well in practical applications of the matrix in a large number of companies.

Portfolio approaches in practice

The company shown in Figure 2 would be a good example of a potentially well balanced portfolio. With a firm foundation in the form of two or three substantial *cash cows*, this company has some well placed *stars* to provide growth and to yield high cash returns in the future when they mature. The company also has some *question marks* at least two of which are probably sufficiently well placed that they offer a good chance of being funded into *star* positions at a reasonable cost, not out of proportion to the company's resources. The company is not without *dogs*, but properly managed there is no reason why these should be a drain on cash.

The sound portfolio, unsoundly managed

Companies with an attractive portfolio of this kind are not rare in practice. In fact Figure 2 is a disguised version of a representation of an actual U.K. company analysed in the course of a Boston Consulting Group assignment. What is much rarer, however, is to find that the company has made a clear assessment of the matrix positioning and appropriate strategy for each business in the portfolio.

Ideally, one would hope that the company in Figure 2 would develop strategy along the following lines. For the *stars*, the key objectives should be the maintenance of market share; current profitability should be accorded a lower priority. For the *cash cows*, however, current profitability may well be a primary goal. *Dogs* would not be expected to be as profitable as the *cash cows*, but would be expected to yield cash. Some *question marks* would be set objectives in terms of increased market share; others, where gaining dominance appeared too costly, would be managed instead for cash.

The essence of the portfolio approach is therefore that strategy objectives must vary between businesses. The strategy developed for each business must fit its own matrix position *and* the needs and capabilities of the company's overall portfolio of businesses. In practice, however, it is much more common to find all businesses within a company being operated with a common overall goal in mind. 'Our target in this company is to grow at 10 per cent per annum and achieve a return of 10 per cent on capital'. This type of overall target is then taken to apply to every business in the company. *Cash cows* beat the profit target easily, though they frequently miss on growth. Nevertheless, their managements are praised and they are normally rewarded by being allowed to plough back what only too frequently amounts to an *excess* of cash into their 'obviously attractive' businesses. Attractive businesses, yes: but *not* for growth investment. *Dogs* on the other hand rarely meet the profit target. But how often is it accepted that it is in fact unreasonable for them *ever* to hit the target? On the contrary, the most common strategic mistake is that major investments are made in *dogs* from time to time in hopeless attempts to turn the business around without actually shifting market share. Unfortunately, only too often *question marks* are regarded very much as *dogs*, and get insufficient investment funds ever to bring them to dominance. The *question marks* usually do receive some investment, however, possibly even enough to maintain share. *This is throwing money away into a cash trap.* These businesses should either receive enough support to enable them to achieve segment dominance, *or none at all.*

These are some of the strategic errors which are regularly committed even by companies which have basically sound portfolios. The result is a serious sub-optimization of potential performance in which some businesses (e.g. *cash cows*) are not being called on to produce the full results of which they are actually capable, and resources are being mistakenly squandered on other businesses (*dogs, question marks*) in an attempt to make them achieve performance of which they are intrinsically incapable without a fundamental improvement in market share. Where mismanagement of this kind becomes positively dangerous, is when it is applied within the context of a basically unbalanced portfolio.

The unbalanced portfolio

The disguised example in Figure 3 is another actual company. This portfolio is seriously out of balance. As shown in Figure 3(a), the company has a very high proportion of *question marks* in its portfolio, and an inadequate base of *cash cows*. Yet at the time of investigation this company was in fact taking such cash as was being generated by its mature businesses and spreading it out amongst all the high growth businesses, only one of which was actually receiving sufficient investment to enable it even to maintain share! Thus the overall relative competitive position of the portfolio was on average declining. At the same time, the balance in the portfolio was shifting: as shown in the projected portfolio in Figure 3(b), because of the higher relative growth of the *question marks* their overall weight in the portfolio was increasing, making them even harder to fund from the limited resources of the mature businesses.

If the company continued to follow the same strategy of spreading available funds between all the businesses, then the rate of decline could only increase over time leading ultimately to disaster.

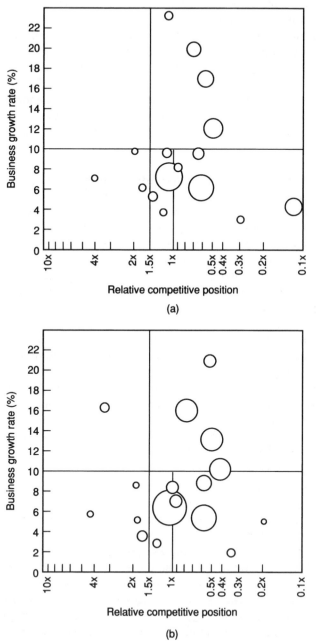

Figure 3 *An unbalanced portfolio. (a) The company today; (b) in five years' time, following same strategy*

This company was caught in a vicious circle of decline. To break out of the circle would require firm discipline and the strength of will to select only one or two of the *question marks* and finance those, whilst cutting off investment in the remainder. Obviously the choice of which should receive investment involves rather more than selection at random from the portfolio chart. It requires careful analysis of the actual nature of the businesses concerned and particularly the characteristics and behaviour of the competitors faced in those businesses. However, the nature of the strategic choice facing the company is quite clear, when viewed in portfolio terms. Without the clarity of view provided by the matrix display, which focuses on the real fundamentals of the businesses and their relationships to each other within the portfolio, it is impossible to develop strategy effectively in any multibusiness company.

Implications for strategy development today

The need for an approach of this kind is more acute than ever today. In recent times business managers and planners have had to adapt to a new norm of continual change and unpredictability in economic affairs. The difficulty of adapting has been compounded over the last few years by persistent pressures of inflation and recession. Inflation of course, results in pressure on profits – certainly on 'real' profits – and even more importantly on cash. More cash is required for the same physical stocks, net debtors inflate and, of course, investment in plant and equipment becomes much more costly in cash terms. Apparent profits can normally be increased in inflationary times, though taxes and dividends take their share. The net result, however, especially in a climate of price and marginal control, is that cash available for reinvestment is insufficient to finance real growth at anything like historic rates. Introduction of accounting changes, spearheaded by the provision of tax relief on 'stock profits', helps the situation but is by no means a complete solution in itself. The influence of recession, superimposed on the inflation, has been to increase further the pressure on profits. In a few instances, recession may have reduced cash needs as working capital needs declined and short-term capacity expansion requirements were revised downwards. But that has been cold comfort, at best.

The predictable reactions

How are companies reacting to these pressures? It is, of course, difficult and dangerous to generalize. It appears however, that the most common corporate response has been simply a general 'tightening of the belt'. The call has gone out to all businesses both to generate more profits in the short-term, and to control cash tightly. The results have been predictable. Prices have been increased as much as is legally possible. Expenditures which look 'postponable' have been eliminated. This has covered everything from company cars and office painting to more important expenditures – such as plant overhaul market research, product research and development – which may produce only 'intangible' short term benefits. Cash has been conserved both by tight stock control, and by energetically trying to take increased supplier credit at the same time as reducing the level of one's own debtors. Significantly, investments in plant and equipment have frequently been refused, unless they offered a very high return and rapid payback. And perhaps most importantly of all, these measures tend to have been applied virtually across the board, affecting all the businesses within large multibusiness companies more or less equally.

Actions such as these are understandable reflex managerial responses. They have alleviated the pressures to which companies have been exposed. Unfortunately, however, they are only acceptable in the short term. They must not be continued now even if the pressures which originally stimulated them persist into the longer term. It is particularly important that they be discontinued if the maximum benefit is to be taken of any near term improvement in trading conditions. If these 'across the board' measures *are* continued, then severe and lasting damage will be done in some businesses for which they are wholly inappropriate long term.

Many companies have been living from day to day for too long. Clear and explicit consideration of long range strategy must be restored to our business consciousness and decision making, or we shall find that we have mortgaged the future irretrievably. Relative competitive position within the context of the portfolio concept can provide the simple and sound individual business objectives which are needed for any company to optimize its strategic opportunities.

Reproduced from Hedley, B. (1976). Strategy and the 'business portfolio'. *Long Range Planning*, **10**, 9-15, by permission of Pergamon Press Ltd.

12 Strategic marketing: Betas, boxes, or basics

Robin Wensley

The problem of resource allocation within the multiproduct, multimarket firm has received considerable attention in both the finance and marketing literature. Although much of the work in finance and marketing has been independent, a number of authors have recognized the potential interrelationships. Wind (1974), for instance, suggested the application of financial portfolio theory to product mix decisions, while Grant and King (1979) proposed that at a corporate level of analysis, the financial approach based on portfolio theory should be considered alongside such marketing classification schemes as the business planning matrix and the directional policy matrix. More recently, Mahajan et al. (1981) have commented on the failure of many marketing schemes to reflect the distinction between risk and return that is so fundamental to the financial approaches.

This paper will develop further the comparison between the financial and marketing approaches. The current financial approach has developed from traditional capital budgeting based on discounting methods to the Capital Asset Pricing Model (CAPM) and the use of discount rates related to the systematic risk of the project, its Beta, whilst the marketing approach has relied on the classification of either products or business units into various boxes. The marketing strategy literature contains numerous individual approaches for such box classifications, but as Wind and Mahajan (1980) imply, it is possible to consider such standardized models in two broad categories: those based on univariate dimensions, best exemplified by the market share/growth matrix; and those based on composite dimensions involving the subjective weighting of a number of factors, exemplified by the directional policy matrix but including others such as the A.D. Little and GE/McKinsey schemes.

In comparing resource allocation models consideration is given first to theoretical assumptions and the supporting empirical evidence and then to the relevance of each approach to crucial strategic issues at the corporate level. It is not possible to include in such a comparison the customized marketing strategy models (Wind and Saaty 1980), since as Mahajan, Wind, and Bradford (1981) recognize, such models tend to rely primarily on management's subjective judgement and, therefore, cannot be tested against either their theoretical assumptions[1] or any general empirical evidence.

A framework for evaluation of corporate level models

In economic terms the underlying principle of corporate level models can be simply stated: They are decision rules or heuristics for detecting areas of sustainable competitive advantage whereby the firm can realize economic profits or rents. Firms have been searching for profit long before the advent of the new strategy models, but at least in principle, such techniques offer an opportunity for a more focused search. To achieve such an objective, however, any particular model must satisfy three requirements:

- An internal consistency in the implied economic processes
- Must be based on established empirical regularities
- Must focus the search along critical dimensions rather than trivial ones, even if it is claimed (Hopkins 1977) that a particular approach is to help managers think rather than give them answers.

The issue of simplicity is in itself not particularly relevant. A simple model that focuses on a particular critical dimension is likely to be more cost effective than a more complex one that concentrates on the same dimension. Indeed it has been argued that effective strategic analysis is more likely from simple add-on models that contradict the results of established analysis under certain conditions and, hence, generate a level of surprise. Provided such models are based on established empirical regularities, the simplicity of the model increases the likelihood that the surprises will be acted upon rather than the model ignored (Wensley 1979a).

Financial models for resource allocation

Although the concept of discounting future cash flows has existed in economics for a long time, it was during the fifties and sixties that the Discounted Cash Flow (DCF) approach towards project selection became widely adopted in both U.S. and U.K. corporations. Considerable efforts were extended, both academically and practically, to establish the relevant

---

[1]Customized strategy models do, of course, make implicit assumptions about the economic value of a more systematic and consistent appraisal of project characteristics. As such there are close relationships with the arguments for procedural rationality (Burton and Naylor 1980). These assumptions could also be tested against the evidence, but this is outside the scope of this paper.

Weighted Average Cost of Capital (WACC), which could then be used as the criterion for project selection or rejection (Merrett and Sykes 1963). In a number of instances it became clear that such a DCF approach was being used not only as a method of identifying attractive opportunities but also as a means of generating an exclusive ranking on the basis of each opportunity's internal rate of return.

Such developments led some strategic analysts to voice strident criticisms of such a rigidly quantified and unidimensional perspective:

> In evaluating the deployment of assets, the rigidity of quantification (DCF, for example) can distort the true picture of the various alternatives open to the firm seeking growth; those factors which do not lend themselves under conventional methods to numerical analysis tend to be left to intuition (e.g., risk analysis).
>
> The reinforcement of 'minimum rates' or uniform return criteria can often result in foreclosing growth through implicitly limiting a company's strategic choices.
>
> Failure to come to grips explicitly with risk/return tradeoffs often displaces logical strategic analysis with traditional policies or 'conventional wisdom' (Zakon 1971, p. 1).

The general criticism that overreliance on the now traditional means of project selection based exclusively on ranking by internal rate of return could lead to undesirable effects, became widely recognized. New developments occurred in both the areas of finance and marketing partially at least in response to such problems. Such developments were, however, independent and have remained virtually unrelated; as Anderson recently commented (1979, p. 325): 'A virtual revolution has occurred in financial thinking in the last two decades, but few of the new technologies and approaches from finance have filtered into marketing.'

Portfolio theory and the capital asset pricing model

The finance approach starts from the appropriate rules to construct an efficient portfolio of financial investments. The most widely developed approach is that based on the mean-variance rule suggested by Markowitz (1952). At a technical level, however, it has been recognized that the mean-variance rule is only optimally efficient under certain assumptions, in particular that the investor's utility function is quadratic and the probability distribution of returns is normal. Such issues have led to the development of rather different rules under stochastic dominance principles (Mahajan *et al.* 1981). Whether such concerns will in the end prove significant in the area of strategic marketing is a moot point. At the moment it seems likely that the basic principles underlying the CAPM approach, which is the means to apply Markowitz' portfolio theory to resource allocation decisions both at the level of the individual investor (Linter 1965, Mossin 1966, Sharpe 1964, and Weston 1973) and of the firm (Rubinstein 1973), will prove to be fairly robust to most of these issues.

The CAPM approach is concerned with the selection of the appropriate discount rate to apply to the cost and benefit stream for any particular project. The approach rejects the use of the same discount rate for all projects the WACC approach discussed earlier, and recommends a project specific rate related to the systematic risk of the project. The systematic risk is not the total risk but only that portion of total risk that is nondiversifiable from the point of view of the portfolio investor.

In the usual finance terminology, the level of systematic risk is characterized by its 'Beta,' which is strictly the covariance between the asset returns and returns from a fully diversified market portfolio. The higher the Beta of any particular project, the higher the required return for that project. A number of financial analysts have argued that there is a general relationship between increased market uncertainties and systematic risk. This would imply, for instance, that new product ventures may involve higher systematic risks than line extension projects for established products. On this basis, projects should first be sorted into different general classes:

> Various types of projects are separated into risk classes according to their perceived risk, and each risk class is assigned a discount rate . . . for example, cost reduction projects are put into Class A (low risk), scale expansion projects into Class B (average risk), new projects into Class C (high risk). (Franks and Broyles 1979, p. 118)

Then higher return targets should be set for the higher risk categories so that, for instance, the required ROI is higher for new products than for line extensions to mature products.

Limitations in the CAPM

Because the CAPM has been derived from finance theory, it has a high degree of internal consistency. There are, however, a number of problems in extending the CAPM to resource allocation decisions on projects within the firm. An analysis of the project cash flows on the basis of a discount rate related to the project's Beta gives reasonable answers. The problem is that the determinants of the correct Beta in this case are complicated and related to such factors as the link between cash flow forecast errors and the forecast errors of market return as well as asset life, the growth trend in cash flows, and the pattern of expected cash flows over time (Myers and Turnbull 1977).

On the issue of empirical evidence, despite extensive testing of the CAPM, Roll (1977) has shown that the many empirical tests purporting to show that the CAPM is descriptively valid, i.e., that the actual pricing of capital assets in the market follows the predicted behavior of the model, are, in reality, joint tests of both the CAPM and market efficiency, and that the CAPM cannot be tested directly on its own.

Finally, it has been recognized that the existence of a positive Net Present Value (NPV) against the appropriate risk adjusted discount rate cannot be taken as the automatic indicator of acceptance. A large NPV must reflect anticipated scarcity or competitive advantage. Management must, therefore, decide how much effort should be expended on the basic application of the CAPM compared with a strategic analysis of competitive advantage in any resource allocation decision.

Box models for resource allocation

The market share/growth matrix

The development of the approach derived from the CAPM can be seen as one means of responding to many of the criticisms of the traditional capital budgeting methodology. Another approach to such problems has been the market share/growth box classification system, probably best described by Hedley (1977) and principally attributed to the Boston Consulting Group (BCG).

The BCG approach focuses the analysis on the two axes of market share and market growth. Market share or relative market share is seen to be important as an indicator of relative competitive position, particularly in cost terms. Such an assumption is supported by the empirical evidence of the relationship between market share and profitability (Buzzell *et al.* 1975) as well as the somewhat more indirect evidence of the experience curve effect (Hedley 1976). Market growth is, on the other hand, seen to be important partly because of the substantial cash costs of funding activity in high growth markets; the need for substantial annual additions to both fixed and working capital often dominates any cash generated by the operation. Market growth is also seen as significant because of a hypothesized interaction effect with market share itself: It is suggested that it is easier to gain market share in high growth markets.

The BCG matrix, therefore, appears to be an appropriate means of comparing market position, in terms of share and growth, with the cash performance of any particular product. It also has the advantage that in many cases it is simple and easy to use, although problems of market definition and measurement have been recognized by other commentators (Channon 1979, Day 1977).

Limitations in the BCG matrix

The BCG matrix has, however, been commonly extended from a simple diagnostic tool to a framework within which future strategic actions can be proposed. In such a situation we are not considering an approach derived from financial economic theory, as in the case of the CAPM, but one that is essentially ad hoc, and we need to look much more closely at two critical assumptions:

- The need for the corporation to maintain a degree of cash balance by the recycling of cash between products within the corporate portfolio
- Preferential investment in high market growth businesses.

The need for cash balance

The capital market as a source of funds seems to be almost ignored in some approaches. Hedley (1977), for instance, states that most companies will have to divest themselves of certain activities solely because they will not be able to generate enough cash from other areas. The extent to which such an approach can only be effective with strict cash budgeting is left somewhat unclear, but the strong implication in this direction has been developed much further by other authors (Gray and Green 1976, Hall 1978).

This whole approach brings us back to the strategic mistake in seeing the corporation as an independent cash recycling entity. There are times in any corporation's history when it is difficult to raise either debt or equity, but this is very different from the assumption that in the long run the corporation cannot raise funds even if it can offer a portfolio of attractive projects to the market. This is back to defining the attractiveness of any particular investment from the market point of view. If we argue that we need an internal cash control policy to avoid investing in reasonable return projects in mature markets, then logically this must be because we are claiming that the opportunity cost of cash within the firm is above such a rate for relatively low risk projects. In this case, the corporation should probably be out in the market raising further funds.[2]

Preferential investment in high market growth businesses

In a similar approach to that of Hedley, Zakon (1971) implies that cash should be preferentially directed towards high growth markets and away from established businesses in slower growth markets. The logic behind the need for such redirection seems to rest on two further assumptions: there are more opportunities for investing in high growth areas, and the payoff for such investment is better, or at least it is easier to gain market share in high growth markets.

In a simple sense, the question of more opportunities is clearly irrelevant because there is no need to direct cash towards a particular area when it already generates a large number of demands. The more subtle argument for such a bias rests on the assumption that it is in high growth markets that technology is changing fastest, and so the competitive advantage of investing in the latest technology is the greatest. This was an argument used very effectively by the BCG (1975) to explain the rapid demise of the U.K. motorcycle industry at the hands of the Japanese. However, while there may be some correlation between market growth and the rate of technological change, it would seem more appropriate to focus the analysis on the critical

[2] This principle also works in the reverse situation. If the corporation is unable to find sufficient projects with adequate returns to use up all the funds available from its retained earnings, it should be returning such additional funds to its shareholders rather than investing in projects with inadequate returns.

variable of technological change rather than a partial proxy such as market growth, particularly in the context of a market such as a worldwide motorcycle market.

The issue of better payoffs is potentially very relevant, but the model is not well formulated. It is, therefore, not clear to what extent the ease of gaining share in high growth markets refers to the short run cost of gaining market share or to the long run incremental benefit of increasing market share. There is very little empirical evidence, but Kijewski (1978) did undertake an analysis of the PIMS data in an attempt to estimate the cash costs of gaining market share points in different market environments. By looking at the difference between the cash flow/investment ratios for businesses that gained share as opposed to those that held share steady over one year as a means of estimating the short-term cash flow costs of gaining share, she concluded:

> Contrary to conventional wisdom, we do not find that the cash costs of gaining share vary substantially between moderate and rapid growth markets. When the cash costs are appropriately adjusted for average point change in market share in each environment, the cost of a point in share is only slightly lower in the more rapidly growing markets (and, indeed, lowest in low growth markets). (Kijewski 1978, p. 8)

On such evidence it would be difficult to make a good general case for investing in market share gains in rapid growth markets because the short-term costs were substantially lower. Indeed on such criteria there might even be a bias towards investments in low growth markets. To justify a general bias towards high growth markets there must be significant evidence that the long run incremental benefits of market share gains in such markets are greater.

If we were willing to postulate a model in which all product/markets followed the same Product Life Cycle (PLC) pattern of the same duration, then gains in market share would have greater longevity in terms of benefits if they were achieved at earlier stages in the cycle. Such a model would in fact appear to be fairly close to that implicitly assumed by those who attempt to tie budgeting procedures to the PLC (Savich and Thompson 1978). The PLC, however, has been a notable empirical failure if the analysis focuses too directly on the issue of stages (Dhalla and Yuspeh 1976, Polli and Cook 1969). Such failure led a recent reviewer to comment that 'The concept of PLC stages may be hindering PLC research by diverting attention from other issues concerning product life cycles' (Rink and Swan 1979, p. 232).

It would seem that the current limited state of empirical knowledge about the costs and benefits of investing in market share shifts does not support the contention that, on average, the payoff is better from investing cash in gaining market share in rapid growth markets. The market share/growth matrix approach also fails to reflect the considerably greater degree of risk attached to major and substantial diversification moves, which has been widely recognized in more traditional work on corporate strategy since Ansoff's (1965) famous four boxes.

In conclusion, any attempt to use the market share/growth matrix for resource allocation decisions implies a preference for high market growth businesses and the need to maintain a cash balance within the firm. There is little current empirical or theoretical work to justify such a preference.

The directional policy matrix

A number of other criticisms have been levelled against the market growth/ share matrix. Day (1977) in the most comprehensive critique focused on the problems of assumptions, measurement, and strategic feasibility. In particular he indicated that feasibility was often dominated by other factors beyond share and market growth, which was suggestive of the nine box classification. Some other critics have chosen to concentrate solely on the oversimplistic nature of the market growth/share approach (*Marketing News* 1978). Such critics have often been much more emphatic than Day in advocating the Directional Policy Matrix or its cousins (Hussey 1978, Robinson *et al.* 1978). In principle the Direction Policy Matrix involves expanding the dimensions of the BCG matrix so that market growth becomes a part of a composite measure of market attractiveness, and market share equally becomes a part of a composite measure of business position.

Limitations in the DPM

Applications of the DPM approach is complicated by the problem of weighting and combining different factors to generate the two dimensions, and it is in grave danger of leading the analyst to the tautological position of recommending preferential investment in those areas of highest market attractiveness and strongest business position. Hussey (1978) implicitly recognizes this with his tentative conclusion that the DPM analysis results in no surprises and, even to a limited extent, that there was a direct correlation between the discount rates shown by the projects via the normal appraisal system and those predicted by the position of the projects on the DPM. This would come as no surprise to those who see a positive net present value as a reflection of competitive advantage anyway, but Hussey does not address the question of whether he is claiming that a DPM approach would prove to be a less costly means of achieving the same result as the traditional method.

The DPM approach brings us back to the basic search for areas of sustainable competitive advantage, but there is limited evidence that it provides a useful additional form of analysis in such circumstances beyond a fairly comprehensive checklist and an idiosyncratic weighting of factors by corporate management.

Betas or boxes: projects or business units

The evaluation of the CAPM, BCG, and DPM schemes as corporate level models is given in Table 1.

Table 1   An Evaluation of Corporate Level Models

Approach	Exemplar	Internal consistency	Empirical evidence	Critical issue
Risk/return	CAPM	OK	OK	Unlikely because numbers less important than competitive market assumptions
Unidimensional classification	BCG	Dubious assumption about the importance of market growth	No supporting evidence for costs of gaining market share	Very unlikely because of doubts about the validity of the whole approach
Composite dimensions	DPM	No clear theoretical or empirical statements to be assessed – seems broadly in line with competitive advantage approach but no additional empirical tests		Unlikely because it depends on management to make their own idiosyncratic assessments and adds little to current procedures

We should have severe doubts about the theoretical and empirical support for the BCG market share/growth boxes when used to identify areas of sustainable competitive advantage. Both the CAPM and the DPM do remain focused on such an economic principle, but there remain considerable doubts as to the extent to which either can be seen as the critical determinant.

In practice the difference between financial approaches such as the CAPM and box classification systems is greater. A CAPM approach is related to individual projects, whereas box classification systems are most often applied at higher levels of aggregation, in particular Strategic Business Units. Indeed, it would be difficult to justify the cost effectiveness of box classification at the level of individual projects, since in most cases this would involve adding a more superficial approach onto the existing appraisal process within the firm.

In the context of project appraisal most evidence suggests that the sustainable competitive advantage resides in the specifics of the particular project. Hence, much of the current work on the issues of Strategic Business Units (SBUs) is likely to be based on an inappropriate grouping of product-market opportunities into a single unit. For instance, the current literature on the problems of managing units in mature markets contains the implicit assumption that few, if any, worthwhile projects will be generated by such SBUs (Hall 1978). Such an assumption challenges not only economic logic but market evidence. Goodyear, for instance, has decided quite consciously to commit its resources to increasing market share in the low growth auto tire business (*Business Week* 1978), while most of its major competitors such as Goodrich are clearly planning to reduce capacity and future capital commitments in the market. Many firms will have also experienced the fact that it is often economic for the major supplier to expand production in apparently low growth markets as have Philips N.V. in the worldwide electric light bulb market; even more will have encountered the considerable number of highly profitable cost saving investments in such areas.

It is not, of course, difficult to see why such opportunities are genuinely attractive. As the more marginal firms drop out of the business, there are real opportunities for the dominant firm(s) to pick up additional sales. Such opportunities are reinforced when technical change requires all firms to reinvest in new facilities as the switch to radial tires has done in the U.S. market. Similar situations often occur when extra market effects such as tighter pollution regulations require significant incremental investment and, therefore, often encourage marginal firms to leave the market. The dominant firm that invests in such situations is really doing no more than building on its existing market strengths.

This all suggests that corporate management cannot avoid ensuring that each particular strategic investment proposal is assessed individually. A critical component of such an appraisal is the interrelatedness of the particular project with other current or potential activities of the firm, but such interrelatedness is not adequately represented by the generalized dimensions of box classification systems such as the DPM. Conceptually this implies that the distinction between the corporate level approach and the product/market level as proposed by Grant and King (1979) cannot yet be sustained. In principle, if we could identify classificatory systems at the corporate level that meet the classical criterion that the intraclass variability of projects was substantially less than the interclass variability, then we could maintain the distinction. We have argued that against such a criterion we really have nothing better than the traditional budgetary limits method in which projects are essentially classified purely by size or the broad categories of cost saving, line or volume extension, and new products proposed by financial analysts.

The basic issue: aids to assessing competitive advantage

We have argued that any analytical approach in marketing strategy must not be followed to monopolize the search for areas of sustainable competitive advantage. Wensley (1981) has argued that no economic theory can be expected to give us all the right answers, but can provide useful diagnostic questions that will indicate things to be done. Such approaches suggest, as already discussed, that any competitive advantage is much more likely to reside in the specific nature of a particular project rather than the broad characteristics of the particular business division that is sponsoring it. Economic analysis starts from the assumption that any such competitive advantage is essentially temporary but that it can be extended if the firm faces few direct competitors.

The economic analysis of barriers to direct competition starts from Bain's (1956) initial study. Bain's conception of such barriers was that new entrants into a particular market were likely to face substantial costs before being able to compete on equal terms with the established firms. The rather simplified conception of distinct but homogeneous markets inherent in this approach was, however, at variance with the market realities of customer segmentation, alternative distribution channels, and product differentiation. The Caves and Porter (1977) have recently extended the barriers concept to mobility barriers reflecting the initial costs faced by any firm that wishes to change its overall position in the marketplace by opening up a new distribution channel, extending the product line, etc. The whole approach implies that because of such barriers, the level of competitive activity in any market will be less than it would otherwise be since existing firms are in some senses protected from further competition. Porter has also extended the concepts to the implication that in certain declining markets the competition may also be more intense than it would otherwise be because of analogous barriers to exit (Porter 1976).

Mobility barriers distinguish between the performance of established firms in a particular market and that of new entrants. In developing markets the overall entry costs will be different for different firms; some will be better placed to develop production opportunities, while others will have better access to distribution channels and face lower entry costs in terms of this dimension. However, since there is by definition no such thing as established competition, the analysis of actual outcomes has to consider game theoretic assumptions (Shubik 1975), which creates further complications (Salop 1979).

Porter (1979) has argued that the principal empirical base of the BCG approach – the experience curve effect – can be seen as a particular form of a barrier to entry. However, the learning curve phenomena (Andress 1954, Hirschmann 1964) has been extended from direct production costs first to production overhead costs and then to all other value added items in the product. This development means that experience economies can be categorized in two ways:

- Some value added elements such as advertising should be assessed much more on the demand effect rather than actual cost.
- Experience in the various value added components in the final product market can be shared with developments in other, sometimes apparently unrelated areas.

As Day (1977) has indicated, the oversimple extension of the experience curve concept to all value added elements has created the danger that analysis is conducted in terms of building experience curve economies in the production and marketing of Product X.

More comprehensive analysis of experience

In practice, in any experience analysis we should distinguish between both cost and demand effects and also specific and shared benefits. In particular, we should recognize the problems of cost based, specific analysis and the benefits of other approaches.

For instance, an obsession with reaping the benefits of experience curve cost economies can result in a strategic posture in the marketplace that is severely disadvantaged in the case of significant shifts in market response. Such a problem is clearly documented for Ford and the Model T by Abernathy and Wayne (1974), and should be uppermost in the minds of any executives if they feel they are being persuaded to take major investment decisions based on relatively naive and unchanging models of market behavior.

However, some cost based approaches require a broader sense of the related markets. For instance, the burgeoning market for solid-state devices in autos will substantially affect the scale economies for the production of such items in apparently unrelated markets (Boyd and Headen 1978) but the problem goes much further than this. The value added structure of particular products is likely to change over time, hence, the questions of relevant experience become more complex: Will the calculator market become an area where much of the value added is in distribution and marketing? If this is the case, the critical experience curve economies may well switch from production to such areas and thus change the set of corporations that are most competitively placed.

Demand based approaches may offer a way of avoiding some of these problems. For specific products the process of branding offers a way in which, if successful, a premium in the market can be maintained often over a long period. Shared opportunities come from activities in the market that provide future options for further development, such as the opening up of a new distribution channel.

We can, therefore, summarize the four broad options for experience-based strategies, and the examples in Table 2.

Table 2 Examples of Experience Based Strategies

	Specific	*Shared*
Cost Based	Model T	Solid-state components
Demand Based	Branding	Distribution channel

To avoid an overemphasis in our strategic analysis on specific, cost based benefits, we should recognize some of the additional advantages of the other approaches.

Additional considerations

Demand based approaches have the advantage that, if successful, they are often difficult to imitate:

> In general there may be a high level of uncertainty as to the outcome of an advertising campaign. If advertising is successful or a new styling takes, an opponent may not be able to make a strategically successful countermove. If a price cut is successful, an opponent can counter by also cutting prices. (Shubik 1959, p. 349)

In mobility barriers terms certain demand based investments can carry the additional benefit that the relevant barrier grows for those following, either because of a direct increase in costs or the need to use less effective measures because direct imitation is not feasible.

Shared experience approaches offer two potential benefits: a greater degree of flexibility in the face of market uncertainties, and the development of positions that can be exploited at a later date. Within the study of the economics of internal organizations (Alchian and Demsetz 1972, Williamson 1975), it has been recognized that firms already in a particular market have the opportunity to adapt their behavior more efficiently than potential new entrants by selective managerial intervention.

There has also been a growing body of literature on strategic analysis that has focused on this issue either directly or indirectly (Ackoff 1970, Ball and Lorrange 1979, Per Strangert 1977). However, the limited empirical evidence is rather pessimistic about the ability of particular activities to adapt to major environmental change (Cooper and Schendel 1976), and indeed suggests that such activities as more effective environmental scanning (Montgomery and Weinberg 1979) often only delay rather than avoid the threatened demise. This would suggest that corporate management should assess the flexibility in any particular project in terms of monitoring as well as future potential changes, rather than rely on statements about general management skills.

The benefit of building a position, particularly in distribution and customer terms, resides in the options that are made possible before, and often long before, these options are actually realized (Wensley 1979b). Logically, such benefits are a result of the original investment decisions, and the additional value of these optional benefits should have been considered at the time when the investments were being made to develop a positional strength.

The basic conception of positional advantages is very close to the multidimensional definition of corporate strengths proposed by Simmonds (1968), but includes the explicit recognition that today's strategy is tomorrow's history and, therefore, the strategic decisions of today are shaping the strengths and weaknesses of tomorrow. In this direction, certain strategic actions will have much greater payoffs in terms of potential benefits to future actions than others. It is important in the strategic analysis of any particular action that the nature, scale, and value of such benefits is evaluated.

Conclusion

In undertaking strategic marketing analysis of any particular investment option it is important to avoid the use of classificatory systems that deflect the analysis from the critical issue of why there is a potential sustainable competitive advantage for the corporation. /The market growth/share portfolio approach advocated by BCG encourages the use of general rather than specific criteria as well as implying assumptions about mechanisms of corporate financing and market behavior that are either unnecessary or false. The DPM approach, on the other hand, appears to add little to a more specific project based form of analysis.

Both classificatory schemes would be positively harmful if used to justify some form of cash budgeting, since it is essential that any major project is assessed independent of its box classification. The financial basis of such an assessment should be an evaluation of the project's benefits against the appropriate discount rate related to the project's systematic risk or Beta. It is critical, however, that the financial analysis should not dominate a thorough evaluation of the competitive market assumptions upon which the project is based. Such a project based evaluation must focus not only on direct cost experience effects but also on the degree to which the project can be effectively imitated by others if it proves to be successful, the extent to which the project's progress will be adequately monitored and suitable changes implemented at a later date, and the particular ways in which the project will beyond its direct substantive benefits, also enhance the firm's ability to exploit further opportunities at a later stage.

References

Abernathy, William J. and Kenneth Wayne (1974), 'Limits of the Learning Curve,' *Harvard Business Review*, 52 (Sept-Oct.), 109-119.

Ackoff, R.L. (1970), *A Concept of Corporate Planning*, New York: John Wiley.

Alchian, A.A. and H. Demsetz (1972), 'Production, Information Costs and Economic Organization,' *American Economic Review*, 62 (December), 777-795.

Anderson, Paul F. (1979), 'The Marketing Management/Finance Interface,' in *1979 AMA Educators Proceedings*, N. Beckwith *et al.*, eds., Chicago: American Marketing Association, 325-329.

Andress, Frank J. (1954), 'The Learning Curve as a Production Tool,' *Harvard Business Review*, 32 (January-February) 87-97.

Ansoff, I. (1965), *Corporate Strategy*, New York: McGraw Hill.

Bain, J.S. (1956), *Barriers to New Competition*, Cambridge, MA: Harvard University Press.

Ball, Ben C., Jr., and Peter Lorange (1979), 'Managing Your Strategic Responsiveness to the Environment,' *Managerial Planning*, 28(3), (November/December), 3-9.

Boston Consulting Group (1975), *Strategic Alternatives for the British Motorcycle Industry*, London: Her Majesty's Stationery Office.

Boyd, Harper W., and Robert S. Headen (1978), 'Definition and Management of the Product-Market Portfolio,' *Industrial Marketing Management*, 7 (no. 5), 337-346.

Burton, Richard M. and Thomas N. Naylor (1980), 'Economic Theory in Corporate Planning,' *Strategic Management Journal*, 1 (no. 3), 249- 263.

Business Week (1978), 'Goodyear's Solo Strategy: Grow Where Nobody Else Sees It,' (August 1), 67-104.

Buzzell, R.D., B.T. Gale, and R.G.M. Sultan (1975), 'Market Share – A Key to Profitability,' *Harvard Business Review*, 53 (Jan.-Feb.), 97-106.

Caves, R.E., and Porter, M.E. (1977), 'From Entry Barriers to Mobility Barriers, Conjectural Decisions and Contrived Deterrence to New Competition,' *Quarterly Journal of Economics*, XCI (May), 241-261.

Channon, Derek F. (1979) 'Commentary on Strategy Formulation,' in *Strategic Management: A New View of Business Policy and Planning*, D.E. Schendel and C.W. Hofer, eds., Boston: Little, Brown and Co.

Cooper, A.C. and D. Schendel (1976), 'Strategic Responses to Technological Threats,' *Business Horizons*, 19 (February), 61-69.

Day, George (1977), 'Diagnosing the Product Portfolio,' *Journal of Marketing*, 41 (April), 29-38.

Dhalla, Nariman K. and Sonia Yuspeh (1976), 'Forget the Product Life Cycle Concept,' *Harvard Business Review*, 54 (Jan.-Feb.), 102-109.

Franks, J.R., and J. Broyles (1979), *Modern Managerial Finance*, Chichester: Wiley.

Grant, John H. and William R. King (1979), 'Strategy Formulation: Analytical and Normative Models,' in *Strategic Management: A New View of Business Policy and Planning*, D.E. Schendel and C.W. Hofer, eds., Boston: Little, Brown and Co.

Gray, E.G. and H.B. Green, (1976), 'Cash Throw-Off: A Resource Allocation Strategy,' *Business Horizons*, 19 (June), 29-33.

Hall, W.K. (1978), 'SBUs: Hot, New Topic in the Management of Diversification,' *Business Horizons*, 21 (February), 17-25.

Hedley, Barry (1976), 'A Fundamental Approach to Strategy Development,' *Long Range Planning*, 9 (December), 2-11.

Hedley, Barry (1977), 'Strategy and the Business Portfolio,' *Long Range Planning*, 10 (Feb.), 9-15.

Hirschmann, W.D. (1964), 'Profit from the Learning Curve,' *Harvard Business Review*, (Jan.-Feb.), 125-139.

Hopkins, D.S. (1977), 'New Emphasis in Product Planning and Strategy Development,' *Industrial Marketing Management*, 6 (no. 6), 410-419.

Hussey, D.E. (1978), 'Portfolio Analysis: Practical Experience with the Directional Policy Matrix,' *Long Range Planning*, 11 (August), 2-8.

Kijewski, V. (1978), 'Marketing Share Strategy: Beliefs vs. Actions,' PIMS letter 9/2, Strategic Planning Institute, Cambridge, MA.

Linter, John (1965), 'Security Prices, Risk, and Maximal Gains from Diversification,' *Journal of Finance*, 20 (December), 587-615.

Mahajan, Vijay, Yoram Wind, and John W. Bradford (1981), 'Stochastic Dominance Rules for Product Porfolio Analysis,' *Management Science, special issue on Marketing Policy Models*, Andy Zoltners, ed.

Marketing News (1978), 'Market-Share ROI Corporate Strategy Approach Can be an "Oversimplistic" Snare,' 12 (December 15), 12.

Markowitz, H. (1952), Portfolio Selection,' *Journal of Finance*, 7 (March), 77-91.

Merritt, A. and A. Sykes (1963), *The Finance and Analysis of Capital Projects*, London: Longmans.

Montgomery, David B. and Charles B. Weinberg (1979), 'Towards Strategic Intelligence Systems,' *Journal of Marketing*, 43 (Fall), 41-52.

Mossin, Jan (1966), 'Equilibrium in a Capital Asset Market,' *Econometics*, 34 (October), 768-783.

Myers, S. and S.M. Turnbull (1977), 'Capital Budgeting and the Capital Asset Pricing Model: Good News and Bad News,' *Journal of Finance*, 32 (May), 321-333.

Per Strangert (1977), 'Adaptive Planning and Uncertainty Resolution,' *Futures*, 9 (February), 32-42.

Polli, R. and V. Cook (1969), 'The Validity of the Product Life Cycle,' *Journal of Business*, 42 (October), 385-400.

Porter, Michael, E. (1976), 'Please Note Location of the Nearest Exit,' *California Management Review*, XIX (Winter), 21-33.

Porter, Michael, E. (1979), 'How Competitive Forces Shape Strategy,' *Harvard Business Review*, 57 (March/April), 137-145.

Rink, David R. and John E. Swan (1979), 'Product Life Cycle Research: A Literature Review,' *Journal of Business Research*, 78 (September), 219-242.

Robinson, S.J.Q., R.E. Hichens, and D.P. Wade, (1978), 'The Directional Policy Matrix-Tool for Strategic Planning,' *Long-Range Planning*, 11 (no. 3), 8-15.

Roll, Richard (1977), 'A Critique of the Asset Pricing Theories Tests,' *Journal of Financial Economics*, 4 (March), 129-176.

Rubinstein, M. (1973), 'A Mean-Variance Synthesis of Corporate Finance Theory,' *Journal of Finance*, 28 (March), 167-181.

Salop, Steven, C. (1979), 'Strategic Entry Deterrence,' *American Economic Review*, 69 (May), 335-338.

Savich, R.S. and L.A. Thompson (1978), 'Resource Allocation within the Product Life Cycle,' *MSU Business Topics*, 26 (Autumn), 35-44.

Sharpe, W.F. (1964), 'Capital Asset Prices: A Theory of Market Equilibrium Under Conditions of Risk,' *Journal of Finance*, 19 (September), 425- 442.

Shubik, M. (1959), *Strategy and Market Structure*, New York: Wiley.

Shubik, M. (1975), *Games for Society, Business and War*, New York: Elsevier.

Simmonds, K. (1968), 'Removing the Chains from Product Strategy,' *Journal of Management Studies*, 5 (no. 1), 29-40.

Wensley, J.R.C. (1979a), 'The Effective Strategic Analyst,' *Journal of Management Studies*, 16 (October), 283-293.

Wensley, J.R.C. (1979b), 'Beyond the CAPM and the Boston Box: The Concept of Market Location,' Bristol, England: Marketing Educators Group Conference.

Wensley, J.R.C. (1981), 'PIMS and BCG: New Horizons or False Dawn in Strategic Marketing,' *Strategic Management Journal*.

Weston, J. Fred (1973), 'Investment Decisions Using the Capital Asset Pricing Model,' *Financial Management*, 2 (Spring), 25-33.

Williamson, O.E. (1975), *Markets and Hierarchies: Analysis and Antitrust Implications*, New York: Free Press.

Wind, Yoram (1974), 'Product Portfolio: A New Approach to the Product Mix Decision,' *Proceedings of the 1974 AMA Conference*, 460-464.

Wind, Yoram, and Vijay Mahajan (1980), 'Design Considerations in Portfolio Analysis,' working paper, Wharton School, University of Pennsylvania.

Wind, Yoram, and T. Saaty (1980), 'Marketing Applications of the Analytic Hierarchy Process,' *Management Science*, 76 (July), 641-658.

Zakon, A. (1971), 'Growth and Financial Strategies,' working paper, Boston, MA: Boston Consulting Group.

Reproduced from Wensley, R. (1981). Strategic marketing: betas, boxes, or basics. *Journal of Marketing*, **45**, 173-82, by permission of the American Marketing Association.

13 The Directional Policy Matrix – tool for strategic planning

S. J. Q. Robinson, R. E. Hichens and D. P. Wade

In diversified business organizations one of the main functions of the management is to decide how money, materials and skilled manpower should be provided and allocated between different business sectors in order to ensure the survival and healthy growth of the whole. Good management allocates resources to sectors where business prospects appear favourable and where the organization has a position of advantage.

In a reasonably stable economic environment the normal method of comparing the prospects of one business sector with another, and for measuring a company's strengths and weaknesses in different sectors, is to use historical and forecast rates of return on capital employed in each sector to provide a measure of the sector's prospects or the company's strength. This is because a sector where business prospects are favourable and the company's position is strong tends to show higher profitability than one in which business prospects are less attractive and the company's position is weak. But records and forecasts of profitability are not sufficient yardsticks for guidance of management in corporate planning and allocation of resources.

The main reasons are:

(a) They do not provide a systematic explanation
   (1) Why one business sector has more favourable prospects than another.
   (2) Why the company's position in a particular sector is strong or weak.
(b) They do not provide enough insight into the underlying dynamics and balance of the company's individual business sectors and the balance between them.
(c) When new areas of business are being considered, actual experience, by definition, cannot be consulted. Even when entry to a new area is to be

achieved by acquiring an existing business the current performance of the existing business may not be reliable as a guide to its future.

(d) World-wide inflation has severely weakened the validity and credibility of financial forecasts, particularly in the case of businesses which are in any way affected by oil prices.

Corporate managements which recognize these shortcomings bring a variety of other qualitative and quantitative considerations to bear on the decision-making process in addition to the financial yardsticks. These are described in the following sections.

Outline of technique

In building up a corporate plan, a company will normally have available a number of plans and investment proposals for individual business sectors. These will include historical data on the company's past financial performance in the sector, and financial projections embodying the future investment plans. Such projections will reflect the expectations of those responsible for the company's business in that particular sector in relation to:

(a) Market growth
(b) Industry supply/demand balance
(c) Prices
(d) Costs
(e) The company's future market shares
(f) Manufacturing competitiveness
(g) Research and development strength
(h) The activities of competitors
(i) The future business environment.

The basic technique of the Directional Policy Matrix is to identify:

(a) The main criteria by which the prospects for a business sector may be judged to be favourable or unfavourable; and
(b) Those by which a company's position in a sector may be judged to be strong or weak.

Favourable in this context means with high profit and growth potential for the industry generally.

These criteria are then used to construct separate ratings of 'sector prospects' and of 'company's competitive capabilities' and the ratings are plotted on a matrix. It is convenient to divide the matrix into three columns and three rows, but other layouts are equally feasible. The ratings can be plotted in various ways. Figure 1 displays the position of a number of different sectors in a hypothetical company's portfolio. Alternatively, the matrix can be used to display all the competitors in one particular business sector, since the method lends itself to evaluating competitors' ratings as well as those of one's own company.

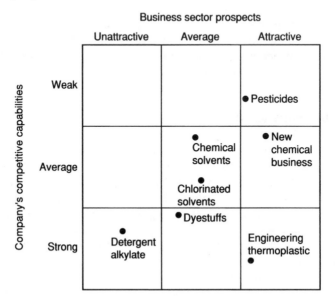

Figure 1   *Positions of business sectors in a hypothetical company's portfolio*

Details of technique

Scope of the analysis

The detailed techniques have been developed by reference to the petroleum-based sector of the chemical industry, but the general technique is applicable to almost any diversified business with separately identifiable sectors. It could be applied to a diversified shipping company where the separate business sectors might be different types of cargo, or to an engineering company offering a range of products and services. In most cases there is no difficulty in identifying a logical business sector to analyse. In the chemical industry business sectors can generally be identified with product sectors, since these form distinct businesses with well defined boundaries and substantial competition within the boundaries.

Any particular geographical area may be defined for study. For the majority of petroleum-based chemicals it has been found most convenient to consider economic blocs (e.g. Western Europe) since there is generally greater movement of chemicals within these blocs than between them.

The time scale of assessment is the effective forecasting horizon. This will vary according to the business growth rate and the lead time needed to install new capacity or develop new uses. For most petroleum-based chemicals a time scale of 10 years has been found appropriate.

Analysis of business sector prospects

There are four main criteria by which the profitability prospects for different sectors of the petroleum-based chemical business may be judged. These are:

(a) Market growth rate
(b) Market quality
(c) Industry feedstock situation
(d) Environmental aspects.

Some of these criteria are not applicable to other industries and other criteria have to be introduced. Industry feedstock situation, for example, would not be of significance in evaluating sectors of the engineering industry. Market growth and market quality, however, are fundamental to any analysis of business sector prospects.

The significance of these four criteria and the way in which they are rated is as follows:

Market growth Sectors with high market growth are not always those with the greatest profit growth. Nevertheless market growth is a necessary condition for growth of sector profits even if it is not a sufficient condition. It has therefore been included in the rating of sector prospects on the basis of an appropriate scale. For sector analysis in the chemical industry the scale given below is the one used in Shell chemical companies. The centre point or average rating, corresponds roughly with the 5 year average growth rate predicted for the heavy organic chemical industry in Western Europe. A star rating system gives more visual impact than a display of numerals.

Sector growth rate per year	*Market growth rating*
0-3 per cent	* (minimum)
3-5 per cent	**
5-7 per cent	*** (average)
7-10 per cent	****
10 per cent and over	***** (maximum)

When applying this rating system to another industry it would be necessary to construct a different scale with a centre point appropriate to the average growth rate for that industry.

The other criteria are used to qualify the basic forecast of growth of demand so far as their effect on growth of profits is concerned.

Market quality   Certain sectors of the chemical industry show a consistent record of higher and/or more stable profitability than others. These differences can be ascribed in part to differences in the quality of the markets which the various sectors serve. For example, in some sectors, notably those of a commodity type, profitability can be highly variable as profit margins contract and expand over a wide range as market conditions swing between under- and over-supply. This problem is often most severe in the case of commodity type products with a large number of producers. Again some sectors may have a chronically poor profitability record because the market is dominated by a small group of powerful customers who are able to keep prices down.

Other sectors remain profitable even in depressed periods of the economic cycle. This may be due to a variety of causes. For example, the market may be supplied by a few well entrenched producers who are content to let sales fall when demand goes down, rather than reduce prices. Or it may be that the consuming industry, able to add a high value, and having a prospect of further substantial growth accepts the need for suppliers to earn a reasonable living. Or, again, the determining factor may be the high technical content of the product, the performance of which has been carefully tailored to the needs of the consumer.

Market quality is difficult to quantify; in order to arrive at a sector rating it is necessary to consider a number of criteria in relation to the sector and try to assess their impact. The following are some of the more important questions:

(a) Has the sector a record of high, stable profitability?
(b) Can margins be maintained when manufacturing capacity exceeds demand?
(c) Is the product resistant to commodity pricing behaviour?
(d) Is the technology of production freely available or is it restricted to those who develop it?
(e) Is the market supplied by relatively few producers?
(f) Is the market free from domination by a small group of powerful customers?
(g) Has the product high added value when converted by the customer?
(h) In the case of a new product, is the market destined to remain small enough not to attract too many producers?
(i) Is the product one where the customer has to change his formulation or even his machinery if he changes supplier?
(j) Is the product free from the risk of substitution by an alternative synthetic or natural product?

A sector for which the answers to all or most of these questions are yes would attract a four or five star market quality rating.

Industry feedstock situation   Normally in the chemical industry, expansion of productive capacity is often constrained by uncertainty of feedstock supply. If this is the case, or if the feedstocks for the sector in question have a strong pull towards an alternative use, or are difficult to assemble in large quantities, this is treated as a plus for sector prospects and attracts a better than average rating.

Conversely if the feedstock is a by-product of another process, and consumption of the main product is growing faster than the by-product, pressure may arise, either from low prices or direct investment by the by-product producer, to increase its consumption. This would attract a lower than average rating.

Environmental (regulatory) aspects   Sector prospects can be influenced by the extent of restrictions on the manufacture, transportation or marketing of the product. In some cases the impact of such restrictions is already quantifiable and has been built into the forecasts of market growth. If it has not, it must be assessed if there is a strongly positive or negative environmental or regulatory influence to be taken into account for the product.

Analysis of a company's competitive capabilities

Three main criteria have been identified by which a company's position in a particular sector of the chemical business may be judged strong, average or weak. With suitable adaption they can probably be applied to the analysis of companies' positions in almost any business sector. The three criteria are:

(a) Market position
(b) Production capability
(c) Product research and development.

The significance of these criteria and the ways in which they are rated is shown below. In general it is convenient to review the position of one's own company in relation to that of all the significant competitors in the sector concerned as this helps to establish the correct relativities.

Normally the position being established is that of the companies *today*. Other points can be plotted for one's own company to indicate possible future positions which might result from implementing alternative investment proposals and product strategies.

Market position   The primary factor to consider here is percentage share of the total market. Supplementary to this is the degree to which this share is secured. Star ratings are awarded against the following guidelines:

***** Leader. A company which, from the mere fact of its pre-eminent market position is likely to be followed normally accompanied by acknowledged technical leadership. The market share associated with this position varies from case to case. A company with 25 per cent of West European consumption in a field of ten competitors may be so placed. A company with 50 per cent in a field of two competitors will not be.

**** Major producer. The position where, as in many businesses, no one company is a leader, but two to four competitors may be so placed.

*** A company with a strong viable stake in the market but below the top league. Usually when one producer is a leader the next level of competition will be three star producers.

** Minor market share. Less than adequate to support R & D and other services in the long run.

* Current position negligible.

Production capability   This criterion is a combination of process economics, capacity of hardware, location and number of plants, and access to feedstock. The answers to all the following questions need to be considered before awarding a one to five star production capability rating:

Process economics. Does the producer employ a modern economic production process? Is it his own process or licensed? Has he the research and development capability or licensing relationships that will allow him to keep up with advances in process technology in the future?

Hardware. Is current capacity, plus any new capacity announced or building, commensurate with maintaining present market share? Does the producer have several plant locations to provide security to his customers against breakdown or strike action? Are his delivery arrangements to principal markets competitive?

Feedstock. Has the producer secure access to enough feedstocks to sustain his present market share? Does he have a favourable cost position on feedstock?

Product research and development   In the case of performance products this criterion is intended to be a compound of product range, product quality, a record of successful development in application, and competence in technical service. In other words, the complete technical package upon which the customer will pass judgment. In awarding a one to five star rating, judgment should be passed on whether a company's product R & D is better than, commensurate with, or worse than its position in the market.

In the case of commodity products, this criterion is not relevant and is not rated.

Assignment of ratings – plotting the matrix

The most straightforward method of assigning ratings for each of the criteria is discussion by functional specialists. They should be drawn from the particular sector of the company's business which is being studied and assisted by one or two non-specialists to provide the necessary detached viewpoint and comparability with other sector assessments.

Although members of the group may differ in the initial ratings which they assign, it is usually possible to arrive at a set of consensus ratings. Where there are still unresolved differences, a representative rating can generally be obtained by averaging. More sophisticated methods of sampling opinion have been designed, using computer techniques, but experience shows that the group discussion method was to be preferred as the end result is reached by a more transparent series of steps which make it more credible both to those participating and to management.

Simplified system

In the simplified form of the technique each of the main criteria is given an equal weighting in arriving at an overall rating for business sector prospects and for company's competitive capabilities. This system of equal weighting may be open to question in comparing certain business sectors but has been found to give good results when applied to a typical chemical product portfolio.

In converting star ratings into matrix positions it is necessary (in order to avoid distortion) to count one, two, three, four and five stars as zero, one, two, three, four points respectively. One star is thus equivalent to a nil rating and a three star rating scores two points out of four and occupies a midway position where three points out of five would not.

It is also convenient in practice to quantify the criteria in half star increments so that there are effectively eight half star graduations between one star and five star. Half stars are shown as: (*).

The working of the system is illustrated by the hypothetical example in Table 1. In this, the technique is being used to assess the competitors in a particular business sector. In general it is desirable to record the arguments and supporting data in considerable detail but in this case the results of the matrix analysis are summarized in highly abbreviated form.

Weighting system

In certain businesses it is unrealistic to suppose that each factor is equally important, in which case an alternative method of analysing company's competitive capabilities can be used, introducing objectively determined weightings.

Table 1.   Examples of simplified weighting system

Product sector: Product X is a semi-mature thermoplastic suitable for engineering industry applications. There are two existing producers in Western Europe and a third producer is currently building plant.

Sector prospects analysis (Western Europe, 1975-1980)

		Stars	*Points*
Market growth	15-20 % per year forecast	*****	4
Market quality			
Sector profitability record?	Above average.		
Margins maintained in over-capacity?	Some price-cutting has taken place but product has not reached commodity status.		
Customer to producer ratio?	Favourable. Numerous customers; only two producers so far.		
High added value to customer?	Yes. The product is used in small scale, high value, engineering applications.		
Ultimate market limited in size?	Yes. Unlikely to be large enough to support more than three or four producers.		
Substitutability by other products?	Very limited. Product has unique properties.		
Technology of production restricted?	Moderately. Process is available under licence from Eastern Europe.		
Overall market quality rating:	Above average.	****	3
Industry feedstock	Product is manufactured from an intermediate which itself requires sophisticated technology and has no other outlets	****	3
Environmental aspects	Not rated separately.	–	–
Overall sector prospects rating			10

Companies competitive capabilities analysis (Competitors, A, B and C)

	A	*B*	*C*	*A*	*B*	*C*
Market position						
Market share	65%	25%	10%	*****	***	***
Production capability						
Feedstock	Manufactures feedstock by slightly out-dated process from bought-in precursors	Has own precursors. Feedstock manufactured by third party under process deal	Basic position in precursors. Has own second process for feedstock			
Process economics	Both A and B have own 'first generation' process supported by moderate process R & D capacity		C is licensing 'second generation' process from Eastern Europe			
Hardware	A and B each have one plant sufficient to sustain their respective market shares		None as yet. Market product imported from Eastern Europe			
Overall production capability ratings				****	***	**(*)
Product R & D (in relation to market position)	Marginally weaker	Comparable	Stronger	****	***	**(*)
Overall competitors' ratings				10/12	6/12	4/12

An example of such weightings is given in Table 2. This is taken from a particular study on speciality chemicals, in which the four functions

(a) Selling and distribution
(b) Problem solving
(c) Innovative research and development
(d) Manufacturing were considered to be the most important.

Table 2 Example of weightings on company's competitive capabilities axis

	Businesses			
	W	*X*	*Y*	*Z*
Selling and distribution	2	3	6	3
Problem solving	2	4	3	1
Innovative R & D	4	1	0	1
Manufacturing	2	2	1	5
	10	10	10	10

In addition to giving a more refined approach to the company competitive axis, the set of weighting factors is useful in its own right, indicating what sort of organizational culture is more apt in this particular business.

Interpretation of matrix positions

The results of the hypothetical example in Table 1 can be plotted on the matrix as shown in Figure 2.

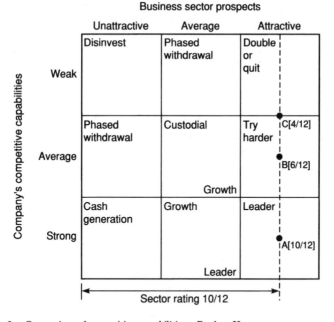

Figure 2 *Comparison of competitive capabilities – Product X*

Since the various zones of the matrix are associated with different combinations of sector prospects and company strengths or weakness, different product strategies are appropriate to them. These are indicated by the various key words which suggest the type of strategy or resource allocation to be followed for products falling in these zones.

The zones covered by the various policy key words are not precisely defined by the rectangular subdivision arbitrarily adopted for the matrix. Experience suggests that:

(a) The zones are of irregular shape.
(b) They do not have hard and fast boundaries but shade into one another.
(c) In some cases they are overlapping.

The most appropriate boundaries can only be determined after further practical experience of comparing business characteristics with positions plotted in the matrix.

Matrix positions in the right hand column

Leader   Competitor A, the largest producer with the lowest unit costs and a commanding technical situation, is in the highly desirable position of leader in a business sector with attractive prospects. His indicated strategy is to give absolute priority to the product with all the resources necessary to hold his market position. This being a fast growing sector he will, before long, need to install extra capacity. Although in all probability he is already earning satisfactory profits from Product X his current cash flow from this source may not be sufficient to finance a high rate of new investment. In that case the cash must be found from another sector of his business. Later, as the growth rate slows down Product X should be able to finance its own growth and eventually to become a net generator of cash.

However, in this hypothetical example, competitor A's position on process and feedstock economics is threatened by second generation processes. This suggests that he may need to strengthen his process R & D. A production capability of one star below market position reflects A's slight weakness in this area.

Try Harder   Competitor B is in this position. It implies that products located in this zone can be moved down towards at least an equality position by the right allocation of resources. However competitor B does not appear to have any very special advantages in this sector and unless he can strengthen his position by, for example, licensing one of the new processes, he may be condemned to remain No. 2. This is not necessarily an unacceptable position in the short term but is likely to become increasingly vulnerable with the passage of time.

Double or Quit   This is the zone of the matrix from which products that are destined to become the future high fliers should be selected. A company should not normally seek to diversify into any new sector unless the prospects for it are judged to be attractive. Only a small number of the most promising should be picked for doubling and the rest should be abandoned. Competitor

C, on the strength of his successful feedstock process development and his licensing relationships with Eastern Europe for the X process has already decided to double, i.e. invest in a commercial plant. He is therefore on the borderline of the Double or Quit and Try Harder zones: his production capability and product R & D ratings are both higher than his present market rating. Competitor C faces a more uncertain prospect of reaching a viable position in this sector than if he had been first in the field like competitor A.

Matrix positions in the middle column

Business sectors falling in the middle column of the matrix are in general those in which market growth has fallen to around the average for the industry. In many cases they are the high growth sectors of a decade or two previously which have now reached maturity. Sector prospects can range, however, from 0.33 (below average) to 0.66 (above average) according to market quality, industry feedstock situation and environmental considerations. The significance of the key words in this column is as follows:

Growth Products will tend to fall in this zone for a company which is one of two to four major competitors (four star market position) backed up by commensurate production capability and product R & D. In this situation no one company is in a position to be a leader and the indicated strategy for the companies concerned is to allocate sufficient resources to grow with the market in anticipation of a reasonable rate of return.

Products in this zone will in general be earning sufficient cash to finance their own (medium) rate of expansion.

Custodial A product will fall in the custodial zone of the matrix when the company concerned has a position of distinct weakness either in respect of market position (below three star), process economics, hardware, feedstock or two or more of these in combination. Typically, custodial situations apply to the weaker brethren in sectors where there are too many competitors. The indicated strategy in these situations is to maximize cash generation without further commitment of resources.

Experience shows that for any individual company's portfolio there tend to be more products in the centre box of the matrix than in any other, and that these products do not just fall into the custodial and growth zones but also occupy intermediate positions between the two. In such cases the matrix gives less clear cut policy guidance but the relative positions of the sectors still enable a ranking to be drawn up for resource allocation.

Matrix positions in the left hand column

Business sectors falling in this column are those in which a growth rate below the average for the industry as a whole is combined with poor market quality and/or weaknesses in the industry feedstock situation and environmental

outlook. A typical case would be a sector in which the product itself is obsoles-
cent and is being replaced by a quite different product of improved performance and environmental acceptability or one in which the product is serving
a customer-dominated industry which has fallen into a low rate of growth.

Cash Generation   A company with a strong position in such a sector can still
earn satisfactory profits and for that company the sector can be regarded as a
cash generator. Needing little further finance for expansion it can be a source
of cash for other faster growing sectors.

Phased Withdrawal   A company with an average-to-weak position in a low-
growth sector is unlikely to be earning any significant amount of cash and the
key word in this sector is phased withdrawal. This implies that efforts should
be made to realize the value of the assets and put the money to more profitable
use. The same policy would apply to a company with a very weak position in
a sector of average prospects.

Disinvest   Products falling within this zone are likely to be losing money
already. Even if they generate some positive cash when business is good, they
will lose money when business is bad. It is best to dispose of the assets as
rapidly as possible and redeploy more profitably the resources of cash,
feedstock and skilled manpower so released.

   In general, unless the prospects for the sector have been completely
transformed as the result of some rapid technological or environmental
change, it will be rare for a well managed company to find that any of its
business sectors lie within the disinvest area; it will be more usual for a
company to be able to foresee the decline in sector prospects in the phased
withdrawal stage.

The second order matrix

The second order matrix enables one to combine two parameters of an *investment* decision. This is distinct from examining the parameters of product
strategy, the object of the first order matrix. In this instance we are relating
the product strategy parameters with our priorities in non-product strategy
notably location and feedstock security aspects.

   Table 3 shows a classification of the business sectors in Figure 1, in order
of priority for resources. It will be noted that new ventures and double or quit
businesses only receive attention after those with proven profitability or cash
generation have been allocated sufficient resources to get the best advantage
from existing commitments.

Table 3 Classification of business sectors in order of priority

Criteria	– Matrix position
	– Profit record
	– Other product related criteria
	– Judgement
Category I	Hard core of good quality business consistently generating good profits.
	Example: Engineering thermoplastic
Category II	Strong company position. Reasonable to good sector prospects.
	Variable profit record.
	Examples: Dyestuffs. Chlorinated solvents
Category III	Promising product sectors new to company.
	Example: New chemical business
Category IV	Reasonable to modest sector prospects in which the company is a minor factor.
	Variable profit record
	Example: Chemical solvents
Category V	Businesses with unfavourable prospects in which the company has a significant stake.
	Example: Detergent alkylate

Table 4 shows a list of non-product strategic options. These will usually have been developed at the corporate level and the company management will have a clear idea of relative preferences.

Table 4 Non-product strategic options

Category	
1	Joint venture to make olefins with petroleum company having secure oil feedstocks.
2	Make maximum use of land and infrastructure at existing sites.
3	Develop new major coastal manufacturing site in the EEC
4	Develop a foothold in the US market.
5	Reduce dependence upon investment in Europe in order to spread risk. Develop manufacturing presence in, *inter alia*, Ruritania.

These two desiderata can then be combined in the second order matrix shown as Figure 3. It will be noted that three of the businesses appear twice, as their future development can be used to satisfy alternative non-product priorities, whereas three of them do not appear at all.

This matrix gives a very convenient method of presentation of priorities and feasible alternatives, from which the most appropriate decisions can be more easily resolved.

Other uses of the DPM

In addition to the applications described, the Directional Policy Matrix can be used in several other ways.

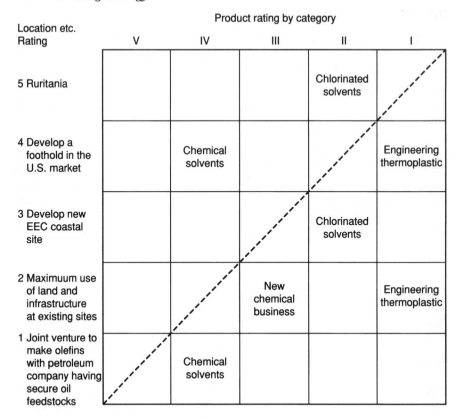

Figure 3   *Second order matrix*

Analysing the dynamics and financial balance of the portfolio

The general shape of the product matrix plot for a diversified business will give an insight into its financial position. Thus a company in which the majority of products plotted fall in the mature phase (cash generator or custodial) may be expected to generate more cash than it needs to pursue its total strategy. If so it must either seek new areas of business in the double or quit or try harder areas, or else act in effect as a banker to other businesses.

Conversely a company that has the majority of its individual product sectors in the double or quit, try harder or leadership areas will need more cash if it is to pursue the opportunities open to it.

Ideally the overall strategy should aim at keeping cash surplus and cash deficit sectors in balance, with a regular input or promising new business coming forward from research or to take up the surplus cash generated by the businesses already in or moving into the mature phase.

Building up a picture of competitors

The DPM can also be used to build up a qualitative picture of the product portfolios of other companies. Some insight into competitors' market positions, production capability and product R & D is in any case a prerequisite to arriving at one's own company's ranking in a particular sector. The matrix analysis will perform a useful function in codifying this information and highlighting areas where more needs to be obtained.

Once competitors' matrices have been plotted, and assuming that competitors will base their investment decisions on broadly the same logic, one can gain an insight into their likely future moves. For example, the matrix analysis will identify the points at which a competitor's production capability is weaker than his market position and hence will indicate that he is likely to lose market share unless he strengthens his position by further investment in manufacturing plant. Conversely it will also identify where production capability is stronger and a competitor is likely to seek to gain market share.

Bibliography

Planning a Chemical Company's Prospects, published by the Royal Dutch/ Shell Group of companies.
Perspectives: The Product Portfolio. The Growth Share Matrix. The Boston Consulting Group.
Barry Hedley, Strategy and the 'Business Portfolio', *Long Range Planning*, 10, February (1973).

Part Four

Strategy Implementation

The strategic planning process so elaborately described in texts on strategic marketing are clearly aimed at generating a detailed plan that describes the strategies to be pursued on a business or product level. As *strategic* plans they *should* embrace all the different activities (finance, manufacturing, etc.), each of which has an important role in their operationalization. Our focus is, though, on marketing, the activities of which will be subsumed in the overall plan; however, if there is a separate marketing function, this may formulate its own marketing plans.

It is assumed that these plans can be employed as a blueprint for action so that their prescriptions are applied as detailed in the plan by the marketing implementators. Appropriate feedback mechanisms in place detect any deviation from plan and appropriate actions can be taken to put the business back on course. The results of these plans may form an input into the next strategic planning cycle, acting as some form of baseline for future activities. In theory, there should be analyses of under-, and indeed, over-achievement as part of the internal audit.

In formulating the general strategic direction various analytical frameworks have been proposed, one of the earliest being Ansoff's (1968) directional matrix. From this four general growth strategies can be identified:

- *Market penetration*, with the aim being to increase volume sales through increased market share; higher per capita consumption from, for example, new uses for the product
- *Market development*, through entry into new market segments, or new territories, from, for example, international expansion
- *New product development*], involving the development of new products for sale within existing markets
- *Diversification*, the riskiest option of all, involving the development of new businesses which may or may not be related to existing businesses.

Economics grounded approaches would draw the distinction between organic or internal development, founded on, for example, the development of new and existing products in house, and external development, using acquisitions and mergers. The latter may involve diversification into unrelated business areas, or vertical or horizontal integration. Mintzberg's (1988) analysis of strategies is essentially a summary of these different approaches. He writes of *distinguishing* a core business, *elaborating* it, *extending* it and finally *reconceiving* it.

The importance of economies of scale and learning effects became part of a widely acknowledged component of the strategic paradigm during the post-second world war era, even though, of course, they had been accepted and acted on significantly earlier. Through centralization of production in large plants, companies could secure significant cost advantages. The focus then was on selling of the large output to ensure high utilization of capacity and naturally market share became a major objective. This perspective is summarized by Hedley (1976), in the first article of Part Four, who suggests that for every product or service it is possible to identify an experience curve which applies to the total costs involved in manufacturing, distributing and selling a product. According to Hedley, it has been found that real unit cost falls 20–30% for each doubling of cumulative experience. Theoretically companies could, assuming they were active in ensuring that experience gains were realized, pursue an aggressive low pricing strategy on the assumption that the reduction in costs required would be realized through higher volume.

More recently, Porter (1980) has put forward a matrix that outlines four major strategic options. According to Porter, companies can only establish a competitive advantage on the basis of cost leadership, demanding lean, no frills operations; or differentiation, based on such pillars as quality of the product, high service support and a premium image. Because differentiation involves additional costs, it is not compatible with a cost leadership stance. Each of these can be pursued for the general market or for specific segment(s) of the market, the latter being termed focus strategies. Companies which do not excel at either differentiation or cost leadership are, according to Porter, likely to be 'stuck in the middle', being good at little and having a poor performance as a consequence.

However, the notion of 'stuck in the middle' has been criticized (Cronshaw *et al.*, 1994) as lacking any empirical foundation. As Hall's (1980) study of 64 firms in 'mature' sectors indicates, firms which achieve both low costs and a differentiated status had outstandingly good performances. However, in general his study suggests that performance could be related to either the attainment of the lowest cost position, coupled with both an acceptable delivered quality, and pricing aimed at securing profitable volume and market share growth; or to the achievement of the highest product/service/ quality differentiated position relative to competition combined with both an acceptable cost structure and pricing to gain margins sufficient to fund reinvestment in product/service differentiation. The methodology employed to obtain these categorizations is, however, vague. Overall, the major and hardly insightful conclusion might be that firms that are not good at either being efficient or achieving 'quality' do not perform well.

The general lack of empirical evidence underlying the prescriptions on strategy should naturally generate scepticism, while the methodologies that are employed in some research are often less than robust (because of issues relating to how performance is measured and over what time period, the categorization of 'markets', the meaning of such terms as 'high' and 'low'). The tendency to focus on competitors *per se* rather than on the changing values and requirements of customers has also been criticized by Ohmae (1988) who believes there has been a shift far too much in favour of the former. This can lead to 'tit-for-tat' competitive rivalry, perhaps at the expense of providing adequately satisfactory offerings to customers, thereby opening up an opportunity to those, including new entrants, which do.

Perhaps more questionable is the emphasis on generic strategies *per se*. By very definition they are so *general* as to be at best bland; whilst the essence of competitiveness is surely the ability to distinguish the company in some way from its rivals in a way that buyers find more acceptable. Successful organizations might be expected to be individualistic and innovative, and not follow some accepted strategic recipe. However, nothing is imitated more than success, so that the high-performing companies need to maintain their differentiated position with values perceived as important by customers; they also need to have in place programmes for continuing to ensure that they change according to manifest or anticipated adjustments in the environment within which they are operating – and to do so ahead of competitors. Peters and Waterman (1982), among others, have emphasized the need for the 'excellent' organization to innovate:

> . . . *innovative companies are especially adroit at continually responding to change of any sort in their environments* . . . when the environment changes, these companies change too. As the needs of their customers shift, the skills of their competitors improve, the mood of the public perturbates, the forces of international trade realign, and government regulations shift, these companies tack, revamp, adjust, transform, and adapt. In short, as a whole culture, they innovate. (p. 12)

The need for continual development and innovation is emphasized in numerous articles and studies. For example, Levitt (1965) highlights the importance of having a strategy for adapting products in order to extend product lives through developing new uses for the product, entering or establishing new markets, extending the brand and so on. Various innovation strategies have been identified, ranging from 'first-to-market' (Ansoff and Stewart, 1967), or pioneering strategy, through the defensive, imitative, entrepreneurial and 'do-nothing' strategies.

Evolutionary perspectives on market development reinforce the need for a more dynamic view of strategy. Even the simple life cycle view points to the way strategy can be expected to progress from a state where the major features are innovation and high costs to a state where products generally have a perceived commodity status. At this stage, there is consequently intense price competition so that efficiency is the hallmark of the competitive firm. Eventually, though, there may be a move towards delivering high perceived value from the equilibrium low cost base. According to Gilbert and Strebel (1987), in the second article of Part Four, firms can anticipate the shift by adopting various strategies, such as the *pre-emptive strategy* aimed at moving the industry life cycle from the emergent to the growth stage, thereby securing an advantage over unprepared competitors.

Although there is something unappealingly deterministic about such cyclical models, there does appear to be a pattern to product market development along the lines suggested by Gilbert and Strebel, and perhaps the art is ensuring that the company shapes the market evolution to an agenda that suits its own requirements. There are also at least two general lessons: that of carefully monitoring the competitive moves and the way in which the product market develops; and of having in place the strategies and structures which enable the company to be competitively effective in contexts that have dramatically different requirements. The necessary organizational metamorphosis implied by such a shift to a high level of efficiency from differentiation based on innovation may not be easily effected by some organizations which will either be compelled to exit from the product market or, realizing their inability to adjust, leave voluntarily and in some cases at a profit.

The paper by Wong *et al.* included as the third article of Part Four suggests that it is important to adopt an assertive but structured approach towards market development. In a study which compares UK subsidiaries of Japanese companies with UK equivalents, it emerged that the Japanese followed strategies aimed at stimulating primary demand and creating new markets, while paying higher regard than the UK firms to the essentials of marketing, such as segmentation of markets and the clear development of customer value. The UK firms, on the other hand, tended to focus on defending their existing market positions through cost reductions. It can reasonably be argued that the comparative analysis is biased in that the sample of Japanese subsidiaries would by the very nature of the selection be more strategically aggressive. It would have been more interesting to compare subsidiaries of UK and Japanese firms in some overseas markets. Nevertheless, some of the important elements of an overall effective strategy, especially in foreign markets, emerge from the study.

It is generally argued that the supporting detail on *how* the strategies are to be implemented is embodied in a written document generally referred to as the *strategic marketing plan*. This should ensure that at least the organization has in place the rudiments for implementing, monitoring and controlling the strategy (Bonoma and Crittenden, 1988). The plan might contain the specific objectives in terms of, for example, sales, profits and market share; the pricing strategy and policies; the communications strategy; and various other elements of the traditional marketing mix necessary for the organization to meet its strategic objectives. As Ross and Silverblatt (1987) found, many firms at least pay lip service to some notion of strategic planning.

Marketing plans can naturally assume various levels of detail and comprehensiveness. They may be written for businesses as a whole, as well as being prepared for specific product groups and even products, if their importance merits this. The impression that has widespread currency is that the planners devise the product plans which are then handed down as 'tablets from the mount' to be implemented. Action then is somehow seen as divorced from the formulation of strategy which, according to Bonoma and Crittenden (1988), has tended to receive the greater emphasis from academics.

Issue might justifiably be taken with this widely held perception. The implementation of strategy might itself be significant in shaping the way in which it emerges. Those at the coalface, as it were, will often be faced with issues, on a day-to-day basis, that the planners remote from customers and the ebb-and-flow of the market will not necessarily have a firm understanding of; while the plan formulators could not possibly anticipate all the issues and changes which may arise. These may demand pragmatic responses which in turn can have an effect on the strategy as it emerges. Mintzberg (1990) criticized the view of what he termed the 'design school' which views formulation and application as separate stages:

> Our critique of the Design School revolves around one central theme: its promotion of thought independent of action, strategy formation above all as a process of *conception*, rather than as one of *learning*. (p. 182)

Given the uncertainties with which organizations have to cope, it would be realistic to assume that organizations to be effective need to have the flexibility to adjust, reshape and augment what may have been originally proposed in response to new information, the consequences of previous actions, competitor reactions and newly emerging opportunities. There is also, of course, a web of internal influences on strategy. Decision-makers bring their own baggage of experience, prejudices and values; organizational history can be a powerful directive; while the relative power of different interest groups within the organization in often complex bargaining processes will often affect the emerging strategic development of an organization. Effective implementation may, according to Piercy (1990), in the fourth article of Part Four, be an iterative process which takes cognizance of the different power relationships and which involves the major protagonists. Whittingham and Whipp (1992), in the fifth article of Part Four, suggest that in the process of shaping strategy, marketing should be able to draw on authority derived from its unique position with the market. However, it could be that this is being progressively undermined by the emphasis on organizations as a whole having a market-orientation, with the possible result that marketing may in essence be increasingly regarded as not the exclusive prerogative of the marketing function.

Against this background perhaps the strategist may be more appositely depicted as someone who crafts strategy in the light of their experience and skills; the often complex political context within which they operate; and the manner in which they perceive the market to be evolving. As Mintzberg expresses in his article 'Crafting Strategy' included here as the sixth article of Part Four:

> In my metaphor, managers are craftsmen and strategy their clay. Like the potter, they sit between a past of corporate capabilities and a future of market opportunities. As if they are truly craftsmen, they bring to their work an equally intimate knowledge of the materials at hand. That is the essence of crafting strategy.

It is not surprising, then, that strategy might be seen to emerge rather than be hatched by a deliberately conceived and detailed plan. Such a process is described in the article by Hutt *et al.* (1988), in the seventh article of Part Four. In their case study, they identify in particular the pivotal role of the salesperson as the initiator of an innovation and the marketing manager as the champion of the innovation. They conclude that:

> Marketing managers potentially can have a vital role in initiating entrepreneurial activities within large, complex firms. Here opportunities that depart from the firm's mainstream areas of business are defined, assessed, and then pursued informally within the planning process.

Quinn (1978) proposes a slightly different perspective. He notes that organizations, generally under the direction of their Chief Executive, are purposeful; so that they may be viewed as being moved towards general goals, the specifics of which become clearer together with the trajectories to be followed in achieving them as more information becomes available and the results of different approaches are tried and emerge.

This is not to argue that planning *per se* is inappropriate. Indeed, as Mintzberg (1973) argues it can be viewed as one of a set of three general strategy styles and it may be suited to organizations operating in relatively stable and predictable environments with the resources to be able to undertake the detailed analyses it demands. However, there may be large organizations with complex decision-making processes whose goals remain relatively unclear where a more bargaining or adaptive strategic style prevails. Public sector organizations are traditionally regarded as falling into this category. The third mode, generally a dominant form in the small firm, is termed entrepreneurial. This tends to involve bold decision-making, often by the chief executive.

Strategic marketing may well be founded on a structured marketing plan, but at best this may act as a framework for guiding overall organizational development and assessing organizational performance. Strategy can be significantly affected by the unexpected, and contingencies for dealing with what might happen may well be an important part. Moreover, luck and the ability to capitalize on it may be the essence of effective strategy.

Finally, it is worth bearing in mind Mintzberg's view of the strategic decision-making process (Mintzberg *et al.*, 1976). He saw this as:

> . . . characterised by novelty, complexity and openendedness, by the fact that the organization usually begins with little understanding of the decision situation it faces or the route to its solution, and only a vague idea of what the solution might be and how it will be evaluated . . . Only by groping through a . . . discontinuous process involving many different steps and a host of dynamic factors over a considerable period of time is a final choice often made.

References

Ansoff, H.I. (1968) *Corporate Strategy*, Penguin, London.

Ansoff, H.I. and Stewart, J.M. (1967) 'Strategies for a Technology Based Business', *Harvard Business Review*, November-December.

Bonoma, T.V. and Crittenden, V.L. (1988) 'Managing Marketing Implementation', *Sloan Management Review*, Winter, 7-14.

Cronshaw, M., Davis, E. and Kay, J. (1994) 'On Being Stuck in the Middle or Good Food Costs Less at Sainsbury', *British Journal of Management*, Vol. 5, 19-32.

Gilbert, X. and Strebel, P. (1987) in Guth, W.D. (ed.), 'Developing competitive advantage', *The Handbook of Business Strategy: 86-87 Yearbook*, Wartree, Gorham and Lamont.

Hall, W.K. (1980) 'Survival Strategies in a Hostile Environment', *Harvard Business Review*, September-October, 75-85.

Hedley, B. (1976) 'A Fundamental Approach to Strategy Development' *Long Range Planning* Vol. 9, No. 6, December, 2-11.

Hutt, M.D., Reingen, P.H. and Ronchetto, J.R. (1988) 'Tracing Emergent Processes in Marketing Strategy Formation', *Journal of Marketing*, January, 4-19.

Levitt, T. (1965) 'Exploit the Product Life Cycle', *Harvard Business Review*, 43, No. 6, 81-94.

Mintzberg, H. (1973) 'Strategy Making in Three Modes' *California Management Review*, Winter, 44-53.

Mintzberg, H. (1988) 'Generic Strategies: Toward a Comprehensive Framework' in *Advances in Strategic Management*, Vol. 15, JAI Press, 1-67.

Mintzberg, H. (1990) 'The Design School: Reconsidering the Basic Premises of Strategic Management, *Strategic Management Journal*, Vol. 11, No. 3, March-April, 171-195.

Mintzberg, H., Raisingnani, D. and Theoret, A. (1976) 'The Structure of Unstructured Decision Processes', *Administrative Science Quarterly*, 246-275.

Ohmae, K. (1988) 'Getting back to Strategy', *Harvard Business Review*, November-December, 149-156.

Peters, T.J. and Waterman Jr, R.H. (1982) *In Search of Excellence*, Harper and Row, New York.

Piercy, N. (1990) 'Marketing Concepts and Actions: Implementing Marketing-led Strategic Change', *European Journal of Marketing*, 24, No. 2, 24-42.

Porter, M.E. (1980) *Competitive Strategy*, Free Press, New York.

Quinn, J.B. (1978) 'Strategic Change: "Logical Incrementalism" ', *Sloan Management Review*, Vol. 1, No. 20 (Fall), 7-21.

Ross, J.E. and Silberblatt, H. (1987) 'Developing the Strategic Plan', *Industrial Marketing Management*, 16, 103-108.

Whittington, R. and Whipp, R. (1992) 'Professional Ideology and Marketing Implementation', *European Journal of Marketing*, 26, No. 1, 52-63.

14 A fundamental approach to to strategy development

Barry Hedley

Strategy for individual businesses

At its most basic, long term strategic success in an individual business depends on a company's ability to achieve a position such that its cost incurred in making the product concerned and delivering it to the relevant market are as low or lower than its competitors'. Since all competitors in a given business will tend to enjoy similar price levels for their products, having lower costs than competition will naturally result in superior profitability. This will be true regardless of general fluctuations in economic conditions and indeed the lower cost competitor should enjoy both superior and more stable profitability, as illustrated schematically in Figure 1. Developing sound strategy for an individual business thus requires a good understanding of the factors influencing long run costs.

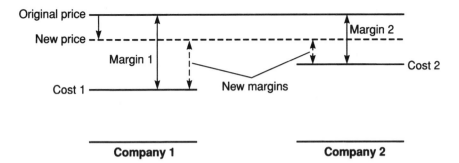

Figure 1 *The Benefits of Lower Costs (Schematic). Company 1 has lower costs than Company 2 in the same business. It thus enjoys superior profitability. Should economic conditions change adversely, as represented by the price fall indicated by the broken line, Company 1's margins will drop proportionately less than Company 2's (by roughly one-third less versus one-half in the diagram as indicated).*

The experience curve effect

It has long been recognized that the labour input required to manufacture a product tends to decline systematically with increases in accumulated production.[1] The Boston Consulting Group has found that the type of relationship involved – originally called the 'learning curve' – frequently applies also to the *total cost* involved in manufacturing, distributing and selling a product. The relationship can be expressed simply as follows:

> Each time the accumulated experience of manufacturing a particular product doubles, the total unit cost in real terms (i.e. in 'constant money', net of GDP inflation) can be made to decline by a characteristic percentage. The decline is normally in the region of 20-30%.

The fundamental nature of this relationship – note especially that it deliberately factors out the influence of inflation – makes it a particularly useful tool for product management and strategy development. The relationship has now been explored in a broad range of industries in many different countries, and it has been found to apply extremely widely. It is best illustrated by plotting real unit cost against cumulative production volume (a quantitative measure of 'accumulated experience'). If logarithmic scales are used a straight line normally results, as shown in the actual examples in Figure 2. This line typically has a slope such that the real unit cost drops to around 70-80% of its former value for each doubling of cumulative volume and is usually referred to as an 'experience curve'.[2]

There are a variety of factors which contribute to the cost reduction performance implicit in the experience curve effect. These include:

- Productivity improvement due to technological change and/or 'learning' effects leading to adoption of new production methods
- Economies of scale and of specialization
- Displacement of less efficient factors of production, especially investment for cost reduction and capital-for-labour substitution
- Modifications and redesign of product for lower costs.

For present purposes, however, it is less important to catalogue all the means by which real costs can be reduced than it is to note the key strategic implications of the experience curve:

- Failure to reduce costs along an appropriate experience curve slope (i.e. equivalent to that achieved by competitors) will lead to an uncompetitive cost position.

---

[1] One of the earliest references to this phenomenon was Wright, T.P., 'Factors Affecting the Cost of Airplanes', J.Aeron. Sci., 3 122–128, February (1936).

[2] For a full description of the experience curve effect and further examples of its application in practice see The Boston Consulting Group, 'Perspectives on Experience', 1968, 1970, 1972. (Available from The Boston Consulting Group Limited at 5 Burlington Gardens, London W1X 2QS.)

- Failure to grow as rapidly as competitors will lead to an uncompetitive cost position: the competitor with the largest market share and hence, over time, the largest accumulated experience, should have the lowest costs and thus the highest profitability.

Real costs have to be aggressively managed downwards. Poor control of operations; lack of investment in new methods enabling cost reduction; allowing an excessive build-up of no-productive overhead: these can all lead to adverse real cost performance. The overwhelming evidence is, however, that given good management real costs *can* be made to decline *for ever*. After all, this simply means that over time, and as a function of experience, we should get rather better (in real terms) in making and selling things – that we do not 'un-learn' as experience builds. This is hardly counterintuitive!

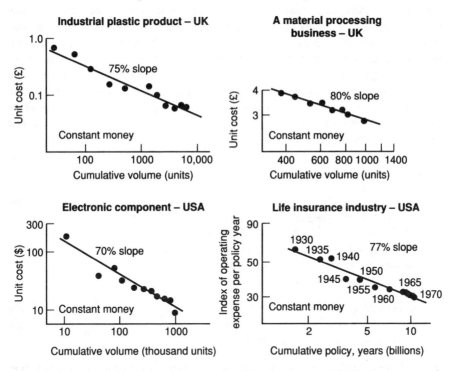

Figure 2 *Some examples of cost experience curves. (With the exception of the life insurance example, which is derived from published data, the other curves were derived for products of clients in the course of consulting assignments performed by the Boston Consulting Group. The curves are therefore presented anonymously).*

It is often easiest to find means for real cost reduction in high growth businesses. Production scale is expanding, and there is plenty of scope for the introduction of new technology and labour-saving production methods without redundancy programmes. Under these conditions alert management will find many opportunities for reducing the level of 'laggards' in the overall cost mix. In experience curve terms, the growth is simply resulting in rapidly expanding accumulated experience and speedy progress is made along the cost curve. The rates of real cost decline which result can easily outstrip inflation, so that costs even decline expressed in current money terms.

An example: electronic calculators

Electronic calculators, which in the space of a few years have been transformed from expensive luxuries into every day items, provide a very good example of this. Events in the calculator market also illustrate the strategic need for management to understand the dynamics of experience curve cost reduction if they are to remain effective competitors. A simplified history of the development of solid state electronic calculators is outlined in Table 1. Electronic calculators first appeared on the scene around the beginning of the 1960s, various rival firms claiming their invention. In the very early days it seems that the major element of cost was that of the discrete semiconductor devices (transistors, diodes) from which the calculators were made. The leading competitors were probably those based in the USA close to the best source of solid state components and technology.

Table 1 Electronic Calculators (Solid State)

	Major cost elements	*Dominant competitors*
Phase 1	Semiconductors (discrete devices)	Americans (e.g. Wang)
Phase 2	Assembly	Japanese (e.g. Sharp, Casio), S.E. Asia
Phase 3	Integrated circuits	Americans (e.g. Texas Instruments)
Phase 4	Assembly plus distribution	? (Unresolved) (Tesco, Woolworth, Boots)

At this time the calculators were extremely expensive. As a result the market was limited to those few applications for which they were cost effective. Meanwhile, however, tremendous expansion was taking place in solid state electronics in general: the market for solid state diodes, for example, regularly expanded in unit volume at a rate in excess of 50% per annum during the early and mid–1960s. This rapid growth engendered correspondingly rapid experience curve based cost and price declines in discrete devices: for example, between 1960 and 1965 the price of the average germanium diode in the USA fell by a factor of seven in real terms. Before long, the main concern in calculator costs became the labour costs, largely related to assembly.

As a result of this, during the mid-1960s the advantage passed to the low labour countries including – at that time – Japan. Japanese companies had assumed virtual control of the market by the end of the decade. Costs continued to come down on an experience curve basis and the market expanded as prices dropped lower and lower, bringing electronic calculators within the range of more pockets. The overall size of the market was now beginning to look very attractive and in the early 1970s the American semiconductor manufacturers themselves entered the market. They realized that with the use of integrated circuits – the so-called LSI ('large scale integration') chips – many assembly operations could be made unnecessary. The overall cost advantage thus lay with the integrated circuit manufacturers themselves, and these companies entered the market in a big way, most notably Texas Instruments who clearly set out to dominate the business.

Calculators were now at price levels such that they were becoming a consumer item. Growth was large: the annual market for consumer (as opposed to desk-top) calculators expanded from only 2 million units in 1972 to almost 20 million units by the end of 1974. Prices dropped dramatically, both as a result of experience curve cost reductions and also under the influence of aggressive competition for market shares: a 'shakeout' was occurring, rather as had happened in discrete semiconductor devices themselves early in the 1960s. This shakeout is not yet complete, and in cost experience curve terms there are some interesting considerations for the protagonists to bear in mind.

First, under the influence of the experience curve, the cost structure of making calculators must unquestionably be changing again: the integrated circuits and displays will be becoming a smaller part of the total cost. Labour costs and assembly in particular will be resuming their relative importance. This could well return the advantage to the low labour cost countries unless overall volume and experience have now reached a level at which highly automated assembly methods can be used enabling cost-effective manufacture in the USA and other advanced countries. The other consideration is the relative importance of distribution costs now that calculators themselves are so cheap. This encourages the distribution of calculators through mass merchandising outlets such as those indicated in Table 1 rather than through speciality business machine stores. The manufacturers who win in the end may well be those with the best distribution links. Meanwhile, costs and prices continue to decline. Prices are probably declining even more rapidly than costs, for some competitors at least: Bowmar, the second largest USA manufacturer, quit the business in mid-1975 and filed for reorganization under USA bankruptcy laws. Texas Instruments, the largest manufacturer – not even in the business at the start of the decade – appears to be prepared to tolerate heavy losses in order to make the market its own. The competitive struggle continues.

The story of calculators is, of course, a dramatic tale of rapid growth and spectacular cost and price declines. A clear understanding of experience curve effects is obviously necessary for effective strategic management in that business. Electronic watches will undoubtedly be the next significant market to undergo similar dynamic changes as a result of high growth compounding the effects of the experience curve.

Low growth businesses

It should not be thought that, based on this extensive discussion of the calculator business, the experience curve is only relevant in high growth businesses. In low growth businesses, too, real cost reductions are possible, but at a lower rate given the slower rate of accumulation of experience. Thus even in a mature business, any competitor who is not achieving the appropriate experience curve cost reductions can expect to be in profit trouble over the long term.

This is the first simple and fundamental strategic message of the experience curve: never relax on cost control. In many growth businesses, US companies actually control cost monthly on an experience curve basis. All companies, in all businesses, should at least ensure that their real costs are not rising on trend. Analysis often reveals that companies who pride themselves on good cost control are not in fact as tough as this in practice. They should be: the experience curve shows it can be done in the majority of cases.

Profitability and market share

The second of the two strategic implications listed earlier has an even more far-reaching significance, which certainly applies in both high and low growth businesses. This implication suggests that – even given good experience curve cost control – profitability, over the long term, will be directly related to market share. It is interesting that extensive independent business research – of which perhaps the best-known example is the recent 'PIMS' study – is also confirming the ubiquitous nature of this relationship.[3] Market share of the acquired firm has also been identified as the critical success requirement in a recent study of European acquisitions.[4] Only rarely is it possible to find explicit cost data for a number of competitors in a single business in order to verify directly the fact that the experience curve effect is at the root of this profit/market share relationship. One example is, however, given by the cost data made public in the USA in anti-trust hearings concerning the business of manufacturing steam turbine electricity generators.

These data are displayed on an experience curve basis in Figure 3. General Electric, the largest competitor, at any point in time had the lowest unit costs. All three competitors tended to move in step over time down a common experience curve. While the market shares remained stable, relative cost level

---

[3] A concise report of the main findings of the 'PIMS' study is given in Robert D. Buzzell, Bradley T. Gale, and Ralph G.M. Sultan, 'Market Share: Key to Profitability', *Harvard Business Review*, January-February (1975).

[4] John Kitching, 'Winning and Losing with European Acquisitions', *Harvard Business Review*, March-April (1974).

stayed stable. General Electric were consistently more profitable than Westinghouse who in turn were more profitable than Allis Chalmers. Despite making real cost reductions on trend over time, Allis Chalmers could never catch up with the leaders unless the relative market share positions were changed. And indeed it looks as though Allis Chalmers even failed to secure real cost reductions on trend over the last 5 or 6 years of the period. It is perhaps not surprising that this has been a perennial problem business for Allis Chalmers.

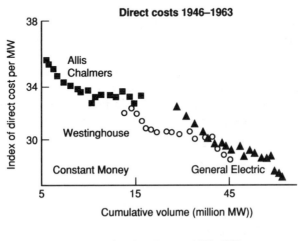

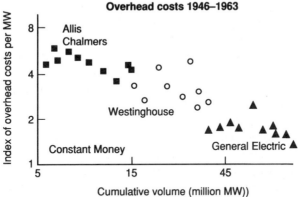

Figure 3 *US steam turbine generators: competitive cost comparison. (Source: Antitrust Hearings)*

Incidentally, it is worth noting that the slope of the experience curve relating the three companies' direct costs to each other is closer to 90% than to 70-80%. This is not uncommon for such 'cross-sectional' experience curves and can arise from a variety of factors such as: equal raw material costs for all competitors; commonly available elements of production technology; tendency for the larger share competitor to spend more per unit on marketing to stabilize his higher share; and so forth. The slope is nevertheless sufficiently steep to lead to very marked profitability differences: at a price level yielding Allis Chalmers no margin above direct costs, General Electrics margin on these costs would be in excess of 20%. This type of profitability/market share relationship is exhibited in a large range of effectively 'single business' industries.

An example: the motor industry

Perhaps the best known example of the profit/market share relationship is in another low growth business: the motor industry. GM, Ford, Chrysler and American Motors form a very clear pecking order in terms of size and profits. What may be less well known is the closely similar pattern displayed by the higher growth Japanese motor industry, as shown in Figure 4.

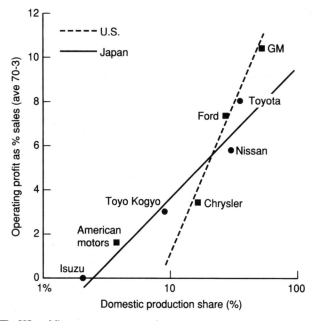

Figure 4   *The US and Japanese motor companies*

Despite very active competition at an 'operational' level between these companies, the experience curve effect indicates that they cannot achieve long term changes in profitability without changes in market share and hence, over time, relative experience and costs. The strategy implications for a low share competitor, such as American Motors or Chrysler, must include resignation to low profitability as long as market share remains low. This may well seem like a hopeless situation, given that gaining share in a major way against GM would probably be a long and extremely costly task, virtually impossible to fund given the lower present profitability of the companies.

The need for 'segmentation'

There is, however, an alternative. Curiously, a guide to the solution can be found in the British motor industry, a cursory analysis of which would appear initially to refute the experience curve effect. As shown in Table 2, the profit relationship between Ford, Vauxhall and Chrysler is much as one would predict from the experience curve. British Leyland, however, which is almost twice the size of Ford in turnover, has been significantly less profitable on trend. The likely reason for this apparent anomaly is revealed on more detailed examination.

Table 2 The British Motor Industry

	Average 1970-1973	
	Sales (£m)	Op. profit margin (%)
British Leyland	1261	4.1
Ford (UK)	716	4.8
Vauxhall	262	0.3
Chrysler (UK)	249	0.6

In Table 3, the basic product offerings of the UK motor companies are listed. The tremendous breadth of Leyland's product line relative to the other manufacturers is startling. This is, of course, partly a legacy of the way Leyland was put together by merger. Yet undoubtedly a detailed experience curve analysis would show that the main determinant of cost in an individual car model is production scale of that basic model, although the potential cost level is also likely to be influenced by the overall accumulated experience of the firm as a whole. Clearly Leyland's average volume *per model* is in fact lower than Ford's and this will put a strategic limitation on the cost level which Leyland can attain even given the good labour relations, smooth production operations, and competitive manning which the CPRS study of the industry showed to be so necessary.[5]

Any future for Leyland in popular cars must surely lie at least in part in the direction of a strategy developing greater volume per model, either through increased market share, increased rationalization or specialization, or some combination of the two. The same could be said of Chrysler in either the UK or, indeed the USA though here the degree of focus would need to be even greater. Again, this conclusion would tend to be supported by the findings of the CPRS study. It is certainly true, however, that huge overall size is not essential for profitability in the car industry: Rolls Royce Motors, with a turnover of the order of £50–60m, shows a before tax return on

[5]The Central Policy Review Staff *The Future of the British Car Industry*, Her Majesty's Stationery Office, London (1975).

Table 3   UK Car Manufacturers Base Product Offerings (Mid 1975)

Leyland	Ford	Vauxhall	Chrysler
Allegro	Escort	Viva	Imp
Maxi	Cortina	Chevette	Avenger
1800/2200	Capri	Victor	Hunter
MG Midget	Consul/Granada		
MGB			
Mini			
Marina			
Rover Saloon			
Range Rover			
Triumph Spitfire			
Toledo/Dolomite			
2000/2500 Saloon			
TR 6			
TR 7			
Stag			
Jaguar XJ6 12			
V12 Open E-Type			
(Daimler Limousine)			
(Taxi)			

capital of almost 20%; Group Lotus, with a turnover of around £10m, has even higher profitability. Of course, seeking profitability by specialized *segment* based dominance can be risky, as other speciality car manufacturers have discovered from time to time (e.g. Jensen, Aston Martin). But this is the only approach for a small manufacturer if he is to have any chance of profitable survival.

At the other end of the scale, the most secure approach to profitability is to dominate the industry both overall *and* on a segment basis: in the USA, GM is not only the largest manufacturer overall, it also offers the broadest product range. Unlike Leyland, however, its overall volume is such that it is still the largest manufacturer in terms of unit volume per basic model type, whether one is talking about body types or engines (Table 4). As a result it should enjoy superior costs (though even GM has suffered from specialist volume-based European and Japanese competition in small cars), and *hence* the higher profitability noted previously in Figure 4, which is now seen to be an oversimplification of the way the experience curve effect applies in this particular industry.

The manufacturing approach adopted by the US manufacturers is such that quite a broad range of superficially different vehicles can be produced on a few identical chassis.

The motor industry example is particularly useful, since it demonstrates the need for explicit examination of business segmentation before applying the experience curve concept for purposes of strategy development. Most broad business areas do in fact break down into a number of business segments which have fairly distinct economics. However, the process of developing an understanding of the basis on which a strategic segmentation should be made is often very complex. It normally involves making a detailed examination of each major element of cost and value addition in the business, and exploring the possible basis on which an experience based advantage relative to competition could exist within each element. The reason American Motors lies so much above the profit trend of the other three USA manufacturers undoubtedly results to a significant degree from a market segmentation approach on their part (e.g. focus on smaller cars).

Table 4 US Car Manufacturers: Volume by Model (1974)

Company	Total Volume	Base body types No. offered	Vol. per type	Engine types No. offered	Vol. per type
GM	4440	6	740	4	1110
Ford	2300	5	460	4	580
Chrysler	1270	4	320	3	420
American Motors	260	4	65	2	130

The manufacturing approach adopted by the US manufacturers is such that quite a broad range of superficially different vehicles can be produced on a few identical chassis.

The overall aim of segmentation can be summarized, then, as the identification of product-market segments which are sufficiently distinct, economically and competitively, that it is meaningful to develop strategy for them separately as 'individual businesses'. The segmentation process must also identify clearly the experience curve basis on which a superior cost position can be developed in the business segment, to enable competitive strategy to be properly developed. In some cases simple relative market share in the segment may not be the sole determinant: all elements of cost do not always have the same experience base, also, some cost elements may share in experience with other business segments. In these cases, it may be necessary to focus directly on likely relative costs by synthesizing a view of the effects of the company's varying position in the different experience bases into its implications for overall costs.

Summary: the experience curve and individual business strategy

It is in practice at the more detailed business segment level that the concept of the value of relative scale and market share is applicable. The basic strategic message of the experience curve can thus be summarized as follows.

The manufacturing approach adopted by the US manufacturers is such that quite a broad range of superficially different vehicles can be produced on a few identical chassis.

- The largest competitor in a particular business area should have the potential for the lowest unit costs and hence greatest profits.

    If he is unprofitable he is probably either being 'out-segmented' by more focused competition, or he is defective in experience curve cost control.

- Smaller competitors in a business area are likely to be unprofitable, and they will remain so unless a strategy can be devised for gaining dominant market share at reasonable cost.

    If achieving overall dominance is not feasible, then the smaller competitor should seek to identify the economically distinct segment of the business in which he can dominate the relevant experience bases sufficiently to attain a viable cost position overall.

    If this is not feasible, then the smaller competitor must resign himself to inadequate profitability for ever. Under these circumstances the business should really be phased out.

These are the fundamental rules of individual business strategy. They focus on position *relative to competitors*. Relative competitive position thus provides the required simple and unchanging objective towards which strategy development efforts should be single-mindedly focused. This objective will remain valid in spite of unpredictable changes in the economic environment. Come inflation or deflation, boom or bust, the superior business performers will be those in strong market positions relative to competition in the relevant business segment. Strategic planning must concentrate on achieving dominance as its primary object. Any efforts directed towards environmental forecasting or extrapolative long range planning are really only useful in so far as they contribute to this goal.

These conclusions at the individual business level imply that in any multibusiness company, the best performers over the long term will tend to be those businesses in which the company has a superior market share; 'problem' businesses or divisions will tend to be those where market shares are marginal. This simple observation, coupled with an appreciation of the effect and value of long term growth, leads to an extremely useful integrated approach to overall strategy development for the multibusiness company.

Reproduced from Hedley, B. (1976). A fundamental approach to strategy development. *Long Range Planning*, **9** (6), 2-11, by permission of Pergamon Press Ltd.

15 Developing competitive advantage

Xavier Gilbert and Paul Strebel

Different industries offer different competitive opportunities and, as a result, successful strategies vary from one industry to another. Identifying which strategies can lead to competitive advantages in an industry may be done in three main steps:

1 *Industry definition* This involves defining the boundaries of the industry, learning its rules of the game and identifying the other players.
2 *Identification of possible competitive moves* Competitive moves exploit the possible sources of competitive advantages in the industry. Their degree of effectiveness evolves with the industry life cycle and is influenced by the moves of other competitors.
3 *Selecting among generic strategies* Successful strategies rely on a sequence of competitive moves. There are only a few such successful sequences corresponding to different industry situations.

We shall discuss each of these steps in turn.

Industry definition

The arena of competition within which an industry member should fight will be described in terms of its boundaries, its rules of the game, and its players.

Identifying the boundaries of the industry

In identifying what constitutes the industry, we must take into account all the activities that are necessary to deliver a product or service that meets the expectations of a market. In this regard, many definitions of a company's business, or of its industry, have been too narrow: there is more to its business than a product, a process and a market; there is in fact an entire chain of activities, from product design to product utilization by the final customer, that must be mobilized to meet certain market expectations.

The most commonly accepted term to designate this chain of activities is the *business system*. The concept, or some variation of it, has been used frequently under different names, such as 'industry dynamics' or 'value chain'; the term 'business system' was coined in the Seventies by the consulting firm McKinsey & Company, from whom we borrow it. Some examples will illustrate why it is important to take into account the entire chain of activities represented by the business system when deciding how to compete.

The first example is provided by the personal computer industry (Figure 1). The business system of the personal computer industry includes a wide range of activities: product design, component manufacturing, different stages of assembly, software development, marketing, selling, distribution, service and support to the customer, and the utilization of the product by the customer. Each of these activities is expected to add value to the product so that it meets the needs of the customer. A view of all the activities necessary to serve customer expectations, as provided by the industry's business system, is thus the starting point of industry analysis.

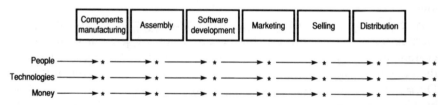

Figure 1 *The PC industry*

Different competitors have made different choices with respect to how these activities should be dealt with. Some have designed their product around the 'IBM industry standard' in order to have access to software, while others have been using a proprietary operating system. Some are designing their own components, while others are finding sources for them outside. Some have selectively authorized dealers to sell their products, while others use mass-retailing channels and others again sell directly to the final customer. This shows that there may be different ways to use the activities in the business system to provide value to the final customer.

Rather than considering the company as competing *in an industry*, it should thus be seen as competing *within a business system*, in the same way as a chess player uses the resources of a chessboard. A chess player does not try to win by asking simply, 'How do I win at chess?' Instead, the player asks, 'How should I use my pawns, my rooks, my knights, my bishops, my queen, and even my king?' Similarly, each personal computer company should see itself as competing with other companies on design, on component manufacturing, on assembly of specific configurations, on software development, on marketing, on selling, on distribution, and on service support to the customer, and not simply as competing 'in the personal computer industry.'

Learning the rules of the game

Each activity in the business system adds perceived value to the product or service. Value,[1] for the customer, is the perceived stream of benefits that accrue from obtaining the product or service. Price is what the customer is willing to pay for that stream of benefits. If the price of a good or service is high, it must provide high value, otherwise it is driven out of the market. If the value of a good or service is low, its price must be low, otherwise it is also driven out of the market. Hence, in a competitive situation, and over a period of time, the price customers are willing to pay for a good or service is a good proxy measure of its value.

The 'game' is to create a disequilibrium between the perceived value offered and the price asked by either increasing the former or by reducing the latter. This modifies the terms of competition and potentially drives competitors out of the market. Competitors will have to respond by either offering more perceived value for the same price, or by offering the same value at a lower price.

At the same time, each activity in the business system is performed at a cost. Getting the stream of benefits that accrue from the good or service to the customer is thus done at a certain 'delivered cost' which sets a lower limit to the price of the good or service if the business system is to remain profitable. Decreasing the price will thus imply that the delivered cost be first decreased by adjusting the business system. As a result, the rules of the game may also be described as providing the highest possible perceived value to the final customer, at the lowest possible delivered cost.

In addition, the intrinsic logic of the business system must also be taken into account. This logic is dictated by the fact that the business-system activities must be coordinated to provide a specific final product. This requirement is best examined at the level of the resources needed for each activity: people, technologies and money.

The personal computer industry again illustrates the point. Among the resources needed to perform the various activities of the business system, the technologies will be used as an example. First, the final customers are not supposed to be computer experts. Their technological know-how might be in the areas of financial analysis, accounting or text processing, not in programming or establishing communication protocols with peripherals. This implies technological choices at the level of product and software design that will make the machine user-friendly. It also implies that the technology required to service the machine and to assist customers, also selected at the time of

---

[1] 'Value' is used here with the meaning it is given by economists in the utility theory.

product design, be compatible with the technology available in the distribution channels.

Similar consistency requirements could be observed with respect to the other resources: people and money. If these rules of the game were not respected, the business system could not deliver a product or service of desired perceived value. Laying out the activities of the business system and the resources required by each of them is thus necessary before the game can be played effectively.

Identifying the other players

'Players' in a business system do not consist only of competitors; they may be other participants in the business system that perform vital activities. For the provider of a product or service, managing the business system can be complicated by players up- and down-stream in the system. By playing an optimal game from their perspective, these other participants may suboptimize the whole business system and put pressure on other activities.

Consider for example the Swiss watch industry (Figure 2). As long as competition was limited, the Swiss watch manufacturers, who were essentially fragmented assemblers, enjoyed satisfactory margins, even though their value added was small relative to the entire business system. But the industry experienced intense global competition during the Seventies and Eighties, leading to sharp price decreases. The first reaction was to believe that competition among watchmakers was the source of these difficulties. Attempts were made to restructure the Swiss watch industry so as to obtain economies of scale similar to those of global competitors.

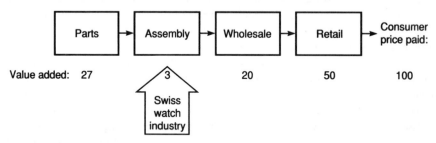

Figure 2   *The Swiss watch industry*

However, the business system shows clearly that competition among watchmakers was not the biggest problem. Producing cheaper watches was necessary, but not sufficient. The Swiss watchmakers were competing fiercely for the consumers' money with costly distribution channels whose added value was questionable for a fast growing mass market. Developing a watch which would not only be inexpensive, but could also be sold through low-margin distribution channels with no service, such as the Swatch, was the way to effectively circumvent this form of competition.

Competitive moves

Competitive advantages are built on the ability to utilize the business system to provide final customers with the desired perceived value, at the lowest delivered cost. However, not all the activities of a business system offer the same potential to build these competitive advantages. In addition, their choice is affected by the stage of development of the industry as well as by the moves of other competitors. This leads to the identification of a limited number of generic moves to gain competitive advantages.

Competitive advantages offered by the business system

Superior profitability requires either higher perceived value and/or lower delivered cost than the competition. This is achieved either through superior performance in at least one of the business-system activities, or through a creative and innovative combination of several activities. Such *competitive formulas* are the basis of all successful strategies.

For example, in the watch industry the main activities of the business system include design, manufacturing of movement parts, movement assembly, case manufacturing and assembly, wholesaling, and retail. Each of these activities can be performed to maximize the perceived value for the final user, or to minimize the delivered cost. Design, for example, can emphasize luxury and elegance, or it can ensure low cost manufacturing. Traditional distribution channels through wholesalers and specialty stores will provide more perceived value, while mass distribution directly through low-margin outlets will contribute to a low delivered cost. A range of competitive formulas can thus be developed, combining the various activities of the business system in a manner that will provide the desired perceived value at the desired delivered cost.

Two observations, however, suggest that this range of possible competitive formulas is not very wide. The first one is that there is an internal logic to each business system. The balance between perceived value and delivered cost cannot be established for one activity independently of the others. For example, it is not possible to use traditional distribution channels to distribute the Swatch. Because of the high distribution margins and of the limited volume the delivered cost would be higher than the perceived value. This is indeed what is meant by a competitive formula. The various activities of the business system must combine high perceived value and low delivered cost in a coherent manner.

The second observation, is that high perceived value and low delivered cost constitute the only possible generic competitive moves. Experience shows that there are no other possibilities. There are only variations around these two main themes, as allowed by the expectations of different market segments. Strategic advantages are obtained by combining them in a sequence, one being implemented preferably in a way that prepares the implementation of the other at a later time.

Many failures have been caused by the inability to put together coherent business systems, with respect to low delivered cost and high perceived value. This was exactly how the Swiss watch industry got into trouble, trying to compete in markets expecting low delivered cost with a business system designed for high perceived value. When the promoters of the Swatch saw that the biggest revolution in the industry was not a technological one, but a distribution one, they engineered a fine-tuned competitive formula in which each business-system activity contributed to delivering a watch for less than SFr 50 (about $25). Even though the Swatch is very precise and carries an element of snobbish appeal, the move was quite clearly a low-delivered-cost one, with a formula that provided maximum perceived value within the low-delivered-cost constraint.

Stage of development of the industry

Although it would be theoretically feasible to choose either of these two moves – high-perceived-value or low-delivered-cost – at any point in time, the actual possibilities are in fact strongly influenced by the stage of industry development. The personal computer industry will be used as an example of the inferences that can be drawn from an industry life cycle to assist in the diagnosis of potential competitive advantages.

Consider first the personal computer industry in the second half of the seventies. The characteristics of the product were in a state of flux, with many competing versions. The manufacturing process was not yet a matter of real concern, as the technology was still evolving. The business system of the industry had not stabilized. Competition was restricted to product innovation and development. These characteristics are typical of an emerging industry offering *high perceived value* to a limited market (Figure 3).

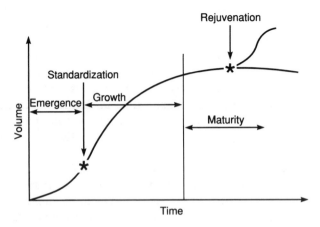

Figure 3 *Industry life cycle*

Consider now the personal computer industry after IBM's entry. Even though IBM's product was not regarded by seasoned users as particularly innovative on the technological side, it had the perhaps unintended advantage of embodying an acceptable common denominator of characteristics desired by a wide cross section of the market. Not the least of these characteristics was the image of IBM's reliability. The IBM PC was soon perceived as the industry standard.

Standardization marks the first important transition to another phase of industry evolution during which competitive advantages shift to *low delivered cost*. This new phase is characterized by *rapid market development*. The personal computer industry was no exception as it moved into a period of very rapid growth in unit sales. Attention had to be shifted to the production process, while most manufacturers were adopting the 'IBM standard'. Rather than further product development, resources were now directed towards the entire business system: process technology, market positioning and distribution efficiency were key.

When IBM and others began to use prices strategically, many of the early competitors could not follow. Those who did survive had joined the industry-standard bandwagon and had the necessary resources to invest in the manufacturing process. The key competitors were now large, professional firms which followed a similar, low-delivered-cost industry discipline.

At the end of 1984 and in 1985, however, a new turn took place in the industry. Signs of *industry maturity* were appearing in the U.S., while activity was starting again on the side of product improvement. IBM itself launched its PC-AT and the need for networks was receiving increasing attention from competitors. Such renewed interest in the perceived value of the product is typical at this stage of an industry's evolution, often called rejuvenation (Figure 3). However, the entire process that made the business system work was still getting much attention. Resources were now channelled both to the process and to a new product generation: integrated computer networks. These developments were in the hands of a few large competitors who could be active on two fronts, process and product.

In a *maturing industry, rejuvenation* is the second important evolutionary transition. It marks the shift to product differentiation and innovation, in addition to cost reduction and process efficiency. At this stage, competitive advantage must be maintained on two fronts: *low delivered cost* and, again, *high perceived value*. As a result of this combination, however, perceived-value advantages can only be marginal and short-lived. This is a time when marketing activity is at its peak.

The effectiveness of high-perceived-value and low-delivered-cost advantages thus varies with the stage of development of the industry. The two generic moves that lead to these advantages must be implemented at the right stage of development of the industry, either to acelerate its evolution, or to follow it.

Identifying strategic groups

The competitors in an industry can be positioned according to which generic moves thay are making at a given time. The resulting mapping may be examined for signs of strategic groups of competitors.

Identifying strategic groups can serve several purposes. An important one is to assess how the moves of competitors may affect the evolution of the industry. The life cycle of an industry is not only pulled by changes in market expectations. It is also pushed by the move of some of the competitors. For example, IBM's entry in the personal computer industry accelerated the transition to market development. Subsequently, IBM's low-delivered-cost move accompanied with decreasing prices accelerated the transition to maturity. As we have seen, assessing the industry evolution is an important input in deciding which competitive move to implement next.

In addition, the identification of strategic groups can serve two other purposes. First, by observing how the key competitors are playing the business system to obtain their competitive advantages, it is possible to develop a better understanding of the business system and of the possible competitive advantages it offers. Second, identifying which competitive positions are occupied and by whom helps decide which competitors may be confronted or avoided.

Although the movements of competitors can be assessed quantitatively, since both perceived value and delivered cost can be measured, an example of how it can be done qualitatively will be provided here. This example is based on the personal computer industry (Figure 4).

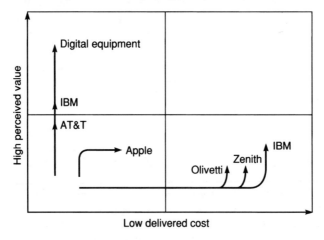

Figure 4   *Strategic groups: the PC industry*

Three main groups could be identified in early 1986. The first group included the industry-standard competitors, of course led by IBM. A low-delivered-cost obsession was clear with this group, as indicated by the price decreases that marked 1985 and were continuing in 1986. In addition to IBM, the group included Compaq, Zenith, for example in the U.S., Sharp, Epson and Toshiba from Japan, and Olivetti from Europe. All were offering basically the same commodity-like product. All were seeing low price as a necessary condition to stay in the game. However, and this is characteristic of a mature industry, all were also trying to offer something else in addition to low price, such as more speed, more capacity, more user-friendliness, wider distribution. But none of these features could yield a lasting advantage.

There was a second group that was trying to exploit the fact that the rules of the game could perhaps be changed. If networking of personal computers, with each other and with mainframes, became critical, which seemed to be the case, the personal computer would become a standard work-station in a decentralized data processing system. It would no longer be the 'force de frappe' and future competitive advantages would accrue from the ability to provide communication hardware and software.

Among the companies competing effectively in this direction were Digital Equipment and other mini-computer vendors, who had traditionally net-worked their machines. IBM was also trying to compete on this front, with its usual follower approach, but it was hampered by its traditionally centralized approach to data processing. AT&T and other telecommunication companies were other credible contenders. The strategies in this group were clearly on the side of high perceived value. The battle of communication standards that was taking place at that time was characteristic of these strategies.

There was finally a third group of those who were beginning to look as if they had missed the boat. Apple was still its most successful member, fighting with low prices and product uniqueness, but a uniqueness of increasingly questionable relevance. However, Apple's statements of intention concerning a future compatibility of the Macintosh with IBM's personal-computer standard and with Digital Equipment's network architecture, demonstrated some understanding of the emerging new rules of the game.

Generic strategies

Two generic moves, leading either to high-perceived-value, or to low-delivered-cost advantages, have been identified and their relevance at different stages of evolution of an industry has been discussed. Successful competitors, however, appear to be combining these moves within overall strategies that allow them to maintain a superior competitive position throughout the evolution of their industry. Two types of generic strategies can be identified:

- One-dimensional strategies, either high-perceived-value, or low-delivered-cost
- Outpacing strategies, either pre-emptive or pro-active.

One-dimensional strategies

One-dimensional strategies rely on the continued repetition of one move, either a high-perceived-value one, or low-delivered-cost one. The situations where this seems possible are not numerous. Only in industries with very short life cycles, like fashion, is it possible to pursue indefinitely a high-perceived-value strategy. Only in industries with very long life cycles, like commodities, is it possible to stick continuously to a low-delivered-cost strategy. In other instances, one-dimensional strategies often hide an inability to implement a new move at the right time and lead to disasters.

The Japanese entry into Western automobile markets is an illustration. In the Sixties, Western manufacturers were pursuing high-perceived-value strategies. In the U.S., this led to yearly model changes. In Europe, ingenious, over-engineered small cars were being produced with rather primitive processes. In the late sixties, Japanese manufacturers began to sell basic and very inexpensive cars thanks to their highly efficient way of playing the business system, of which the manufacturing process was only a part. Success was almost immediate. Western manufacturers failed to see the need for a radical change in their competitive thrust and several were never able to respond.

However, this was not the end of the story. Both the price umbrella offered by Western manufacturers and the superior productivity of the Japanese allowed the latter to reinvest their cash-flow into product improvements and to offer more value for the same price. In Europe, this shift towards higher perceived value was welcomed because it brought new attraction to a standardizing product entering the maturity stage. In the U.S., it essentially met an unsatisfied need for a lower-value, lower-price car to which U.S. manufacturers could never respond. This is evidenced by the instant success achieved by Hyundai by providing the same value as a Japanese car maker, but for less money.

Outpacing strategies

The example of the automobile industry showed clearly that the formulation of a successful strategy rarely relies on the repeated implementation of the same move to maintain a static position. Successful strategies generally consist of a planned sequence of moves from one position to another, at the right time. The sequential implementation of competitive moves should not be seen as strategy changes. It must be planned, one move creating the conditions for the implementation of the next. The dynamic nature of successful strategies is reflected in their description as *outpacing* strategies (Figure 5). Outpacing strategies can be pre-emptive or pro-active.

A pre-emptive strategy is needed by an industry leader to prevent the occurrence of a situation such as the one in the automobile industry. If successful, this strategy will shift the industry life cycle from the emergence stage to the growth stage. Its purpose is to prevent followers from developing secure low-price positions. This is achieved by shifting at the right time from a high-perceived-value position to a low-delivered-cost one. This implies the establishment of a product standard and the development of a *pricing reserve*.

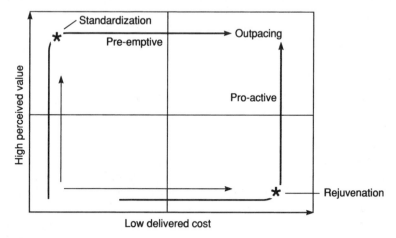

Figure 5 *Outpacing strategies*

Establishing a standard is not only a matter of technology, as was well demonstrated by the IBM Personal Computer. It is rather a question of business system: establishing a formula that meets the expectations of a larger number of potential customers than do other competitive formulas. It is the desired outcome of a high-perceived-value move.

Developing a pricing reserve simply means investing in process improvements to enable the shift to a low-delivered-cost strategy, as soon as a standard is accepted. Experience shows that very few companies can make this shift effectively. It is nevertheless the condition for the tactical use of prices to prevent followers from generating the cashflow that will be necessary to go through the next industry transition, from low delivered cost, back to high perceived value, when the industry matures, if not to discourage them from entering at all. Such a strategy was followed by IBM, immediately after the IBM PC was accepted as a standard.

The timing of a pre-emptive, outpacing strategy is clearly critical. Launched too early, considerable investments in process improvement will be started before the formula is accepted as a standard. Should another standard emerge rapidly, the company will not be able to write off its previous process investments. Launched too late, further investments will have been made into product improvements which the market will not be willing to pay for. This will make it difficult to defend market share against the lower priced standards and will waste resources that would otherwise be needed for process investments.

Pro-active, outpacing strategies are required after the industry transition to lower growth and maturity, so characteristic of many industries, where price wars often equate with self destruction. Often implemented by followers, they consist in building a solid low-delivered-cost position from which to launch a high-perceived-value move. While a pre-emptive strategy focuses on a mass market, a proactive one focuses on selected market segments to which more perceived value can be offered through a range of possibilities, from simple formula differentiation to rejuvenation of the industry. All these possibilities imply essentially the same approach: changing the rules of the game of the business system.

This is done by 'un-bundling' the perceived value added by each activity of the business system: what does each activity really provide to the selected market segment, and at what cost? The process of unbundling will identify elements of perceived value that are not worth their delivered cost. Then additional elements of perceived value, desirable for the market segment, can be included in the formula at an acceptable cost.

An example of this approach is the way in which the Swedish firm, IKEA, redesigned its business system in order to compete effectively in furniture mass distribution. IKEA eliminated or modified the activities that increased the delivered cost and did not add essential perceived value from the consumer point of view. Carefully monitored sub-contracting of production to specialized manufacturers ensured quality at a lower cost. The furniture was no longer assembled, but flat-packed. It was not displayed in city-centre stores, but in hyper-stores, outside cities. A trade-off was made between minimum inventories, to decrease the delivery cost, and immediate availability. Furthermore, by doing its own product design, IKEA could ensure a low-delivered cost consistency throughout its business system.

On the other hand, perceived value was added where this could be done for a low delivered cost. A very wide range of home products was offered under the same roof and could be looked at and tried by the consumer in the display section of the stores, rather than only seen in different stores or in catalogues. The furniture was normally available immediately and could be taken back home by car. Doing its own design, IKEA could offer a homogenous, modular product range. The desirable image of Scandinavian furniture was skilfully exploited to add perceived value. Last but not least, by redesigning its entire business system, IKEA built an additional powerful competitive advantage: the know-how necessary to operate this formula.

Developing competitive advantage: an intrinsic part of corporate strategy

Analysis of competitive advantage is thus an intrinsic part of strategic management, rather than a separate exercise, as it is often presented. Indeed, it cannot be performed linearly in a way that leads to one end product, the 'knowledge of the industry.' It is performed through an iterative process, leading to hypotheses concerning possible strategies, testing them against the company's capabilities and against the positions of competition, and going back to the drawing board to assess other possibilities. This iterative process is the foundation on which each move can lead to sustainable competitive advantages by being part of an overall strategy to fight in the dynamic battle-field of an industry. Bringing this iterative process to life is a permanent responsibility of the general manager of a business unit.

Reproduced from Gilbert, X. and Strebel, P. (1986-7). Developing competitive advantage. In: *The Handbook of Business Strategy*, by permission of Faulkner & Gray, New York.

16 The Japanese marketing strategies in the United Kingdom

Veronica Wong, John Saunders and Peter Doyle

Introduction

Over the 1960s and early 1970s, the United States and other major Western European nations saw a flurry of industrial growth. Over this period, many firms grew. As they became more diversified and complex corporations, many felt the need for greater integration of the firm's key functional activities (e.g. financial, marketing, production, etc.). Out of this emerged the establishment of more formal, systematic approaches to planning. Over the 1970s, long-range or strategic planning evolved and became an important corporate management function. Its rise in popularity was accompanied by a proliferation of strategic planning tools.[1] But, by the early 1980s, corporate planners, managers and academics[2] began to question not only the techniques of, but the very processes for, strategic planning. Questions were increasingly posed about the clarifying, communicating and implementing of strategy and policies. Additionally, the ascendance of Japanese multinationals in the United States, United Kingdom and key Western European markets[3] began to cast doubt upon Western management techniques. Increasingly, Japanese approaches were touted as the new keys to success.

Not unlike many previous studies into Japanese management success factors, the present study seeks to explore what British managers can learn from the practices of their Japanese counterparts. In particular it focuses on marketing as one of the explanatory factors of the Japanese's success and dynamism in Britain: in some sectors where free trade has been relatively unrestricted, the Japanese have swept away all but a handful of British, American and European competitors (e.g. motor cycles, watches, 35 mm cameras, advanced machine tools). More specifically, this paper compares the marketing strategies, policies and organizational characteristics of Japanese subsidiaries and local competitors in the British market. It examines two key questions. First, what are the differences in the marketing approach of the Japanese and their British competitors? Second, what are the obstacles to the local companies emulating the practices of the successful Japanese competitors?

Hypotheses

Studies on Japan's success are well documented and there are many, interlinked, explanations. Major emphasis has been placed on the sociocultural features of Japanese society which support a strong, competitive drive,[4] the government's industrial policies,[5] its manufacturing skills and high levels of industrial efficiency,[6] the strong domestic inter-firm competition[7] and the supportive financial system.[8]

However, two aspects have received less attention. First, previous studies have concentrated overwhelmingly on how these businesses are organized in Japan, less so on the features of Japanese manufacturing, sales and distribution subsidiaries overseas. Second, there have been few detailed empirical studies of Japanese marketing strategies. This lack of research in marketing is partly explained by the difficulty of making generalizations about marketing policies as, unlike Japan's production efficiency, which is a common factor, marketing policies are normally affected by the idiosyncrasies of customers, competition and distribution systems in different countries. For example, a video tape recorder or CNC machine tool is marketed quite differently in Japan, Saudi Arabia, the United States and the United Kingdom. Because of the need to match local conditions, marketing decisions tend to be decentralized with local subsidiaries having considerable autonomy.[9,10]

Certainly, there is much incidental evidence from case studies and business comment that marketing has been a significant factor in the success of the Japanese overseas.[11-13] A comprehensive survey of these sources together with implications from major studies of Japanese industrial performance points to several clear hypotheses about marketing which can be tested for the United Kingdom. The main hypotheses which form the basis for the design of this study are:

1 *Market share vs short-term profits* The marketing of Western companies is oriented to profitability, that of the Japanese to market share. Two factors have been used to rationalize this dichotomy: the characteristics of the Japanese financial system,[14,15] and their need to provide long-term employment security.[7,16]

2 *Greater orientation to new environmental opportunities*   Japanese companies appear more adept at exploiting 'strategic windows'[17] – opportunities created by new market segments, changes in technology or new distribution channels. Such an orientation is strongly encouraged from the centre by MITI 6 and appears to be enthusiastically endorsed by many Japanese companies.[18]

3 *Fast market adaptation rather than innovation*   Unlike some of the famous Western companies, Japanese firms have not been technological pioneers. This has been ascribed to a risk averse culture,[19] but for many companies, like Matsushita, it has been a matter of policy. Re-design, upgrading and rapid commercialization of innovations made elsewhere appears the common priority.[16]

4 *More aggressive marketing tactics*   The drive for market share leads to hypotheses about Japanese low prices, rapid product line extensions and high expenditures on advertising, promotion and dealer incentives. Certainly, these aspects have received frequent comment.[20-22]

Besides strategy, hypotheses on the organization of marketing are also developed. Borrowing the McKinsey framework,[18,23] organization here included the 6 Ss of structure, skills, style, staff systems and shared values. The major studies imply the following hypotheses about Japanese organizations:

5   A greater commitment to lifetime employment.[24]
6   Market focused rather than functional organizational structures.[18]
7   Greater efforts to socialize personnel in shared organizational values.[19,25]
8   Organization, planning and control procedures would be more informal.[26,27]
9   A greater commitment to training, especially broad on-the-job development.[28]
10 A stronger belief in experimentation and entrepreneurship.[16]

Methodology

Data for the study were obtained from personal interviews with senior marketing decision-makers for defined product groups in 15 leading Japanese companies operating in the United Kingdom and their 15 major British competitors. The interviews, which took place during 1984, used a semi-structured questionnaire to obtain information about the marketing performance, strategy and organization of the business. Companies interviewed were chosen from three categories: (1) audio/hi-fi, (2) machine tools (CNC lathes and machining centres), and (3) miscellaneous (plain paper copiers, microwave ovens and industrial bearings).

Semi-structured interviews were chosen to broaden the scope of the information gathered, to check for bias and misunderstanding in the responses, to obtain valuable qualitative judgements, yet at the same time, to obtain data providing measures which would be broadly consistent and comparable across companies. Industries were selected on the bases of being significant nationally in terms of size or growth (all were listed in the 10 'sensitive product areas' in the 1983-84 EEC-Tokyo trade discussions), of being within the top 20 UK imports from Japan, and of having some local competitors with which to form comparisons. The Japanese share of the UK market in 1984 was approximately 60 per cent for audio/hi-fi, 55 per cent for the machine tool categories studies, 60 per cent for plain paper copiers and 55 per cent for microwave ovens.

Companies within the industries were chosen by purposive sampling. Random sampling was not viable given the small population of firms available, the need to find pairs in the industry which were reasonably matched in terms of products, and the desirability of having the limited sample reflect the practices and attitudes of the firms making up the most significant proportion of the industry. Companies were approached via letter and telephone. Confidentiality of individual responses was offered as an inducement to participation. Only five of the firms originally approached declined to be interviewed. Table 1 lists the participating companies.

Table 1   Companies participating in the study

Japanese
Akai, Canon, Hitachi-Seiki, Nakamura Tome, Nugata, National Panasonic,
NSK Bearings, Pioneer, Ricoh, Sansui, Sharp, Sony, Takisawa, Toshiba, Yamazaki

British
Alba, Amstrad, Beaver Machine Tools, Binatone, Colchester Lathe,
Ferguson, Fidelity Radio, Gestetner, Kearne and Trecker Marwin, Rank-Xerox, RHP
Industrial Bearings, TI Creda, TI Matrix and Herbert Churchill, Tricity, Wadkin

Findings: British vs Japanese subsidiaries

Marketing strategy

Figure 1 summarizes the accepted view of the elements of marketing strategy, the information inputs needed and the decision outputs from it.[29,30] The key requirements are: (1) a business needs a set of *strategic objectives* defining the market share, profit or cash flow it is seeking from the product; (2) it requires a *focus* for achieving these objectives, this may entail stimulating primary demand, winning competitor's customers or improving productivity; (3) it must define the target *customer segments* it is seeking to serve; (4) it should identify its major *competitor's strategies*; (5) the company must affirm its *competitive advantage* and market positioning; (6) it will define its *marketing mix* – the four Ps which activate the plan; and finally (7) it will audit its organization and procedures to successfully implement the strategy.

This section employs the framework depicted in Figure 1 to compare how the managers of the British companies and Japanese subsidiaries perceived their marketing in the United Kingdom.

There was a striking contrast between the two national groups in the confidence displayed about their marketing strategies: only one-third of the British (compared with two-thirds of the Japanese) felt they were 'good at efficient sales and marketing' (Table 2).

Table 2 How well does 'Good at Efficient Sales and Marketing' describe your company?

British (%) 34	Japan (%) 66

Sample size = 30 in all tables

Strategic objectives A company's ambition and commitment are reflected in its marketing objectives. There was a striking contrast between the two groups in these strategic objectives. When entering a new market, the British usually arrived late, and few had a strong commitment to it. Two-thirds of British companies gave defensive entry reasons: 'we had to in order to survive'. Several admitted they 'had never really thought it out'. In contrast, the Japanese were much more professional and clearer in their objectives: over 70 per cent acknowledged that their moves were 'part of a planned global expansion', or related to the 'potential of the UK market'. Once in the market, the British lack of commitment to beating competition was again striking. Some 87 per cent of the Japanese gave 'aggressive growth' or 'market domination' as their goal, compared to only 20 per cent of the British who thought these targets applied to them (Table 3). Indeed, 'maintenance' of the status quo, or the 'prevention of decline' was more typical of the objectives cited by the British. As hypothesized, the British emphasized short-term profitability much more than the Japanese (93 per cent vs 40 per cent). The former were willing to cut costs and allow their market position to be eroded in order to bolster short-run profit.

Table 3 What was your Market Share/Sales Strategy?

%	Prevent decline	Defensive	Maintain position	Steady growth	Aggressive growth	Dominate market
British	20	20	40	0	13	7
Japanese	0	0	0	13	60	27

How well does 'Good short-term profits are the objective' describe your Company?

British (%) 93	Japanese (%) 40

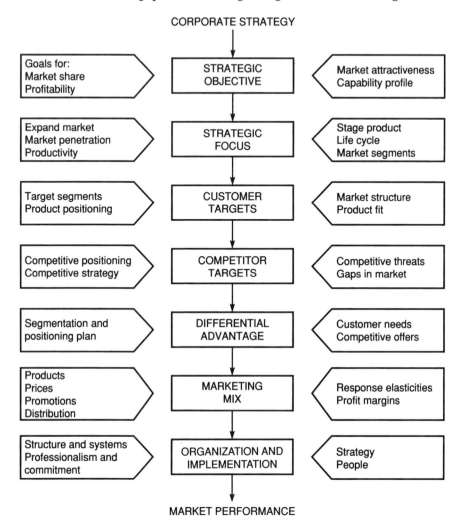

CORPORATE STRATEGY

	STRATEGIC OBJECTIVE	
Goals for: Market share Profitability		Market attractiveness Capability profile
Expand market Market penetration Productivity	STRATEGIC FOCUS	Stage product Life cycle Market segments
Target segments Product positioning	CUSTOMER TARGETS	Market structure Product fit
Competitive positioning Competitive strategy	COMPETITOR TARGETS	Competitive threats Gaps in market
Segmentation and positioning plan	DIFFERENTIAL ADVANTAGE	Customer needs Competitive offers
Products Prices Promotions Distribution	MARKETING MIX	Response elasticities Profit margins
Structure and systems Professionalism and commitment	ORGANIZATION AND IMPLEMENTATION	Strategy People

MARKET PERFORMANCE

Figure 1 *Components of marketing strategy*

Strategic focus A company can improve profitability by a strategic focus based upon raising volume or by cutting costs and improving productivity (Figure 2). The Japanese were clearly ambitious in that they overwhelmingly chose volume (Table 4): 73 pr cent sought to stimulate primary demand (47 per cent of the British): 67 per cent saw 'entering newly emerging market segments' as a principal means of expanding volume (vs 27 per cent of the British); and 87 per cent aimed to increase market share by winning over competitors' customers (53 per cent of the British). By contrast, the conservative focus on volume by the British meant that rather than pushing into growth markets or competing for market share, they often cut investments, discretionary costs (e.g. advertising, selling and market research) and new product development in a vain attempt to prevent margin erosion. It would appear that British companies quickly lost market positions because of their preoccupation with defending short-term profit. The consequences of such defensive strategies – the vicious circle of relatively higher unit costs and lower margins – have been noted elsewhere,[31,32] but seemed not to have concerned the average British company.

Table 4 Components of marketing strategy

'Good at stimulating primary demand'	
British (%) 47	Japanese (%) 73
'Enter newly emerging market segments'	
British (%) 27	Japanese (%) 67
Winning share by beating competition'	
British (%) 53	Japanese (%) 87
'Focus on cost reduction and improved productivity'	
British (%) 86	Japanese (%) 53

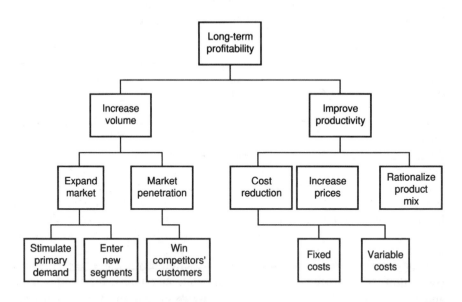

Figure 2 *Marketing strategy: the strategic focus*

Customer targets At the heart of successful modern marketing are two key principles – segmentation and positioning. Successful firms are invariably those that divide the market into relatively uniform groups of customers and target their offerings to those with the most potential. Quite alarmingly, 47 per cent of British firms (vs 13 per cent of Japanese) admitted they were unclear about the principal categories of customers and their special needs.

The following comments, one by the marketing director of a British consumer durables company and the other by the sales director of a British engineering company, were typical:

> We have not broken the customers down. We have always held the opinion that the market is wide . . . and the product has wide appeal therefore why break the market down at all.

> We do not see the market as being made up of specific segments. Our market is made up of the whole industry.

Where British companies (both consumer and industrial) did segment, it was noted that they tended to be positioned at the lower, cheaper end of the market (Table 5). Customers of CNC machine tools and hi-fi equipment increasingly perceived the Japanese, rather than the British, product as offering higher quality and status. Thus, 40 per cent of the Japanese competitors categorize their customers as 'up-market' vs only 13 per cent of the British. It appears that while the Japanese concentrated their marketing resources and efforts on the high potential segments, the British tended to dissipate theirs across the entire market.

Table 5   Characteristics of Customer Targets

	Down-market			Up-market	
	1	2	3	4	5
British (%)	7	27	53	13	0
Japanese (%)	0	0	60	27	13

Competitor targets   It is always vital for a company to identify the position and relative strength of strategic competitive groups in the industry and anticipate the strategies of their most important competitors.[33] Interestingly, only 20 per cent of the Japanese firms regarded a European product as their major rival, the rest seeing their main competitors as Japanese. Sixty per cent of the British saw their major rival as Japanese, 40 per cent as British. Strategically, the Japanese were most concerned about new products and quality levels being developed by their competitors; the British worried more about price competition.

These observations confirm that the Japanese companies are as much competitors in export markets as at home. They also suggest that the Japanese and British are increasingly forming separate strategic groups: the former are positioning themselves in the quality, high value-added sector of the market whilst the latter are retreating to the price-sensitive, commodity end of it.

Differential advantages   To achieve market success, a company has to be able to match the needs of a customer segment at least as effectively as competition. In the absence of a clear or decisive positioning strategy, it was not surprising to find many British companies weak at differentiating themselves from competition (Table 6). Identifying their own perceived advantages, 87 per cent of the Japanese cited 'superior quality and reliability' as a key advantage (vs 47 per cent of the British). Twice as many Japanese as British companies also cited 'customer service' as a major differential advantage. The British tended to see themselves as possessing a price (lower than competition) advantage, in addition to 'being British' and carrying a 'traditional brand name'. The sales director of an industrial company expressed with satisfaction, 'There is still a strong "buy-British" attitude in this country. Our customers know we are an established British company – "British-made" is the benefit we are offering them'. Such statements reveal the complacency in attitude held by many of the British companies interviewed. It is therefore not surprising to discover that many of them also found themselves to be weaker at R & D, design, volume manufacturing process development and cost reduction capabilities.

Table 6   How well do these statements describe your Differential Advantages?

'Good at product differentiation'
British (%) 20   Japanese (%) 53

'Strong on advanced research capabilities'
British (%) 47   Japanese (%) 66

'Strong on product design capabilities'
British (%) 47   Japanese (%) 86

'Strong on process development and cost reduction capabilities'
British (%) 27   Japanese (%) 60

'Strong on efficient large scale manufacturing'
British (%) 40   Japanese (%) 93

Marketing mix   The marketing mix policies deployed by the Japanese were consistent with their focused strategic thrust. Their product policy emphasized superior quality and range extensions to broaden market appeal. The vast majority of Japanese competitors (87 per cent against only 34 per cent of the British) believed their products to be superior in quality to competition (Table 7). Cost-cutting and rationalization had left British firms with fewer product offerings than competition.

Table 7   How superior is your Marketing Mix to competition generally?

Product range
British (%) 27   Japanese (%) 74

Product quality
British (%) 34   Japanese (%) 87

Dealer support
British (%) 36   Japanese (%) 83

As implied by their positioning strategy, the Japanese prices were not lower than those for British products. They did not appear to offer more 'extras'.

The two groups seemed to attach similar importance to advertising. However, the Japanese tended to spend more on promotions, the British more on personal selling. This could be explained in terms of the Japanese more ambitious market share goals: personal selling is more viable for small numbers of customers.

No significant differences were found in distribution policies although a clear difference was noted in the provision of dealer support, the Japanese (83 per cent) claiming superiority in this much more than the British (only 36 per cent). Dealer support from the Japanese parent was manifested in the way of ample stock for immediate delivery, more technical and training support to dealers and frequent underwriting of promotional and advertising spending by dealers.

It would appear that the majority of Japanese subsidiaries had more clearly defined and professional marketing strategies. They were more committed in their market share objectives, strategically focused on volume expansion and targeted at higher value-added market sectors. Quality and a broad offering targeted at different market segments were their principal differential advantage. With some notable exceptions, British companies showed little conception of marketing strategy. Their lack of commitment and professionalism resulted in their defensive reaction to the Japanese penetration of their markets. Cost cutting and range reduction seemed to have left them with weak competitive advantages and withdrawal in lower price, down-market segments in the market.

Organization

Our study shows that the Japanese subsidiaries are overwhelmingly run and managed by local personnel who do not differ in age, experience or background from those of the British competitors. So, how is it that British managers in Japanese subsidiaries often operate with such professionalism and commitment compared to counterparts in British companies who appear to function with neither. Is this due to the organization of Japanese business? For example, Tsurumi[34] and many others have advanced the hypotheses that the lifetime employment commitment of Japanese employers, their continuous training and intensive socialization of employees to company values generate an extra dimension of commitment and effort. Or, can these differences be better explained by 'Western' philosophies of good management and organization? This section reviews differences in the organization and implementation of marketing by the two groups.

Parent company-subsidiary relationship As Table 8 shows, all the Japanese subsidiaries acknowledge they enjoyed complete or virtually complete autonomy in marketing matters covering choice of products for sale, pricing, promotion and distribution policies. Nevertheless, their performance was very closely monitored by their head offices in Japan. Interestingly, control was not effected by formal methods imposed by Japan or those so favoured by Western multinationals such as standard planning systems, international product management and marketing committees[35] but rather by continuous *informal monitoring.*

Table 8   Japanese subsidiaries: have you responsibility for Marketing and Distribution decisions?

	Not responsible			Sole responsibility	
	1	2	3	4	5
Japanese (%)	0	0	0	50	50

All the subsidiaries indicated that reporting was a 'daily' or 'constant' process. The telephone and, increasingly, facsimile were the main means of communication with Japan. In 80 per cent of the subsidiaries, a Japanese national as managing director was the key person in the reporting process.

Head offices were extremely well informed of activities, progress and problems. It would appear that Japanese HQ-subsidiary relations reflected two key attributes of Peters and Waterman's[23] excellent companies – 'operational autonomy to encourage entrepreneurship' and 'simultaneous loose-tight controls'.

Organization structure

The typical organization of the British and Japanese subsidiaries were quite different. Two-thirds of the Japanese were organized along specific product-market lines. The British companies employed traditional, functional structures instead. Most British organizations were broadly based autonomous subsidiaries within the characteristic British holding company structure. The weakness of the functional approach[36] was that few managers felt totally dedicated to the overall performance of key products. The sales or marketing director would supervise sales of a whole portfolio of products (hi-fi, video, TVs, computers, etc.), but he did not have the knowledge, incentive or time to champion an individual line. Few of the British companies had budgeting or information systems showing performance at the market or product line level. Rather, these were designed to show factory or production profitability. So, market or product performance were often obscured and with them the individual commitment and responsibility for overall results. By contrast, organization, responsibilities and systems in the Japanese subsidiaries generally centred around the product or market. The usual explanation was that 'the parent company in Japan is set up this way – every division is a profit centre'.

Management style   The Japanese subsidiaries showed a stronger tendency towards teamwork and informality (Table 9). Sixty-four per cent of senior management in Japanese subsidiaries were consciously concerned about promoting group responsibility and teamwork, compared with only 27 per cent of the British. The latter often appeared to have rigid and bureaucratic structures; 60 per cent of the British vs only 18 per cent of the Japanese rated themselves as strongly hierarchical. The Japanese were also more inclined to have variable and *ad hoc* job specifications (73 per cent of the Japanese compared to 27 per cent of the British). Communications flows were also equally hierarchical in the British companies in contrast to the looser, informal, task-oriented approach of the Japanese.

Table 9   How well do these statements describe your company's Management Style?

'Group responsibility and teamwork'
British (%) 27   Japanese (%) 64

'Strong hierarchical distinctions in management'
British (%) 60   Japanese (%) 18

'Variable and *ad hoc* job specifications'
British (%) 27   Japanese (%) 73

'Both top-down and bottom-up communications'
British (%) 7   Japanese (%) 64

It would appear that the informal teamwork and group responsibility, propagated by Japanese subsidiaries, give their (largely British) managers a greater sense of commitment than that appearing among British competitors. Also, their strategies become clear and gain in acceptance as a result of a 'sequential decision-making' process. In the Japanese subsidiary, marketing plans appear first to be developed by the British managers alone. The 'collective decision' is then communicated to the Japanese managing director, usually by the senior British manager. Once accepted, the Japanese director acts to report and implement this plan in the continual dialogue with headquarters. Simplicity and clarity are necessary largely because of the substantial language and cultural barriers which still usually separate the British and Japanese managers.

Staff, systems and shared values   Interestingly, these features, previously identified as distinguishing characteristics of Japanese companies,[18] were not so strongly apparent in Japanese subsidiaries in the United Kingdom. There were few differences in the age, education, experience and background of the managers from both groups of companies. Training and promotional practices of the two groups were very similar. There was also little support for the 'lifetime employment' hypothesis. Only a third of the Japanese subsidiaries reported that the Japanese corporate policy on lifetime employment extended to local employees.

Formal planning, control and information systems did not differ greatly between Japanese and British competitors – except that the former tended to overlay formal systems with greater informal, daily communications.

Surprisingly, the Japanese subsidiaries did not possess strongly held shared values, or entertain corporate principles about 'sincerity', 'harmony', 'integrity' or 'family spirit', so commonly ascribed to their parent companies. Subsidiary managers recognized that their parent companies probably held such values but no attempt was made to imbue UK staff with them.

It would therefore seem that the Japanese subsidiaries were not very different from their British competitors in terms of staff, systems and culture. Perhaps this is not so surprising when we see that, except for the very top executives, the managers in Japanese subsidiaries were all British, and often recruited in mid-career from British companies, to which many eventually expect to return.

Conclusions

Overall, the results strongly support the four initial hypotheses about Japanese marketing. Most of the Japanese subsidiaries were more oriented to long-term market share than short-term profits, to exploiting new environmental opportunities and to fast market adaptation. They were also more ambitious! They had a clearer view of their customers and how their products competed in the market. As new segments emerged, they quickly introduced new models to match and exploit these developments. In some markets (e.g. audio/hi-fi), they have positioned in the quality, higher value-added segments, their products being seen as more expensive and desirable than the British offering which is seen as the cheap alternative. By sharp contrast, British companies were frequently production or financial-oriented. They sought short-term profits at the expense of longer-term market position. Their weakness lies in inadequate knowledge of how the market is segmented, buyer expectations and the requirements of successful growth strategies. Their objectives were short-sighted and failed to appreciate basic market dynamics – a failure to invest in growth markets leads to losses of market share which not only affect sales but reduce cost competitiveness; that adaptive repositioning is required to remain in growing high-value-added market segments. Many British firms also failed to see the dynamics of competition, notably their multinational competitors' commitment to aggressive market share policies. Whilst they mistakenly sought only survival, their competitors aimed to be winners.

It would seem that, in terms of strategy, the major differences between the British and Japanese competitors in Britain reside in attitude and thinking. The former case is clearly reflected in the Japanese aggressive aspirations for market share growth and/or domination. The latter may be expressed as strategic thinking and is appropriately reflected by the Japanese competitors' greater awareness and anticipation of market and competitive dynamics. It would seem that, contrary to popular opinion, Japanese companies concentrate on product quality, on teamwork, and on asking the right questions, not on 'fancy planning techniques'.[37,38] As noted in our study, the Japanese competitors demonstrated a clearer appreciation of customer needs, they were more adept at segmentation, they created significant competitive advantages, they were aware of and quick at exploiting environmental opportunities, they were market-focused and implemented decisive positioning strategies. All these imply that the Japanese competitors study their industries and competitors. They seek answers to pertinent questions about their markets, customers and competition. Such information has very important implications for planning (e.g. designing marketing material, setting prices and delivery schedules, developing new models, etc.).

Although formal planning and control procedures did not vary much between Japanese and British competitors, the former tended more to employ continuous, informal monitoring and shared communications to gauge progress and guide action. Such processes ensure that managers are kept informed of the subsidiary's daily actions as well as circulate information vital to the running of their business.

Our present findings suggest that many of the conventional theories about Japanese organizations do not apply to their subsidiaries in Britain. They were not more committed to lifetime employment, to training or to imbuing shared values and company culture in personnel. Their managers were similar in age, background and experience.

However, the Japanese subsidiaries did differ in structure – the use of product/market divisions – and the process of strategy formulation – involvement of the whole management team, in addition to informal, continuous monitoring of progress as noted above. It appears that in the Japanese subsidiaries, strategy and structure are related. Their product/ market-focused organization centred information and responsibility on the overall performance of a product. The functional structure favoured by the British companies results in dissipation of focus and responsibility. Unlike the hierarchical, top-down approach of the British companies, group decision-making and informal, continuous feedback found in the Japanese subsidiaries facilitate implementation of marketing strategy by reinforcing the commitment and clarity of strategy more effectively. It seems clear that market success is not based entirely on Japanese product quality and production efficiency. Indeed some of the British firms in our sample also had excellent products. Their weakness lay in inadequate market knowledge and adherence to strategy and structure that were out of synchronization with the imperatives of their competitive environment. By contrast, the Japanese subsidiaries were clearly market-focused. They had systems and structure that reinforced and assured the commitment and initiatives necessary to carry strategy and plans through effectively.

Recommendations

Three major themes or recommendations emerge from this study:

1   Many British companies should break-down their top-heavy functional organizations into smaller business units oriented around a product and market. Responsibility, planning, control and information systems need focusing around the performance of individual products rather than production of financial aggregates.
2   Most British companies need to develop more of a 'marketing culture'. Too many are dominated by short-term profit considerations or over-emphasis on internal production capabilities. To improve their competitiveness, there is need for reorientation at the top. The chief executive should take the lead in demonstrating his commitment to marketing and stimulate continuous, informal monitoring and anticipation of developments in the market. Marketing planning and implementation should not be seen as separate from other functions in the company. The Japanese take a holistic view of marketing, seeing it as a conceptual framework for integrating the entire management process from product development to manufacturing, selling and after-sales service, and then back to product development.
3   Better professional education in marketing is required. Too many British managers appear completely unaware of basic marketing skills. Strategy and performance suffer as predictable trends in market segments, competitive strategies and product developments are missed because managers lack the knowledge base.

References

1   G.S. Day, 'Diagnosing the product portfolio', *Journal of Marketing*, 29-38, April (1977).
2   R.H. Hayes and W.J. Abernathy, 'Managing our way to economic decline', *Harvard Business Review*, 67-77, July (1980).
3   OECD, *Import Penetration in OECD Countries, 1970-80*, OECD, Paris (1984).
4   Y. Tsurumi, *The Japanese are Coming: a Multinational Interaction of Firms and Politics*, Ballinger, Cambridge (1976).
5   N. McCrae, 'Pacific Century 1975-2075', *The Economist*, 38-54, 4 July (1975).
6   NEDC, *Transferable Factors in Japanese Economic Success*, NEDC, London (1983).
7   R. Gibbs, 'Industrial Policy', in *More Successful Economies – Japan*. NEDC, London (1980).
8   'The financing of Japanese industry', *Bank of England Quarterly Bulletin*, 28-36, December (1981).
9   V. Terpstra, *International Marketing*, 3rd edn, Holt, Rinehart and Winston, New York (1983).
10 R.Z. Sorenson and H.E. Wiechmann, 'How multinationals view marketing standardization', *Harvard Business Review*, 38-56, May (1975).
11 'Beware Japanese bearing gifts', *Financial Times*, 8, 16 July (1984).
12 'Xerox quietly narrows its focus in office automation', *Business Week*, 36-37, 2 July (1984).
13 'Rank organisation – for whom the gong tolls', *The Economist*, 17- 21, 5 March (1983).
14 Boston Consulting Group, *Strategy Alternatives for the British Motorcycle Industry*, HMSO, London (1975).

15 G.C. Allen, *The Japanese Economy*, St Martin's Press, London (1981).

16 K. Ohmae, *The Mind of the Strategist*, McGraw Hill, New York (1982).

17 D.F. Abell, Strategic windows, *Journal of Marketing*, 21-25, July (1978).

18 R.T. Pascale and A.K. Athos, *The Art of Japanese Management*, Allen Lane, London (1982).

19 W. Ouchi, *Theory Z*, Avon Books, New York (1981).

20 F. Furstenberg, *Why the Japanese Have Been So Successful in Business*, Leviathan House, London (1974).

21 N. Suzuki, 'The changing pattern of advertising strategy by Japanese business firms in the US market: content analysis', *Journal of International Business Studies*, 63-72, Winter (1980).

22 'The secret of Japan's export prowess', *Fortune*, 49-53, 30 January (1978).

23 T.J. Peters and R.H. Waterman, Jr, *In Search of Excellence*, Harper and Row, New York (1982).

24 K. Nagata, 'On-the-job training – a key feature of Japanese management education', *Journal of the Business Graduate*, 13, 127-129 (1983).

25 T.P. Rohlen, *For Harmony and Strength: Japanese White-Collar Organisation in Anthropological Perspective*, University of California Press, Berkeley (1974).

26 M. Beresford, 'Why the Japanese excel at personnel management', *International Management*, 203-206, March (1982).

27 I. Nonaka and J.K. Johansson, 'Japanese management: what about the hard skills?', *Academy of Management Review*, 181-191, April (1985).

28 C. Johnson, *MITI and the Japanese Miracles: The Growth of Industrial Policy, 1925-1975*, Stanford University Press, California (1982).

29 J. O'Shaughnessy, *Competitive Marketing*, George Allen and Unwin, Boston (1984).

30 R. Wensley, 'Strategic marketing: Betas, boxes or basics', *Journal of Marketing*, 173-182, Summer (1981).

31 P. Kotler, L. Fahey and S. Jatusripitak, *The New Competition*, Prentice-Hall, Englewood Cliffs, New Jersey (1985).

32 R.A. Thietart and R. Vivas, 'Success strategies for declining activities', *International Studies of Management and Organisation*, 77-92, Winter (1983).

33 M.E. Porter, *Competitive Strategy: Techniques for Analysing Industries and Competitors*, Free Press, New York (1980).

34 Y. Tsurumi, *Multinational Management Business Strategy and Government Policy*, 2nd edn, Ballinger, Cambridge (1984).

35 *Managing Global Marketing*, Business International, New York (1976).

36 P. Drucker, *Management*, Penguin Books, London (1980).

37 'The state of strategic thinking', *The Economist*, 21-28, 23 March (1987).

38 M.E. Porter. 'From competitive advantage to corporate strategy', *Harvard Business Review*, 43-59, May-June (1987).

17 Marketing concepts and actions: implementing marketing-led strategic change

Nigel Piercy

Introduction

The sources of the work discussed in this article are four-fold, reflecting: consultancy with major organizations concerned with developing their marketing effectiveness; training and development work with individual managers concerned with their own personal effectiveness in shaping marketing strategies and actions; the development of formal programmes in business policy and marketing management, as well as the results of empirical work of the more conventional type.

A focus on implementation and change in marketing

The theme to be addressed here is that of implementation and change in marketing strategies. However, rather than approaching this issue from the traditional route of literature survey leading to the statement of testable propositions, the model developed here is closer to the 'inductive realism' described by Anderson[1] in his study of the advancement of marketing and strategic planning, or the 'direct research' into management problems proposed by Mintzberg.[2]

The central point of the article is that one of the most significant frontiers for marketing is that of implementation, and thus the organizational changes required to achieve that implementation. In the most straightforward terms the central issue is the manager's pragmatic question, 'We know what marketing *is*, but how do we *do* it?' Indeed, one recent analysis has summarized just this problem in the following way:

> marketing for a number of years has been long on advice about *what to do* in a given competitive or market situation and short on useful recommendations for *how to do it* within company, competitor and customer constraints . . . experiences with both managers and students argue strongly that these parties are often strategy-sophisticated and implementation-bound.[3]

This certainly identifies part of the problem aptly, although Bonoma's treatment is perhaps less satisfactory in the largely tactical view he takes of the requirements for attacking the implementation problem in marketing.

It certainly does appear that, with relatively few exceptions, the prescriptively-based literature of marketing relies on the notion of 'rational' management decision making. This approach is characterized by the existence of a number of discrete decision areas, defined by formalized frameworks, using information collected and analysed through a set of accepted scientific techniques.

It is only very recently, and then somewhat infrequently, that the marketing literature has recognized the barriers faced routinely by marketing executives in such areas as: the diversity of organizational structures in which marketing executives operate and the impact of conflicts of interests with other functions;[1,4,5] the interaction between organizational structure and the effectiveness of marketing activities;[6-9] and the manipulation of marketing information.[10-12]

Although it is far from a complete answer, one theme emerging from the literature is that the received marketing literature has tended to portray marketing decision making as something isolated from, and independent of, the organizational context in which actual marketing decisions are made. It is this weakness in the marketing paradigm on which we focus here.

In fact, to return to Bonoma's analysis of the problem, this writer's view is that the problem is no longer simply that the implementation issue is ignored by the marketing literature. As stated, a number of recent works have emerged around this question[13,3,14] and even the mainstream textbooks have explicitly recognized the need for 'implementation skills'[15] and 'strategies of change'.[16]

The central difficulty is that even when we have recognized and accepted the problem delineated above, let alone its logical extensions, the marketing literature still lacks the conceptual framework or analytical tools with which to attack the issues raised – particularly if we aspire to a *strategy* of marketing implementation, rather than simply tactical responses to short-term problems.

This suggests that if we want to implement marketing strategies and to cope with the changes involved, then we have yet to provide marketing executives with the tools and skills they require. Accordingly, the perspective of this article is shaped by findings such as those of Kanter,[17] whose studies of organizational change and innovation suggested that there was no single 'mould' out of which innovative companies came, but that the real strategic implementation question at the company level was 'what will work for us?'

The first goal was to develop the basic proposition that a critical lacuna in the received theory of marketing, and hence in the conventional paradigms for marketing education and training, relates to implementation and change. In practical terms, we have tended not to provide a satisfactory answer to the manager's question, which was cited above. The implication is the need to develop a framework for generating effective implementation and change strategies in marketing.

With this goal behind us, the second objective is to examine a variety of empirical and conceptual contributions which are relevant to this theme, in that they share a focus on what will be called the 'corporate environment' for marketing. It is here that we attempt to build a link between the focus of the 'excellence' literature on corporate culture, and work on the power and politics of structure, information, and process in marketing decision making. The outcomes of the basic propositions which this argument produces are two-fold. They lead to a management agenda to be addressed in the development of implementation strategies for marketing plans and to a discussion of some of the diagnostic tools developed for use with managers who are confronting the problems of marketing change. These approaches are based on a model of the barriers to applying models of strategy generation and planning in marketing which arise from the degeneration of organizational behaviour from the 'rational' to the 'political'. This provides managers with a mechanism for 'making sense' of marketing theories in the practical setting and attempting to match their strategies to the corporate realities they face. Finally, we underline the potential for research developments and the direction currently being taken.

The corporate environment for marketing

Interest in the 'corporate environment' for marketing management has been discussed elsewhere.[18] In spite of its limitations, this concept has served to provide a generalized description of those organizational characteristics which have an impact on marketing, as a counterpart to the more familiar notion of a marketing environment external to the organization.

Indeed, there are various fragments of the marketing literature which pertain to the 'corporate environment', and these form a parallel to the more widely propagated 'excellence' literature and its focus on corporate culture. Such accumulating, if fragmented, evidence has focused on the intervention of various organizational variables between markets, marketing plans and strategies, and marketing actions. For example, Cravens[19] has taken organizational structure as a determinant of marketing strategies; Leppard and McDonald[20] have related the effectiveness and appropriateness of marketing planning to stages of organizational evolution; John and Martin[7] and Martin[8] have analysed the credibility and use of marketing plans in terms of the surrounding organizational structure; Cunningham and Clarke[21] studied product managers as manipulators of targets and marketing information; Deshpande[6] and Deshpande and Zaltman[10] have attempted to relate marketing research use to organizational context; and Parasuraman and Deshpande[22] have attempted an analysis of the cultural context of marketing management, and commented on the lack of a marketing theory of culture, while Bonoma[3] has commented on the importance of the 'marketing culture'.

'Excellence' and corporate culture

However, by far the largest literature in this area is that surrounding the Pascale and Athos,[23] Deal and Kennedy[24] and Peters and Waterman[25] McKinsey-based studies of corporate 'excellence' and the 'culture' of the excellent organization. For these purposes, culture is used in the simple sense of 'the way we do things here'[26] as part of the 'organizational software' surrounding performance,[25] rather than a more technical definition (which is itself problematic[27]). These works have attracted both 'clones',[28-30] but also detractors and critics.[31,32]

The most critical attention given to the 'excellence' works in the marketing literature has been concerned mainly with attempts to validate their central propositions empirically. For example: Saunders and Wong[32] found only limited support for the Peters and Waterman propositions in a sample of UK companies; on the other hand, Dunn *et al.*[33] found in a survey of US companies that the relationship between marketing performance and corporate culture was valid, and Birley *et al.*[34] reported an association between marketing effectiveness and various dimensions of corporate culture – particularly a preoccupation with quality and service; while Leppard[20] has used a proxy measure of corporate culture as a factor significant to explaining the effectiveness of marketing planning. It must be said that Peters and Waterman have certainly backed off from any implication that their findings provide a definitive model for corporate development – in Waterman's reported words 'It's not a bible you know!'[35]

In fact, culture in this broad, non-technical sense is very similar to what has been called here the 'corporate environment',[18] and is virtually indistinguishable from what others have referred to as: the 'ideology' of the organization;[36] the 'institutionalized power' structure;[37] the 'dominant reality' which exists and shapes managerial behaviour,[38] or more simply climate and management style.[17,32,39] Perhaps the major difference between these formulations and those of the 'excellence' writers is that the former take 'culture' as something which is negotiated, created or managed, not simply as an innate quality of the organization which reflects such factors as the founders' philosophy. It appears also that power skills and political actions are implicit in that process of negotiation, creation, or manipulation.

While disparate in their empirical and conceptual sources, these views are also linked by a focus on 'the way we do things here' as a determinant of strategic choices and their implications. They do, moreover, suggest certain insights into the 'inner workings' of the marketing organization,[22] which are largely neglected by the 'excellence' writers. These relationships and the implications to be explored are summarized in Figure 1.

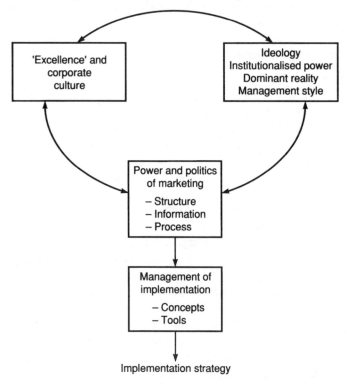

Figure 1 *The corporate environment for marketing and implementation strategy*

Basic propositions

The arguments above lead to three basic propositions, which are at the heart of this paper.

1 The corporate environment is a key to managing marketing implementation and change

This article shares with others the conclusion that to understand the marketing decision-making process, and the implementation of marketing strategies, it is necessary to analyse the organizational context in which that process operates.

The reasoning underlying this proposition has been articulated elsewhere,[5,9,18,40] and similar arguments have been expressed by Ohmae,[13] Bonoma,[3] Parasuraman and Deshpande,[22] Dunn *et al.*[33] and others, and most recently by Birley *et al.*[34] and Martin.[8] Saunders and Wong[32] have quite appropriately expressed some reservations about the danger inherent in the 'excellence' literature's focus on organizational issues to the exclusion of customer and competitive strategy factors. Indeed, it may be this reservation which has led to the scant attention given to organizational issues in marketing until relatively recently.[4,18,41] In fact, this suggests that the corporate environment concept should probably be seen as somewhat broader than that of culture alone.

The view taken here is that the corporate environment underpins not simply the implementation and tactics of marketing – i.e. problems of *doing* – but also the perceptions of the opportunities and threats in the marketing and the strategic choices made in the first place – i.e. problems of bias and selectivity in strategic *thinking*.

Our conception of the corporate environment is thus broad, pervasive, and largely covert, as opposed to the 'hoop-la' of culture in the Peters and Waterman sense. Nonetheless, for the reasons already discussed, the concept of culture is too rich to ignore in pursuing an analysis of the corporate environment for marketing.

The suggestion made here is that the marketing concept may provide a route to the external orientation characterized by Deal and Kennedy[24] as a 'strong' culture. This statement is not as simplistic as it might at first seem, particularly if we are to think in terms of changing or shaping corporate culture rather than accepting it simply as a constraint.

Clearly, this last point hinges on the degree to which we perceive culture as something capable of change through deterministic management action, or more simply an intractable factor that simply exists. It is apparent that some controversy surrounds this point. Robbins[42] suggests that the real issue is not whether culture can be manipulated (for if it cannot, then the whole culture and 'excellence' debate becomes of very limited practical interest), but rather under what conditions it may be changed, citing such contingent factors as: the emergence of a crisis; leadership change; the organizational life cycle; the age, size, strength of the current culture; and the absence of strong subcultures. Others suggest that culture change is 'awesome if not impossible',[43] and that the attempt should be avoided if at all possible,[44] with culture remaining primarily as a constraint on the acceptability and feasibility of the strategic.[45]However, if we accept the ends of a continuum of choice as either: to reject strategies that are incompatible with the corporate culture; or to change the culture to match the strategies chosen, then this implies the existence of a range of choices for aligning strategies and cultures, which may be possible in different situations, as suggested in Figure 2. This model is hypothetical, but is a stimulus to debate over the direction and form of change efforts (e.g. see Piercy and Peattie[46] for an expansion of this argument), and it leads directly to the next proposition.

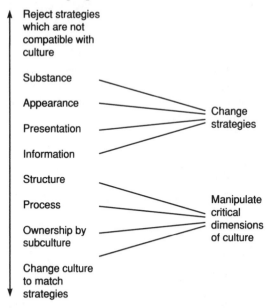

Figure 2   *Strategy and culture matching*

2   Corporate culture is a political phenomonen

The underlying point of the structure in Figure 1 is that if we are to approach culture as a variable to be managed rather than simply accepted as a constraint, or indeed to be actively controlled as a resource, then the power and politics of culture move from being arguably implicit to becoming quite explicit.

For example, Deal and Kennedy[24] talk of the importance of the management of symbols compared to 'rational' management, while Peters and Waterman[25] note the force of 'gamesmanship', the productivity of the 'skunkworks' and 'bootlegging', as well as the significance of internal competition and the manipulation of information sharing. They also discuss the management of symbols and rituals in terms of myths, legends and metaphors.

It is here that there is a direct parallel between such notions and the links which Mintzberg[36] has developed between the 'ideology' of the organization and its power structure, and the more explicit view of Pfeffer[37] that culture represents the 'institutionalized power' of the dominant interests in an organization.

Even more appositely, Culbert and McDonough's[38] model of 'radical' rather than 'rational' management makes explicit the argument that politics precede culture change, and that to change the 'dominant reality' in an organization requires the management of the political context. Indeed, those concerned specifically with the management of change in organizations have increasingly adopted a political perspective. For example: De Luca[47] has analysed the 'sociopolitical context for planned change'; Tichy[48] has proposed a 'technical-political-cultural' model to manage change strategically; while Kanter[17] has studied innovation and her 'change masters' in organizations explicitly in terms of their power skills and the processes necessary to empower innovators.

3 Corporate culture can be operationalized in marketing through power and politics, i.e. structure, information and process

We make the following assumptions: (a) for the reasons given above it is acceptable to conceive of corporate culture and culture change in political terms and (b) that the process of marketing decision making is also susceptible to analysis in terms of the power and politics of the organization.

If these premises are granted then it is possible to use the conceptual framework provided by power and politics to construct an agenda which addresses the issues of structure (power) and process and information (politics) in marketing, in such a way that culture can be operationalized, as a variable to be managed, in both strategy formulation and implementation in marketing. It should also follow that such an agenda should lead towards the development of tools for use in approaching the practical problems faced in coping with culture in marketing operations and planning.

The first of these critical assumptions has been discussed above, and is taken as given for the moment. The second assumption is considered below.

The power and politics of marketing

The proposal that marketing can be analysed in terms of the power and politics of the organization has provided a theme through a number of works.

First, in studying the development of *information* systems in marketing,[49] it was found that to analyse managerial information needs in planning the implementation of information systems, it was first necessary to cope with the notion that information was a source of power in the organization, and that behaviour associated with information use was inherently political. However, analysis of the organizational context in which marketing decisions were made was found to be almost wholly neglected in the marketing literature. More generally, the organizational context for marketing decision-making processes was found to be capable of analysis in terms other than those of rational economic behaviour or bureaucratic systems. By recognizing a political paradigm, it was argued that the contingencies typically surrounding marketing decision making were frequently those favouring the emergence of political behaviour – primarily goal and technology dissensus[37] – and that where those contingencies exist the use of power and politics is inevitable to resolve the conflict implied by the pluralism of interests in organizations.

Taking information as one important element in this argument, subsequent empirical testing has suggested that the 'ownership' of critical information processing activities, such as sales forecasting, may be linked both directly and through strategic and political contingencies with the relative power of the marketing organization and its ability to implement change.[12] Another study has empirically validated a model of information restriction by marketing executives, suggesting that political behaviour by marketing executives in restricting the access of other managers to information is a form of substitute for formal power.[11] In effect it was observed that information control was manipulated to gain influence in the absence of formal organizational power.

At the same time, accepting the parallel between information flows and organizational structure, in evaluating *marketing organization*,[18] rather than following the traditional route of describing structural alternatives, a contingency approach was adopted, which recognized the impact of political processes in organizations.[18] The model of organizational design to which this led was based on the assumption that matching marketing organizational structures to surrounding contingencies could only be approached pragmatically in the context of the distribution of power and the political systems operating in an organization.

The empirical support for this element of the work has taken a number of forms. Firstly, in a study of UK medium to large manufacturing firms we were able to observe a relatively low level of departmentalization of marketing, but also a number of stereotypical forms of marketing organization: the strategy/services; the limited/staff role; the selling-oriented; and the full-service integrated marketing departments.[50] These forms were found to be related to the power of the marketing department, and to the critical problems identified by executives in gaining the implementation of marketing strategies. Subsequent studies have found essentially the same marketing structures to exist in the UK retail sector[51] and in the UK financial services sector.[52] In the last study it was also possible to model marketing effectiveness as dependent not simply on formal structure, but also on information dissemination and key corporate values.[53]

Developing out of this work on information and structure in marketing, we have developed a focus on *process*. First, the resource allocation process in marketing was modelled as a political process, where empirical investigation[5,9,54] has suggested that variations in budget outcomes could be 'explained' in terms of the power of the marketing department relative to other sub-units in the organization (measured in its positional, perceived and participative dimensions), the relative political strength of the marketing department (taken primarily as the ability to control information flows), and the related factor of the 'control' of the marketing budgeting process. This suggested an agenda of contextual variables to be managed in achieving control of resource allocation in marketing.

The current emphasis in these process studies is on the marketing planning process. One study demonstrates a relationship between 'behavioural planning problems' in marketing, compared to planning technique sophistication, corporate culture variables, and the credibility and utilization of marketing plans.[55] Other elements of this work have examined the 'internal marketing' process as a route to the implementation of marketing plans in resistant cultures.[56,57]

These works provide some empirical support in the marketing context for what some managers appear to understand implicitly – that decision-making processes in organizations are frequently political in nature. The main implication drawn is that if management seeks to influence the outcomes of decision-making processes in marketing, then there may be greater effectiveness in operating not simply on the use of decision-making techniques or even formal authority systems (except in so far as they influence power and politics), but to reallocate the critical sources of power and stimuli for political behaviour – for instance to reallocate boundary-spanning functions and the influence they bring; to redesign structures to modify the institutionalization of rules and procedures and the 'ownership' of critical contingencies by power holders; to modify information flows, for example through the innovation of new technology; or to influence social interaction patterns. We concluded that effective control of decision-making processes in marketing could be approached through acting on structure (power), on information, and perhaps most importantly on process (politics) to reshape those factors which influence outcomes.

For present purposes the proposition is that the conceptual framework provided by research into the power and politics of marketing provides a starting point in actually managing the matching of marketing strategies with corporate culture, to achieve implementation and the organizational change this implies.

However, on its own this conclusion is of limited practical value. As Culbert and McDonough[38] have suggested, many managers appear to see power and politics as a 'black box', and to understand only 'tactical' politics for short-term advantage, rather than 'strategic' politics for shaping the 'dominant reality' of the organization. Actual implementation and change are linked to the skills and tools of power and politics rather than to the concept.[17,42]

This leads to the final elements of the article: the construction of an agenda for management to address, and the discussion of the planning and analytical tools which can be provided to develop implementation strategies in marketing. It is apparent that the marketing literature offers no 'off-the-shelf' answers, but it is possible to develop instruments to structure better the reality faced by marketing managers in their organizations.

A management agenda for marketing-led organizational change

The content of the management agenda implied by the commentary above is concerned with those variables which are capable of being managed to influence decision-making *processes* in marketing management.

Organization structure

The classic thesis that 'structure follows strategy' has been amended by the notion that 'strategy follows structure'[18] because structure represents the power of the dominant interest groups. In this sense the formal organizational arrangements surrounding marketing are part of 'agenda-setting' for the decision-making unit. For example, consider the use of product management as a device for empowering new champions, and the reallocation of responsibilities for critical contingencies and the amendment of patterns of dependence and influence within the organization.

Marketing information

If we accept the argument that the marketing information system is a major clue to the result of the process of environmental enactment in an organization,[40] then changing the structure of that system and its content may provide a route to changing the 'model of the world' to which executives subscribe. At one level this may mean no more than acting on the patterns of information 'ownership' and control in the organization. However, if executives are to change their implicit assumptions and attitudes towards the marketplace, they may have to be confronted with new, possibly unwelcome, flows of information.

Decision-making units

One part of empowering change agents may be to operate on the nature and functioning of the major decision-making units concerned with marketing. While the structure surrounding the DMU provides certain imperatives, and the information system may be used to challenge underlying assumptions and shape the process of environmental enactment, the covert aspects of the DMU and, indeed, its constitution are equally susceptible to management control. For example, the amount or form of participation in a process like marketing planning can be varied, as can the mandate for formal membership of the DMU. The opportunities for social interaction, the location of the political 'fixers', the mix of levels of seniority and functional specializations, are all capable of managerial control to redefine the task environment for key areas of marketing decision making.

Management style

Finally, the way in which marketing processes are seen to be managed is a critical issue. The use of rewards and sanctions, the focusing of myths and stereotypes, the informal pressures produced and examples provided are all likely to be significant to marketing decision makers.

Comparisons may be drawn between this type of listing and the parallel conclusions of others, for example: Kanter's[17] 'agenda for change'; Doyle's[58] discussion of a 'revitalization process' in marketing; Quinn's[59] 'leadership' tasks of empowerment and the political management of strategy; Tichy's[48] matrix separating technical, political and cultural issues in relation to strategy and structure and more specifically in the marketing literature, Martin's[8] 'Dioplan' model of human factors in marketing planning.

The shared frame of reference of all these works is the need to manage the organizational context for decision making as well as its analytical content.

Diagnostic and development tools for marketing

However, even if an agenda such as that above succeeds in sensitizing management to the need to operate on the corporate environment to implement marketing-based change, it will have done no more than this. We have still done little to provide the planning tools needed by executives. Two approaches discussed below represent attempts to reduce these complex issues to a level where they can be structured and operated on by managers at a practical level, implying the quest for pragmatism, possibly at the expense of conceptual purity.

A structured iterative marketing planning process

A 'structured iterative marketing planning' (SIMP)[60] process provides a vehicle for stimulating the type of marketing-led organizational change discussed above. In effect, this is a covert route to implementing what Peters and Waterman[25] have described as 'chunking'. The SIMP operates by tasking a cross-functional team of managers with the job of constructing a marketing plan for a market or market segment selected by top management for attention.

Briefly, the SIMP process[60,61] is a redesign of the traditional marketing planning process, which is based on managers' consensus of how to attack a market. The process is structured around a set of analytical tools which then challenge and refine that vision. The managers' initial view of their target market is challenged and refined through a focused marketing audit, which requires a continual iteration, forcing participants to go backwards and forwards through the process. The output is a conventional marketing plan – albeit one which is likely to represent a high degree of commitment and 'ownership' among those responsible for creating the plan.

Much of the attraction of the SIMP is that it specifically addresses the issue of 'how we do things here', and challenges participants to design better ways of doing things for 'their' market. The SIMP process provides a vehicle through the dynamics of group interaction to allow managers to say the 'unsayable' and even to think the 'unthinkable' in terms of their companies' ideologies.

However, particularly appositely, this mechanism implicitly provides a point of focus for the type of agenda discussed earlier: it focuses on a real business problem, but it is possible to manipulate the way in which that problem is defined, as well as such variables as the level and type of *membership* of the group (with regard to level, mix of functions and opportunities for social interaction, and so on), the *information* which is supplied to it, the type and level of *pressure* provided by top management, and the location of 'fixers'. Such manipulation provides a mechanism for shaping the type of output which is produced and is comparable to the more general notion of managing the 'human side of planning' proposed by Lyles and Long.[62]

In essence the SIMP process is a political tool for designing and creating marketing-led change in a company – what Leppard and McDonald[20] have referred to, somewhat suspiciously, as marketing planning 'as a change mechanism with "political undertones"'. Our major exception to the Leppard and McDonald argument is that they conclude mainly that the marketing planning process should be adapted to the culture, while we see marketing planning proactively as a tool to operate on the culture.

At the present stage much of this agenda remains implicit and the issues are addressed as 'rational' management choices rather than political issues, and it must be said that much remains to be done in measuring the impact of the process in the longer term, although the short-term case evidence is impressive.[54,60]

Developing implementation strategies in marketing

The next stage is the development of strategies for implementing marketing plans in the real corporate environment faced by the individual company. We see this as an extension of the SIMP, which asks managers to face the issues of the constraints imposed by the nature of their companies. While the SIMP addresses the issues of how to free managers' *thinking* from the culture of the organization, an Implementation Strategy is concerned with finding effective ways of *doing* things in the companies.

This part of the marketing change process is relatively novel in two respects: it forces managers to confront the implicit issues of power and politics which surround implementation and change in marketing; and it asks managers to focus on the match between the strategies which have been generated in the planning process and the realities of the corporate environment which they face.

The first of these issues is addressed through a 'Rational-Power-Politics' model, which is a crude device used to recognize that in most areas of marketing it is possible to identify approaches which have characteristics of each of these types as suggested by Figure 3.

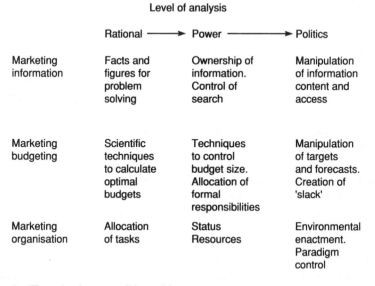

Level of analysis		
Rational ⟶	Power ⟶	Politics
Marketing information		
Facts and figures for problem solving	Ownership of information. Control of search	Manipulation of information content and access
Marketing budgeting		
Scientific techniques to calculate optimal budgets	Techniques to control budget size. Allocation of formal responsibilities	Manipulation of targets and forecasts. Creation of 'slack'
Marketing organisation		
Allocation of tasks	Status Resources	Environmental enactment. Paradigm control

Figure 3 *The rational–power–politics model*

The model is accompanied by a set of self-completion diagnostic question-naires, some of which are summarized in the Appendix. These instruments focus on such questions as the 'type' of marketing organization in operation in a company, the existence and availability of marketing information, the control of resources in marketing budgeting systems, and the consolidation of these into an Implementation Strategy for the marketing plan.

While the tools are crude, and only in the earlier stages of development they do appear to have achieved some effectiveness in providing a counterpart to the marketing planning process, and establishing a means for actually allowing managers to address the agenda suggested by the concept of the corporate environment for marketing. A more complete coverage of a set of diagnostic instruments for planning implementation strategy has been provided elsewhere.[63]

Conclusions

If Peters and Waterman are an easy target for 'academic nitpicking',[32] then so equally is this article, since it lacks an integrated theory.

In summary the basic contentions of the paper started from the point that the literature and research tradition of marketing has been remiss in the provision of effective tools for the implementation of marketing, with the organizational changes which are implied by this. The tools we have tradition-ally provided have been for strategy generation rather than implementation.

One attack on this problem area is represented by those works focusing on the 'corporate' environment for marketing. The largest contribution in this area has been from the 'excellence' writers, and others seeking to analyse the impact on the 'inner workings' of organizations on the process of generating marketing strategies and of implementing them.

It was here that a parallel was drawn with work on the impact of power and politics on marketing decision making. If this premise is granted, then it follows that the tools drawn from this conceptual framework are of direct relevance to achieving the types of change in organizations with which we are concerned. This suggests that it is possible to build an agenda for management which focuses on the management of *process* in the marketing organization through the manipulation of the context provided by structure and information.

We considered some of the practical opportunities which are represented by the work on the 'structured iterative marketing planning' process, and the tools used with managers to assist in developing implementation strategies in marketing.

While those tools are described (and readers are invited to use them in their own work and to communicate their experience with the writer), they are as yet relatively exploratory, and inevitably this article concludes with a note of the research directions which are being pursued.

First, we are attempting to evaluate the impact of the SIMP in organiza-tions, and attempting to systematize the factors which contribute to the effective use of the technique. We are starting this work with some general rules of marketing planning systems in operation in the UK, but then focusing more specifically on companies where the SIMP approach is used, where we are undertaking 'before-and-after' measurements of the corporate context, and comparing across cases the factors internal and external to the process which are associated with its successful use.

Second, we are using post-experience executive programmes as a vehicle for recruiting cases where the goal of marketing-based change is approached by executives with the diagnostic tools which have been discussed here.

The hypotheses underpinning these developments are:

1 That the marketing planning process offers a route to organizational change by re-shaping corporate culture
2 That marketing planning processes and outputs can be shaped by manipu-lating variables of structure, process and information to influence outcomes
3 That the diagnosis of structure, process and information systems with a political frame of reference, provides managers with tools needed to develop and effect implementation strategies for their marketing plans.

While these studies are in progress, it is suggested that they represent an attack on the pursuit of 'excellence' in marketing linked to shortcomings in our analysis of implementation and change which are currently constraining marketing. Comments on the basic propositions and the logic upon which they are based, and the hypotheses we are pursuing would be received with great interest by the writer.

References

1 Anderson, P.F., 'Marketing Strategic Planning and the Theory of the Firm', *Journal of Marketing*, Vol. 46, Spring 1982, pp. 15-26.
2 Mintzberg, H., 'An Emerging Strategy of "Direct" Research', *Administrative Science Quarterly*, Vol. 24, December 1979, pp. 582-9.
3 Bonoma, T.V., *The Marketing Edge – Making Strategies Work*, Free Press, New York, 1985.
4 Ruekert, R.W., Walker, O.C. and Roering, K.J., 'The Organization of Marketing Activities: A Contingency Theory of Structure and Performance', *Journal of Marketing*, Vol. 49, Winter 1985, pp. 13-25.
5 Piercy, N., *Marketing Budgeting – A Political and Organisational Model*, Croom Helm, Beckenham, 1986.
6 Deshpande, R., 'The Organizational Context of Market Research Use', *Journal of Marketing*, Vol. 46, Fall 1982, pp. 91-101.
7 John, G. and Martin, J., 'Effects of Organizational Structure of Marketing Planning on Credibility and Utilization of Plan Output', *Journal of Marketing Research*, Vol. 21, May 1984, pp. 170-83.
8 Martin, J., 'Marketing Planning Systems and the Human Element', *Irish Marketing Review*, Vol. 2, 1987, pp. 34-42.
9 Piercy, N., 'Advertising Budgeting: Process and Structure as Explanatory Variables', *Journal of Advertising*, Vol. 16 No. 2, 1987, pp. 134-40.
10 Deshpande, R. and Zaltman, G., 'A Comparison of Factors Affecting Researcher and Manager Perceptions of Market Research Use', *Journal of Marketing Research*, Vol. 21, February, 1984, pp. 32-8.
11 Piercy, N., 'Information Control and the Power and Politics of Marketing', *Journal of Business Research*, Vol. 18, 1989, pp. 229-43.
12 Piercy, N., 'The Power and Politics of Sales Forecasting: Uncertainty Absorption and the Power of the Marketing Department', *Journal of the Academy of Marketing Science*, Vol. 17 No. 2, 1989, pp. 109-20.
13 Ohmae, K., 'The Strategies Triangle and Business Unit Strategy', *Marketing Quarterly*, Winter 1983, pp. 9-24.
14 Bonoma, T.V., 'Making your Marketing Strategy Work', *Harvard Business Review*, March/April 1984, pp. 69-76.
15 Kotler, P., *Marketing Management: Analysis, Planning and Control*, 5th ed., Prentice-Hall International, London, 1984.
16 O'Shaughnessy, J., *Competitive Marketing – A Strategic Approach*, 2nd ed., Allen and Unwin, Boston, 1988.
17 Kanter, R.M., *The Change Masters – Corporate Entrepreneurs at Work*, Unwin, London, 1983.
18 Piercy, N., *Marketing Organisation – An Analysis of Information Processing, Power and Politics*, Allen and Unwin, London, 1985.
19 Cravens, D.W., 'Strategic Forces Affecting Marketing Strategy', *Business Horizons*, September/October, 1986, pp. 77-86.
20 Leppard, J. and McDonald, M., 'A Re-appraisal of the Role of Marketing Planning', in Wensley, R. (Ed.), *Proceedings 1987 Marketing Education Group Conference*, University of Warwick, 1987.
21 Cunningham, M. and Clarke, C.J., 'The Product Management Function in Marketing', *European Journal of Marketing*, Vol. 9 No. 2, 1979, pp. 129-49.

22 Parasuraman, A. and Deshpande, R., 'The Cultural Context of Marketing Management', in *Proceedings of American Marketing Association*, American Marketing Association, Chicago, 1984.

23 Pascale, R.T. and Athos, A.G., *The Art of Japanese Management*, Warner, New York, 1981.

24 Deal, T.E. and Kennedy, A., *Corporate Cultures – The Rites and Rituals of Corporate Life*, Addison-Wesley, Reading, Mass., 1982.

25 Peters, T.J. and Waterman, R., *In Search of Excellence – Lessons from America's Best-Run Companies*, Harper & Row, New York, 1983.

26 Bower, M., *The Will to Manage*, McGraw-Hill, New York, 1966.

27 Wilkins, A.L., 'The Culture Audit: A Tool for Understanding Organizations', *Organizational Dynamics*, Autumn 1983, pp. 24-38.

28 Goldsmith, W. and Clutterbuck, D., *The Winning Streak*, Penguin, Harmondsworth, 1985.

29 Lessem, R., *The Roots of Excellence*, Fontana, London, 1985.

30 Pilditch, J., *Winning Ways*, Harper & Row, London, 1987.

31 Carroll, D.T., 'A Disappointing Search for Excellence', *Harvard Business Review*, November/December 1983, pp. 78-88.

32 Saunders, J. and Wong, V., 'In Search of Excellence in the UK', *Journal of Marketing Management*, Vol. 1 No. 2, 1985, pp. 119-38.

33 Dunn, M.G., Norburn, D. and Birley, S., 'Corporate Culture – A Positive Correlation with Marketing Effectiveness', *International Journal of Advertising*, Vol. 4, 1985, pp. 65-73.

34 Birley, S., Norburn, D. and Dunn, M., 'Marketing Effectiveness and its Relationship to Customer Closeness and Market Orientation: The British Experience', in Wensley, R. (Ed.), *Proceedings Marketing Education Group Conference*, University of Warwick, 1987.

35 Lorenz, C., 'Excellence Takes a Knock', *Financial Times*, 1 November 1984, p. 23.

36 Mintzberg, H., *Power In and Around Organizations*, Prentice-Hall, Englewood Cliffs, NJ, 1983.

37 Pfeffer, J., *Power in Organizations*, Pitman, Marshfield, Mass., 1981.

38 Culbert, S.A. and McDonough, J.J., *Radical Management – Power Politics and the Pursuit of Trust*, Free Press, New York, 1979, pp. 129-49.

39 White, J., 'Corporate Culture and Corporate Success', *Management Decision*, Vol. 22 No. 4, 1984, pp. 14-19.

40 Piercy, N., 'Developing Marketing Information Systems', in Baker, M.J. (Ed.), *The Marketing Book*, Heinemann, London, 1987.

41 Spillard, P., *Organisation and Marketing*, Croom Helm, Beckenham, 1986.

42 Robbins, S.P., *Organization Theory – Structure, Design and Applications*, 2nd ed., Prentice-Hall International, London, 1987.

43 Fombrun, C.J., 'Corporate Culture, Environment and Strategy', *Human Resource Management*, Vol. 22 Nos. 1/2, 1983, pp. 139-52.

44 Uttall, B., 'The Corporate Culture Vultures', *Fortune*, 17 October 1983, pp. 66-72.

45 *Business Week*, 'Corporate Culture – The Hard-to-change Values that Spell Success or Failure', *Business Week*, 27 October 1980, pp. 148-60.

46 Piercy, N. and Peattie, K.J., 'Matching Marketing Strategies to Corporate Culture', *Journal of General Management*, Vol. 13 No. 4, Summer 1988, pp. 33-44.

47 De Luca, J.R., 'Managing the Socio-political Context in Planned Change Efforts', in Kakabadse, A. (Ed.), *Power, Politics and Organizations: A Behavioural Science View*, Wiley, Chichester, 1984.

48 Tichy, N.M., 'Managing Change Strategically: The Technical, Political and Cultural Keys', *Organizational Dynamics*, Autumn, 1982, pp. 59-80.

49 Piercy, N. and Evans, M.J., *Managing Marketing Information*, Croom Helm, Beckenham, 1983.

50 Piercy, N., 'The Role and Function of the Chief Marketing Executive and the Marketing Department', *Journal of Marketing Management*, Vol. 1 No. 3, 1986, pp. 265-90.

51 Piercy, N., 'The Role of Marketing in UK Retailing Organizations', *International Journal of Retailing*, Vol. 4 No. 2, 1989, pp. 46-65.

52 Piercy, N. and Morgan, N., 'Marketing Organisation in the UK Financial Services Industry', *International Journal of Bank Marketing*, Vol. 7 No. 4, 1989, pp. 3-10.

53 Piercy, N. and Morgan, N., 'Corporate Culture, the Fomalisation of Marketing, and Marketing Effectiveness', Proceedings: Marketing Education Group Conference, Glasgow, 1989, pp. 225-57.

54 Piercy, N., 'The Marketing Budgeting Process: Marketing Management Implications', *Journal of Marketing*, Vol. 51, October 1987, pp. 45-59.
55 Piercy, N. and Morgan, N., 'Behavioral Planning Problems versus Planning Techniques in Predicting Marketing Plan Credibility and Utilization', in Bloom, P. *et al.* (Eds.), *Enhancing Knowledge Development in Marketing*, American Marketing Association, Chicago, 1989, pp. 314-19.
56 Piercy, N. and Morgan, N., 'Internal Marketing: Managing the Corporate Environment for Marketing', Proceedings: Marketing Education Group Conference, Glasgow, 1989, pp. 404-24.
57 Piercy, N. and Morgan, N., 'Internal Marketing Strategy as a Lever for Manufacturing Marketing-led Strategic Change', forthcoming, 1990.
58 Doyle, P., 'Marketing and the Competitive Performance of British Industry: Areas of Research', *Journal of Marketing Management*, Vol. 1 No. 1, 1985, pp. 87-98.
59 Quinn, J.B., 'Formulating Strategy One Step at a Time', *Journal of Business Strategy*, Winter 1981, pp. 42-63.
60 Giles, W., 'Marketing Planning for Maximum Growth', in Thomas, M.J. (Ed.), *The Marketing Handbook*, Gower Press, London, 1988.
61 Giles, W., 'Marketing Planning and Customer Policy', *Management Decision*, Vol. 24 No. 3, 1986, pp. 19-27.
62 Lyles, M.A. and Long, R.T., 'Managing the Planning Process: A Field Study of the Human Side of Planning', *Strategic Management Journal*, Vol. 3, 1982, pp. 105-18.
63 Piercy, N., 'Diagnosing and Solving Implementation Problems in Strategic Planning', *Journal of General Management*, Winter, 1990.

Appendix Summary of training and development diagnostics

1 Marketing organization

1 Locate the company's department on the proforma.
2 Are there desirable changes in positioning on the model?
3 What will we have to do to obtain these changes?
4 What are the particular problems of operating with this type of marketing organization? What are the sources or causes of these problems?

2 Marketing information strategy

The underlying logic of what we are trying to do here is shown below:

Level	Focus	Marketing information implications
Rational	Facts and figures	Information gaps we need to fill to present and implement the Marketing Plan.
Power	Ownership of information	Information 'owned' by others and the information sources *we* need to 'own'.
Political	Communication of information (targets and contents)	'Games' being played against us by others, and the tactics we may need to adopt.

Marketing Department Proforma

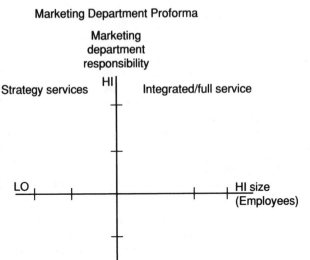

We follow the logic that first, we collect together the straightforward information gaps we have identified and then we look at the rational information systems (data gathering needed); then we turn to the problems associated with the information power situation ('ownership', resource control etc.) and with the politics of information.

The results feed into an implementation strategy for our marketing plans.

3 Marketing budgeting

1 What are the existing budgeting techniques – how are they used?
2 What is the form of budgeting process – who owns the budgeting in our company?
3 Who are the most influential people in fixing the marketing resource allocation, how influential are they, and what are our choices of gaining their support?
4 Locate the key players on the matrix below.

Key Player Matrix

'Influence over marketing budgeting' score

How can we influence the actors in the top left of the matrix?

How can we make the actors in the bottom left of the matrix more persuadable?

Can our allies in the top right of the matrix be used to influence others – or can they become more central to the budgeting process?

5   What scope is there for forming coalitions with others in the company to gain the power and influence we need?

6   What do we have to bargain with to get what we want from others – can we do more to increase this without sacrificing what the plan is all about?

7   What is the 'saleability' of our marketing plan *within* the company – can we do more to increase this without sacrificing what the plan is all about?

8   What is the scope for making the marketing budgeting process and the marketing planning process more participative, and using this to shape the outcomes that are reached?

The results go into our Implementation Strategy

4   Marketing Implementation Strategy

The questions to be confronted in developing our implementation strategy for the marketing plan are:

● What will we have to do to get other people in the company to reach the same conclusions as us about this market?

● What will we have to change in the company to put this plan into effect – i.e. what are the targets we have to achieve within the organization before we are in a position to go after the targets we have identified in the marketplace?

● Who in the company will try to stop us going after the market we have identified – and what strategies can we develop to overcome this? – and who will support us in the company – and how can we best use this resource?

A structure for the marketing planning is:

	Stage
Goals	1 Mission statement
Audit	2 Market analysis
	3 Competition
	4 Strengths and weaknesses
	5 Opportunities and threats
Plan	6 Marketing strategies
	7 Tactics and actions
	8 Financial plan
Implementation	9 Implementation problems
	10 Implementation strategy

Stage 9 asks what the obstacles are for our chosen strategies and the real source of those obstacles in the company.

Stage 10 asks us to look at what we need to do to overcome the obstacles identified for important strategies.

Reproduced from Piercy, N. (1990). Marketing concepts and actions: implementing marketing-led strategic change. *European Journal of Marketing*, **24** (2), 24-42, by permission of MCB University Press.

18 Professional ideology and marketing implementation

Richard Whittington and Richard Whipp

The issue of marketing implementation is gaining increasing attention, in this journal (*European Journal of Marketing*) especially.[1-5] This interest has been reinforced by the apparently chronic weakness of British and American manufacturers at marketing.[6,7] A persistent failing, it seems, is that marketing is only superficially implemented, achieving the trappings of change but not the substance.[8]

This article will analyse the implementation problem from two perspectives that have developed outside the marketing discipline over the last decade: the 'contextualist' approach to organizational change, and recent literature on the competition between the professions. The two are linked. The contextualist approach has demonstrated the importance to organizational change not only of managing complex internal processes, but also of mobilizing resources from the social context outside the organization itself.[9,10] A potentially crucial resource from this social context is the availability of an exclusive professional apparatus capable of conferring both technological competence and ideological credibility on the particular groups leading change. Recent studies of the professions have suggested that accountancy and finance have been especially successful at developing such a professional apparatus, at the expense of engineers and marketers in particular.[11,12]

Here the focus will be on how managerial change initiatives can depend on the mobilization of professional ideologies. Examining the two cases of marketing implementation, the article will show both how change initiatives can run against the entrenched interests of other organizational professions, and how successful change management required, in each case, the securing of superior organizational legitimacy. In these two cases, the effective mobilization of marketing ideology was important to the achievement of organizational change. It will be suggested, finally, that the extension of marketing's influence, depends not only on the refinement of its techniques, but also on a more self-conscious development of its own professional ideology. In concentrating on the substance of marketing, the profession may be neglecting its trappings.

Professional competition and ideology

The particular pre-eminence in Britain of accounting and finance professionals in senior managerial positions has been widely noted.[11,13] This pre-eminence has been at the expense of other professions, marketing included. In a survey of the top 1,000 British firms, Doyle[14] found that only 49 per cent had marketing directors on the main board, against 89 per cent with finance directors, and that non-executive directors were overwhelmingly more likely to have financial rather than marketing backgrounds.

In recent work, this relative success of accounting and finance professionals has been attributed not simply to the technical superiority of their methods but also to their collective political skills as a profession.[11,12,15] The accountancy profession has extended beyond its hard technological core (centred on the provision of quantitative information) to claim a competence in management in general. Accountants have projected themselves to the top by promoting the managerial problems which accounting is best suited to solve, while systematically denigrating the expertise of competing professional groups.[11] As Burchell et al.[16] put it, they have been able to transform their technological core from an informational 'answering machine' into an 'ammunition machine' for organizational politics. Indeed, Hines[17] suggests that the generation of more-and-more sophisticated 'conceptual frameworks' in the accounting discipline can be seen as a set of 'strategic manoeuvres' designed to advance the collective interests of the profession as much as 'technical enterprises' to improve effectiveness.

Thus accountants have constructed around their technology a 'professional ideology'[18] of superior expertise that, while transcending the boundaries of any particular organization, yet provides them with a crucial legitimizing resource in their organizational politics. Access to this ideological resource is rigorously controlled by examination systems and professional regulation. The contrast between accounting and marketing is strong. Marketing remains only a 'quasi-profession', with very little control over its membership or its practices.[19] Compared with accountants and even with R&D professionals, Child et al.[20] allege, marketing still suffers from a poorly developed professional ideology, failing to establish a domain of specialist expertise and discretion. Unlike those of the rival accounting profession, therefore, the ideological resources of marketing are neither exclusive nor credited.

Yet marketing does not lack ideological materials.[21,22] Its closeness to the market is a potent advantage. This allows its practitioners to proffer themselves as servants of the consumer: 'the marketing concept . . . calls for most of the effort to be spent on discovering the wants of a target audience and then creating the goods and services to satisfy them' (Ref. 23, p. 5). The profession promises organizations greater profits: other things being equal, 'the greater the marketing orientation, the higher its business performance' (Ref. 24, p. 13). And, in return for all this, marketing promotes its right to positions of power and influence: 'Marketing today sets company operating policy in the short term. It will come to influence long-term policy more and more . . . More than any other function, marketing must be tied to top management' (Ref. 25, p. 38).

These are strong claims, but the problems for marketing remain those of credibility and exclusivity. The assumption of consumer sovereignty, so central to the marketing concept, has been particularly challenged. Houston and Gassenheimer[26] and Dickenson *et al.*[27] have pointed out that much marketing activity is actually about the avoidance of competition and the dominance of markets. In this sense, marketing benefits the firm not by satisfying customers but by establishing quasi-monopolistic power over them. Even so, doubts continue about marketing's technological effectiveness. As Kohli and Jaworski[24] have recently observed, the marketing literature has produced only the most tentative evidence for the proposition that marketing orientations are necessarily associated with better profits. Indeed, the more independent strategy literature suggests that the relationship between profitability and marketing-oriented leadership is at best highly contingent.[28,29,30] The credibility of marketing's claims are thus still at issue.

The profession has also not succeeded in establishing privileged control over its technological and ideological apparatus. The rhetoric of the market is too widely available. Boreham[31] suggests that the power and autonomy of a profession depends on the creation of 'an aura of indeterminacy', a mystique that excludes rivals and superiors. The challenge for marketing, therefore, is that in propagating itself, it should not popularize itself. Other groups should not too easily be able either to turn marketing's tools to their own use, or to appropriate its ideological resource to legitimize their own, possibly contrary, purposes.

In sum, the power of particular groups within organizations can be heavily influenced by the status of their professions within society at large. The following sections will examine how, in change initiatives that challenge the relative power of professional groups, ideological credibility and control can prove to be critical resources.

Implementing change

Implementation remains a neglected area in marketing research, with few case studies of the practicalities of organizational change.[1,2] Traditionally, the discipline has relied heavily on 'cognitive' approaches to marketing implementation, emphasizing training and informational strategies aimed at broadening attitudes and improving skills.[4,7,14,32] Recently, however, a more complex 'micropolitical' perspective has emerged, warning of potential opposition from rival functional interest groups highly resistant to cognitive approaches to change.[2] This article will build on this recognition of complexity and politics, but add a contextualist perspective that emphasizes the ideological resources that may be drawn into organizations from the social context outside.

This contextualist approach is being increasingly adopted within the wider literature on strategic and organizational change.[9,33,34] The contextualist method of detailed case study reveals the dense social and political textures of the firms and environments in which managers must struggle for initiative and control. Stressing the internal complexity of organizations, the contextualists warn not only of the plurality of sectional interests involved in change, but also of the range of parallel movements and issues in which any particular initiative may become embroiled. Emphasizing the way in which organizations became embedded within their environments, the contextualist perspective also situates organizational micropolitics firmly within their societal contexts.[35] Here, the contextualist approach will be used to link internal micropolitical competition to the prestige and influence of professions within society as a whole.

The previous section highlighted the importance of professional ideologies which, while transcending particular organizations, offer their adherents critical resources in organizational politics. The accountants' success appears to be based not only on their quantitative technologies, but also on a professional ideology that extends their credibility in general management while excluding the claims of others. For marketers too, therefore, the contextualist perspective suggests that dissemination of the marketing orientation within organizations requires more than just cognitive and micropolitical change strategies – important though these may be. Marketing implementation involves ideological struggle. Marketers need reinforcement from a wider social context that makes available a well-developed professional ideology giving them credibility and confidence, identity and *élan*.

A well-developed marketing ideology could be mobilized in favour of more than just marketing change. Once more, accounting illustrates this potential. The legitimacy of accountancy figures can be harnessed to much broader projects of change than simple financial control. As Nahapiet[36] shows in her study of the Resource Allocation Working Party in the National Health Service, the introduction of accounting into the public sector has not just brought in a new set of techniques, it has imported a new 'language of discourse'. This new language provides a way of conceptualizing the NHS and its purposes that has increasingly displaced the traditional concepts of the medical profession. Thus, according to Hopwood,[37] the infusion of accounting into the public sector has legitimized widespread structural changes, quite distant from purely financial initiatives. In particular, he argues, this new accounting language has pushed public sector culture into becoming much more 'market-oriented'.

While accountancy has access to the legitimacy of figures, marketing appeals directly to the common sense acceptance of market mechanisms within society. With its foundations in notions of sovereign consumers operating in competitive markets, marketing already supplies a powerful rhetoric that can be applied to justifying all kinds of change. As Whalley[38] shows in his study of the adoption of customer-contractor principles in the engineering industry, technical staff were prepared to accede to consequent losses of professional autonomy because these changes were legitimized by the language of the market. In this sort of change process, marketing's ready access to market language provides a powerful ideological resource. More than just a set of techniques for the management of external markets, marketing can be an instrument in legitimizing internal control and change.

Thus, part of the utility of marketing may lie in the flexible way in which managers can appropriate its language to quite diverse causes. As one example, British Telecom's massive changes under 'Project Sovereign' are justified as making the company more 'customer-oriented'.[39] But a large part of BT's staff are not being redeployed to deal more directly with customer enquiries and demands; they are being made redundant. With up to 80,000 jobs in jeopardy, one staff representative has warned: 'This opportunity to make the company more customer-facing . . . has been undermined by those who have sought to use it (Sovereign) simply as a means to cut staff'.[40]

Herein lies the danger. The ideological power of marketing can rebound. Complex organizations are likely at any one time to be the site for a number of managerial initiatives. The threat to marketing is that its flexible ideology will become confused with, or deliberately hijacked by, quite different programmes for change. Marketing in its purer sense risks becoming tainted by broader initiatives opportunistically exploiting its legitimacy. The challenge for marketers, therefore, is to retain control over their own ideological resource.

Case studies of marketing-led change

Thus the contextualist perspective draws attention to the complex nature of organizational change processes, highlighting not only rival groups and initiatives within the organization but also ideological resources mobilized from outside. The following two cases will illustrate some of these themes. First, the Longman's publishing case will examine how marketing changes can run into entrenched professional interests and, besides, become embroiled in far wider changes. (The Longman case is extracted from research also reported in Pettigrew and Whipp.[9]) Second, the 'Electron' R&D laboratory case demonstrates how the ideological elements of marketing can be deployed positively to achieve change and secure legitimacy. (The Electron case is extracted from research also reported by Whittington.[41])

Longman

During the 1980s, Longman occupied a leading position in the UK publishing industry, with 10 per cent market share overall and strength in specialist markets ranging from English language teaching (ELT) to reference books. The company had also developed a major international presence, with 70 per cent of its turnover outside the UK and subsidiaries all over the world.

Despite this success, by the late 1980s Longman's senior management feared that its traditional strengths might exercise a distorting influence on its current operations. The problem lay with the company's editorial staff – those who commission new books. Longman's editors were renowned for the technical integrity and professional quality of their publications. Senior management's concern, however, was that deeply held beliefs in publishing standards should not become detached from changes in market demand. The shifts associated with curriculum reform in the UK and the growth of demand for ELT were cases in point. The emerging tension between editorial and marketing criteria was expressed in the 1988 corporate plan which formulated the objective of 'supplying the highest possible quality in relation to market needs'.

Longman has undertaken a number of initiatives in order to strengthen the organization's marketing orientation. A new director of marketing has been brought in from outside the trade, a move unheard of in the industry. Extensive training in marketing has been offered with outside experts brought in. New forms of organization have been tried in order to place staff in the closest possible touch with their markets. For instance, 'publishing cells' have been established in the higher education and medical areas to exploit niche opportunities.

However, the introduction of marketing has not been entirely smooth. The marketing creed sits uneasily with the traditional values of the editorial profession. Within the British context, editors tend to claim a commitment to publishing that is almost vocational and a creativity that is unsusceptible to management controls. In the case of Longman, this has enabled a subtle but nonetheless pointed resistance to marketing.

Articulate, highly educated and steeped in the trade, editors have often been able to undermine the credibility of marketing propositions. Emphasizing the uniqueness of the publishing industry, they point to ways in which the individuality of every book, none competing directly, and the special nature of the relationship between editor and author, seem to confound simple marketing orthodoxies. According to one editor:

You can do an audit on a market and come up with a technical specification of a product but then of course you need the creative ability of the publisher to interpret that into an appropriate product.

These reservations are more than technical. They manifest the professional values on which editorial power and autonomy has traditionally been based.

Thus the clash has not been simply one of technology or values, but also about management control. The appointment of marketing specialists to senior positions has challenged the old pre-eminence of editors in management. As well as the main board appointment of a marketing 'outsider', two new overseas ELT divisions are now headed by marketers. Moreover, attempts to introduce a clearer marketing direction have run against the traditional team-oriented working styles. Longman's had traditionally operated with 'a light management touch', with 'management being the people who you work alongside'. In this consensual atmosphere, marketing might be listened to, but would have no necessary priority. But now marketing was claiming to be more equal than the others.

Further difficulties have been created by marketing's relationship with parallel initiatives at Longman's. During the 1980s, management had also been investing heavily in improved accounting controls and information technology. These other sets of specialists have been making competing demands on editorial attention, and promoted their own solutions at the expense of marketing's. Thus reform of the editorial process has not been the sole preserve of the marketers.

The relationship with parallel initiatives has not always been simply competitive. Sometimes the problem has been more of uncomfortable association. Faced with all kinds of new criteria and controls, editors have not differentiated the sources of change, but seen them – rightly – as part of an interrelated set of changes, all challenging to their traditions. Marketing has thus been tarred with the same brush as finance, and vice versa. In particular, the separation of the computing, production and distribution divisions from editorial functions, and the introduction of market-type trading relations between them, have mixed the marketing initiative with others. Aimed at achieving greater efficiency and financial control, these structural changes were couched in the language of markets and marketing. Again marketing appeared to be implicated in a challenge to traditional flat, team-oriented organizational structures.

At Longman, then, structural and educative attempts at change were insufficient to win editorial adherence to the new consumer orientation. The introduction of marketing directly challenged not only the professional ideology of editors, but also the very real interests in autonomy and access to management positions which this ideology was designed to serve. Moreover, at a time of substantial change, marketing had to compete for editorial attention with other initiatives, and even found its own rhetoric hijacked by these competitors.

Electron R&D

The ideological potential of marketing in wider material and cultural change can be seen in this case of change in a large research and development laboratory during the 1980s. This laboratory had 1,300 staff in 1982, serving a major high-tech British company called here 'Electron'. The laboratory was a central facility, separate from its parent group's subsidiary companies, and drew 80 per cent of its funds directly from headquarters.

The laboratory had developed a high reputation for research, with nearly 200 of the staff having master's or doctoral degrees. These strong academic roots sustained a professional ideal of scientific progress – they were a 'university without teaching'. Powerful technical directors headed up twelve divisions based on scientific or technological disciplines. As one manager recalled later, in the early 1980s, 'the name of the game was technology, almost for its own sake'.

During the mid-1980s, however, poor results, takeover threats and new top management, led Group headquarters suddenly to increase the pressure on R&D. The very need for a central laboratory came under question. Central funding was cut to only 15 per cent of the total, with the remainder to be supplied by Electron's subsidiary companies or external clients on a customer-contractor basis. This change imposed not simply a significant loss of funding but also a direct challenge to the traditional research ethos.

Cost-cutting was felt directly through job losses of nearly 400, with compulsory redundancies. This was combined with a deliberate shift of the laboratory 'from R to D', with applications work focused on short-term benefits replacing more fundamental research. The shift from a technological to a commercial ethos was reinforced by changes in senior laboratory management. A new chief was brought in from outside without a R&D background, and the layer of 12 technical directors was abolished, with several of the older and more traditional directors forced to depart.

One manager summed up the extent of the changes: 'Prior to the cuts, there was no control over the type of work that was done here: the R was very defocused. It was controlled by a group of technical directors who were not attached to the businesses in any way whatever. Now we've gone to a position where the control is very close from the businesses.' With a highly trained workforce, previously committed to research, it was essential to find a means of justifying this shift in the nature and control of work. Still under threat of possible closure, it was important too that the laboratory re-establish its legitimacy within the Group as a whole. For both tasks, the language and ideas of marketing played a key role.

The incoming chief adopted a new slogan for the laboratory: 'Serving Customers through Partnership'. The end users of Electron's products were identified now as the laboratory's true 'customers', with R&D presenting itself to its client companies as a 'partner' in serving them. The new chief also reorganized the 12 technical divisions into four main divisions, focused on the four basic business areas of the Group. Each division was to be 'the prime marketing and sales focus with the business units and external customers'. Quite possibly such marketing-inspired changes would, over time, bring about an improvement in R&D's capability in satisfying its clients. But at least as important in the short term was how the language and rationales borrowed from marketing immediately impressed both headquarters and client companies with the laboratory's determination to break with the past and deliver the future. The threat of possible closure receded.

Internally, as well, marketing played a significant legitimizing role. The 150 most senior staff were pushed through short training courses, first in sales awareness then in basic marketing principles. The technical content of the courses was important, but they had a more general impact: 'Training is the key to changing the culture . . . They've got to learn the message ("Serving Customers through Partnership") – not just learn it, but actually live, agree with, understand, imbibe and be comfortable with it.' Marketing courses, then, were a medium for changing the whole R&D culture, providing a rationale for reduced resources, a shift towards short-term development and more direct control from outside.

Not everyone accepted these changes. Marketing challenged head-on the scientists' own professional ideology: that R&D should be guided by scientific judgement of potential benefit, and that the clients could not know what they really needed in the long term. Some laboratory staff found subservience to clients unacceptable, reducing them to continuous 'fire-fighting': they left. But for those who stayed, management believed that the marketing language had provided a new, invigorating *raison d'être*:

> Now everything is very focused, they are very, very motivated. Often they will forget about research. They get a buzz from talking to people out in the business unit. They would rather hear 'Can you come down and help me with this' than 'Look here, here's £100,000 to develop this new high-tech supernut'. They're needed; they feel wanted.

It is hard to tell whether the new customer-focused regime actually met customer needs better than before or whether it really did sacrifice long-term advantages, as the diehard scientists feared. But judgement of marketing on this basis alone would be to concentrate merely on its technical function, ignoring its ideological role. As legitimizer, there can be no doubt about marketing's effectiveness. Under threat of closure, the laboratory had quickly clothed itself in marketing's language to regain legitimacy in the eyes of its clients and the Electron main board. Undergoing a radical redefinition of work, the laboratory's management had vigorously indoctrinated key staff in a new marketing rationale. Internally and externally, the trappings of marketing had been as important as the substance.

Conclusions

There are no easy answers to the implementation problem. The case study approach reveals the complex and contextual nature of change in practice. Longman's experience certainly demonstrates that, when faced by entrenched and confident professional interests, cognitive-based training strategies are unlikely to be enough. At Longman too, the issues involved more than simple functional competition: marketing and finance initiatives got continually mixed up. If marketers are to be effective in marketing implementation they will have to become shrewd organizational operators who are sensitive to a variety of approaches and cautious to their expectations.

Yet the case studies also demonstrate the potential value to marketers of professional ideologies developed outside their organizations. At Electron, imported marketing rhetoric provided a ready screen to the external world behind which longer-term processes of commercial indoctrination could safely proceed. At Longman, a new marketing language did finally challenge the moral superiority of the traditional editorial ideology, and gave legitimacy to a whole raft of changes involving financial control and organizational restructuring. It seems that marketing ideology can indeed be a powerful resource.

Even so, the marketing profession still appears to lack influence. The contextual argument here suggests that gains at the organizational level will demand change at the professional level. The example of parallel professions, especially the success of rival accountants, indicates that marketing too needs to develop its professional apparatus. The earlier discussion highlighted the issues of credibility, exclusivity and generalizability.

The two cases did demonstrate the ability of change agents at both companies to harness marketing language to a broad range of initiatives, extending beyond marketing strictly defined. Marketing, with its easy access to the legitimacy of the market, proved to be a potent ideological resource. Seemingly, then, the profession shows a capacity to be accepted as offering legitimate approaches to management problems in general. In this sense, marketing may have the same potential to generalize its claims to relevance and expertise as accountancy and finance. The profession has the opportunity to exploit its legitimacy not only to reinforce purely marketing initiatives, but to extend marketers' influence as widely as the accountants have done.

But the problem of control over this ideological resource remains. The rhetoric of the market is not the exclusive property of marketers. As the case of British Telecom's Project Sovereign may warn, market language and legitimacy can be appropriated by rival initiatives and professions. Marketers offer themselves as high priests of the marketplace, sole interpreters of the entrails of captive consumers, and yet too often they see their liturgies stolen from them. Marketing has to develop and defend its priestly mystique.

The marketing profession is not likely, in the near future, to gain the same formal control over its members and practices that the older professions enjoy. Yet the 'strategic manoeuvres'[17] of accounting can still teach marketing ways of defending its exclusiveness. Important to the power of accounting and finance has been the development of increasingly sophisticated mathematical models that are not only technically effective but also impressively forbidding to outsiders. The exclusivity of marketing may require, then, further research investment into developing more sophisticated, and less accessible, quantitative technologies. Marketing may thus steal back from the accountants some of the legitimacy of numbers.

Research effort should also be dedicated to improving the credibility of marketing. This must involve conceptual clarification as well as empirical evidence. Too often, still, the very definition of the marketing concept reduces the relationship between profitability and marketing to the comfortable level of near tautology: 'the marketing concept means that an organization aims all its efforts at satisfying its customers – at a profit' (Ref. 42, p. 35). The marketing discipline needs to separate out profitability more clearly as a dependent variable, and to establish self-critically the extent of its contribution to this end. Empirical evidence on the true contribution of marketing to performance remains unconvincingly thin.[24,43]

Indications are that the credibility of the marketing profession will need further bolstering. The legitimacy of markets, its prime ideological resource, is not secure. In the British public sector, the early 1980s were the years of accounting, with its emphasis on efficiency and cost. The late 1980s may have seen the advantage passing to marketing, with the introduction of internal markets to the National Health Service and opting-out in education. But, in the 1990s, markets may not be able to sustain their current legitimacy. In this changing context, the profession will need to develop new technological and ideological resources if marketing is to protect, let alone extend, its present influence.

References

1 Gummesson, E., 'Marketing Orientation Revisited: The Crucial Role of the Part-Time Marketer', *European Journal of Marketing*, Vol. 25 No. 2, 1991, pp. 60-75.
2 Piercy, N., 'Marketing Concepts and Action: Implementing Marketing-led Strategic Change', *European Journal of Marketing*, Vol. 24 No. 2, 1990, pp. 24-42.
3 Darling, R.J. and Taylor, R.E., 'A Model for Reducing Internal Resistance to Change', *European Journal of Marketing*, Vol. 23 No. 7, 1989, pp. 34-41.
4 Payne, A.F., 'Developing the Marketing-Oriented Organisation', *Business Horizons*, May-June 1988, pp. 46-53.
5 Bonoma, T.V., *The Marketing Edge: Making Strategies Work*, Free Press, New York, 1985.
6 Webster, F.E., 'The Rediscovery of the Marketing Concept', *Business Horizons*, May-June 1988, pp. 29-39.
7 Wong, V., Saunders, J. and Doyle, P., 'The Barriers to Achieving Stronger Marketing Orientation in British Companies: An Exploratory Study', in *Proceedings of the 22nd Marketing Education Group Conference*, Vol. 3, Glasgow Business School, 1989.
8 Ames, B.C., 'Trappings versus Substance in Industrial Marketing', *Harvard Business Review*, Vol. 48, 1970, pp. 93-102.
9 Pettigrew, A. and Whipp, R., *Managing Change for Competitive Success*, Basil Blackwell, Oxford, 1991.
10 Pettigrew, A., *The Awakening Giant*, Basil Blackwell, Oxford, 1985.
11 Armstrong, P., 'Changing Management Control Strategies: The Role of Competition between Accounting and other Organizational Professions', *Accounting, Organizations and Society*, Vol. 10 No. 2, 1985, pp. 129- 48.

12 Richardson, A.J., 'Accounting Knowledge and Professional Privilege', *Accounting, Organizations and Society*, Vol. 13 No. 14, 1988, pp. 381-96.

13 Handy, C., *The Making of Managers*, Pitman, London, 1988.

14 Doyle, P., 'Left or Right-handed Companies?', *MBA Review*, Vol. 2 No. 1, 1990, pp. 5-8.

15 Willmott, H., 'Organizing the Profession: A Theoretical and Historical Examination of the Major Accountancy Bodies in the UK', *Accounting, Organizations and Society*, Vol. 11 No. 6, 1986, pp. 555-80.

16 Burchell, S., Clubb, C. and Hopwood, A., 'The Role of Accounting in Organizations and Society', *Accounting, Organizations and Society*, Vol. 5 No. 1, 1980, pp. 5-27.

17 Hines, R.D., 'Financial Accounting, Conceptual Framework Projects, and the Social Construction of the Accounting Profession', *Accounting, Auditing & Accountability Journal*, Vol. 2 No. 2, 1989, pp. 72-92.

18 Elliot, P., 'Professional Ideology and Social Situation', *Sociological Review*, Vol. 21, 1973, pp. 211-28.

19 Walker, D.S. and Child, J., 'The Development of Professionalism as an Issue in British Marketing', *European Journal of Marketing*, Vol. 13 No. 1, 1979, pp. 27-54.

20 Child, J., Fores, M., Glover, I. and Lawrence, P., 'A Price to Pay? Professionalism and Work Organisation in Britain and West Germany', *Sociology*, Vol. 17 No. 1, 1983, pp. 63-78.

21 Smith, N.C., 'Consumer Boycotts and Consumer Sovereignty', *European Journal of Marketing*, Vol. 21 No. 5, 1987, pp. 7-19.

22 Morgan, G., 'Marketing Discourse and Practice: A Critical Analysis', in Alvesson, M. and Willmott, H. (Eds), *Critical Theory and Management Studies*, Sage, London, 1992.

23 Kotler, P. and Zaltman, G., 'Social Marketing: An Approach to Planned Social Change', *Journal of Marketing*, Vol. 35, 1971, pp. 3-12.

24 Kohli, A.J. and Jaworski, B.J., 'Market Orientation: The Concepts, Research Propositions and Managerial Implications', *Journal of Marketing*, Vol. 54, April 1990, pp. 1-18.

25 Keith, R.J., 'The Marketing Revolution', *Journal of Marketing*, Vol. 24, January 1960, pp. 35-388.8.

26 Houston, F.S. and Gassenheimer, J.B., 'Marketing and Exchange', *Journal of Marketing*, Vol. 51, October 1987, pp. 3-18.

27 Dickenson, R., Herbst, A. and O'Shaughnessy, J., 'The Marketing Concept and Customer Orientation', *European Journal of Marketing*, Vol. 20 No. 10, 1988, pp. 18-23.

28 Miles, R.E. and Snow, C.C., *Organization Strategy, Structure and Process*, McGraw-Hill, New York, 1978.

29 Hambrick, D.E., 'Some Tests of the Effectiveness and Functional Attributes of Miles and Snow's Strategic Types', *Academy of Management Journal*, Vol. 26 No. 1, 1983, pp. 5-26.

30 Lawless, M.W. and Finch, L.K., 'Choice and Determinism: A Test of Hrebiniak and Joyce's Framework on Strategy-Environment Fit', *Strategic Management Journal*, Vol. 10, 1989, pp. 351-65.

31 Boreham, P., 'Indetermination: Professional Knowledge, Organisation and Control', *Sociological Review*, Vol. 31, 1983, pp. 693-718

32 Kotler, P., 'From Sales Obsession to Marketing Effectiveness', *Harvard Business Review*, November/December 1977, pp. 67-75.

33 Whipp, R. and Clark, P., *Innovation and the Auto Industry*, Frances Pinter, London, 1986.

34 Child, J. and Smith, C., 'The Context and Process of Organizational Transformation: Cadbury Limited in its Sector', *Journal of Management Studies*, Vol. 24 No. 6, 1987, pp. 563-93.

35 Whittington, R., 'Social Structures and Resistance to Strategic Change', *British Journal of Management*, Vol. 1 No. 3, 1990, pp. 201-13.

36 Nahapiet, J., 'The Rhetoric and Reality of an Accounting Change', *Accounting, Organizations and Society*, Vol. 13 No. 4, 1988, pp. 333-58.

37 Hopwood, A., 'Accounting and Organisation Change', *Accounting, Auditing & Accountability Journal*, Vol. 3 No. 1, 1990, pp. 7-17.

38 Whalley, P., 'Markets, Managers and Technical Autonomy', *Theory and Society*, Vol. 15 No. 1, 1986, pp. 223-47.

39 'British Telecom Plans 80,000 Job Cuts in Efficiency Drive', *Financial Times*, 27 November 1990, p 1.

40 Simon Petch, General Secretary, Society of Telecom Engineers, letter to *Financial Times*, 2 October 1990, p. 23.

41 Whittington, R., 'Changing Control Strategies in Industrial R&D', *R&D Management*, Vol. 21 No. 1, 1991, pp. 43-53.
42 McCarthy, E.J. and Perrault, W.D., *Basic Marketing*, 8th ed., Irwin, Homewood, IL, 1984.
43 Narver, J. and Slater, S., 'The Effect of a Marketing Orientation on Business Profitability', *Journal of Marketing*, Vol. 54, October 1990, pp. 20-35.

19 Crafting strategy

Henry Mintzberg

Imagine someone planning strategy. What likely springs to mind is an image of orderly thinking: a senior manager, or a group of them, sitting in an office formulating courses of action that everyone else will implement on schedule. The keynote is reason – rational control, the systematic analysis of competitors and markets, of company strengths and weaknesses, the combination of these analyses producing clear, explicit, full-blown strategies.

Now imagine someone *crafting* strategy. A wholly different image likely results, as different from planning as craft is from mechanization. Craft evokes traditional skill, dedication, perfection through the mastery of detail. What springs to mind is not so much thinking and reason as involvement, a feeling of intimacy and harmony with the materials at hand, developed through long experience and commitment. Formulation and implementation merge into a fluid process of learning through which creative strategies evolve.

My thesis is simple: the crafting image better captures the process by which effective strategies come to be. The planning image, long popular in the literature, distorts these processes and thereby misguides organizations that embrace it unreservedly.

In developing this thesis, I shall draw on the experiences of a single craftsman, a potter, and compare them with the results of a research project that tracked the strategies of a number of corporations across several decades. Because the two contexts are so obviously different, my metaphor, like my assertion, may seem farfetched at first. Yet if we think of a craftsman as an organization of one, we can see that he or she must also resolve one of the great challenges the corporate strategist faces: knowing the organization's capabilities well enough to think deeply enough about its strategic direction. By considering strategy making from the perspective of one person, free of all the paraphernalia of what has been called the strategy industry, we can learn something about the formation of strategy in the corporation. For much as our potter has to manage her craft, so too managers have to craft their strategy.

At work, the potter sits before a lump of clay on the wheel. Her mind is on the clay, but she is also aware of sitting between her past experiences and her future prospects. She knows exactly what has and has not worked for her in the past. She has an intimate knowledge of her work, her capabilities, and her markets. As a craftsman, she senses rather than analyzes these things; her knowledge is 'tacit'. All these things are working in her mind as her hands are working the clay. The product that emerges on the wheel is likely to be in the tradition of her past work, but she may break away and embark on a new direction. Even so, the past is no less present, projecting itself into the future.

In my metaphor, managers are craftsmen and strategy is their clay. Like the potter, they sit between a past of corporate capabilities and a future of market opportunities. And if they are truly craftsmen, they bring to their work an equally intimate knowledge of the materials at hand. That is the essence of crafting strategy.

In the pages that follow, we will explore this metaphor by looking at how strategies get made as opposed to how they are supposed to get made. Throughout, I will be drawing on the two sets of experiences I've mentioned. One, described in the Appendix, is a research project on patterns in strategy formation that has been going on at McGill University under my direction since 1971. The second is the stream of work of a successful potter, my wife, who began her craft in 1967.

Strategies are both plans for the future and patterns from the past

Ask almost anyone what strategy is, and they will define it as a plan of some sort, an explicit guide to future behavior. Then ask them what strategy a competitor or a government or even they themselves have actually pursued. Chances are they will describe consistency in *past* behavior – a pattern in action over time. Strategy, it turns out, is one of those words that people define in one way and often use in another, without realizing the difference.

The reason for this is simple. Strategy's formal definition and its Greek military origins notwithstanding, we need the word as much to explain past actions as to describe intended behavior. After all, if strategies can be planned and intended, they can also be pursued and realized (or not realized, as the case may be). And pattern in action, or what we call realized strategy, explains that pursuit. Moreover, just as a plan need not produce a pattern (some strategies that are intended are simply not realized), so too a pattern need not result from a plan. An organization can have a pattern (or realized strategy) without knowing it, let alone making it explicit.

Patterns, like beauty, are in the mind of the beholder, of course. But anyone reviewing a chronological lineup of our craftsman's work would have little trouble discerning clear patterns, at least in certain periods. Until 1974, for example, she made small, decorative ceramic animals and objects of various kinds. Then this 'knick-knack strategy' stopped abruptly, and eventually new patterns formed around waferlike sculptures and ceramic bowls, highly textured and unglazed.

Finding equivalent patterns in action for organizations isn't that much more difficult. Indeed, for such large companies as Volkswagenwerk and Air Canada, in our research, it proved simpler! (As well it should. A craftsman, after all, can change what she does in a studio a lot more easily than a Volkswagenwerk can retool its assembly lines.) Mapping the product models at Volkswagenwerk from the late 1940s to the late 1970s, for example, uncovers a clear pattern of concentration on the Beetle, followed in the late 1960s by a frantic search for replacements through acquisitions and internally developed new models, to a strategic reorientation around more stylish, water-cooled, front-wheel-drive vehicles in the mid-1970s.

But what about intended strategies, those formal plans and pronouncements we think of when we use the term *strategy?* Ironically, here we run into all kinds of problems. Even with a single craftsman, how can we know what her intended strategies really were? If we could go back, would we find expressions of intention? And if we could, would we be able to trust them? We often fool ourselves, as well as others, by denying our subconscious motives. And remember that intentions are cheap, at least when compared with realizations.

Reading the organization's mind

If you believe all this has more to do with the Freudian recesses of a craftsman's mind than with the practical realities of producing automobiles, then think again. For who knows what the intended strategies of a Volkswagenwerk really mean, let alone what they are? Can we simply assume in this collective context that the company's intended strategies are represented by its formal plan or by other statements emanating from the executive suite? Might these be just vain hopes or rationalizations or ploys to fool the competition? And even if expressed intentions exist, to what extent do others in the organization share them? How do we read the collective mind? Who is the strategist anyway?

The traditional view of strategic management resolves these problems quite simply, by what organizational theorists call attribution. You see it all the time in the business press. When General Motors acts, it's because Roger Smith has made a strategy. Given realization, there must have been intention, and that is automatically attributed to the chief.

In a short magazine article, this assumption is understandable. Journalists don't have a lot of time to uncover the origins of strategy, and GM is a large, complicated organization. But just consider all the complexity and confusion that gets tucked under this assumption – all the meetings and debates, the many people, the dead ends, the folding and unfolding of ideas. Now imagine trying to build a formal strategy-making system around that assumption. Is it any wonder that formal strategic planning is often such a resounding failure?

To unravel some of the confusion – and move away from the artificial complexity we have piled around the strategy-making process – we need to get back to some basic concepts. The most basic of all is the intimate connection between thought and action. That is the key to craft, and so also to the crafting of strategy.

Strategies need not be deliberate – they can also emerge

Virtually everything that has been written about strategy making depicts it as a deliberate process. First we think, then we act. We formulate, then we implement. The progression seems so perfectly sensible. Why would anybody want to proceed differently?

Our potter is in the studio, rolling the clay to make a waferlike sculpture. The clay sticks to the rolling pin, and a round form appears. Why not make a cylindrical vase? One idea leads to another, until a new pattern forms. Action has driven thinking: a strategy has emerged.

Out in the field, a salesman visits a customer. The product isn't quite right, and together they work out some modifications. The salesman returns to his company and puts the changes through; after two or three more rounds, they finally get it right. A new product emerges, which eventually opens up a new market. The company has changed strategic course.

In fact, most salespeople are less fortunate than this one or than our craftsman. In an organization of one, the implementor is the formulator, so innovations can be incorporated into strategy quickly and easily. In a large organization, the innovator may be ten levels removed from the leader who is supposed to dictate strategy and may also have to sell the idea to dozens of peers doing the same job.

Some salespeople, of course, can proceed on their own, modifying products to suit their customers and convincing skunkworks in the factory to produce them. In effect, they pursue their own strategies. Maybe no one else notices or cares. Sometimes, however, their innovations do get noticed, perhaps years later, when the company's prevalent strategies have broken down and its leaders are groping for something new. Then the salesperson's strategy may be allowed to pervade the system, to become organizational.

Is this story farfetched? Certainly not. We've all heard stories like it. But since we tend to see only what we believe, if we believe that strategies have to be planned, we're unlikely to see the real meaning such stories hold.

Consider how the National Film Board of Canada (NFB) came to adopt a feature-film strategy. The NFB is a federal government agency, famous for its creativity and expert in the production of short documentaries. Some years back, it funded a filmmaker on a project that unexpectedly ran long. To distribute his film, the NFB turned to theaters and so inadvertently gained experience in marketing feature-length films. Other filmmakers caught onto the idea, and eventually the NFB found itself pursuing a feature-film strategy – a pattern of producing such films.

My point is simple, deceptively simple: strategies can *form* as well as be *formulated*. A realized strategy can emerge in response to an evolving situation, or it can be brought about deliberately, through a process of formulation followed by implementation. But when these planned intentions do not produce the desired actions, organizations are left with unrealized strategies.

Today we hear a great deal about unrealized strategies, almost always in concert with the claim that implementation has failed. Management has been lax, controls have been loose, people haven't been committed. Excuses abound. At times, indeed, they may be valid. But often these explanations prove too easy. So some people look beyond implementation to formulation. The strategists haven't been smart enough.

While it is certainly true that many intended strategies are ill conceived, I believe that the problem often lies one step beyond, in the distinction we make between formulation and implementation, the common assumption that thought must be independent of (and precede) action. Sure, people could be smarter – but not only by conceiving more clever strategies. Sometimes they can be smarter by allowing their strategies to develop gradually, through the organization's actions and experiences. Smart strategists appreciate that they cannot always be smart enough to think through everything in advance.

Hands and minds

No craftsman thinks some days and works others. The craftsman's mind is going constantly, in tandem with her hands. Yet large organizations try to separate the work of minds and hands. In so doing, they often sever the vital feedback link between the two. The salesperson who finds a customer with an unmet need may possess the most strategic bit of information in the entire organization. But that information is useless if he or she cannot create a strategy in response to it or else convey the information to someone who can – because the channels are blocked or because the formulators have simply finished formulating. The notion that strategy is something that should happen way up there, far removed from the details of running an organization on a daily basis, is one of the great fallacies of conventional strategic management. And it explains a good many of the most dramatic failures in business and public policy today.

We at McGill call strategies like the NFB's that appear without clear intentions – or in spite of them – emergent strategies. Actions simply converge into patterns. They may become deliberate, of course, if the pattern is recognized and then legitimated by senior management. But that's after the fact.

All this may sound rather strange, I know. Strategies that emerge? Managers who acknowledge strategies already formed? Over the years, our research group at McGill has met with a good deal of resistance from people upset by what they perceive to be our passive definition of a word so bound up with proactive behavior and free will. After all, strategy means control – the ancient Greeks used it to describe the art of the army general.

Strategic learning

But we have persisted in this usage for one reason: learning. Purely deliberate strategy precludes learning once the strategy is formulated; emergent strategy fosters it. People take actions one by one and respond to them, so that patterns eventually form.

Our craftsman tries to make a freestanding sculptural form. It doesn't work, so she rounds it a bit here, flattens it a bit there. The result looks better, but still isn't quite right. She makes another and another and another. Eventually, after days or months or years, she finally has what she wants. She is off on a new strategy.

In practice, of course, all strategy making walks on two feet, one deliberate, the other emergent. For just as purely deliberate strategy making precludes learning, so purely emergent strategy making precludes control. Pushed to the limit, neither approach makes much sense. Learning must be coupled with control. That is why the McGill research group uses the word *strategy* for both emergent and deliberate behavior.

Likewise, there is no such thing as a purely deliberate strategy or a purely emergent one. No organization – not even the ones commanded by those ancient Greek generals – knows enough to work everything out in advance, to ignore learning en route. And no one – not even a solitary potter – can be flexible enough to leave everything to happenstance, to give up all control. Craft requires control just as it requires responsiveness to the material at hand. Thus deliberate and emergent strategy form the end points of a continuum along which the strategies that are crafted in the real world may be found. Some strategies may approach either end, but many more fall at intermediate points.

Effective strategies develop in all kinds of strange ways

Effective strategies can show up in the strangest places and develop through the most unexpected means. There is no one best way to make strategy.

The form for a cat collapses on the wheel, and our potter sees a bull taking shape. Clay sticks to a rolling pin, and a line of cylinders results. Wafers come into being because of a shortage of clay and limited kiln space in a studio in France. Thus errors become opportunities, and limitations stimulate creativity. The natural propensity to experiment, even boredom, likewise stimulate strategic change.

Organizations that craft their strategies have similar experiences. Recall the National Film Board with its inadvertently long film. Or consider its experiences with experimental films, which made special use of animation and sound. For 20 years, the NFB produced a bare but steady trickle of such films. In fact, every film but one in that trickle was produced by a single person, Norman McLaren, the NFB's most celebrated filmmaker. McLaren pursued a *personal strategy* of experimentation, deliberate for him perhaps (though who can know whether he had the whole stream in mind or simply planned one film at a time?) but not for the organization. Then 20 years later, others followed his lead and the trickle widened, his personal strategy becoming more broadly organizational.

Conversely, in 1952, when television came to Canada, a *consensus strategy* quickly emerged at the NFB. Senior management was not keen on producing films for the new medium. But while the arguments raged, one filmmaker quietly went off and made a single series for TV. That precedent set, one by one his colleagues leapt in, and within months the NFB – and its management – found themselves committed for several years to a new strategy with an intensity unmatched before or since. This consensus strategy arose spontaneously, as a result of many independent decisions made by the filmmakers about the films they wished to make. Can we call this strategy deliberate? For the filmmakers perhaps; for senior management certainly not. But for the organization? It all depends on your perspective, on how you choose to read the organization's mind.

While the NFB may seem like an extreme case, it highlights behavior that can be found, albeit in muted form, in all organizations. Those who doubt this might read Richard Pascale's account of how Honda stumbled into its enormous success in the American motorcycle market. Brilliant as its strategy may have looked after the fact, Honda's managers made almost every conceivable mistake until the market finally hit them over the head with the right formula. The Honda managers on site in America, driving their products themselves (and thus inadvertently picking up market reaction), did only one thing right: they learned, firsthand.[1]

Grass-roots strategy making

These strategies all reflect, in whole or part, what we like to call a grass-roots approach to strategic management. Strategies grow like weeds in a garden. They take root in all kinds of places, wherever people have the capacity to learn (because they are in touch with the situation) and the resources to support that capacity. These strategies become organizational when they become collective, that is, when they proliferate to guide the behavior of the organization at large.

[1]Richard T. Pascale, 'Perspective on Strategy: The Real Story Behind Honda's Success,' *California Management Review*, May-June 1984, p. 47.

Of course, this view is overstated. But it is no less extreme than the conventional view of strategic management, which might be labeled the hot-house approach. Neither is right. Reality falls between the two. Some of the most effective strategies we uncovered in our research combined deliberation and control with flexibility and organizational learning.

Consider first what we call the *umbrella strategy*. Here senior management sets out broad guidelines (say, to produce only high-margin products at the cutting edge of technology or to favor products using bonding technology) and leaves the specifics (such as what these products will be) to others lower down in the organization. This strategy is not only deliberate (in its guidelines) and emergent (in its specifics), but it is also deliberately emergent in that the process is consciously managed to allow strategies to emerge en route. IBM used the umbrella strategy in the early 1960s with the impending 360 series, when its senior management approved a set of broad criteria for the design of a family of computers later developed in detail throughout the organization.[2]

Deliberately emergent, too, is what we call the *process strategy*. Here management controls the process of strategy formation – concerning itself with the design of the structure, its staffing, procedures, and so on – while leaving the actual content to others.

Both process and umbrella strategies seem to be especially prevalent in businesses that require great expertise and creativity – a 3M, a Hewlett-Packard, a National Film Board. Such organizations can be effective only if their implementors are allowed to be formulators because it is people way down in the hierarchy who are in touch with the situation at hand and have the requisite technical expertise. In a sense, these are organizations peopled with craftsmen, all of whom must be strategists.

Strategic reorientations happen in brief, quantum leaps

The conventional view of strategic management, especially in the planning literature, claims that change must be continuous: the organization should be adapting all the time. Yet this view proves to be ironic because the very concept of strategy is rooted in stability, not change. As this same literature makes clear, organizations pursue strategies to set direction, to lay out courses of action, and to elicit cooperation from their members around common, established guidelines. By any definition, strategy imposes stability on an organization. No stability means no strategy (no course to the future, no pattern from the past). Indeed, the very fact of having a strategy, and especially of making it explicit (as the conventional literature implores managers to do), creates resistance to strategic change!

[2]James Brian Quinn, IBM (A) case, in James Brian Quinn, Henry Mintzberg, and Robert M. James, *The Strategy Process: Concepts, Contexts, Cases* (Englewood Cliffs, N.J.: Prentice-Hall, forthcoming).

What the conventional view fails to come to grips with, then, is how and when to promote change. A fundamental dilemma of strategy making is the need to reconcile the forces for stability and for change – to focus efforts and gain operating efficiencies on the one hand, yet adapt and maintain currency with a changing external environment on the other.

Quantum leaps

Our own research and that of colleagues suggest that organizations resolve these opposing forces by attending first to one and then to the other. Clear periods of stability and change can usually be distinguished in any organization: while it is true that particular strategies may always be changing marginally, it seems equally true that major shifts in strategic orientation occur only rarely.

In our study of Steinberg Inc., a large Quebec supermarket chain headquartered in Montreal, we found only two important reorientations in the 60 years from its founding to the mid-1970s: a shift to self service in 1933 and the introduction of shopping centers and public financing in 1953. At Volkswagenwerk, we saw only one between the late 1940s and the 1970s, the tumultuous shift from the traditional Beetle to the Audi-type design mentioned earlier. And at Air Canada, we found none over the airline's first four decades, following its initial positioning.

Our colleagues at McGill, Danny Miller and Peter Friesen, found this pattern of change so common in their studies of large numbers of companies (especially the high-performance ones) that they built a theory around it, which they labeled the quantum theory of strategic change.[3] Their basic point is that organizations adopt two distinctly different modes of behavior at different times.

Most of the time they pursue a given strategic orientation. Change may seem continuous, but it occurs in the context of that orientation (perfecting a given retailing formula, for example) and usually amounts to doing more of the same, perhaps better as well. Most organizations favor these periods of stability because they achieve success not by changing strategies but by exploiting the ones they have. They, like craftsmen, seek continuous improvement by using their distinctive competencies in established courses.

While this goes on, however, the world continues to change, sometimes slowly, occasionally in dramatic shifts. Thus gradually or suddenly, the organization's strategic orientation moves out of sync with its environment. Then what Miller and Friesen call a strategic revolution must take place. That long period of evolutionary change is suddenly punctuated by a brief bout of revolutionary turmoil in which the organization quickly alters many of its established patterns. In effect, it tries to leap to a new stability quickly to

---

[3]See Danny Miller and Peter H. Friesen, *Organizations: A Quantum View* (Englewood Cliffs, N.J.: Prentice-Hall, 1984).

reestablish an integrated posture among a new set of strategies, structures, and culture.

But what about all those emergent strategies, growing like weeds around the organization? What the quantum theory suggests is that the really novel ones are generally held in check in some corner of the organization until a strategic revolution becomes necessary. Then as an alternative to having to develop new strategies from scratch or having to import generic strategies from competitors, the organization can turn to its own emerging patterns to find its new orientation. As the old, established strategy disintegrates, the seeds of the new one begin to spread.

This quantum theory of change seems to apply particularly well to large, established, mass-production companies. Because they are especially reliant on standardized procedures, their resistance to strategic reorientation tends to be especially fierce. So we find long periods of stability broken by short disruptive periods of revolutionary change.

Volkswagenwerk is a case in point. Long enamored of the Beetle and armed with a tightly integrated set of strategies, the company ignored fundamental changes in its markets throughout the late 1950s and 1960s. The bureaucratic momentum of its mass-production organization combined with the psychological momentum of its leader, who institutionalized the strategies in the first place. When change finally did come, it was tumultuous: the company groped its way through a hodgepodge of products before it settled on a new set of vehicles championed by a new leader. Strategic reorientations really are cultural revolutions.

Cycles of change

In more creative organizations, we see a somewhat different pattern of change and stability, one that's more balanced. Companies in the business of producing novel outputs apparently need to fly off in all directions from time to time to sustain their creativity. Yet they also need to settle down after such periods to find some order in the resulting chaos.

The National Film Board's tendency to move in and out of focus through remarkably balanced periods of convergence and divergence is a case in point. Concentrated production of films to aid the war effort in the 1940s gave way to great divergence after the war as the organization sought a new raison d'etre. Then the advent of television brought back a very sharp focus in the early 1950s, as noted earlier. But in the late 1950s, this dissipated almost as quickly as it began, giving rise to another creative period of exploration. Then the social changes in the early 1960s evoked a new period of convergence around experimental films and social issues.

We use the label 'adhocracy' for organizations, like the National Film Board, that produce individual, or custom-made, products (or designs) in an innovative way, on a project basis.[4] Our craftsman is an adhocracy of sorts too, since each of her ceramic sculptures is unique. And her pattern of strategic change was much like that of the NFB's, with evident cycles of convergence and divergence: a focus on knick-knacks from 1967 to 1972; then a period of exploration to about 1976, which resulted in a refocus on ceramic sculptures; that continued to about 1981, to be followed by a period of searching for new directions. More recently, a focus on ceramic murals seems to be emerging.

Whether through quantum revolutions or cycles of convergence and divergence, however, organizations seem to need to separate in time the basic forces for change and stability, reconciling them by attending to each in turn. Many strategic failures can be attributed either to mixing the two or to an obsession with one of these forces at the expense of the other.

The problems are evident in the work of many craftsmen. On the one hand, there are those who seize on the perfection of a single theme and never change. Eventually the creativity disappears from their work and the world passes them by – much as it did Volkswagenwerk until the company was shocked into its strategic revolution. And then there are those who are always changing, who flit from one idea to another and never settle down. Because no theme or strategy ever emerges in their work, they cannot exploit or even develop any distinctive competence. And because their work lacks definition, identity crises are likely to develop, with neither the craftsmen nor their clientele knowing what to make of it. Miller and Friesen found this behavior in conventional business too; they label it 'the impulsive firm running blind'.[5] How often have we seen it in companies that go on acquisition sprees?

To manage strategy is to craft thought and action, control and learning, stability and change

The popular view sees the strategist as a planner or as a visionary, someone sitting on a pedestal dictating brilliant strategies for everyone else to implement. While recognizing the importance of thinking ahead and especially of the need for creative vision in this pedantic world, I wish to propose an additional view of the strategies – as a pattern recognizer, a learner if you will – who manages a process in which strategies (and visions) can emerge as well as be deliberately conceived. I also wish to redefine

[4]See my article 'Organization Design: Fashion or Fit?' HBR January-February 1981, p. 103; also see my book *Structure in Fives: Designing Effective Organizations* (Englewood Cliffs, N.J.: Prentice-Hall, 1983). The term *adhocracy* was coined by Warren G. Bennis and Philip E. Slater in *The Temporary Society* (New York: Harper & Row, 1964).

[5]Danny Miller and Peter H. Friesen, 'Archetypes of Strategy Formulation,' *Management Science*, May 1978, p. 921.

that strategist, to extend that someone into the collective entity made up of the many actors whose interplay speaks an organization's mind. This strategist *finds* strategies no less than creates them, often in patterns that form inadvertently in its own behavior.

What, then, does it mean to craft strategy? Let us return to the words associated with craft: dedication, experience, involvement with the material, the personal touch, mastery of detail, a sense of harmony and integration. Managers who craft strategy do not spend much time in executive suites reading MIS reports or industry analyses. They are involved, responsive to their materials, learning about their organizations and industries through personal touch. They are also sensitive to experience, recognizing that while individual vision may be important, other factors must help determine strategy as well.

Manage stability Managing strategy is mostly managing stability, not change. Indeed, most of the time senior managers should not be formulating strategy at all; they should be getting on with making their organizations as effective as possible in pursuing the strategies they already have. Like distinguished craftsmen, organizations become distinguished because they master the details.

To manage strategy, then, at least in the first instance, is not so much to promote change as to know when to do so. Advocates of strategic planning often urge managers to plan for perpetual instability in the environment (for example, by rolling over five-year plans annually). But this obsession with change is dysfunctional. Organizations that reassess their strategies continuously are like individuals who reassess their jobs or their marriages continuously – in both cases, people will drive themselves crazy or else reduce themselves to inaction. The formal planning process repeats itself so often and so mechanically that it desensitizes the organization to real change, programs it more and more deeply into set patterns, and thereby encourages it to make only minor adaptations.

So-called strategic planning must be recognized for what it is: a means, not to create strategy, but to program a strategy already created – to work out its implications formally. It is essentially analytic in nature, based on decomposition, while strategy creation is essentially a process of synthesis. That is why trying to create strategies through formal planning most often leads to extrapolating existing ones or copying those of competitors.

This is not to say that planners have no role to play in strategy formation. In addition to programming strategies created by other means, they can feed ad hoc analyses into the strategy-making process at the front end to be sure that the hard data are taken into consideration. They can also stimulate others to think strategically. And of course people called planners can be strategists too, so long as they are creative thinkers who are in touch with what is relevant. But that has nothing to do with the technology of formal planning.

Detect discontinuity Environments do not change on any regular or orderly basis. And they seldom undergo continuous dramatic change, claims about our 'age of discontinuity' and environmental 'turbulence' notwithstanding. (Go tell people who lived through the Great Depression or survivors of the siege of Leningrad during World War II that ours are turbulent times.) Much of the time, change is minor and even temporary and requires no strategic response. Once in a while there is a truly significant discontinuity or, even less often, a gestalt shift in the environment, where everything important seems to change at once. But these events, while critical, are also easy to recognize.

The real challenge in crafting strategy lies in detecting the subtle discontinuities that may undermine a business in the future. And for that, there is no technique, no program, just a sharp mind in touch with the situation. Such discontinuities are unexpected and irregular, essentially unprecedented. They can be dealt with only by minds that are attuned to existing patterns yet able to perceive important breaks in them. Unfortunately, this form of strategic thinking tends to atrophy during the long periods of stability that most organizations experience (just as it did at Volkswagenwerk during the 1950s and 1960s). So the trick is to manage within a given strategic orientation most of the time yet be able to pick out the occasional discontinuity that really matters.

The Steinberg chain was built and run for more than half a century by a man named Sam Steinberg. For 20 years, the company concentrated on perfecting a self-service retailing formula introduced in 1933. Installing fluorescent lighting and figuring out how to package meat in cellophane wrapping were the 'strategic' issues of the day. Then in 1952, with the arrival of the first shopping center in Montreal, Steinberg realized he had to redefine his business almost overnight. He knew he needed to control those shopping centers and that control would require public financing and other major changes. So he reoriented his business. The ability to make that kind of switch in thinking is the essence of strategic management. And it has more to do with vision and involvement than it does with analytic technique.

Know the business Sam Steinberg was the epitome of the entrepeneur, a man intimately involved with all the details of his business, who spent Saturday mornings visiting his stores. As he told us in discussing his company's competitive advantage:

'Nobody knew the grocery business like we did. Everything has to do with your knowledge. I knew merchandise, I knew cost, I knew selling, I knew customers. I knew everything, and I passed on all my knowledge; I kept teaching my people. That's the advantage we had. Our competitors couldn't touch us.'

Note the kind of knowledge involved: not intellectual knowledge, not analytical reports or abstracted facts and figures (though these can certainly help), but personal knowledge, intimate understanding, equivalent to the craftsman's feel for the clay. Facts are available to anyone; this kind of knowledge is not. Wisdom is the word that captures it best. But wisdom is a word that has been lost in the bureaucracies we have built for ourselves, systems designed to distance leaders from operating details. Show me managers who think they can rely on formal planning to create their strategies, and I'll show you managers who lack intimate knowledge of their business or the creativity to do something with it.

Craftsmen have to train themselves to see, to pick up things other people miss. The same holds true for managers of strategy. It is those with a kind of peripheral vision who are best able to detect and take advantage of events as they unfold.

Manage patterns Whether in an executive suite in Manhattan or a pottery studio in Montreal, a key to managing strategy is the ability to detect emerging patterns and help them take shape. The job of the manager is not just to preconceive specific strategies but also to recognize their emergence elsewhere in the organization and intervene when appropriate.

Like weeds that appear unexpectedly in a garden, some emergent strategies may need to be uprooted immediately. But management cannot be too quick to cut off the unexpected, for tomorrow's vision may grow out of today's aberration. (Europeans, after all, enjoy salads made from the leaves of the dandelion, America's most notorious weed.) Thus some patterns are worth watching until their effects have more clearly manifested themselves. Then those that prove useful can be made deliberate and be incorporated into the formal strategy, even if that means shifting the strategic umbrella to cover them.

To manage in this context, then, is to create the climate within which a wide variety of strategies can grow. In more complex organizations, this may mean building flexible structures, hiring creative people, defining broad umbrella strategies, and watching for the patterns that emerge.

Reconcile change and continuity Finally, managers considering radical departures need to keep the quantum theory of change in mind. As Ecclesiastes reminds us, there is a time to sow and a time to reap. Some new patterns must be held in check until the organization is ready for a strategic revolution, or at least a period of divergence. Managers who are obsessed with either change or stability are bound eventually to harm their organizations. As pattern recognizer, the manager has to be able to sense when to exploit an established crop of strategies and when to encourage new strains to displace the old.

While strategy is a word that is usually associated with the future, its link to the past is no less central. As Kierkegaard once observed, life is lived forward but understood backward. Managers may have to live strategy in the future, but they must understand it through the past.

Like potters at the wheel, organizations must make sense of the past if they hope to manage the future. Only by coming to understand the patterns that form in their own behavior do they get to know their capabilities and their potential. Thus crafting strategy, like managing craft, requires a natural synthesis of the future, present, and past.

Appendix Tracking strategy

In 1971, I became intrigued by an unusual definition of strategy as a pattern in a stream of decisions (later changed to actions). I initiated a research project at McGill University, and over the next 13 years a team of us tracked the strategies of 11 organizations over several decades of their history. (Students at various levels also carried out about 20 other less comprehensive studies). The organizations we studied were: Air Canada (1937–1976), Arcop, an architectural firm (1953–1978), Asbestos Corporation (1912–1975), Canadelle, a manufacturer of women's undergarments (1939–1976), McGill University (1829–1980), the National Film Board of Canada (1939–1976), Saturday Night Magazine (1928-1971), the Sherbrooke Record, a small daily newspaper (1946–1976), Steinberg Inc., a large supermarket chain (1917-1974), the U.S. military's strategy in Vietnam (1949–1973), and Volkswagenwerk (1934–1974).

As a first step, we developed chronological lists and graphs of the most important actions taken by each organization – such as store openings and closings, new flight destinations, and new product introductions. Second, we inferred patterns in these actions and labeled them as strategies. Third, we represented graphically all the strategies we inferred in an organization so that we could line them up to see whether there were distinct periods in their development – for example, periods of stability, flux, or global change. Fourth, we used interviews and in-depth reports to study what appeared to be the key points of change in each organization's strategic history.

Finally, armed with all this strategic history, the research team studied each set of findings to develop conclusions about the process of strategy formation. Three themes guided us: the interplay of environment, leadership, and organization; the pattern of strategic change; and the process by which strategies form. This article presents those conclusions.

Author's note: Readers interested in learning more about the results of the tracking strategy project have a wide range of studies to draw from. Works published to date can be found in Robert Lamb and Paul Shivastava, eds., *Advances in Strategic Management*, Vol. 4 (Greenwich, Conn.: Jai Press, 1986), pp. 3-41; *Management Science*, May 1978, p. 934; *Administrative Science Quarterly*, June 1985, p. 160; J. Grant, ed., *Strategic Management Frontiers* (Greenwich, Conn.: Jai Press, forthcoming); *Canadian Journal of Administrative Sciences*, June 1984, p. 1; *Academy of Management Journal*, September 1982, p. 465; Robert Lamb, ed., *Competitive Strategic Management* (Englewood Cliffs, N.J.: Prentice-Hall, 1984).

20 Tracing emergent processes in marketing strategy formation

Michael D. Hutt, Peter H. Reingen and John R. Ronchetto, Jr.

Marketing theorists argue that there is a gap between our rational and comprehensive descriptions of marketing strategy formulation and our empirical understanding of how decisions are made and marketing strategies are formed within organizations (Day and Wensley 1983; Wind and Robertson 1983). Recent literature reflects a growing interest in viewing marketing strategy formulation as a political process (Anderson 1982). The traditional paradigms of marketing are expanded to incorporate negotiated exchanges with internal and external coalitions in the pursuit of competitive advantage. In spite of this important paradigm shift, very limited attention has been given to exploring these internal exchange processes or to the role of the marketing function in the strategic dialogue of the firm.

The study we report explored the strategic decision processes in a division of a large electronics firm. Specifically, the study traced the communication patterns that emerged during the formation of marketing strategy for a set of new technical products. The marketing literature has given only limited attention to the change agent or championing role (Schön 1967) that managers often assume in nurturing innovative activity in the firm. Such autonomous initiatives often involve advocacy of a markedly different strategic course for the firm, informal rather than formal networks, and political rather than administrative tools of analysis. Previous systematic research on marketing decision making has focused on particular marketing mix elements, such as the advertising budgeting or pricing decision, and has failed to consider the interdependencies between marketing and other business functions. (See Hulbert 1981 for a comprehensive review of descriptive research on marketing decision making.) Particular attention was given in our study to exploring interfunctional communication patterns and to defining the key roles that various organizational members assumed in the formation of marketing strategy. Thus, the central focus of the research was on the decision processes leading to strategic choice, rather than on the content of the strategies.

Our discussion is divided into four parts. First, we provide a synthesis of the strategic decision-making literature that is particularly relevant to our study. Special attention is given to the theoretical and empirical contributions issuing from the process school of strategic decision making. Second, we introduce the concept of autonomous strategic behavior (Burgelman 1983b) and link it to strategic marketing processes within the firm. Third, we report research results and offer several research propositions to guide future studies. Fourth, we highlight key implications for strategic marketing management and process research on marketing strategy development.

Strategic decision-making perspectives

Researchers differ in their conceptualizations of strategic decision making. Some adopt a normative position and conceptualize strategic decision making primarily in terms of the content or outcome of strategy. Others conceptualize it in terms of a process leading to a particular decisional outcome.

The fields of marketing and strategic management traditionally have been dominated by an emphasis on normative models of strategy formulation (e.g., Andrews 1980; Hofer and Schendel 1978; Kotler 1984). These models describe the strategy formulation process as involving activities such as establishing goals, monitoring the environment, assessing internal capabilities, searching for and evaluating alternative actions, and developing an integrated plan to achieve the goals. The accent of the rational approach is on strategy content. Pettigrew (1985, p. 276) charges that, as applied to the formulation of strategy, the rational approach assumes the '. . . firm speaks with a unitary voice or can be composed of omnipotent, even heroic general managers or chief executives, looking at known and consistent preferences and assessing them with voluminous and presumably apposite information, which can be organized into clear input-output relationships.'

The image of the organizational decision maker as a rational, calculating being contrasts rather sharply with emerging strategic management conceptualizations that '. . . depict strategic decisions as messy, disorderly, and disjointed processes around which competing factions contend' (Pennings 1985, p. 10). Advocates for this process perspective of strategic decision making include, for example, Mintzberg (1978), Quinn (1978, 1980), Murray (1978), Pettigrew (1977), and Narayanan and Fahey (1982).

The foundation for the process school of strategic decision making can be traced to the work of Simon and his colleagues (Simon 1945; March and

Simon 1958; Cyert and March 1963). Organizational actors have a limited capacity for processing and storing information. Hence alternatives and their associated consequences are rarely known with clarity and choices, when made, are often of a satisficing nature – reflecting the discovery and selection of a satisfactory, rather than an optimal, alternative (March and Simon 1958). Thompson and Tuden (1959) argue that different types of decisions confront organizations and each type suggests a different group process and structure. They offer a typology of decision-making situations and suggest, for example, that strategic decisions are most likely to be made by *computation* (e.g., addressed by specialists in a programmed manner) when there is agreement about goals and the consequences of various alternatives, but by *compromise* when there is agreement about the consequences without agreement on appropriate goals. Because organizations undergo a variety of pressures from coalitions with different goals (Cyert and March 1963), decision-making processes are less stable, predictable, and defined than early management theorists assumed.

Emphasizing the ambiguity of organizational decision making, Cohen *et al.* (1972) view an organization as a collection of choices searching for problems, solutions searching for issues to which they might represent the answer, and decision makers searching for problems or gratification. Within this formulation, which they term a 'garbage can' model of organizational choice, a decision represents an outcome or an interpretation of the streams of problems, choice opportunities, solutions, and participants within the organization. These streams are channeled and shaped, to a degree, by elements of the organizational and social structure (March and Olsen 1976). Thus, organizations, through the use of various administrative mechanisms, regulate connections among problems, choice opportunities, solutions, and the energy and time of decision participants.

The process school of strategic decision making has been influenced also by Lindblom (1965; see also Lindblom 1979), who conceptualizes decision making, most notably in the formation of public policy, as an incremental process of 'muddling through'. Because different units in the decision-making domain have divergent preference orderings and develop different sensitivities to certain lines of consequences, the decision-making process tends to encompass mechanisms for partisan mutual adjustment and often produces a stream of incremental, disjointed decisions (Braybrooke and Lindblom 1963).

Anderson (1982) argues that these behaviorally oriented theories capture the reality of marketing's internal and external relationships. The strategic position of the firm is shaped by a bargaining process among various functional areas. The marketing function contributes to the strategic planning process by identifying optimal long-term competitive positions that will ensure customer support and satisfaction, by developing strategies designed to capture these preferred positions, and by serving as a strong advocate for these strategic options with top management and other internal coalitions.

Strategy research: process perspectives

Though a process perspective has been adopted in emerging conceptualizations of strategic marketing, only limited research attention has been given to process issues in marketing strategy research. Several studies drawn from the strategic management literature provide a foundation for exploring marketing strategy from a process perspective.

An early study in the decision process school of research was conducted by Cyert, *et al.* (1956). Through observation, document analysis, and personal interviews, they traced and described the decision process followed by a firm in purchasing a computer. On the basis of their analysis, they documented three dimensions of the decision process: (1) common processes that recur within the organization at various stages in the decision, (2) communication processes that represent the transmission and filtering of information within the organization, and (3) problem-solving processes that involve the search for desirable courses of action. The researchers noted that '. . . the problem to be solved was in fact a whole series of "nested" problems, with each alternative solution to a problem at one level leading to a new set of problems at the next level' (p. 247). Their study was an initial step leading to important pioneering efforts (Cyert and March 1963; March and Simon 1958; Newell and Simon 1972).

Bower (1970) conducted a carefully designed longitudinal field study of the strategic capital investment process in four large corporations. He observed the allocation of resources to be basically a bottom-up, three-phase political process in which business and investment planning are closely coupled and in which multiple levels of management participate. Proposals are defined at the product/market level in technical and economic terms (*definitional process*). Importantly, Bower observed that projects survive only if given impetus from division-level management. This *impetus process* is highly political as managers weigh the benefits and costs of project sponsorship in light of the organization's reward and measurement system. Corporate-level managers participate in the strategic process by manipulating the *structural context* within which proposal generation takes place, thereby influencing the type of proposals that will be defined and given impetus.

Mumford and Pettigrew (1975) explored the process of implementing strategic decisions in four organizations over periods ranging from two to five years. Employing a case research approach, they examined the introduction of a large-scale computer system in each organization from the point when a decision was made to consider a new system through the implementation of the system in the organization's operations. Because the technology enabled the organizations to develop more complex service offerings and pursue new and different market segments, the purchase represented a strategic decision. Mumford and Pettigrew found that as the organization attempted to cope with the uncertainty in its environment by introducing more advanced information systems, new uncertainties were spawned within the organization. These uncertainties were introduced when long-established methods and procedures were abandoned in favor of new ones. In turn, political behavior among different interest groups became prevalent as each group maneuvered to maintain its position in the organization. Such interest groups have different goals, time horizons, values, and problem-solving styles (Pettigrew 1977). Pettigrew (1985, p. 281) argued that the '. . . strategy formulation and change processes in organizations may be understood in part as the outcome of processes of competition between these rationalities expressed through the language, priorities, and values of technologists, of accounting and finance – the bottom line; or of the rather more diffuse perspectives adopted by specialist groups from planning, operations research, organizational development, or personnel.'

Mintzberg *et al.* (1976) conducted a field study of 25 strategic decision processes. The objective of the research was to identify how organizations make 'unstructured strategic' decisions. Such decisions were defined to include (1) decision processes that have not been encountered in the same form in the past and for which the organization has no established set of ordered responses (unstructured) and (2) decisions that are important in terms of resources committed, action initiated, or precedents set (strategic). By reviewing the original stimuli, the decision process, and the solution, Mintzberg *et al.* proposed a general model of the strategic decision-making process. The model does not suggest a steady, undisturbed progression from one step to another in a strategic decision process, but rather that '. . . the process is dynamic, operating in an open system where it is subjected to interferences, feedback loops, dead ends, and other factors' (p. 263).

From an analysis of 25 decision-making situations, the researchers concluded (p. 250-1 that the

> . . . strategic decision process is characterized by novelty, complexity, and openendedness, by the fact that the organization usually begins with little understanding of the decision situation it faces or the route to its solution, and only a vague idea of what that solution might be and how it will be evaluated when it is developed. Only by groping through a recursive, discontinuous process involving many different steps and a host of dynamic factors over a considerable period of time is a final choice made.

Mintzberg (1978; see also Mintzberg and Walters 1985) argued that such findings highlight the importance of distinguishing *deliberate* strategies (intended strategies that become realized) from *emergent* strategies (realized strategies that, at least initially, were not intended).

Emergent strategy patterns are evident in Quinn's research (1980). He used a case research approach to explore strategic change processes in 10 large corporations. In contrast to the rational, analytical systems often described in the strategic planning literature (e.g., Lorange 1980), Quinn offered the concept of 'logical incrementalism' to characterize the process of strategic change operative in these organizations. According to this view, the organization moves step by step from early generalities to later specifics, further refining the strategic course incrementally as new information emerges and organizational or political constraints allow or dictate (Quinn 1980, 1982). As initial strategic positions become clarified, champions may emerge to lead specific strategic courses or component groups within the organization may establish internal momentum around partial decisions. 'The choice and selective nurturing of these champions and groups will inevitably shape the direction of the strategy itself . . .' (Gladstein and Quinn 1985, p. 212; see also Quinn 1979, 1985). Quinn (1978) emphasized that such incrementalism is not 'muddling', but instead is a purposeful and effective management technique for integrating both the analytical and behavioral dimensions of strategy formulation.

Extending the work of Bower (1970), Burgelman (1983a) explored the internal corporate venturing process in a large, diversified corporation. Six ongoing venturing projects were the focus of the field study. The historical development of the projects was traced and the progress of each was monitored carefully over a 15-month period. The findings indicated that the '. . . motor of corporate entrepreneurship resides in the autonomous strategic initiatives of individuals at the operational levels in the organization' (p. 241). On the basis of the research, Burgelman presented a process model delineating the strategic process by which new ventures take shape. The model suggests that successful new ventures depend on (1) the presence of autonomous entrepreneurial effort among operational-level participants (product-championing activities), (2) the ability of middle-level managers to evaluate and conceptualize the strategic implications of these initiatives in more general terms (organizational championing activities), and (3) the capacity of top management to permit entrepreneurial initiatives to alter the direction of corporate stategy. The study highlights the significant role of middle-level managers in the strategy formulation process by linking promising strategic initiatives to the corporation's concept of strategy.

Collectively, the studies cited, spawned by the decision process school, provide significant insights into strategic decision making and change. Strategic processes are seen not as a linear progression from strategy formulation to strategy implementation, but as multilevel processes where the outcomes of decisions are shaped by the interests and commitments of individuals and groups, the forces of organizational momentum, important changes in the environment, and the manipulation of the structural context surrounding decisions (Pettigrew 1985). Clearly, this research tradition highlights the importance of examining the role of the marketing function and individual marketing managers in adaptive, emergent strategies.

Autonomous strategic behavior

Insights into the processes that can trigger emergent strategies can be gained by examining an alternative concept of strategy. On the basis of his research on internal corporate venturing, Burgelman (1983b, c) presented a model of the strategic process in large, complex organizations. He proposed that strategic activity within the firm fits into two broad categories, *induced* and *autonomous* strategic behavior.

Induced strategic behavior is consistent with the firm's traditional concept of strategy and takes place in relationship to the firm's familiar external environment. By manipulating various administrative mechanisms, top managers can influence the perceived interests of managers at the middle and operational levels of the organization and keep strategic behavior in line with the current strategy course. Thus, organizational structures and systems often direct the attention of organizational members to routine, not innovative, activities (Starbuck 1983; Van de Ven 1986). Examples of induced strategic behavior might emerge in product development efforts for present markets. Induced strategic initiatives can be judged within the established evaluation and measurement system of the firm (Burgelman 1983b).

Autonomous strategic behavior, in contrast, is conceptually equivalent to entrepreneurial activity and introduces new categories for the definition of opportunities into the firm's strategic planning process. During any period, most strategic activity in large, complex firms is likely to fit into the induced behavior category. However, Burgelman (1983c) proposed that large, resource-rich firms are likely to have a pool of entrepreneurial potential at operational levels that will be expressed in autonomous strategic initiatives. Here, managers at the product/market level conceive new business opportunities, then engage in project-championing activities to mobilize resources and create momentum for the project's further development. Emphasizing political rather than administrative channels, middle managers question the firm's current concept of strategy and '. . . provide top management with the opportunity to rationalize, retroactively, successful autonomous strategic behavior' (Burgelman 1983c, p. 1352). Through the activation of these political mechanisms, successful autonomous strategic initiatives can become integrated into the organization's concept of strategy.

Occupying a boundary role position, marketing managers pursue activities that are within both categories of strategic behavior. New product development efforts for present businesses or market development projects for the firm's present products are the outgrowth of induced strategic initiatives. Taking shape outside the firm's current concept of strategy, autonomous strategic efforts depart from the current course and center on new categories of business opportunity. Middle managers initiate the project, nurture its development, and if successful see the project integrated into the firm's concept of strategy. Day and Wensley (1983) charged that traditional conceptualizations have given little recognition to the role of the marketing function as an initiator of innovative activity in the organization. This role, however, is fundamental to marketing's contribution to the strategic management process in the firm. By gathering critical environmental information about threats and opportunities (Wind and Robertson 1983), serving as an advocate for desirable strategic options (Anderson 1982), and channeling organizational attention to those options (Day and Wensley 1983), marketing managers assume a central role in the management of innovation within the firm. Van de Ven (1986) argued that organizational actors who experience direct personal confrontations with problem sources, opportunities, and threats are more likely to recognize the need for strategic change and pay attention to innovative ideas. Limited attention, however, has been given to exploring the autonomous strategic behavior of marketing managers and how their activities are interconnected with those of managers representing other functional areas and other layers of the strategic hierarchy.

Our study complements the work of Burgelman (1983a, b, c) and affords further insights into autonomous strategic behavior. Several characteristics that distinguish autonomous from induced strategic behavior are proposed in Table 1. Whereas induced strategic initiatives are likely to center on new product development for present markets, autonomous strategic initiatives often extend the firm's product and market domain in new directions through internally generated new resource combinations. Observe from Table 1 that autonomous and induced strategic initiatives are expected to involve different sets of actors and evoke different forms of strategic dialogue. An individual manager, the product champion, assumes a central role in sensing an opportunity and in mobilizing an informal network to assess the technical feasibility and market potential of the idea. In comparison with induced strategic behavior, autonomous initiatives are more likely to involve a communication process that departs from regular work flow and hierarchical decision-making channels. The decision roles and responsibilities of partici-pants in this informal network are poorly defined in the early phases of the strategy formulation process but become more formalized as the process evolves. In contrast, induced strategic behavior is characterized by well-defined roles and responsibilities.

If the efforts of the product champion are successful, the autonomous strategic initiative blends into the firm's planning routine or, in essence, becomes more like an induced initiative. Thus, the communication structure is likely to become more complex as the participants in the strategy formulation process become interconnected in a web of product-related communications (i.e., high network density). Note from Table 1 that autonomous strategic behavior entails a creeping commitment toward a particular strategic course. In contrast, induced strategic initiatives are more likely to involve administra-tive mechanisms that encourage a more formal and comprehensive assess-ment of strategic alternatives at various levels in the planning hierarchy.

Our research explored several of the characteristics of autonomous strategic behavior proposed in Table 1. Using an exploratory case research approach in combination with network analysis, we traced over time a strategic decision process that centered on a significant autonomous strategic initiative. Developing a detailed description of the properties of the formal and informal communication network and identifying key organizational players enabled us to isolate and explore in depth selected dimensions of autonomous strategic behavior. Particular attention was given to exploring the composition and properties of the communication network, the nature of interfunctional and hierarchical communication patterns, and the key roles of various organizational members in the formation of marketing strategy.

Table 1 Induced Versus Autonomous Strategic Behaviour: Selected Characteristics of Marketing Strategy Formulation Process

	Induced	*Autonomous*
Activation of strategic decision process	Individual manager defines market need that converges with organization's concept of strategy	Individual manager defines market need that diverges from organization's concept of strategy
Nature of screening process	Formal screening of technical and market merit by established administrative procedures	Reliance on informal network in assessing technical and market merit
Type of innovation	Incremental (e.g., new product development for present markets using present organizational resources)	Major (e.g., new product development projects requiring new combinations of organizational resources)
Nature of communication process	Consistent with organizational work flow pattern	Departs from organizational work flow pattern in early phase of decision process
Major actors	Prescribed by regular channel of hierarchical decision making	Informal network emerges based on mobilization efforts of product champion
Decision roles	Well-defined roles and responsibilities for participants in strategy formulation process	Roles and responsibilities of participants poorly defined in initial phases but become more formalized as strategy formulation process evolves
Properties of communication network	High density throughout decision process	Low density in early phases; high density in later phases
Implications for strategy formulation	Strategic alternatives considered; commitment to particular strategic course evolves	Commitment to particular strategic course emerges in early phases through sponsorship efforts of product champion

Method

We traced the formation of marketing strategy for a set of new technical products. The products represented a significant departure from the firm's current business. To secure a comprehensive view of the strategy formation process, we selected a qualitative research method. Concerns of external validity were traded against opportunities to explore interaction patterns, which have been given limited attention in the marketing literature. Bonoma (1985) suggested that qualitative research techniques should be considered when the marketing phenomena under investigation meet the dual conditions of little technical knowledge and high complexity. Noting that certain marketing issues defy quantification, he offers the following illustration: '. . .

good practice in marketing management and the coordination of marketing activities with other business functions are currently nonquantifiable phenomena; they are so complex it is impossible at this early stage of theory development to know what to count' (p. 202).

Network analysis

We used network analysis in conjunction with a case research approach; each contributes to understanding the complex phenomena of the marketing strategy formulation process. Network analysis provides a means of describing and analyzing individuals or aggregations of individuals by focusing explicitly on their interrelationships. (See Tichy 1981 for a comprehensive review of network research in an organizational context.) In network analysis terms, an organization can be treated as a set of roles linked by several networks that transmit information, influence, and affect. Discussing organizational research approaches, Fombrun (1982, p. 286) stated that '. . . network analysis improves case methodology by providing a skeleton on which to hang the rich descriptive data.' We extended past exploratory assessments of strategic decision processes by adopting a network perspective.

A strength of network analysis is its focus on the nature of emergent subgroups in the organization. Thus, the network approach provides a means for exploring the structural characteristics of communication patterns associated with autonomous strategic behavior. In turn, case research provides insights into the functioning of key departments, reporting relationships, formal systems for evaluating marketing performance, and the history of particular projects and related areas.

Research setting

The research was conducted in a division of a large, diversified high technology firm. In evaluating candidate firms and screening possible projects within those firms, we sought to identify a project that would generally fit the definition of an autonomous strategic initiative – one that departs from the firm's mainstream business and concept of strategy (Burgelman 1983a). Such a project would involve a complex strategy situation characterized by extensive problem solving. High task uncertainty, high information requirements, unfamiliar alternatives, and poorly defined decision rules are features of marketing strategy situations characterized by extensive problem solving (Howard *et al.* 1975; Hutt and Speh 1984).

The selected project, which centered on avionics equipment, fits the definition. The project was in a very early stage of development, departed from the traditional technical and market strengths of the division, and represented a potentially significant new business opportunity. The avionics equipment involved different customers, a different technology base, and a higher degree of value added than the products, primarily component parts, traditionally manufactured and sold by the division. Though the project had not been formally funded or screened within the division, selected marketing and R&D personnel had been exploring the project on a tentative basis for several months.

Data collection

A combination of data collection methods was used. First, several interviews were conducted with key participants in the new product development effort to trace the historical development of the project. Second, document analysis was used to verify the information obtained in the interviews. The company provided access to internal memos, telephone logs, and selected planning documents. From the interviews and the document analysis, four milestones were identified.

1 An individual manager initiates informal assessment of the market and the technical feasibility of the technology.
2 Selected marketing and R&D personnel meet with the potential customer to describe and partially demonstrate the capabilities of the proposed technology before the project receives funding or formal endorsement in the organization.
3 A modest grant is authorized to explore some technical dimensions of the project.
4 The project receives formal organizational endorsement and funding.

These milestones correspond to key events or activities that took place as the project progressed from the idea stage to a formally recognized and endorsed marketing effort. Likewise, a preliminary list was developed to identify the organizational members who had some direct or indirect involvement in the project. This list, which included diverse functional representation, was updated as the project was monitored over a 12-month period.

Questionnaires were sent to organizational members who had been identified as having had some role in the project. Respondents were given a listing of those individuals and were encouraged to add others who may have been missed inadvertently by the investigators. As a result of this process, a total of 23 organizational members were identified who had been involved in at least one milestone of the project. They were asked to indicate their communications relations with each individual for each of the identified milestones. Communication patterns then were developed for the 23 organizational members. The resulting network included personnel from four divisions, several functional specialties, and multiple layers in the organizational hierarchy.

Results

Autonomous strategic behavior

The communication networks corresponding to each of the four milestones of the project are depicted in Figure 1. Initial insights into the marketing strategy formulation process can be gained by exploring the pattern of communication in the preliminary phase of the project (milestone 1). The idea that spawned the proposed project originated with a salesperson (actor 19, Figure 1, A) who

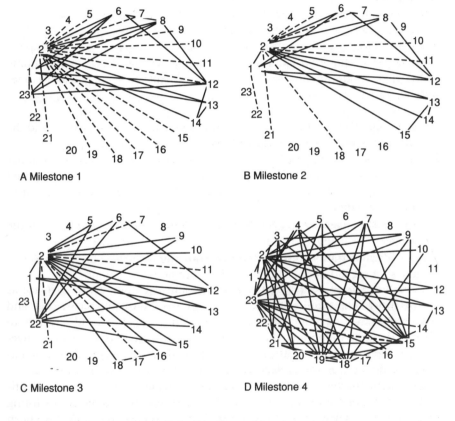

A Milestone 1

B Milestone 2

C Milestone 3

D Milestone 4

——————— Dyadic communication link within groups

- - - - - Dyadic communication link

Figure 1 *Communication structure. Groups consist of at least three individuals, all of whom communicated with each other. For milestone 1, the groups are: 1, 2, 6, 8, 12; 1, 2, 13; 1, 6, 8, 12, 23; 2, 12, 14; and 2, 13, 14. For milestone 2: 1, 2, 6, 8, 12; and 2, 3, 15. For milestone 3: 1, 2, 12, 22; 1, 2, 13; 2, 5, 22; 2, 6, 12, 22; 2, 9, 22; 2, 14, 22; 2, 15, 22; and 2, 16, 18. For milestone 4: 1, 2, 13; 2, 3, 9, 15, 23; 2, 3, 20, 23; 2, 3, 15, 21, 23; 4, 15, 18, 19, 23; 2, 5, 15, 19, 21; 2, 7, 15, 18, 19, 23; 2, 9, 15, 19, 23; 2, 10, 18; 2, 12, 23; 14, 18, 23; 2, 15, 18, 19, 21, 23; and 2, 16, 18, 19, 23. These groups were determined with SONET-1 (Foster and Seidman, 1978), a package of computer algorithms for network analysis.*

had identified a problem that a potential customer was having with a piece of avionics equipment. Because the required product/ technology diverged significantly from the firm's current offerings, the salesperson discussed the potential opportunity with manager 2, who emerged as one of the key actors in the strategy formulation process. Manager 2, a project manager whose responsibilities include both engineering and marketing activities, assumed an active role in assessing the technical and market feasibility of the idea. Here manager 2 departed from established organizational guidelines for assessing a new business opportunity and relied instead on informal organizational channels.

Observe from Figure 1, A that a complex web of project-related communications emerged well before the project was funded and formally recognized within the firm's strategic planning process. The early project-related communications involved key buying influentials in an important customer organization, personnel of other divisions of the firm (e.g., manager 12 and manager 17), and selected personnel within the project initiators' division. Interviews indicated that the personnel in other divisions contributed to the early development of the project by lending equipment and providing information to the project initiators. These exchanges occurred outside prescribed corporate guidelines. At milestone 1, manager 2 obtained informal support for the project from managers 14 (director, R&D), 18 (market manager), and 7 (vice president or business unit manager). Especially crucial to the early development of the initiative was the informal support of the business unit manager (manager 7). This informal endorsement came after the business unit manager had learned of a favorable customer response to a technical demonstration. Given the very preliminary stage of the project, resource support did not accompany this informal endorsement.

Figure 1, A also shows that manager 2 basically was a point from which the vast majority of communications relations radiated. Many of the communications relations were merely dyadic, involving just manager 2 and many other individuals in other divisions, the customer organization, and other functional areas. Observe, however, that the number of communication links that were merely dyadic (i.e., not included in larger groupings of organizational actors) declined as the project progressed through the four milestones. Though 42% of the communications relations in milestone 1 fit into this category, only 4% of the communication links in milestone 4 were purely dyadic. This finding suggests that the communication structure became more complex as the momentum for the project increased within the organization. Manager 2, who had a significant role in nurturing the innovation process, was involved in 87% of the purely dyadic communication links across the four milestones.

Note also the dyadic communication links within groups related to the formative stage of the project (Figure 1, A). These groups included a collection of individuals who assumed a vital role in the formative stages of the project: three managers in other divisions (1, 6, 12) and three in the focal division (2, 8, 23). The case data suggest that the exchanges within these groups centered on the technical and market feasibility of the project. A product manager (8) supplied important market information to the groups. These groups remained basically intact at milestone 2 but note that the communication structure assumed more complex properties at milestone 3, a phase dominated by technical dialogue, and milestone 4, a phase dominated by strategic marketing dialogue.

On the basis of the preceding discussion, we offer the following propositions.

P$_1$: Ideas that spawn autonomous strategic initiatives are more likely to originate with boundary-spanning members (e.g., salespersons) of the organization than with those more insulated within the organization.

P$_2$: In comparison with induced strategic behavior, autonomous strategic initiatives are characterized by more purely dyadic communication relations – within and outside prescribed organizational boundaries.

Van de Ven (1980, 1986) argued that direct personal confrontations with problem sources increase the likelihood that an organizational member's action threshold will be triggered, thereby spawning an innovative initiative. In turn, von Hippel (1978) found that ideas for many product innovations come directly from customers. Once issue recognition is triggered, organizational members, relying on informal channels, engage in a diverse set of information and resource exchanges.

The organizational form may likewise influence the nature of strategic behavior.

P$_3$: In comparison with bureaucratic organizational structures, organic structures are more likely to spawn autonomous strategic initiatives.

Exploring the effectiveness, efficiency, and adaptiveness of various organizational forms, Ruekert, Walker, and Roering (1985, p. 23) emphasized '. . . that the structures used to accomplish marketing tasks should reflect the nature of the task and the environment facing the organization . . .' They suggested that a decentralized, nonformalized structure (organic form) is more flexible in responding to a changing environment (see also Weitz and Anderson 1981). Autonomy on the part of organizational actors is replaced by established rules in the bureaucratic structure, which inhibit entrepreneurial initiatives.

Individual level of analysis

Van de Ven (1986) emphasized that the management of innovation depends on an understanding that innovation is not the undertaking of an individual entrepreneur. Instead, innovation involves '. . . a network-building effort that centers on the creation, adoption, and sustained implementation of a set of ideas among people who, through transactions, become sufficiently committed to these ideas to transform them into "good currency" '(p. 601). Clearly, manager 2 assumed a central role in establishing the structure of the network portrayed in Figure 1. This network-building effort can be clarified further by analyzing the communication behavior of individual participants in the strategy formulation process.

Table 2 is a summary of the organizational members who participated in one or more of the milestones, their positions, and three properties of their communication behavior: centrality, hierarchical communications, and functional communication. Observe from Table 2 that a variety of organizational members drawn from four different divisions were involved to varying degrees in the project. In terms of functional representation, 54% were drawn from the technical (R&D) area, 36% from marketing, and the remainder from other areas (finance, public relations, senior management). Of course, functional boundaries often are blurred in organizations that serve complex technological markets.

Championing roles

Particular insights into the marketing strategy formation process can be gained by examining the centrality of individual network participants. *Centrality* refers to the ratio of the aggregate relations involving an actor *i* over all relations in a network; that is, the proportion of all network relations that involve *i* (Knoke and Kuklinski, 1982). Research suggests that actors or units occupying central positions in a network are viewed as potentially powerful organizational members because of their greater access to and possible control over relevant resources (Boje and Whetten 1981; Hinings *et al.* 1974).

The formation of marketing strategy involves an emergent process characterized by changing roles, fluid participation of organizational members, and a significant amount of interfunctional communication. Observe from Table 2 that some actors (e.g., 1) decline in centrality, some increase (e.g., 18), many remain marginally involved (e.g., 5, 14), and some (e.g., 3, 4) are not involved in every phase of the project. Note from Table 2 the central position that manager 2 assumed in the strategy formation process. In fact, manager 2 was the most central actor in all phases. Of all the communication relations at milestone 1, for example, manager 2 was involved in 58%. In the terminology originally offered by Schon (1967), manager 2 assumed the role of a *product champion*. Maidique (1980) described a product champion as a member of an organization who creates, defines, or adopts an idea for a technological innovation and who is willing to assume significant risk (e.g., in terms of position or prestige) to make possible the successful implementation of the innovation. Schon (1967) and more recently Peters and Waterman (1982) and Burgelman (1983a) have emphasized the importance of the product champion's role in many successful innovations.

Table 2 Individual Analysis: Communication Patterns of Network Participants[a]

Actor	Division	Position	M1 C	M1 HC	M1 FC1	M1 FC2	M1 FC3	M1 FC4	M2 C	M2 HC	M2 FC1	M2 FC2	M2 FC3	M2 FC4	M3 C	M3 HC	M3 FC1	M3 FC2	M3 FC3	M3 FC4	M4 C	M4 HC	M4 FC1	M4 FC2	M4 FC3	M4 FC4
1	2	Project manager	.21	.40		.14	.86		.15	.33		.17	.83	.14	.15	.33			1.00		.04				1.00	
2	1	Project manager	.58	.75		.45	.45	.10	.59	.70	.36	.50		.14	.40	.53		.40	.53	.07	.27	.80		.43	.50	.07
3	3	Director, R&D	.03	1.00			1.00			1.00			1.00			1.00					.11	1.00		.50	.50	
4	1	Director, PR	.03	1.00				1.00		1.00				1.00		1.00					.07	1.00				1.00
5	4	Project manager	.03			1.00			.07					.07							.07		.75		.25	
6	2	Research engineer	.15	.50		.20	.80		.11	1.00		.25	.75								.09	1.00				
7	1	Vice president	.03	1.00					.04	1.00	1.00					1.00										
8	1	Product manager	.15	.33	1.00				.16	.50	1.00				.50	1.00					.09	1.00		.40	.60	
9	1	Research engineer	.03	1.00			1.00		.04	1.00			1.00		.50	1.00			1.00		.09	1.00				1.00
10	1	Controller	.03	1.00				1.00	.04	1.00	1.00					1.00			1.00		.04	1.00				
11	1	Product manager	.03	1.00	1.00				.04	1.00	1.00				1.00				1.00		.04				1.00	
12	2	Director, R&D	.18	.40		.17	.83		.15	.50		.25	.75		1.00				1.00		.05				1.00	
13	3	Director, R&D	.09				1.00		.07			.25	.75		1.00				1.00		.05	1.00				1.00
14	1	Director R&D	.09	1.00			1.00		.07	1.00			1.00		1.00				1.00		.40			.33	.67	
15	1	Product manager	.03		1.00				.07	1.00	1.00				.50	1.00	.50	.50			.20	1.00	.40	.50	.10	
16	1	Product planner	.03		1.00				.07	1.00						1.00	1.00				.07	1.00	.50	.50		
17	4	Product manager	.03		1.00				.04		1.00					1.00										
18	1	Market manager	.03	1.00	1.00				.07	1.00	1.00				.50	1.00	.50	.50			.18	1.00	.45	.33		.22
19	1	Marketing represent.	.03	1.00	1.00																.18	.75	.45	.44		.11
20	1	Director, marketing																			.05	1.00	1.00			
21	1	Product manager	.03		1.00				.04		1.00				.04	1.00		1.00			.13	1.00	.43	.57		
22	1	Research engineer	.03			1.00			.30	.50			1.00		.30	.50		.13	.87		.02	1.00	1.00			
23	1	Research engineer	.12	.33		.25	.75														.24	.90		.50	.42	.08

[a] Abbreviations:

C = centrality

HC = hierarchical communications

FC = functional communications

1 = among marketing specialists

2 = between marketing and R&D specialists

3 = among R&D specialists

4 = others (marketing and PR, R&D and finance, etc.)

The case data suggest that manager 2 was instrumental in defining the business opportunity, exploring the technical feasibility of the project, and demonstrating that feasibility to customers using borrowed and adapted equipment. These activities were accomplished, in many instances, outside the regular channels of hierarchical decision making. Note, however, that manager 2 engaged in some hierarchical communication across divisions during each phase of the project (see HC columns in Table 2). A value of .75 for manager 2 (milestone 1), for example, indicates that 75% of project-related communications (up or down) were with members of the same division and 25% were with members of other divisions.

Once market interest had been stimulated, the product champion (manager 2) increased the visibility of the project and pursued it openly within regular corporate channels. As the project progressed toward formal corporate approval, other managers assumed prominent roles in the strategy formation process. First, observe from Table 2 the increased centrality of manager 15 (3% at milestone 1; 20% at milestone 4). A product manager, manager 15 supported the efforts of manager 2, became a strong advocate for the project, and engaged in a web of project-related communications across the division.

Second, note also from Table 2 the increasing centrality of manager 18, a market manager (3% at milestone 1; 18% at milestone 4), and manager 23, a research engineer (12% at milestone 1; 24% at milestone 4). The case data suggest that these managers likewise assumed key championing roles. A manager who provides sponsorship or impetus for a project within the management structure has been referred to as an *organizational champion* (Burgelman 1983a; see Maidique 1980 for a review of alternative conceptualizations). Though largely a political activity, organizational championing also requires the capacity to assess the merits of initiatives of product champions in strategic rather than merely technical terms (Burgelman 1983a). The case data indicate that both managers 18 and 23 were instrumental in (1) keeping top managers informed and enthusiastic about the project, (2) securing support at required points, and (3) positioning the project in a manner consistent with corporate strategy. The emergence of this organizational championing role appears to fit a pattern identified in past research. For example, both Kusiatin (1976) and von Hippel (1977) found that the venture manager's manager assumed a critical role in the success of internal corporate ventures.

A multilayered communication process was operative at milestone 4. Observe, for example, in Figure 1, D the organizational members who are linked to the business unit manager (7). They include the product champion, manager 2; the organizational champions, managers 18 and 23; a product manager, 15; and a marketing salesperson, 19. This pattern corresponds with that found in past research showing the strategy-making process to be basically a bottom-up, multiphase political process in which multiple levels of management are involved (Bower 1970; Burgelman 1983a).

The case research suggests the following propositions.

P_4: For autonomous strategic initiatives, centrality in the strategy communication network is associated positively with influence.

P_5: For autonomous strategic initiatives, hierarchical position, as a source of influence, tends to be more important in the later stages of the strategy formulation process than in the earlier stages.

Brass (1984) found that access to and control of work-related communications in the organization are related to individual influence. In addition, Fombrun (1983) found that the network centrality of an individual is a significant determinant of perceived power in an R&D department. By being centrally positioned, organizational actors can integrate the functional contributions of others during the strategy formulation process. As the autonomous strategic initiative gathers momentum and challenges the firm's concept of strategy, hierarchical authority assumes more significance.

An additional proposition issues from the preceding discussion.

P_6: In comparison with induced strategic behavior, autonomous strategic initiatives are more likely to be characterized by the formation of coalitions during the strategy formation process.

The previous outcomes of coalitional bargaining are reflected in the organizational structure and policies of the firm (Cyert and March 1963). Thus, potential changes in the firm's concept of strategy create opportunities for renewed coalitional activity. (See Stevenson *et al.* 1985 for a review of the concept of coalition in organization theory and research.)

Marketing-R&D interface

Dialogue between the marketing and R&D functions was evident throughout the strategy formation process. However, the proportion of project-related communication crossing the functional areas appears to be contingent on the phase in the emergent strategy process. As an illustration, observe the functional communication data in Table 2 for milestone 3 (see FC). Column 3 provides the proportion of communication links among R&D specialists. Note that R&D personnel tended to be involved in project-related communications only with other technical personnel. Thus, milestone 3 might be termed the technical phase in sharp contrast to milestone 4, the marketing phase, in which marketing-R&D communications became more prominent (see FC column 2 in Table 2).

Organizational members who assumed championing roles nurtured the marketing-R&D interface. Observe the functional communication pattern of manager 2, the product champion, across the four milestones. During the final phase, 43% of the product champion's communication links were with marketing personnel, 50% with R&D specialists, and 7% with other organizational members such as those in public relations. In turn, examine the functional communication patterns of marketing personnel, especially at milestone 4. Observe, for example, the distribution of communication links for manager 18, who assumed an organizational championing role: 45% with marketing personnel, 33% with R&D specialists, and 22% with other organizational members.

The following proposition is offered for the marketing-R&D interface.

P$_7$: In comparison with induced strategic behavior, autonomous strategic initiatives are characterized by a greater number of communication links between marketing and R&D personnel.

This proposition issues from the work of Gupta *et al.* (1986), who adopted a contingency perspective in exploring the marketing-R&D interface. The complex information processing requirements imposed by autonomous strategic initiatives create the need for a close relationship between the two units.

Aggregate level of analysis

Additional insights are provided by examining selected properties of the emergent strategy network at an aggregate level of analysis. In Table 3 are data on three network properties: functional communication, network density, and hierarchical communication. First, the analysis centers on the functional composition of the dyads across the strategy formation process. For example, of all the dyadic communication relations for milestone 1, none were between marketing specialists, 38% involved a marketing specialist and R&D specialist in the dyad, and 56% were between R&D specialists. Also, note the increase in dyads composed of marketing specialists (none at milestone 1 to 17% at milestone 4), as well as dyads composed of marketing and R&D specialists (38% at milestone 1 to 43% at milestone 4). Further evidence highlighting the technical emphasis of the third milestone emerges; 65% of the dyads were composed of R&D specialists. Note how the proportions shift rather dramatically at the fourth milestone.

Table 3 Aggregate Analysis: Selected Communication Patterns

	Milestones			
	1	*2*	*3*	*4*
Functional communication				
Marketing	.00	.00	.04	.17
Marketing/R&D	.38	.38	.27	.43
R&D	.56	.54	.65	.28
Other[a]	.06	.08	.04	.12
Network density	.14	.18	.20	.32
Hierarchical communication	.59	.54	.64	.89

[a]Includes public relations and finance interactions.

Second, Table 3 provides a density score for each of the milestones. 'Density' is defined as the number of all communication ties divided by the number of all possible ties $(N - N^2)$ (Knoke and Kuklinski 1982). At milestone 1, the communication network structure was minimal, as indicated by the network density value of .14. In turn, the case data clearly suggest that the communication flow, spawned by the autonomous initiatives of the product champion, departed in many instances from prescribed organizational patterns. However, the flow of communication began to follow a more predictable or prescribed pattern once the project received a formal organizational endorsement. This pattern underlies the rise in density scores across the four milestones. By milestone 4, the communication network structure had become much more complex: the vast majority of communication relations were in larger groupings of individuals, all of whom engaged in project-related communications with one another.

Third, Table 3 provides a further assessment of hierarchical communication patterns. Of all the dyadic communication relations that were hierarchical (i.e., up or down in the same division, not across the same level), 59% involved personnel with the same division. Observe that this proportion increased to 89% at mlestone 4. The density of the communication network increased sharply as strategy formulation progressed and hierarchical communications began to follow a more prescribed pattern consistent with formal organizational boundaries. Thus, the autonomous strategic initiative became embedded in the firm's planning hierarchy. Significantly, after a commitment to a particular strategic course had been made and strategy implementation was underway, a formal written business plan was developed. This document provided a basis for describing and justifying the project at the corporate level of the planning hierarchy.

The case research suggests that:

P_8: Autonomous strategic initiatives are characterized by an increasing level of network density through the marketing strategy formulation process.

P_9: A commitment to a particular strategic course emerges in an earlier phase of the decision-making process for autonomous initiatives than for induced strategic behavior.

P_{10}: The more senior management encourages risk-taking, the greater the degree of autonomous strategic behavior by organizational members.

Narayanan and Fahey (1982) argue that strategy implementation often is underway before a formal organizational commitment to a particular strategic course is made. The strategy course, set in motion by the product champion, is often in the early stages of implementation before receiving formal recognition within the planning hierarchy. Likewise, senior management can provide an environment that may be conducive or inhibitive to entrepreneurial initiatives (e.g., Shrivastava and Souder 1985; Souder 1981). For example, corporate management can encourage risk-taking through specific performance evaluation and reward systems.

Conclusions and implications

We extend past exploratory assessments to strategic decision processes by assessing the communication patterns that emerged during the formulation of marketing strategy. Our findings suggest the need to extend the conceptualization of the marketing strategy formation process to include the autonomous strategic behavior of marketing managers. Additional research is needed to clarify how such autonomous strategic initiatives differ from more induced forms of strategic behavior. Several research propositions are offered to guide future inquiry. In turn, the case research provides insight into the nature and selected characteristics of autonomous strategic processes.

Autonomous strategic behavior

The marketing literature has given only limited attention to autonomous strategic behavior or to the change agent role that *individual* managers often assume in nurturing innovative activity in the firm. As the case research shows, information supplied by a salesperson triggered the innovative initiative within the organization. Once motivated to act, the marketing manager or, more accurately, a product champion is often instrumental in defining the need, sensing the opportunity, and conceptualizing how the firm's resources might be restructured to take advantage of this opportunity.

The study findings strongly suggest that autonomous strategic initiatives and induced initiatives involve different sets of actors and spawn different forms of strategic dialogue. As a result of the mobilization efforts of the product champion, an informal, multi-functional, and loosely structured network emerges. Thus, project-related communications emanate from the product champion to a loosely connected subset of organizational members.

As the product champion achieves an initial threshold of success in demonstrating a project's potential, the organizational champion assumes a central role in the internal strategic dialogue. Marketing managers, emphasizing market and competitive information, and R&D managers, emphasizing technical data, assume key roles in positioning the project within the firm's concept of strategy. Gradually, the roles and responsibilities of key participants in the process are clarified and the strategy formulation process becomes more formalized. Likewise, the communication structure becomes more complex as the participants in the process become interconnected in a web of project-related communications (i.e., high network density). If the efforts of the product and organizational champions are successful, the autonomous strategic initiative blends into the firm's formal planning routine and concept of strategy.

Our case research suggests that a commitment to a particular strategic course occurs at an early point in the evolution of an autonomous strategic initiative. The impetus for the project comes from an individual manager who concentrates on mobilizing resources and support for a particular strategy direction. As our findings indicate, the product champion's success in internal negotiations hinges on the successful demonstration of the technology in a particular market context. Once that success is achieved, the strategy course is set and implementation is underway. Induced strategic initiatives, in contrast, are more likely to involve a more formal and systematic analysis of strategic alternatives.

Implications for marketing management

The opposing tendencies toward stability and change in the strategic planning process raise a set of challenging implications for marketing managers. First, our analysis affirms the role of the marketing function in the strategic management process of the firm. Marketing managers potentially can have a vital role in initiating entrepreneurial activities within large, complex firms. Here opportunities that depart from the firm's mainstream areas of business are defined, assessed, and then pursued informally within the planning process. To assess and capitalize on these autonomous strategic initiatives, substantiative interaction is necessary among the different levels of planning hierarchy. The marketing function often assumes a key role in this strategic dialogue. There is also a need for a balance between bottom-up and top-down approaches to strategic planning and market analysis (Day 1981a, b).

Second, our findings suggest that entrepreneurial initiatives cannot be planned precisely, but can be encouraged and nurtured. In our study, the product champion had a degree of flexibility and informal management support in exploring market opportunities. Burgelman (1983c, p. 1361) argues that top management '. . . need not encourage entrepreneurship; it need only make sure not to suppress it.' In contrast, Quinn (1979, 1980) recommends that the planning and budgeting process should shift its primary role of resource rationing to one that also emphasizes opportunity-seeking and risk-taking. Peters and Waterman (1982) suggest that companies such as 3M, Hewlett-Packard, and IBM have successfully adopted such a perspective.

Third, our analysis suggests that autonomous strategic initiatives could be aided by facilitating the exchange of information among functional areas and business units of the organization. For example, an inventory of R&D projects underway across the corporation as well as a corresponding list of project leaders would enhance the flow of technical information in the formal and informal networks. Efforts might also be focused profitably on nurturing communication among marketing personnel (including field salespersons) and R&D managers. Clearly, the marketing function can have a pivotal role in the acquisition and dissemination of information crucial to entrepreneurial initiatives.

Limitations

Our study was exploratory and subject to the limitations often associated with comparable process research efforts. First, because the study centered on an in-depth analysis of a single case, the findings may not be generalizable to all organizations. Second, we traced a single decision process over time and did not consider the interrelationship between that process and other strategic decisions unfolding in the organization during the same period. Third, there may be alternative ways of defining and operationalizing the critical milestones in the autonomous strategy formation process. Delineation of the early phases of this process is especially crucial. Care must be exercised in exploring the stimuli that triggered the autonomous initiatives and in exploring the nature of early mobilization efforts.

By providing an analytical emphasis on emergent subgroups within the organization, network analysis is a valuable tool for research such as ours. In the future, researchers might also systematically examine both induced and autonomous strategic behavior in the same organizational setting. In determining critical milestones, they might draw upon the work of Mintzberg, Raisinghani, and Théorêt (1976), who demonstrate that strategic decision processes are amenable to conceptual structuring.

Implications for research

Our discussion raises several broader research issues. First, research is needed to establish the conditions under which different systems are adequate and appropriate for designing and managing innovative activity in organizations. Researchers have suggested that the entrepreneurial process can be institutionalized through established administrative mechanisms (Jelinek 1979), can be planned to a degree by using flexible criteria and the nurturing of top management (Quinn 1979), or can be described best as a process of experimentation and selection spread over multiple levels of management in the firm (Burgelman 1983a). Clearly, there is a need to explore more carefully the effects of alternative organizational designs, reward systems, and control procedures on the level and quality of entrepreneurial initiatives emanating from the marketing function. Such a line of research appears to be especially appropriate in light of a survey in which top managers were critical of marketing managers for a lack of innovative and entrepreneurial thinking (Webster 1981).

Second, research might examine how marketing managers utilize information in organizational decision making. Past research indicates a gap between normative theories of decision making and the empirical understanding of how marketing decisions actually are made within organizations (Hulbert 1981; O'Reilly 1983). What information sources and search procedures do marketing managers employ in exploring autonomous strategic initiatives? How are preferences for particular autonomous strategic initiatives formed? This line of research may provide important insights into autonomous strategic behavior.

Third, the innovation process is characterized by an increasingly complex bundle of transactions among organizational members (Van de Ven 1986).

Clearly, there is a need to examine the internal negotiation processes that are operative during marketing strategy development. Here attention might be given to tracing communication and influence patterns across different types of marketing strategy situations. Ruekert and Walker (1987) provide a useful conceptual framework for examining patterns of interaction between marketing and other functional units. Such research also might systematically examine the importance of various structural sources and intraorganizational power (hierarchical authority and resource control, as well as network centrality) during the strategy formulation process. Likewise, attention might be given to the conflict resolution mechanisms that marketing managers use in negotiating with other functional areas (such as R&D) or with other layers in the planning hierarchy. This line of research is consistent with the emerging constituency-based theory of marketing (Day and Wensley 1983) and may better capture the reality of the strategy formation process as well as the role of the marketing function and individual marketing managers in shaping the strategic position of the firm.

References

Anderson, Paul F. (1982), 'Marketing Strategic Planning, and the Theory of the Firm,' *Journal of Marketing*, 46 (Spring), 15-26.

Andrews, Kenneth R. (1980), *The Concept of Corporate Strategy*, Homewood, IL: Richard D. Irwin, Inc.

Boje, David M. and David A. Whetten (1981), 'Effects of Organizational Strategies and Contextual Constraints on Centrality and Attributions of Influence in Interorganizational Networks,' *Administrative Science Quarterly*, 26, 378-95.

Bonoma, Thomas V. (1985), 'Case Research in Marketing: Opportunities, Problems, and a Process,' *Journal of Marketing Research*, 22 (May), 199-208.

Bower, Joseph L. (1970), *Managing the Resource Allocation Process*. Boston: Graduate School of Business Administration, Harvard University.

Brass, Daniel J. (1984), 'Being in the Right Place: A Structural Analysis of Individual Influence in an Organization,' *Administrative Science Quarterly*, 29 (December), 518-39.

Braybrooke, David and Charles E. Lindblom (1963), *A Strategy of Decision: Policy Evaluation as a Social Process*. New York: The Free Press.

Burgelman, Robert A. (1983a), 'A Process Model of Internal Corporate Venturing in the Diversified Major Firm,' *Administrative Science Quarterly*, 28, 223-44.

Burgelman, Robert A. (1983b), 'A Model of the Interaction of Strategic Behavior, Corporate Context, and the Concept of Strategy,' *Academy of Management Review*, 8 (1), 61-70.

Burgelman, Robert A. (1983c), 'Corporate Entrepreneurship and Strategic Management: Insights from a Process Study,' *Management Science*, 29 (December), 1349-64.

Cohen, Michael D., James G. March, and Johan P. Olsen (1972), 'A Garbage Can Model of Organizational Choice,' *Administrative Science Quarterly*, 17, 1-25.

Cyert, Richard M. and James G. March (1963), *A Behavioral Theory of the Firm*. Englewood Cliffs, NJ: Prentice-Hall, Inc.

Cyert, Richard M., Herbert A. Simon, and Donald B. Trow (1956), 'Observation of a Business Decision,' *Journal of Business*, 29, 237-48.

Day, George S. (1981a), 'Strategic Market Analysis and Definition: An Integrated Approach,' *Strategic Management Journal*, 2 (July- September), 281-99.

Day, George S. (1981b), 'Analytical Approaches to Strategic Market Planning,' in *Review of Marketing 1981*, Ben M. Enis and Kenneth J. Roering, eds. Chicago: American Marketing Association, 89-105.

Day, George S., and Robin Wensley (1983), 'Marketing Theory with a Strategic Orientation,' *Journal of Marketing*, 47 (Fall), 79-89.

Fombrun, Charles J. (1982), 'Strategies for Network Research in Organizations,' *Academy of Management Review*, 7 (2), 280-91.

Fombrun, Charles J. (1983), 'Attributions of Power Across a Social Network,' *Human Relations*, 36 (6), 493-508.

Foster, Brian L. and Stephen B. Seidman (1978), *SONET-1: Social Network Analysis and Modeling System*, Vol. 1. Binghamton, NY: Center for Social Analysis, State University of New York.

Gladstein, Deborah and James B. Quinn (1985), 'Making Decisions and Producing Action: The Two Faces of Strategy,' in *Organizational Strategy and Change*, Johannes M. Pennings and Associates, eds. San Francisco: Jossey-Bass Publishers, 198-216.

Gupta, Ashok K., S.P. Raj, and David Wilemon (1986), 'A Model for Studying R&D-Marketing Interface in the Product Innovation Process,' *Journal of Marketing*, 50 (April), 7-17.

Hinings, Christopher R., David J. Hickson, Johannes M. Pennings, and Rodney E. Schneck (1974), 'Structural Conditions of Intraorganizational Power,' *Administrative Science Quarterly*, 19, 22-44.

Hofer, Charles and Daniel Schendel (1978), *Strategy Formulation: Analytical Concepts*. St Paul, MN: West Publishing Co.

Howard, John A., James Hulbert, and John U. Farley (1975), 'Organizational Analysis and Information-Systems Design: A Decision-Process Perspective,' *Journal of Business Research*, 3 (April), 133-48.

Hulbert, James M. (1981), 'Descriptive Models of Marketing Decisions,' in *Marketing Decision Models*, Randall L. Schultz and Andris A. Zoltners, eds. New York: Elsevier North-Holland Publishing Company, 19-53.

Hutt, Michael D. and Thomas W. Speh (1984), 'The Marketing Strategy Center: Diagnosing the Industrial Marketer's Interdisciplinary Role,' *Journal of Marketing*, 48 (Fall), 53-61.

Jelinek, Mariann (1979), *Institutionalizing Innovation*. New York: Praeger Publishers.

Knoke, David and James H. Kuklinski (1982), *Network Analysis*. Beverly Hills, CA: Sage Publications, Inc.

Kotler, Philip (1984), *Marketing Management: Analysis, Planning and Control*, 5th ed. Englewood Cliffs, NJ: Prentice-Hall, Inc.

Kusiatin, Ilan (1976), 'The Process and Capacity for Diversification Through Internal Development,' Ph.D. dissertation, Harvard University.

Lindlbom, Charles E. (1965), *The Intelligence of Democracy*. New York: The Free Press.

Lindlbom, Charles E. (1979), 'Still Muddling, Not Yet Through,' *Public Administration Review*, 39 (November-December), 517-26.

Lorange, Peter (1980), *Corporate Planning: An Executive Viewpoint*, Englewood Cliffs, NJ: Prentice-Hall, Inc.

Maidique, Modesto A. (1980), 'Entrepeneurs, Champions, and Technological Innovations,' *Sloan Management Review*, 21 (Spring), 59-76.

March, James G. and Johan P. Olsen (1976), *Ambiguity and Choice in Organizations*. Bergen, Norway: Universitets-forlaget.

March, James G. and Herbert A. Simon (1958), *Organizations*. New York: John Wiley & Sons, Inc.

Mintzberg, Henry (1978), 'Patterns in Strategy Formulation,' *Management Science*, 24 (May), 934-48.

Mintzberg, Henry, Duru Raisinghani, and André Théorêt (1976), 'The Structure of "Unstructured" Decision Processes,' *Administrative Science Quarterly*, 21 (June), 246-75.

Mintzberg, Henry and James A. Waters (1985), 'Of Strategies, Deliberate and Emergent,' *Strategic Management Journal*, 6, 257-72.

Mumford, Enid and Andrew Pettigrew (1975), *Implementing Strategic Decisions*. London: Longmans.

Murray, Edwin A. (1978), 'Strategic Choice as a Negotiated Outcome,' *Management Science*, 24 (9), 960-72.

Narayanan, V.K. and Liam Fahey (1982), 'The Micro-Politics of Strategy Formulation,' *Academy of Management Review*, 7 (1), 25-34.

Newell, Allen and Herbert A. Simon (1972), *Human Problem Solving*. Englewood Cliffs, NJ: Prentice-Hall, Inc.

O'Reilly, Charles A., III (1983), 'The Use of Information in Organizational Decision Making: A Model and Some Propositions,' in *Research in Organizational Behavior*, Vol. 5. Greenwich, CT: JAI Press, Inc., 103-39.

Pennings, Johannes M. (1985), 'Toward Convergence in Strategic Theory and Practice,' in *Organizational Strategy and Change*, Johannes M. Pennings & Associates, eds. San Francisco: Jossey-Bass Publishers, 468-94.

Peters, Thomas J. and Robert H. Waterman, Jr. (1982), *In Search of Excellence, Lessons from America's Best-Run Companies*. New York: Harper & Row Publishers, Inc.

Pettigrew, Andrew M. (1977), 'Strategy Formulation as a Political Process,' *International Studies of Management and Organization*, 7 (2), 78-87.

Pettigrew, Andrew M. (1985), 'Examining Changes in the Long-Term Context of Culture and Politics,' in *Organizational Strategy and Change*, Johannes M. Pennings & Associates, eds. San Francisco: Jossey-Bass Publishers, 269-318.

Quinn, James B. (1978), 'Strategic Change: Logical Incrementalism,' *Sloan Management Review*, 20 (Spring), 7-21.

Quinn, James B. (1979), 'Technological Innovation, Entrepreneurship, and Strategy,' *Sloan Management Review*, 21 (Spring), 19-30.

Quinn, James B. (1980), *Strategies for Change: Logical Incrementalism*. Homewood, IL: Richard D. Irwin, Inc.

Quinn, James B. (1982), 'Managing Strategies Incrementally,' *Omega*, 10 (6), 613-27.

Quinn, James B. (1985), 'Managing Innovation: Controlled Chaos,' *Harvard Business Review*, 63 (May-June), 73-84.

Ruekert, Robert W. and Orville C. Walker, Jr. (1987), 'Marketing's Interaction with Other Functional Units: A Conceptual Framework and Empirical Evidence,' *Journal of Marketing*, 51 (January), 1-19.

Ruekert, Robert W., Orville C. Walker, Jr., and Kenneth J. Roering (1985), 'The Organization of Marketing Activities: A Contingency Theory of Structure and Performance.' *Journal of Marketing*, 49 (Winter), 13-25.

Schon, Donald A. (1967), *Technology and Change*. New York: Delacorte Press.

Shrivastava, Paul and W.E. Souder (1985), 'Phase Transfer Models for Technological Innovation,' *Advances in Strategic Management*, Vol. 3. Greenwich, CT: JAI Press, Inc., 135-47.

Simon, Herbert A. (1945), *Administrative Behavior*, 1st ed. New York: The Free Press.

Souder, W.E. (1981), 'Disharmony Between R&D and Marketing,' *Industrial Marketing Management*, 10 (February), 67-73.

Starbuck, William (1983), 'Organizations as Action Generators,' *American Journal of Sociology*, 48 (1), 91-115.

Stevenson, William B., Jone L. Pearce, and Lyman W. Porter (1985), 'The Concept of "Coalition" in Organizational Theory and Research,' *Academy of Management Review*, 10 (2) 256-68.

Thompson, James D. and Arthur Tuden (1959), 'Strategies, Structures and Processes of Organizational Decision,' in *Comparative Studies in Administration*, James D. Thompson *et al.*, eds. Pittsburgh: University of Pittsburgh Press.

Tichy, Noel M. (1981), 'Networks in Organizations,' in *Handbook of Organizational Design*, Paul C. Nystrom and William H. Starbuck, eds. Oxford: Oxford University Press, 225-49.

Van de Ven, Andrew H. (1980), 'Problem Solving, Planning, and Innovation; Part 2, Speculations for Theory and Practice,' *Human Relations*, 33, 757-79.

Van de Ven, Andrew H. (1986), 'Central Problems in the Management of Innovation,' *Management Science*, 32 (May), 590-607.

von Hippel, Eric (1977), 'Successful and Failing Internal Corporate Ventures: An Empirical Analysis,' *Industrial Marketing Management*, 6, 163-74.

von Hippel, Eric (1978), 'Successful Industrial Products from Customer Ideas,' *Journal of Marketing*, 42 (January), 39-40.

Webster, Frederick E., Jr. (1981), 'Top Management's Concerns about Marketing: Issues for the 1980s,' *Journal of Marketing*, 45 (Summer), 9-16.

Weitz, Barton and Erin Anderson (1981), 'Organizing and Controlling the Marketing Function,' in *Review of Marketing 1981*, Ben M. Enis and Kenneth J. Roering, eds. Chicago: American Marketing Association, 134-42.

Wind, Yoram and Thomas S. Robertson (1983), 'Marketing Strategy: New Directions for Theory and Research,' *Journal of Marketing*, 47 (Spring), 12-25.

21 Ten barriers to marketing planning

Malcolm H. B. McDonald

Introduction

The overall purpose of marketing planning, and its principal focus, is the identification and creation of a competitive advantage. Yet after twenty years of doing, researching (McDonald 1984), teaching, and writing about the subject, the author of this paper has experienced little to change his view that *marketing planning* is still the most enigmatic of all the problems facing management as they brace themselves for whatever challenges the 1990s hold.

The purpose of this paper is to expose a few myths about marketing planning and in the process to suggest ways of doing it better in order to create a substantial competitive advantage, for surely, if marketing planning doesn't lead to this, it can't be worth bothering about in the first place.

The paper opens by restating what marketing planning is and how little impact it has had on British industry to date.

The main part of the paper explores what it is that prevents organizations from developing and implementing good strategic marketing plans.

Some solutions to the problem identified are proposed.

What is marketing planning?

Marketing planning is simply a logical sequence and a series of activities leading to the setting of marketing objectives and the formulation of plans for achieving them. Companies generally go through some kind of management process in developing marketing plans. In small, undiversified companies, this process is usually informal. In larger, more diversified organizations, the process is often systematized. Conceptually, this process is very simple and involves a situation review, the formulation of some basic assumptions, setting objectives for what is being sold and to whom, deciding on how the objectives are to be achieved, and scheduling and costing out the actions necessary for implementation.

Why is marketing planning necessary?

Apart from the need to cope with increasing turbulence, environmental complexity, more intense competitive pressures, and the sheer speed of technological change, a marketing plan is useful:

- For *you*

- For *superiors*
- For *non marketing* functions
- For *subordinates*

- To help identify sources of competitive advantage
- To force an organized approach
- To develop specificity
- To ensure consistent relationships
- To inform
- To get resources
- To get support
- To gain commitment
- To set objectives and strategies

Naivety about marketing planning

At the cognitive level, all of this seems delightfully simple. Yet many observers are still bemused by the fact that many meticulous marketing planning companies fare badly, whilst the sloppy or inarticulate in marketing terms do well. Has there ever been any relationship between marketing planning and commercial success, or are we all deluding ourselves?

Greenley's recent (1987) study of marketing planning identified only seven UK empirically based studies into the marketing planning practices of commercial organizations. The remaining mass of publications are largely prescriptive and amount to little more than logically deduced theories based on ungrounded assumptions (what Glaser and Strauss (1967) refer to as 'exampling'). Most of the empirical studies concluded that few companies actually practice the theory of marketing planning so prolifically written about by so many.

But, even more disturbing, those who recognized the need for a more structured approach to planning their marketing and who turned to the formalized procedures found in prescriptive texts, rarely enjoyed the claimed benefits of marketing planning – indeed, the very opposite sometimes happened, in that there were actually *dysfunctional* consequences, which brought marketing planning itself into disrepute.

Herein lies the problem. The claimed benefits of better coordination of inter-related activities, improved environmental awareness, better communication among management and better use of resources, really *are* there for the taking, and there *is* a relationship between marketing planning and commercial success, as the work of McDonald (1984), Thompson (1962), Kollatt *et al.* (1972), Ansoff (1977), Thune and House (1970), Leighton (1966) and others has shown. It is just that the contextual problems surrounding the process of marketing planning are so complex and so little understood, that effective marketing planning rarely happens. What these problems are and how they can be overcome will be dealt with in the main body of the paper.

The fact that financial performance at any one point in time is not necessarily a reflection of the adequacy or otherwise of planning procedures, (since some companies just happen to be in the right place at the right time, usually in growth industries), should not deflect us from this fundamental truth. Those who want to know what marketing planning can add in a situation where a company has a well established position and where success to date has not been based on any particularly rigorous approach to marketing planning, should remember that all leadership positions are transitory, and no industry based in the United Kingdom needs reminding of that today. The rapid and systematic demise of the UK's world leadership position is an insult to the founding fathers of British industry.

It is easy to forget the financially-driven management of the 60s and 70s who milked dry the results of the endeavours of their entrepreneurial forebearers. Rationality to them meant only short-term profits on a product-by-product basis, and if this meant raising the price or deleting the product, who cared as long as the end-of-year profit and loss account came out right? Regard for competitive position, market share, promotion, customer franchise, R & D and the like (all of which, of course, are funded from revenue) seemed irrelevant in those halcyon days of high growth.

Nor should we fool ourselves that this sad state of affairs has changed. A recent study (Wong *et al.* 1988) of Japanese and British companies in the UK concluded that 87% of British firms still have *profit maximization* as their major short-term goal, whilst 80% of their Japanese competitors have *market share growth* as their major short-term goal. It is a sad reflection on our business schools in the UK that so many of our top industrialists still behave like vandals in the way they manage their marketing assets. It is little wonder that so many of our famous industries and names such as Woolworths, Dunlop, British Leyland and countless others, have had to suffer the humility of near bankruptcy, and it is a pity that so many more will have to suffer the same fate before we come to our senses and see that marketing planning is crucial to our long-term survival and prosperity.

There is no escaping the fact that, whatever our size or shape, marketing's contribution to business success lies in analysing future opportunities to meet well-defined customer needs with products or services that deliver the sought-after benefits in a superior way to that of competitors.

Such a process and activities must not be mistaken for forecasts and budgets, which of course we need and already have. Put bluntly, the process of marketing planning is concerned with identifying what and to whom sales are going to be made in the longer term, and how, in order to give revenue budgets and sales forecasts any chance of being achieved.

Let us turn now to the question of why it is that so few companies really master the art of marketing planning.

Barriers to the development of marketing plans

Prescriptive texts on marketing planning describe the process of marketing planning in terms of marketing audits, SWOT analyses, objective setting, and so on, with hardly any thought given to the contextual issues surrounding the process. For example, who is to do all these things, how, when, how often, should it be top down or bottom up, which comes first, the one year or the long-range plan, and so on? Then there are issues such as: company culture; company size; internationalization; diversity; environmental turbulence; market growth rate; technological change; and countless other considerations.

It is very clear that the simplistic approaches of most writers do not adequately address such contextual issues in relation to marketing planning, which partly accounts for the fact that so few companies do it at all, and even fewer do it well.

The remainder of this paper outlines the ten principal reasons for this failure and gives advice on how these pitfalls can be avoided.

1 Confusion between marketing tactics and strategy

The author's own research (1984) has shown that, in peering into the murky depths of organizational behaviour in relation to marketing planning, confusion reigns supreme, and nowhere less than over the terminology of marketing.

Few practising marketers understand the real significance of a *strategic* marketing plan as opposed to a *tactical*, or operational marketing plan.

Why should this be so?

For an answer, we need to look at some of the changes that have taken place during the past two decades. For example, the simple environment of the 1960s and early 1970s, characterized by growth and the easy marketability of products and services, has now been replaced by an increasingly complex and abrasive environment, often made worse by static or declining markets. For most, the days have gone when it was only necessary to ride the tidal wave of growth. There wasn't the same need for a disciplined, systematic approach to the market. A tactical, short-term approach to marketing planning seemed to work perfectly well in such conditions. But by failing to grasp the nettle of strategic orientation in plans that identify and develop their distinctive competence, companies have become, or will increasingly become, casualties during the 1990s.

The problem is really quite simple. Most managers prefer to sell the products they find easiest to sell to those customers who offer the least line of resistance. By developing short-term, tactical marketing plans first and then extrapolating them, managers merely succeed in extrapolating their own short-comings. It is a bit like steering from the wake O.K. in calm, clear waters, but not so sensible in busy and choppy waters! Preoccupation with preparing a detailed one year plan first is typical of those many companies who confuse sales forecasting and budgeting with strategic marketing planning – in our experience the most common mistake of all.

Already, companies led by chief executives with a proactive orientation that stretches beyond the end of the current fiscal year have begun to show results visibly better than the old reactive companies with only a short-term vision.

Figure 1 shows the old style of company in which very little attention is paid to strategy by any level of management. It will be seen that lower levels of management do not get involved at all, whilst the directors spend most of their time on operational/tactical issues.

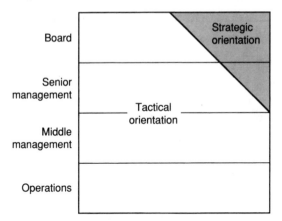

Figure 1

Figure 2 is a representation of those companies that recognize the importance of strategy and who manage to involve all levels of management in strategy formulation.

The rule, then, is simple:

Develop the *strategic* marketing plan first. This entails greater emphasis on scanning the external environment, the early identification of forces emanating from it, and developing appropriate strategic responses, involving all levels of management in the process.

A strategic plan should cover a period of between 3 and 5 years, and only

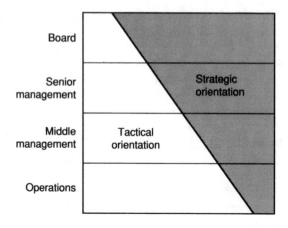

Figure 2

when this has been developed and agreed should the one year operational marketing plan be developed. Never write the one year plan first and extrapolate it.

2 Isolating the marketing function from operations

One of the most common causes of the failure of marketing planning is the belief that marketing is something that a marketing person 'does' in their office. The appointment of a marketing supremo is often a last-ditch attempt to put things right when all else has failed. The trouble is, the new person comes along and, irrespective of their knowledge or skills, quickly finds that all the power is vested in others, particularly for product development (the technical people), pricing (the accountants), customer service (the distribution department) and selling (the sales director). This leaves some bits of the promotional mix for the new person to play around with. Hence the new executive is powerless to influence anything of significance and quickly fails.

Line managers look on the new department with disdain and see requests for information, strategies and plans as a time-consuming task likely to have little impact on their real and more pressing problems.

This has much to do with the general misunderstanding about what marketing really is. Without a corporate driving force centred around customer satisfaction (i.e. a marketing orientation), arguments about where to put marketing are of course pointless, but even when top management is jolted into a realization of the need to take account of the customer, the most frequent mistake is to separate out marketing from operations as if it had the plague.

This is not the place to argue about organizational issues, such as line versus staff, centralization versus decentralization, although the principles are clear:

> For the purpose of marketing planning, put marketing as close as possible to the customer. Where practicable, have both marketing and sales report to the same person, who should not normally be the chief executive officer.

3   Confusion between the marketing function and the marketing concept

The author's close contact with about 2,000 senior managers a year confirms his belief about the depth of ignorance that still abounds concerning what marketing is.

(a) *Confusion with sales*   One managing director aggressively announced to the assembled seminar audience, 'There's no time for marketing in my company 'til sales improve!' Confusion with sales is still one of the biggest barriers to be overcome.

(b) *Confusion with product management*   The belief that all a company has to do is to produce a good product to succeed also still abounds, and neither Concorde, the EMI Scanner, nor the many thousands of brilliant British products that have seen their owners or investors go bankrupt in the past twenty years will convince such people otherwise.

(c) *Confusion with advertising*   This is another popular misconception and the annals of business are replete with examples such as Dunlop, Woolworths and British Airways who, before they got professional management in, won awards with their brilliant advertising campaigns, whilst failing to deliver the goods. Throwing advertising expenditure at the problem is still a very popular way of tackling deep-rooted marketing problems.

(d) *Confusion with customer service*   The 'have a nice day' syndrome is currently having its hey day in many countries of the world, popularized of course by Peters and Waterman in *In Search of Excellence*. The banks are amongst those who have spent millions training their staff to be charming to customers whilst still getting the basic offer fundamentally wrong – the banks are still closed when the public most needs them open. Likewise, in British Rail, whilst it helps to be treated nicely, it is actually much more important to get there on time.

The principle, then, is as follows.

> Marketing is a management process whereby the resources of the whole organization are utilized to satisfy the needs of selected customer groups in order to achieve the objectives of both parties. Marketing, then, is first and foremost an attitude of mind rather than a series of functional activities.

4   Organizational barriers

Closely linked with the issue of marketing powerlessness, is the issue of organizational form.

The most typical organigram is the one which is based around corporate functions such as personnel, finance, production, distribution, operations, and marketing. Whilst the traditional reasons for this type of organization are clear, there is little doubt that it can be very difficult to get people who are loyal to their own 'tribe' to think of subjugating their own goals to the broader goals of customer satisfaction. This is clearly the role of top management and has a lot to do with corporate culture, to be discussed below.

Whilst the team building approach has gone a long way towards overcoming this kind of organizational barrier, of much more importance is to get the task of defining strategic business units (SBUs) right (The Strategic Planning Institute 1986).

A strategic business unit:

- Will have common segments and competitors for most of its products
- Is a competitor in an external market
- Is a discrete, separable and identifiable unit
- Will have a manager who has control over most of the areas critical to success.

But SBUs are not necessarily the same as operating units, and the definition can, and should, be applied all the way down to a particular product of customer or group of products or customers, and it is here that the main marketing planning task lies.

The problem remains of getting organizational support and commitment to the marketing planning process, but this is discussed later.

So the principle is:

Organize company activities around customer groups if possible rather than around functional activities and get marketing planning done in these strategic business units. Without excellent marketing planning in SBUs, corporate marketing planning will be of limited value.

5   Lack of in-depth analysis

Even from well-respected companies, the most common complaint concerns lack of adequate information for the purpose of analysis. On deeper investigation, however, it nearly always turns out to be a case of too much information rather than too little. The real problem is frequent lack of proper analysis. At a recent conference for a builder's merchanting company that had increased its net profit before tax by 60% for the second year running, one of their chief executives did not know the answer to any of the following questions:

How much of the profit increase is due to:
● Market size growth
● Market share growth
● Price increases
● Cost reductions
● Productivity improvements?

Faced with such massive ignorance, it is clear what will happen to this company the moment construction industry trading conditions worsen.

The methodology for developing marketing intelligence systems has been comprehensively covered in the literature during the past twenty years (McDonald 1980), yet it is clear that in Britain at least, industry has a long way to go to get even the basics right concerning trends in:

● The environment
● Markets
● Competitors
● Internal strengths and weaknesses.

It is also clear that, even if an organization has an adequate intelligence system, rarely is there a formal *marketing audit* undertaken by all SBU managers as a *required* activity at a specific time of the year as part of an agreed planning process.

The principle, then, is as follows:

For an effective marketing audit to take place:
● Checklists of questions customized according to level in the organization should be agreed.
● These should form the basis of the organization's M.I.S.
● The marketing audit should be a *required* activity.
● Managers should not be allowed to hide behind vague terms like 'poor economic conditions'.
● Managers should be encouraged to incorporate the tools of marketing in their audits, e.g. product life cycles, product portfolios, and the like.

6   Confusion between process and output

Confusion between the management process itself and the output of the process, the marketing plan, is common. In most cases, plans are too bulky to be of any practical use to busy line managers and most contain masses of data and information which rightly belongs in the company's marketing information system or audit, and whose inclusion in the marketing plan only serves to rob it of focus and impact.

The SWOT device (Strengths, Weaknesses, Opportunities and Threats), whilst potentially a very powerful analytical device to give impact to the ensuing assumptions, objectives, strategies and budgets, is rarely used effectively.

A SWOT should:

- Be focused on each specific segment of crucial importance to the organization's future
- Be a summary emanating from the marketing audit
- Be brief, interesting and concise
- Focus on *key* factors only
- List *differential* strengths and weakness *vis à vis* competitors, focusing on competitive advantage
- List *key* external opportunities and threats only
- Identify and pin down the *real* issues. It should not be a list of unrelated points
- The reader should be able to grasp instantly the main thrust of the business, even to the point of being able to write marketing objectives
- Follow the implied question 'which means that. . . ?' to get the real implications
- Not overabbreviate

This leads to a key point which needs to be made about this vital part of the marketing planning process.

Information is the foundation on which a marketing plan is built. From *information* (internal and external) comes *intelligence. Intelligence* describes *the marketing plan,* which is the intellectualization of how managers perceive their own position in their markets relative to their competitors (with competitive advantage accurately defined – e.g. cost leader, differentiation, niche), what objectives they want to achieve over some designated period of time, how they intend to achieve their objectives (strategies), what resources are required, and with what results (budget).

7 Lack of knowledge and skills

It must be a matter of great disappointment to academics that many of the components of a typical marketing syllabus are rarely used by practising marketing managers, at least in industrial goods organizations. Indeed, in the author's experience, even experienced marketing managers with marketing qualifications often fail to apply the techniques of marketing in their jobs.

The perennial problems have always centred around customer behaviour and market segmentation, and indeed these are extremely difficult concepts to grasp even at the cognitive level. Even more worrying, however, is the blind assumption often made by top management that all the key marketing practitioners in an organization actually possess both the *knowledge* and the *skills* to be effective marketers.

The author has conducted a series of experiments in some of the UK's leading companies during the past two years, and has found that almost two-thirds of marketing practitioners do not know the difference between a corporate objective, a marketing objective, and an advertising objective. Even fewer know what a logarithmic scale is and how it can be used in experience curves and matrices. Very few have heard of the Standard Industrial Classification and virtually no one has heard of P.I.M.S. Very few even understand the significance of Benefit Analysis, let alone Benefit Segmentation. Out of fifty questions, the average score is about 20%.

Whilst these are only examples, and do not prove anything, it must be a matter of concern when thinking seriously about marketing planning, for without an understanding of at least some of the basic tools of marketing, the chance of coming up with strategies based on sustainable competitive advantage is slim.

Communication and interpersonal skills are also prerequisites for marketing planning success, since excellent marketing plans will be ineffective unless those on whom the main burden of implementation lies understand them and are highly motivated towards their achievement.

The principle, then, is:

Ensure all those responsible for marketing in SBUs have the necessary marketing knowledge and skills for the job. In particular, ensure they understand and know how to use the more important tools of marketing, such as:

- Information
  - How to get it
  - How to use it
- Positioning
  - Market segmentation
  - Ansoff
  - Porter
- Product life cycle analysis
  - Gap analysis
- Portfolio management
  - BCG
  - Directional policy matrix
- 4 x Ps management
  - Product
  - Price
  - Place
  - Promotion

Additionally, marketing personnel require communication and interpersonal skills.

8   Lack of a systematic approach to marketing planning

Gorb (1978) talks about the differences between a hunter and a farmer in planning requirements. A hunter travels light, and needs stealth, cunning and know-how, whereas a farmer needs to plan ahead, buy seed, sow, harvest, interpret demand for the crops, and so on. Clearly, then, at the entrepreneurial end of corporate development, marketing planning as a formalized system is not likely to be seen as relevant because of the 'here and now' ethos.

Leppard (1987) discusses the different kinds of planning system that are required by organizations. These range from very informal systems to highly formalized ones, with the degree of autonomy at the top or bottom depending on the organization's size and stage of development. Leppard and McDonald (1987) have evolved an analytical tool for measuring an organization's stage of development to ensure that any marketing planning system is appropriate.

The point here, however, is that for all but very small, undiversified organizations, a marketing planning system is essential to ensure that things happen when they are supposed to happen and that there are at least some basic standards which must be adhered to. In the author's experience even where training has been carried out, the quality and usefulness of SBU marketing plans are so variable as to make headquarters coordination into a central document an impossible task. This is largely due to the different levels of intellect and motivation of participating managers.

The principle, then, is as follows:

It is essential to have a set of written procedures and a well-argued common format for marketing planning. The purposes of such a system are:
1   To ensure all key issues are systematically considered.
2   To pull together the essential elements of the strategic planning of each SBU in a consistent manner.
3   To help corporate management to compare diverse businesses and to understand the overall condition of and prospects for the organization.

9   Failure to prioritize objectives

Even when organizations are successful in producing well reasoned marketing plans, it is not uncommon to find in each marketing plan as many as fifty objectives and many more strategies. This is because of the hierarchy effect of a principal marketing objective leading to a number of sub-objectives, with each of these sub-objectives leading to further sub-objectives. It is rare, however, to find any kind of prioritization of these objectives, and even rarer to find any allocation of time resource to each. The result is that managers can, and do, get sucked into the day-to-day 'In Tray' syndrome, which in turn results in the creeping non-implementation of the marketing plan.

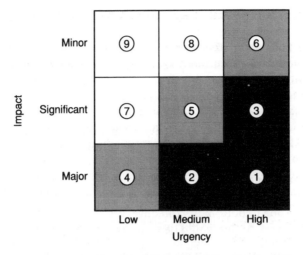

Key : Possible time/resource allocation (%)

1 – 30	4 – 12	7 – 8
2 – 15	5 – 10	8 – 4
3 – 12	6 – 8	9 – 1
57	30	13

Figure 3 *Objectives priority matrix*

The key role of senior management is to concentrate lower level management attention on factors that are both high leverage and actionable in order to get the essential jobs done effectively.

To prevent managers getting sidetracked by trivia, the author has found that it is helpful to get managers to prioritize their next year's objectives using a time allocation planner.

The principle, then, is as follows:

Ensure that all objectives are prioritized according to their impact on the organization and their urgency and that resources are allocated accordingly.

10   Hostile corporate cultures

During the years 1985 and 1986, Leppard (1987) carried out a research study to attempt to provide an explanation for the widespread corporate resistance to marketing planning. Most previous work concentrated on the 'medicine', itself and showed relatively little concern for the 'patient'. In a sense, this is a bit like a doctor dispensing the same drug to all patients irrespective of their condition, a practice that would be at best irrelevant and at worst even dangerous.

Over the years, in promoting the marketing planning nostrum, the product has somehow become more important than the customer. So, just as a good doctor tries to find out more about his patient before prescribing drugs, the author attempted to find out more about the condition of companies before prescribing a marketing planning 'cure'.

This research showed that the acceptance of marketing planning is largely conditioned by the stage of development of the organization and the behaviour of the corporate culture carriers. Thus it is that different modes of marketing planning become more appropriate at different phases of an organization's life.

While the marketing planning process itself is universally consistent, *how* the process is managed must be congruent with the current organizational culture – i.e. top down, bottom up, directive, non-directive, coordination, and so on. The alternative to this would be to attempt to change the organization's culture to make it more amenable to a particular planning process.

Since culture tends to act to maintain the existing power structure and status quo, marketing planning interventions must be recognized as having a 'political' dimension and are not purely educational. Thus, even though requisite training is given to key marketing personnel and an appropriate system is developed, without the active support and participation of the power brokers, marketing planning will not happen. Not least among the political issues is the question of whether or not an organization's management style can adapt sufficiently to enable the marketing planning process to deliver the rewards it promises.

Can managers who have led a company down a particular path suddenly change track? Is it possible for frogs to become princes? Iconoclastic books would claim they can, because this is a much more optimistic message with which to sell copies. However, experienced practitioners and consultants would have some reservations.

If the business pressures on a company are great enough, intelligent behaviour will, of course, win the day, as in the cases of British Airways and Woolworths quoted earlier.

In the meantime, however, standardized, textbook type marketing planning cannot be imposed on organizations with any chance of success, and most definitely not without the active support and participation of the culture leaders. Such participation must involve feeding back to those who have taken part in the process the total results of their efforts.

The final principle, then, is as follows:

Marketing planning will not be effective without the active support and participation of the culture leaders. But even with their support, the type of marketing planning has to be appropriate for the phase of the organizational life line. This phase should be measured before attempting to introduce marketing planning.

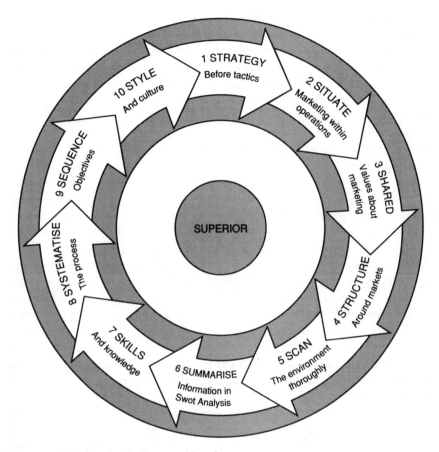

Figure 4   *Marketing planning for competitive advantage*

Conclusion

It will be understood from the foregoing that marketing planning never has been the simple step-by-step approach described so enthusiastically in most prescriptive texts and courses. The moment an organization embarks on the marketing planning path, it can expect to encounter a number of complex organizational, attitudinal, process and cognitive problems which are likely to block progress. By being forewarned about these barriers, there is a good chance of doing excellent marketing planning that will bring all the claimed benefits including a significant impact on the bottom line through the creation of competitive advantage. If they are ignored, however, marketing planning will remain the Cinderella of business management.

The ten barriers described in this paper and the advice provided for overcoming them are summarized in Figure 4.

References

Ansoff, H.I. (1977), 'The state and practice of planning systems', *Sloane Management Review*, 18(2), Winter.

Cannilus, J.C. (1972), 'Evaluating the benefits of formal planning', *Long Range Planning*, June.

Glaser, B.G. and Strauss, A.C. (1967), *The Discovery of Grounded Theory: Strategies for Qualitative Research*, New York, Aldine Publishing Co.

Gorb, P. (1978), 'Management development for the small firm', *Personnel Management*, January.

Greenley, G. (1987), 'An exposition into empirical research into marketing planning', *Journal of Marketing Management*, 3(1), July.

Kollatt, D.T. *et al.* (1972), *Strategic Marketing*, New York, Holt, Reinhart and Winston.

Leighton, D.S.R. (1966), *International Marketing Text and Cases*, New York, McGraw-Hill Book Co. Ltd.

Leppard, J.W. (1987), *Marketing Planning and Corporate Culture*, Cranfield Institute of Technology M.Phil.

Leppard, J.W. and McDonald, M.H.B. (1987), 'A reappraisal of the role of marketing planning', *Journal of Marketing Management*, 3(2).

McDonald, M.H.B. (1984), *The Theory and Practice of Marketing Planning for Industrial Goods in International Markets*, Cranfield Institute of Technology Ph.D.

The Strategic Planning Institute Membership Conference (1986), Keynote Address, Cambridge, Massachusetts.

Thompson, S. (1962), *How Companies Plan*, AMA Research Study, No. 54. AMA.

Thune, S. and House, R. (1970), 'Where long range planning pays off', *Business Horizons*, 7(4), August.

Wong, V., Saunders, J. and Doyle, P. (1988), 'The quality of British marketing: A comparative investigation of international competition in the UK market', *Proceedings of the 21st Annual Conference of the Marketing Education Group, Huddersfield Polytechnic, July*.

Reproduced from McDonald, M.H.B. (1989). Ten barriers to marketing planning. *Journal of Marketing Management*, **5** (1), 1-18.

Index

Marketing Strategy

Books in the series

Managing Business Ethics
John Drummond and Bill Bain

Marketing Strategy
Dale Littler and Dominic Wilson

Mission and Business Philosophy
Andrew Campbell and Kiran Tawadey

New Thinking in Organizational Behaviour
Haridomos Tsoukas

Strategic Information Management
R. D. Galliers and B. S. H. Baker

Strategic Issues in Finance
Keith Ward

Strategic Synergy
Andrew Campbell and Kathleen Sommers Luchs